OFG

Premodifiers in English

The order and behaviour of the premodifier (an adjective, or other modifying word that appears before a noun) has long been a puzzle to syntacti-
cians and semanticists. Why can we say 'the actual red ball', but not 'the
red actual ball'? And why, conversely, do some other premodifiers have free
variation in sentences; for example, we can say both 'German and English
speakers' and 'English and German speakers'? Why do some premodifiers
change the meaning of a phrase in some contexts; for example, 'young
man' can mean 'boyfriend', rather than 'man who is young'? Drawing on
a corpus of over 4,000 examples of English premodifiers from a range of
genres such as advertising, fiction and scientific texts, and across several
varieties of English, this book synthesises research into premodifiers and
provides a new explanation of their behaviour, order and use.

JIM FEIST is an Honorary Research Fellow in the Department of Applied
Language Studies and Linguistics at the University of Auckland, New
Zealand.

Premodifiers in English

Their Structure and Significance

JIM FEIST

University of Auckland, New Zealand

CAMBRIDGE UNIVERSITY PRESS
Cambridge, New York, Melbourne, Madrid, Cape Town,
Singapore, São Paulo, Delhi, Tokyo, Mexico City

Cambridge University Press
The Edinburgh Building, Cambridge CB2 8RU, UK

Published in the United States of America by Cambridge University Press, New York

www.cambridge.org
Information on this title: www.cambridge.org/9781107000865

First published 2012

Printed in the United Kingdom at the University Press, Cambridge

A catalogue record for this publication is available from the British Library

ISBN 978-1-107-00086-5 Hardback

Contents

vii

Acknowledgements

I am very grateful to Professor Jim Miller, for his guidance and encouragement in the research on which this book is based. I am also indebted to Professor Susan Fitzmaurice for her help with the section on grammaticalisation. The editors, Helen Barton and Merja Kytö, and copy editor, Jill Lake, have been very supportive and helpful during the preparation of the book.

Figures

1 Introduction

1.1 The need for this book

This book sets out to explain the nature and arrangement of premodifiers in English nominal phrases by relating their order to their meaning and syntax and to other areas of language, and to show the significance of that structure for other work in linguistics. ('Premodifiers' covers uses like 'the <u>nearby</u> house'; 'a house <u>nearby</u>' has a postmodifier; the words *the* and *a* are excluded, as determiners.)

The book starts from three facts about English that call for explanation. A music reviewer (cited in the British National Corpus) once described the tambourine as 'your actual tinny round percussion instrument'. It is generally agreed among linguists and nonspecialist users of language that the order of modifiers in such a phrase cannot be varied freely: we cannot grammatically say *'your percussion actual round tinny instrument' or *'your tinny round percussion actual instrument', for example. There are evidently rules of some sort for the order; so the fundamental thing to be explained about the order of premodifiers in English nominal phrases is the nature of the rules.

At the place where *tinny* occurred in the phrase quoted above, it is possible to use several modifiers together. You could say 'your actual <u>tinny, cheap, unpleasant</u> round percussion instrument'; and the order of the words underlined may be varied but still be grammatical: 'cheap, tinny, unpleasant', for example. So a second phenomenon to be explained is why the order can sometimes be varied freely, and the nature of the variations.

A novelist wrote of one of her characters, 'Here was a young, impulsive, over-curious young woman.' (P. D. James, cited in Adamson 2000: 58.) That is acceptable and effective English; but most readers will feel intuitively that, while the second *young* is in normal position ('over-curious <u>young</u> woman'), the first *young* is in an abnormal position. So we must explain the acceptability and effect of such flouting of the rules.

Preliminary investigation of those phenomena, by assembling examples of premodifier order, reveals a few other features that call for explanation. Two of them are illustrated with *glassy*, in table 1.1.

Table 1.1 *Uses of* glassy

the	*glassy*	green	*[sea]*	water
the	*simple*	*glassy*	arm	spines
the	*present*	disordered	*glassy*	state

Table 1.2 *Uses of* golden

Sense		Premodifiers		Head
<1> Earliest	*enormous*	*nine-branch*	*golden* 'Made of gold'	*candelabrum*
<3> Later	*lovely*	*golden* 'Of the colour of gold'	skin	tone
<5> Latest	*golden* 'Characterised by great happiness'	*olden*	*[college]*	days

First, table 1.1 shows that the same word can occur in different positions in the phrase. Second, it shows that all uses of the word in different positions can have a common sense element – 'pertaining to glass', in the table – but that they differ in their precise meaning: in the first of its three positions, *glassy* means 'lustrous and transparent as glass' (sense <4> in the *Shorter Oxford English Dictionary* – 'SOED' hereafter); in the second position, it means 'resembling... glass' (part of sense <1> in SOED); in the third position it means 'characteristic of glass' (another part of sense <1>). To sum up: the table illustrates two important features of premodification: that the same word can occur in different positions in the phrase, and that the meaning changes with the change in position.

A third important feature is shown by the history of words. *Golden*, for example, was used in Middle English, to mean 'made of gold' (sense <1> in SOED). A new sense developed by Late Middle English: <2> 'Yielding or containing much gold'. Then sense <3> developed: 'Of the colour of gold...'; then sense <4a> 'Resembling gold in value', and <4b> 'Precious, important, excellent'; then sense <5> 'Characterised by great prosperity and happiness; flourishing'. Those senses are used in different positions in the phrase, with the later senses being used in positions further from the head, as shown in table 1.2.

Putting the three features together, we see a three-way correlation between premodifiers' position in the order, their meaning and their history. That correlation also calls for explanation.

There are several things about premodifiers, then, that need explanation, but many writers have already tried to provide it; so making another attempt needs justification. In general, previous explanations have been incomplete: nearly all writers have evidently been unaware of the variations in position and sense just noted, and, more fundamentally, cannot explain them;[1] and there are other examples they cannot explain. Most writers have been aware that their explanations are incomplete, emphasising that they are 'tendencies', or that the order they describe is only the 'preferred' one.

There are, moreover, some striking gaps. As far as I am aware, no work has studied the historical development of premodifier order as such. None has been based on a detailed modern understanding of semantics, although a couple of short articles have given some consideration to such semantics; for example, Adamson (2000) on *lovely*, and Paradis (2000) on 'reinforcing adjectives' as in '<u>absolute</u> bliss' and 'an <u>awful</u> mess'. Apparently, no treatment has tried to evaluate the different approaches and explanations, or to integrate them.

Cruse (2004: 302) summed up the situation: 'Various partial explanations have been put forward, but none is comprehensively convincing.'

1.2   The approach followed here, to fill the need

The first step in my approach to filling the need for a good explanation has been to examine the data – as many different nominal phrases as possible, from a wide variety of genres and varieties. (I have in effect examined all the nominal phrases I have met in five years of looking for them in research, and in meeting them incidentally in general reading.) The second step has been to seek an explanation for the order. Rather than follow a prior commitment to a particular linguistic theory, I have used explanatory concepts from a range of approaches – provided that they are compatible – treating the varying approaches as complementary, just as plan and elevation are complementary views of a house. For example, I felt forced to include the historical approach, because synchronic study left some things unexplained. The British National Corpus and the Corpus of Contemporary American English have often been used to check proposed explanations.

The theoretical approach I have come to is closest to the Systemic Functional Grammar of Halliday (2004). In particular, I share his view that language is functional, that utterances and even individual phrases may serve several functions at once, and that those functions use syntax, semantics and phonology flexibly as means to a goal. In semantics, my approach is in the tradition of Leech (1974) and Cruse (2004, for example), where meaning includes not only concepts but also expressive and functional elements.

---

[1] Longobardi (2001: 577) and Adamson (2000) are aware of those facts, but do not apply them fully, or explain them.

Table 1.3 *Phrases illustrating the core argument*

Determiner	Premodifiers				Head
	1	2	3	4	
your	actual	tinny	round	percussion	instrument
a	mere	250,000	live	television	audience
a		young, impulsive, over-curious	young		woman
the		present	disordered	glassy	state
the		simple	glassy	arm	spines
the		glassy	green	sea	water
an		enormous	nine-branch	golden	candelabrum
her		lovely	golden	skin	tone
the		golden	olden		days
		little	black and red	iron	fences
		traditional	creamy	vanilla and chocolate	ice-cream

Discussion of syntax will include the effect of words on other words' meaning, as well as their position. Because I expect the approach and particular concepts to justify themselves by their explanatory power, I do not attempt to justify them theoretically. Terms and concepts will be explained as they become relevant; the index will help the reader find the explanations.

1.3   Core of the account to be given

The correlation noted above, among the order of premodifiers, differences in their senses, and their historical development, not only calls for explanation: it also leads to the explanation for the fundamental phenomena of premodifier order given above.

Table 1.3 presents the phrases already cited, and some others, as illustrative data for what follows. The positions in the order are numbered for reference.

The argument is that the premodifier positions, as in table 1.3, are zones of use, which may have one word, or several, or none. The zones have semantic characteristics (for example, words in zone 1 are like the adverb *very* in being intensifiers, not content words); and they have syntactic characteristics, which are interdependent with the semantic ones. That order of zones constitutes the normal order of premodifiers in English. Words within the same zone are in grammatically free order – 'black and red' may be 'red and black'. Premodifiers may be moved for special effect, in marked order (for example, 'a <u>young</u>... young woman').

1.4   Advantages of the account

The account just summarised provides us with rules for premodifier order comparable in simplicity and adequacy with the rules for the order of main clause elements in declarative clauses. The rules for clauses are: (1) the subject must be put first; (2) if there are several words in the subject, or several verbs, they may be put in any order; (3) for certain stylistic purposes, a marked reversal of the order may be used (as with the caption from romantic silent films, 'Came the dawn... '). Similarly with premodifiers: (1) words with a zone-1 sense must be put first, then zone-2 senses, zone-3 senses, and zone-4 senses; (2) if there are several words in one zone, they may be put in any order; (3) for certain stylistic purposes, a marked reversal of the order may be used (as with *young*, above).

That explanation accounts for the variation of sense and position. It also avoids the problems we noted with previous accounts: the distinction between grammatically required and grammatically free order avoids most of the problems with tendencies and preferences; the others are resolved by the marked/unmarked distinction and by the specification that the order is of senses not of words – so 'old fat' and 'fat old' are both possible (see §3.4.2.3), and both 'smooth dark' and 'dark smooth' (see §7.1.2). The explanation accounts for problem examples such as 'impossibly high high heels' (see §2.2.1.2, item (v)), and 'new old' and 'old new' (see §3.4.2.3). The zones have various semantic and syntactic characteristics and can thus serve different functions, which leads to the integration of semantic, syntactic and functional explanations, both synchronic and historical. That allows the explanation to fill the gaps noted previously, and to integrate valid insights from other theories with new insights.

Finally, the account to be given here avoids a further problem that arises from the tendencies-and-preferences theories. If speakers uttering a phrase with several premodifiers had to consider for each one a number of non-binding preferences for order, each relative to other positions and relative to words in the same position, they could not decide quickly what the order should be. Moreover, there is no likelihood that speakers would agree closely on the order. Yet speakers of English in fact arrange premodifiers quickly, without conscious thought, and in the same order as other speakers.

1.5   Outline of the book

The body of the book develops the core outlined above. Chapter 2 presents the zones in more detail. Chapter 3 gives a semantic explanation of the normal order of the zones; chapter 4 gives a syntactic explanation of it; and chapter 5 explains the order within zone 4, which has an internal semantic and syntactic structure of its own. Chapters 6 and 7 explain the free and marked orders, using the same semantic and syntactic concepts. Chapter 8 complements the preceding synchronic explanations with a diachronic one, showing that the Old English order by part of speech became the modern syntactic order in Middle English, which was in turn reanalysed as being also a semantic order. Chapter 9 complements the preceding semantic and syntactic analysis with supporting explanations from the approaches of discourse, psycholinguistics and children's development of language. Chapter 10 is devoted to discussion of the wider significance of the previous analysis of premodifiers and their order – adding to the discussion developed incidentally in the preceding chapters. Chapter 11 concludes.

1.6   Further significance of the explanation to be given

The argument developed through the book, as just outlined, is intended to be satisfying for being based on copious and wide-ranging data, and for being detailed, comprehensive and well integrated. It is put forward as being new in several ways: in its use of modern semantics, which deals with expressive as well as conceptual functions of language, to solve an old problem; in its accounting for the insights of other scholars and other approaches; and in being psycholinguistically credible, while providing for all the subtlety and variety of English.

Along the way, the concepts and distinctions used to explain premodifiers will provide what I trust are insights into various controversies. For example, the historical explanation in chapter 8 will lead to the suggestion that words grammaticalise right through nominal phrases, from head to determiner, and in the other direction. The 'Discussion' chapter (chapter 10) will suggest an answer to the puzzlement about 'compounds'. (Is the phrase 'noun compound' itself a compound? It hardly seems to be, but it should be, shouldn't it?) In the same chapter, the nature of the zones will be shown to imply that we must accept the modern constructional approach to syntax, that the concepts of gradience and prototypes are applied too widely in recent linguistics, and that the traditional concepts of parts of speech such as 'adjective' simply do not apply to Present-Day English nominal phrases. Some oddities can also be explained. Why is it, for example, that although premodifiers are typically 'adjectives' they may be 'adverbs' ('the then prime minister'), 'participles' ('running water'), or 'nouns' ('noun phrase')? And why can numbers be used as premodifiers ('a mere 250,000 live television audience') although they are usually determiners ('250,000 mere mortals')? Finally, the concepts and distinctions used will imply some things that do not seem to have been considered before, such as that the very nature of English semantics has changed, just as English syntax and morphology have.

1.7   Conventions to be used

As well as the usual conventions, the book uses numbers in angle brackets –
as in <2> – to represent the *Shorter Oxford English Dictionary*'s number-
ing of its meanings[2]. The hash sign – # – is used for expressions which I
have constructed and regard as grammatically acceptable. Phrases without
the hash are attested, even when the source is not cited, unless prefaced with
expressions such as 'that could be expressed as'.

---

[2] I generally use the *Shorter Oxford English Dictionary* (SOED) rather than the *Oxford
English Dictionary* (OED) because it gives the historical development of word meanings
more clearly; for my purpose, its being slightly more out of date than the online OED in
some entries does not matter.

2   Zones, and types of order

2.1   Introduction

This chapter sets out the basic structure of premodifier order, which the rest of the book will explain and discuss. It argues for three main points. First, premodifier order is a matter of zones (each containing one word, or several, or none), rather than of individual words. Second, there are four zones. Finally, there are three types of order: (a) 'unmarked' order, across zones, in which words occur in the grammatically set order of the zones; (b) 'marked' order, across zones, in which a user may flout the unmarked order for certain stylistic purposes; (c) 'free' order, within one zone, in which words may grammatically occur in any order. Those points will be asserted as empirical facts evident from the examples given; but the reader may prefer to treat them as working hypotheses, since the chapters to follow will substantiate them by explaining the nature of the zones and their order.

The concept of premodification zone will be introduced, the nature of each zone will be outlined, and each of the zones will be named. The concepts will be developed through much of the chapter. The rest of the chapter sets out the nature of the zones (§2.2), and the types of order (§2.3). The conclusion (§2.4) sums up, and looks forward to later chapters.

2.2   Zones of premodification

2.2.1   *Premodification order as an order of zones*

2.2.1.1   *Four zones of premodification*

I follow Quirk *et al.* (1985) in asserting that the overall order consists of four zones of premodification, approximately as shown in table 2.1 (after Quirk *et al.*, 1985: 1340).

However, I qualify their account of Zone I ('precentral' modifiers). They describe Zone I modifiers as 'intensifying adjectives' (1985: 1338), which are also described (1985: 429) as having 'a heightening effect on the noun that they modify, or the reverse, a lowering effect'; the examples of intensifying adjectives given (1985: 429) include '<u>pure</u> fabrication', '<u>outright</u> lie', '<u>sheer</u> arrogance', and '<u>complete</u> fool'. I accept that description, but assert that

Table 2.1 *Zones of premodification (approximate)*

Determiners	Premodifiers				Head
	Zone I: precentral	Zone II: central	Zone III: postcentral	Zone IV: prehead	
our	*numerous*	*splendid*		*African tourist*	*attractions*
all this			*costly*	*social*	*security*
a		*certain*		*church*	*tower*
these			*crumbling[,] grey*	*Gothic church*	*towers*
some		*intricate*	*old[,] interlocking*	*Chinese*	*designs*
all the		*small*	*carved*	*Chinese jade*	*idols*
both the	*major*			*Danish political*	*parties*

some of their other examples do not fit it. In 'our <u>numerous</u> . . . . . attractions', *numerous* is a quantifying determiner, like *many*, *several* and *two*, as in '<u>several</u> mistakes' and 'too <u>many</u> mistakes' (1985: 262), and #'two tourist attractions'; it is a postdeterminer here, in my judgement. If intended to be descriptive, it would belong in Zone II. *Major* is a synonym of *important*, and adds meaning to its head, *parties* (not intensifying it); it belongs in Zone II. Those two modifiers do not heighten or intensify the meaning of their head words. By hypothesis, I take that quality to be characteristic of Zone I (and will show that to be so, in chapter 3, on semantics), and discount the examples; '<u>pure</u> fabrication' and '<u>outright</u> lie' would be valid examples. With that qualification, I accept the zone structure given by Quirk *et al.* (1985). It will be the basis for my account of premodifier order in the rest of the book. That argument relies on defining determiners as being words that limit ('determine') the referent of the head using presupposed information (working by deixis or quantification); modifiers are words that use asserted information to either limit or describe the referent.

The zone numbers used by Quirk and others (1985) give no indication of the nature of the zones; so, instead of 'Zone I' and so on, I will use more descriptive terms, as follows. I will use 'Reinforcer' for Zone I words (like *sheer, complete, absolute*, as used in table 2.1); they reinforce the sense of the noun they modify; in 'absolute idiot', *absolute* reinforces the concept IDIOCY in the noun. (The term comes from Paradis 2000, 2001.) I will use 'Epithet' for the expressive Zone II words, such as *splendid* and *intricate*. (The term is from Halliday 2004, but applies there to both Zones II and III.) I will use 'Descriptor' for the factually descriptive Zone III words, such as *crumbling, grey, interlocking*. I will

Table 2.2 *General illustration of the zones*

Determiner	Premodifiers				Head
	Reinforcer	Epithet	Descriptor	Classifier	
your	*actual*	*tinny*	*round*	*percussion*	*instrument*
a	*mere*	*useless*	*gibbering*	*stop-the-war-at-any-price*	*pacifist*
	sheer	*desperate*			*necessity*
a	*complete*	*bloody*			*fool*
		little	*black*	*iron*	*fences*
a		*shabby*	*dark*	*city*	*suit*
a		*lissom*	*young*	*TVNZ*	*reporter*
some		*gangbuster*	*new*	*McKinsey*	*idea*
the		*beautiful*	*sunny*	*winter*	*weather*
the		*huge*	*annual*	*ram*	*sales*
		ugly	*trailing*	*overhead*	*wires*
		smooth	*panning*	*camera*	*movements*
her		*lacy*	*tin-roofed*	*row*	*house*
a		*distinctive*	*checked*	*baseball*	*cap*
the		*filthy*	*colonial*	*military*	*compounds*
		traditional	*creamy*	*vanilla*	*ice-cream*

use 'Classifier' for Zone IV words, which commonly subclassify the referent of the head word. (This term is also from Halliday 2004; a number of authors use 'classify' for the <u>function</u> of such words – for example, Teyssier 1968, Warren 1984, Quirk *et al.* 1985: 1340, Adamson 2000: 60, Bauer 2004: 13.) I intend the words' everyday senses to suggest the nature of the zones, and I will characterise the zones in the next two chapters; but I use the words as technical terms to name the zones; the descriptive meaning of the terms does not define them. S ction 2.2.1.2 below identifies the zones more fully.

Since the zones will not be fully explained until I have set out their semantic and syntactic characteristics in the next two chapters, I give further illustrations in table 2.2, to give the reader an intuitive feel for their nature, and to help the discussion in the rest of this chapter. (Some examples are repeated from above.)

There are few phrases which combine Reinforcers with other premodifiers; and there are extremely few with all four zones filled (for reasons that will be made clear in §4.3.1) – the first example in the table is from the British National Corpus, and the second from Fries (2000: 312).

2.2.1.2   The nature of premodification zones

It is important for the argument that we can be confident which zone the word being discussed belongs in, since the examples will be used as

Table 2.3 *Obscure zoning of 'the smart blue bonnet'*

	Det.	Premodifiers				Head
		Reinf.	Epithet	Descriptor	Classifier	
Possible analysis	*the*		? *smart*	? *blue*		*bonnet*
Possible analysis	*the*			? *smart*	? *blue*	*bonnet*

Table 2.4 *Clear zoning of 'the smart blue bonnet'*

Det.	Premodifiers				Head
	Reinf.	Epithet	Descriptor	Classifier	
the		*smart*	*blue*	[*silk*]	*bonnet*

evidence for the assertions about the zones. Once the semantic nature of
the zones has been demonstrated (in chapter 3), we can see what zone any
word belongs in from its semantic structure, even if it occurs as the only
premodifier. Until then, we must rely on seeing its position relative to other
words.

In 'a mere useless gibbering stop-the-war-at-any-price pacifist' (table 2.2),
the assignation of words to zones is clear: four premodifiers in four zones. In
'little black iron fences', it is fairly clear: 'little' cannot be a Reinforcer, since
it is, to our intuition, not of the reinforcing type (e.g. *sheer, absolute, mere*);
so the three modifiers must spread across the other three zones, as shown in
the table. However, in 'the smart blue bonnet' (to be discussed below), *smart*
and *blue* could be thought to belong in either of two columns (*smart* being
intuitively not a Reinforcer), as in table 2.3.

But if we add *silk* to the phrase, it must be the last premodifier, since normal use is #'smart blue <u>silk</u> bonnet', not *'<u>silk</u> smart blue bonnet' or *'smart
<u>silk</u> blue bonnet'; so the assignment of *smart* and *blue* to zones becomes
clear, as in table 2.4. That relies, of course, on the reader's accepting that the
amended phrase is idiomatic English, and that *'smart *silk* blue bonnet' and
similar items, are not. In some of the tables hereafter, I accordingly insert
words into attested examples (marking the insertion by square brackets), to
make clear which zones the attested words belong in. With that proviso clear,
we can now list the characteristics of the zones.

i   Premodification zones form a grammatically set order
The order of premodifier zones in English nominal phrases is set grammatically for most premodifier combinations; for example, 'a <u>heavy trundling</u>
sound' must occur in that order; it cannot grammatically be *'a <u>trundling</u>

Table 2.5 *Two or more words in one zone*

Det.	Premodifiers			Head
	Epithet	Descriptor	Classifier	
the first	*major*	*machine-readable, corpus-based*	*lexical*	*project*
a	*hazy, out-of-focus, 3-dimensional*	*black and white*	*tv*	*image*

heavy sound'; 'lifelong eating habits' cannot be *'eating lifelong habits'. For that assertion, I appeal primarily to the reader's intuition, but also to the judgement of previous writers (see §10.4). An exception to order across zones being grammatically set will be outlined in §3 of this chapter ('Types of order'), and explained in chapter 7, on 'Marked order'.

ii   Zones may contain more than one word
Nominal phrases often have more than one word in the same zone, as shown by several of the phrases in Quirk *et al.*'s table: 'crumbling, grey' in their Zone III, and 'Chinese jade' in their Zone IV. Further examples, within one zone, are as follows. 'True, pure villa' has two Reinforcers. 'A real, human, compelling and enduring character' has several Epithets. 'The pink and green and blue and silver houses' has several Descriptors. 'Computer, software, consumer-electronics, telecoms, cable and internet companies' has several Classifiers. Phrases with multiple zones occupied, and with two or more words in one zone, are given in table 2.5.

iii   Order is variable within a zone
In each phrase with two or more words in a zone, the order of the words within a zone may be changed, and remain grammatical. For example, one could say #'pure, true villa', instead of 'true, pure villa'. Instead of 'a real, human, compelling, and enduring character', one could say #'a real, compelling, human, and enduring character', or 'a real, enduring, human, and compelling character', and so on. Chapter 6, on 'Free order', will discuss that stylistic variation of order within a zone.

iv   Zones affect modification structure
As shown in the examples in the last two subsections, words within one zone are usually co-ordinated. They are co-ordinated in writing by a comma or by a conjunction such as *and*, *or* or *but*, and in speech by a pause and appropriate intonation contour. (I discuss exceptions in §7.1.2) Coordination occurs within all zones; and may not occur across zones. Some examples have already been given; table 2.6 gives more, by varying the first, attested

Table 2.6 *Coordination in each zone*

Det.	Premodifiers				Head
	Reinf.	Epithet	Descriptor	Classifier	
	true, pure	[*modern*]			*villa*
a		*modern, desirable*	*red*		*villa*
a		*modern*	*red and brown*		*villa*
a		*modern*	*red*	*weather-board and tile*	*villa*

example. We could thus say #'a modern, desirable red and brown weather-board and tile villa', but the coordination cannot be changed to *'a modern desirable and red and brown and weather-board tile villa'. The coordination is grammatically set.

Being co-ordinated, words within the same zone modify the head independently (in a 'multi-branching' structure): for example, 'her [[white], [sagging] face]', in which the face is represented as both white and sagging, rather than as a sagging face which is white. The difference in structure becomes important when part of the phrase (e.g. 'sagging face') represents Given information, and other parts represent New information (e.g. 'white'); see §9.3, for explanation. By contrast, words in different zones modify the following part of the nominal phrase (forming a 'right-branching' structure) – just as determiners do, as in 'a [real character]'. For example, 'a [black [oilskin coat]]; or to take a more complex example (with both structures), 'the [first [major [[machine-readable], [corpus-based] [lexical project]]]]'. The earlier premodifiers are syntactically subordinate[1] to the following part of the phrase.

Those assertions on modification structure have sometimes been denied (see, for example, the discussion in Chomsky, 1965: 196–7), so I will support them more fully. First, the contrast between the use of conjunctions, commas and pauses (for coordination) within zones and their absence between zones shows clearly that there is some such difference. Second, there is an exact parallel between this distinction and the distinction between independent or 'paratactic' clauses and dependent or 'hypotactic' clauses: independent (multi-branching) clauses are co-ordinated with commas, or *and, but* or *or*; dependent clauses (in a right- or left-branching structure) are linked by special subordinating conjunctions or run on without commas (for restrictive relative clauses).

---

[1] 'Subordinate' is used here to contrast with 'co-ordinate', without implying that the relation is exactly the same as that of subordinate clauses.

Table 2.7 Smart *in different zones*

| Det. | Premodifiers | | | | Head |
	Reinf.	Epithet	Descriptor	Classifier	
the		*smart*	*blue*	[*silk*]	*bonnet*
a		*tight*	*smart*	*Viking's*	*son*
the		[*successful*]	[*new*]	*American 'smart'*	*bomb*

Further, some examples will show the contrast between co-ordinated and subordinated structures. The unexpected comma in example (1) shows that premodifiers are normally right-branching.

(1)   'My first, disastrous marriage'. (Radford 1993: 82)

Written with a comma, the phrase asserts that this marriage was his first, and was disastrous; the modifiers apply equally and separately to marriage: 'my [[first] [disastrous] marriage]'. Without a comma, 'my first disastrous marriage' would imply that there were other disastrous marriages: 'first' is modifying 'disastrous marriage'; it is right-branching: 'my [first [disastrous marriage]]'. Example (2) illustrates the multi-branching structure, where premodifiers are co-ordinated.

(2)   'a black and green rucksack'.

The adjectives are syntactically co-ordinate – 'a [[black] and [green] rucksack]' – because different parts of the rucksack are of different colours; 'a [black [green rucksack]]' would be a green rucksack that was black – which is absurd.

Further evidence of right-branching structure is provided by how premodifying phrases are interpreted. Byrne (1979) asked subjects in his experiment to interpret phrases like 'a slow fast dog'. Typically, they linked the noun and the adjective closest to it into a generic term ('fast dog'), and interpreted the other adjective as modifying that term: 'a slow fast dog' was interpreted as meaning 'an ageing greyhound'. That is, they interpreted the phrases as right-branching: 'a [slow [fast dog]]'. Finally, there are a number of authorities to support this analysis of premodification structure: Adamson (2000), Biber *et al.* (1999), Bouchard (2002), Chatman (1960), Fischer (2007), Halliday (2004), Huddleston and Pullum (2002), Quirk *et al.* (1985), Ziff (1960).

v   The same word may occur in different zones
The same word may occur in different zones, as noted in chapter 1. For example, *smart* may be an Epithet, a Descriptor, or a Classifier, as in table 2.7.

Table 2.8 *Different senses of* smart

Det.	Premodifiers			Head
	Epithet	Descriptor	Classifier	
a	_smart_ <12> 'Fashionable'	*blue*	[*silk*]	*bonnet*
a	tight	_smart_ <8> 'Quick, active'	*Viking's*	*son*
the	[*successful*]	[*new*]	*American 'smart'* <9b> 'Guided to a target'	*bomb*

Table 2.9 *Change of order and sense*

Det.		Premodifiers			Head
	Reinf.	Epithet	Descriptor	Classifier	
a		[*attractive*]	*red*	_silken_ <1> 'Made of ... silk'	*cloth*
a		_silken_, [*attractive*] <2> '... glossy ...'	*red*	[*nylon*]	*cloth*

Table 2.10 *First structure of 'a big baby'*

Det.	Premodifiers				Head
	Reinforcer	Epithet	Descriptor	Classifier	
a	_big_ reinforcing 'baby'				*baby*

It is very important to note that when a word occurs in a different zone, it occurs in a different sense (though it may have two or more senses within one zone). The different senses of the examples just given are shown in table 2.8. (The definitions are from SOED.)

The same two modifiers may be reversed in order, with one or both words changing their zone and their sense: we can say 'red silken cloth' and 'silken red cloth'; see table 2.9.

The possibility of occurrence in different zones can result in ambiguity. For example 'a big baby' can mean 'very babyish' (Quirk *et al.* 1985: 430) – #'That guy's just a big baby!', we might say scornfully, with the structure shown in table 2.10. 'A big baby' can also mean 'a baby large for its age', as in table 2.11. The phrase 'a big baby' is therefore ambiguous; and the ambiguity is both as to the meaning of *big*, and as to its zone.

Table 2.11 *Second structure of 'a big baby'*

Det.	Premodifiers				Head
	Reinforcer	Epithet	Descriptor	Classifier	
a		*big* 'large ...'			*baby*

Table 2.12 *Words occurring twice in the same phrase*

Det.	Premodifiers				Head
	Reinf.	Epithet	Descriptor	Classifier	
		very high 'very acute in pitch'	[*clear*]	*high* [designating upper part of singer's range]	*notes*
my		*young* <2a> '... immature'	*young* <4> '...not far advanced in life'		*days*

A word can even occur twice in the same phrase, in different zones. Thus we have, 'He's got very high high notes' and 'in my young young days', as in table 2.12. (Both examples are from the British National Corpus. The context for the second indicates that the first *young* meant 'immature'.)

vi   Zone order is an order of word uses

In all of the examples in the last section (*smart, silken, big*, and so on), the word occurring in different zones is used in different ways. That is, it is used in a different sense (for example, *smart* as Epithet means 'fashionable', but *smart* as Descriptor means 'quick, active'); or it is used with a different function (for example, *big* as Reinforcer strengthens the meaning of another word, *baby*, but as Epithet, it conveys a meaning of its own). We thus reach a very important conclusion: the zone order is an order of word <u>uses</u>, rather than an order of <u>words</u>. That fact will be fundamental to the book. (The fact, and the relationship between the word's zone and its meaning and function, will be explored fully in the next two chapters.)

vii   Zone order constitutes premodifier order

The presence of gaps in some lines of these tables indicates that those zones are empty (just as object position in a clause may be empty), and that word uses belong in a zone, irrespective of other premodifiers in the phrase. If that is so, then order is not simply a sequence of word uses;

nor can it be simply a matter of modification structure (since the gaps are meaningless for modification structure). The fundamental issue, then, is the nature of the zones: the order of premodifiers <u>consists of</u> the order of the zones in which they occur. (As a consequence, I will from here on refer to 'order', 'position' or 'zone' almost interchangeably, as suits the context.)

Support for premodification zones comes from Halliday (2004), whose description is very close to that of Quirk *et al.* (1985); and from Bache (1978, 2000), although that work posits only three zones, and of a somewhat different nature. Works such as Strang (1962: 123) acknowledge that one 'position' may have several premodifiers, co-ordinated.

2.2.2   Discussion of zones

2.2.2.1   Determining what zone a modifier is in

The reader may have difficulty in accepting my allocation of words to zones, because many phrases do not have three or four premodifiers, and because there are several potential sources of confusion. This section discusses that problem pending the semantic explanation to be given in the next chapter, which will allow identification when there is a single premodifier.

The first feature which can confuse our perception of a modifier's zone is the presence of submodifiers. Just as a nominal phrase may consist of one word or several (forming one constituent of the clause), so a premodifier may consist of one word or several, as a single constituent of the nominal phrase. That is fairly clear with phrases like 'a <u>very old</u> woman' and '<u>painfully brilliant</u> vertical streaks'; but particular care is needed in analysing phrases with words that can be either a modifier or a submodifier. For example, (i) 'Her [<u>dark</u> red] hair' ('of a dark red colour') has one (submodified) premodifier, but (ii) 'her [<u>dark</u>], [red] hair' ('dark and red') has two premodifiers.

The prosody of speech, and the punctuation of writing, are not wholly reliable as a guide to coordination and subordination, and therefore to zone membership. First, Epithets are sometimes run on without co-ordinating pauses or commas: when they reinforce each other (as in '<u>tiny little</u> bird') as 'intensificatory tautology' (term and example from Huddleston and Pullum 2002: 561), and when one acts in part as a submodifier of the next, as in 'a <u>nice</u> warm room' (that form of modification will be discussed in §4.3). Second, there is a marked use of punctuation (i.e. exceptional use or omission of commas), to be explained in §7.1.2. Finally, some speakers and writers use punctuation idiosyncratically or incorrectly.

Classifiers are another potential source of confusion, since the Classifier zone is more complex than I have indicated so far: we find phrases with several Classifiers, sometimes co-ordinated and sometimes not, as in table 2.13.

Table 2.13 *Co-ordinated and non-coordinated Classifiers*

Det.	Premodifiers			Head
	Epithet	Descriptor	Classifier	
	[*interesting*]	[*recent*]	*political, economic and social*	*comment*
an	[*interesting*]	[*old*]	*Roman pagan fertility*	*festival*

In fact, the Classifier zone is quite complex, having alternative structures, each with subzones. (In this section – and in the next two chapters – I give only the main points, leaving the details to a separate chapter on the Classifier zone – chapter 5.) But the examples in the table do conform to the principle given above in §2.2.1.2: within the Classifier zone (as across all zones), words in different (sub)zones are subordinate to later ones, and words within a single (sub)zone are co-ordinated.

Until the following two chapters have characterised the zones strictly, I will give multiple premodifiers in the phrases, where the identification of a word's zone is not obvious but is important, to show the zones by the sequence.

2.2.2.2   *Whether a premodifier can be on the borderline between zones*

There are many nominal phrases with premodifiers that may appear to be on the borderline between zones or on the borderline between premodifiers and determiners. I deal with the borderlines between zones in the next chapter, but will consider the issue briefly here, to establish one further point about zones.

I take an example from Quirk *et al.* (1985). Possessives are sometimes determiners, as in 'his old friend's cottage' and sometimes modifiers, as in 'his old fisherman's cottage' (1985: 1335–6). The structures are shown in table 2.14.

Each possessive is either a determiner or a premodifier; it cannot be both, nor be <u>on</u> the borderline. Similarly, a premodifier's zone will be apparent if we imagine other premodifiers added to the phrase. For example, as noted previously, *silken* in 'silken cloth' could be intended and understood as either Epithet or Classifier; but when another premodifier is added, its zone becomes clear, as in table 2.15. *Silken* must follow <u>or</u> precede *red*: so words may be close to the borderline between zones (semantically), but they cannot be <u>on</u> the borderline. There are some semantic elements that are gradient across the zones (as we will see in the next chapter), but the zones are distinct.

The point is illustrated wittily in a remark from a political commentator (Mike Moore, *New Zealand Herald*, June 2009). In the days of steam locomotives, the state-run railways employed a driver, a fireman and a brakeman

Table 2.14 *Possessives as determiners and as modifiers*

Det.	Epithet	Descriptor	Classifier	Head
his old friend's				*cottage*
his		*old*	*fisherman's*	*cottage*

Table 2.15 *Zoning of* silken

Det.	Epithet	Descriptor	Classifier	Head
	# [*beautiful*]	[*red*]	*silken*	*cloth*
	# *silken*	[*red*]	[*Chinese*]	*cloth*

Table 2.16 *Zoning of* working

Det.	Ep.	Descriptor	Classifier	Head
the			*working* = 'having a manual occupation'	*man*
the		*working* = 'actively performing a task'		*man*

on each train. After 1981, with diesel locos, there was work for only one man but the other two were kept – although idle – under union pressure: 'It was thought to be a victory for the working man', wrote Moore. Table 2.16 shows how the pun on *working* relies on different zones.

2.3   Types of order

The discussion so far has implicitly set out two patterns of premodifier order: (a) a grammatically prescribed order, where modifiers are in different zones, for example, 'small carved Chinese idols'; (b) a grammatically free order, where modifiers are co-ordinated within one zone, for example, 'political, economic and social comment'. There is a third pattern, however. I illustrate it from a highly descriptive newspaper report (*New Zealand Herald*, 2 August 2005) of a woman arriving at court to be tried. The report mentioned the woman's yellow dress (felt to be a little unusual for an accused), and described her hairstyle as in example (3).

(3)   'her <u>new</u>, curly, <u>Tina Turner</u> bob'.

Table 2.17 *Normal zoning of words in example (3)*

Det.	Reinf.	Epithet	Descriptor	Classifier	Head
her		*curly* *(beautiful, intricate)*	*new* *(old, grey)*	*Tina Turner* *(horse-hair, Chinese)*	*bob*

Table 2.18 *Actual zoning of example (3)*

Det.	Reinf.	Epithet	Descriptor	Classifier	Head
her		*new, curly, Tina Turner*			*bob*

The words in that phrase would normally be arranged and structured as in table 2.17. (To make the allocation of words to zones clearer, I add other words that could occur there.)

In the phrase as quoted in example (3), the journalist has deliberately changed the order and co-ordinated the three modifiers, to change the meaning of some words and achieve a dramatic stylistic effect: *new* and *Tina Turner* are intended to be no longer plain, factual words, but descriptive ones evoking many associations, like *curly*, to which they are co-ordinated – Tina Turner being a stylish and 'sexy' pop singer. The zone structure is given in table 2.18.

It is a marked order – 'marked' in the double sense of being a breach of what is normal, and in being used for special effect. (The definition is from Croft 1991: 57.) This usage is like metaphor: there, the incompatibility of a word's literal meaning and the context spurs the reader to construct a new meaning. Here, the incompatibility of a word's position in the phrase and the position(s) for which it has established meanings similarly spurs a new reading. This usage is an accepted device in English, just as metaphor is. (The nature of this marked order will be set out fully in chapter 7.)

There are, then, three types of premodifier order in English nominal phrases. (a) Unmarked order is the usual and grammatically prescribed order (as set out in the tables above); words are used in an established sense, and without special effect. (b) Free order is the order of words within a zone; speakers may arrange them arbitrarily (although, as we will see later, they often control the order for a stylistic reason); the words retain their sense if the order is changed; the variations are equally grammatical. (c) In marked order, the unmarked order is broken (but by a device which is an established convention), with a change in the normal sense of words, and usually with further special effect.

2.4   Conclusion: the nature of premodifier order

2.4.1   Summary

This chapter has discussed the two fundamental issues for the order of premodifiers in English nominal phrases (modification zones and types of order), and has made a number of assertions.

On modification zones, the chapter has asserted the following. (a) The broad order of premodifiers is grammatically set, not a matter of users' free choice, or of general tendencies. (b) The order is one of zones, rather than of individual words or senses. (c) The zones: there are four of them (Reinforcer, Epithet, Descriptor, Classifier); each is syntactically subordinated to zones that follow; each may contain no words, or one word, or several words; if there are two or more words, they are co-ordinate; coordination is normally shown by a pause and intonation in speech or a comma in writing, or by a conjunction; one word can occur in different zones (even in the same phrase). (d) It is word senses rather than words as such, that have zone membership (since a particular word can occur in different zones).

On types of premodifier order, the chapter has asserted the following. (a) There is an unmarked order – the regular, grammatically set order of successive zones. (b) There is a marked order, which contravenes the grammatical one for a special stylistic purpose, but which is established by usage. (c) There is free order within one zone, to which no grammatical rules apply.

2.4.2   Conclusions

The zones are identified here as observable phenomena (their order and their patterns of coordination and subordination being observable), and as all having what users of the language intuit to be a nature of their own: they are not identified by any linguistic definition of essential qualities. The following chapters set out to explain the intuitions and the phenomena, not to (re)define what has been defined already, which would make the discussion circular; the discussion will confirm the preliminary analysis given in this chapter.

2.4.3   Prospect: the chapters to follow

The concepts established in this chapter will be central to the rest of the book. The two main concepts outlined above (modification zones and types of order) form a foundation on which the next six chapters build directly: the unmarked order of the four zones will be given a semantic explanation in chapter 3 and a syntactic explanation in chapter 4; the unmarked order within the Classifier zone will be given both semantic and syntactic explanations in chapter 5; the free order will be explained in chapter 6; the marked order will be explained in chapter 7; an historical explanation of the zones and orders will be given in chapter 8.

There are further important facts about zones yet to be established: chapter 5 will show that the Classifier zone constitutes a grammatical construction (not simply an arrangement of words, but a structure of categories contributing to the phrase a meaning of its own); and the examination of marked order (in chapter 7) will lead to the conclusion that the other zones constitute constructions as well (§10.2).

3 Semantic explanation of unmarked order across the zones

3.1 Introduction

3.1.1 Purpose and outline of the chapter

The purpose of the chapter is to explain English premodifier order semantically. Starting from the last chapter's analysis of nominal phrase order as one of zones, it argues that the zone order is an order of 'semantic structure', as follows. The first words (those in the Reinforcer zone) are those with a purely 'grammatical' meaning. Those that come in the next zone (Epithets) are words with conceptual 'descriptive' meaning that is scalar. Words in the Descriptor zone have perceptual 'descriptive' meaning that is not scalar. Classifier words have 'naming' or 'referential' meaning. (The terms in quotation marks are explained in the next section.)

In this chapter, the terms 'semantics' and 'meaning' relate to the significance of words individually. They exclude the compositional significance of phrases (that is, the meaning of a phrase as a combination of words), which is treated in the following chapter, on syntax. They also exclude what might be called 'sentence meaning' and 'discourse meaning'; the latter is treated in §9.3. 'Semantic structure' is the combination of types and dimensions of meaning that makes up the meaning of a word (such as 'descriptive' and 'social' meaning). The concept is crucial to the book. Those concepts will be developed in the next section, along with others.

Two potential difficulties should be noted. As stated in the last chapter, the Classifier zone is complex (having subzones within it), and I accordingly deal with it in a separate chapter. Consequently, the treatment of its semantics in this chapter is slightly simplified; I explain in §3.2.2 what the simplification amounts to. Second, understanding the semantics of premodifier order is made difficult not only by the subtleties of word meaning, but also by gradual change of meaning historically. Hence the number of premodifiers which appear to be on the borderline between zones, which was noted in the last chapter. These 'borderline' examples will be discussed in the sections for the various zones.

In the rest of §3.1, I first set out the analysis of meaning which I will use (§3.1.2). It is crucial to this chapter (and much of the book), and some of the concepts and terms may be unfamiliar to readers, so the section is lengthy. I then give a few phrases as data that suggest the scope and direction of the discussion to follow (§3.1.3), and three short word histories (§3.1.4) that give a perspective that should help the main exposition.

The main sections of the chapter are arranged in the order of zones, from the Classifier zone (§3.2) to the Reinforcer zone (§3.5); each section gives a detailed analysis of the semantic properties of the senses that occur in that zone. Discussion follows (§3.6), and a conclusion (§3.7).

3.1.2   Types and dimensions of meaning

3.1.2.1   Introduction

In chapter 1, I said that my approach to the subject is a functional one, and that I regard language as a human activity as well as a structured system. Accordingly, I take 'meaning' in its general sense broadly: it includes some of what might be regarded as function; it is carried by inflections, syntax, the phonology of speech and the punctuation of writing, as well as by words individually. It is whatever contribution the word or other linguistic form makes to the hearer's interpretation of the utterance. (Compare Harder 1996: 103.)

Words interact with each other, and suggest the meaning of the utterance, rather than constituting it by giving successive units which may simply be added up. However, this section, §3.1, focuses on the conventionalised meaning of words (meaning of the sort that dictionaries record, that is). From §3.2 onward, and in the rest of the book, their meaning will be taken in the context of the phrase. I stress that I am dealing primarily with the meaning of individual words; in most contexts, that is equated with 'meaning' and 'semantics'. Meaning that is expressed by the structure of phrases is distinguished by a more specific expression, such as 'constructional meaning'.

I also distinguish between meaning and world knowledge; I treat meaning as the relation between language and the experience, world knowledge and intentions behind it. (World knowledge and meaning are not parallel or opposed areas of mental content.) The distinction will be important; I deal with it in my discussion of naming. (Thus the book is outside both the philosophical approach that treats meaning as propositional content having truth value, and a certain cognitive-linguistic tradition that equates meaning and knowledge.)

This analysis of meaning is taken almost wholly from Cruse (2004). The structuring of types is a little different, but the approach, the main distinctions and most terms are his. The analysis is, in my experience, very little used in linguistics, so it may be unfamiliar to the reader; but it is fundamental to the whole of the book, as well as to this chapter. It is fundamental to the analysis that words commonly have several types of meaning at once, which will be important for the rest of the chapter. However, the words given as examples in this section will mostly have only one type of meaning, for the sake of clarity.

3.1.2.2 Types of meaning

There are 'three ways the speaker aids the hearer in selecting the appropriate referent', which are 'describing, naming, and pointing' (Cruse 2004: 329). For words considered individually, I will accordingly distinguish among referential meaning ('naming'), descriptive meaning ('describing') and deixis ('pointing'); and since we use language expressively (as well as to select referents), I also distinguish expressive and social meaning from the others. Words such as determiners and intensifiers contribute grammatical relations to the hearer's interpretation, so I also distinguish grammatical meaning. This section explains those types of meaning.

i   Naming: referential meaning

The first of the three ways of designating a referent, naming, is used by proper nouns, such as 'London'. Their significance for us comes from the social convention that the word will be the referent's name. That significance has two elements: (a) the bare mental referent (the concept representing the real-world thing named), which is part of the system of language and which does not vary in essentials from person to person; (b) facts about London (e.g. its location, population, and so on), which are part of our general world knowledge, varying considerably from person to person.

Many uses of common nouns are similar to the use of proper nouns. In traditional (and rather philosophical) terms, the use can be explained as follows. Common nouns function as names if they are referentially stable: that is, they would have the same reference even if the abstract concepts that go with them were changed; they denote 'natural kinds'. Cruse (2004: 53) explains it this way: 'Suppose one day it was discovered that cats were not animals ... but highly sophisticated self-replicating robots'; we would still apply the word *cats* to the same things as now, although we would no longer associate with them abstract concepts such as LIVING. In psycholinguistic terms, the explanation is that the simple, fundamental concepts denoted by such nouns are cognitively natural: they are almost forced upon us by experience as a way of partitioning and conceptualising the elements of perception, and children can form such concepts before they have learned any words at all, and without abstractions like LIVING. (See Gentner and Boroditsky 2001.) The semantic or linguistic meaning of *cat*, then, is the bare mental referent to which we attach concepts such as LIVING and MAMMALIAN, not those concepts themselves; it is by world knowledge that we attach those concepts to cats. I regard many premodifying nouns (as in 'mountain valley' and 'steel bar') as having this type of meaning, just as proper nouns do; they identify a referent, rather than describe it. (In other uses, nouns commonly have other types of meaning, as well.)

Thus, this type of meaning, as 'bare' mental referent, is bare of descriptive elements (to be discussed in the next section). It is also bare of shape, size and discreteness. In English, mass nouns have that quality – unboundedness: with *rice*, for example, we must use expressions like 'a grain of' to give any element of shape, and to make the referent countable. (In some languages, all nouns are unbounded; the quality will be discussed further in §3.2.3, and §9.3.4. See also Langacker 2004: 81, on count nouns.)

Bolinger (1986: 103) distinguishes bare referents from descriptive elements in a different way, in distinguishing between using nouns to state qualities (for example, 'It's enough to make a <u>saint</u> swear') and to identify an entity ('It was the <u>saint</u>'). Similarly, *animal* may be used merely to denote a referent, as in the linguists' example 'Every farmer who owns a donkey feeds the wretched <u>animal</u>' (cited by Seuren 1998: 388) – a referential use. It may also be used to evoke descriptive qualities, as in, 'Despite Stan's perpetual grogginess, he is a real <u>animal</u> when it comes to business dealings' – a descriptive use. Compare also the use of *thingummy* and *what's-his-name*, for identification without description.

I will call this type of meaning (identifying a mental entity as referent) 'referential meaning'. The term does not imply any referent in the external, physical world; and it is distinct from 'reference' as the speech act of directing a hearer's attention to some 'real', external entity.

The distinction I have just made between world knowledge and meaning is much more difficult and controversial for premodifiers other than nouns. I assume that whereas 'a <u>London</u> street' relates to world knowledge directly, '<u>warm</u> water' relates to it more distantly and indirectly – through meaning (which is linguistic) and remembered perceptions of warm objects; that 'a <u>dangerous</u> situation' relates to it still more distantly and indirectly; and that 'an <u>utter</u> fool' has only a very tenuous relation to it. I assume likewise that while the significance to us of 'naming' or 'identifying' words (such as 'a <u>London</u> street') is almost wholly from world knowledge, the significance of words such as '<u>warm</u> water' is partly world knowledge and partly linguistic (that is, 'meaning'); and that of words like *utter* is wholly linguistic. That view is supported more or less directly by Giegerich (2005) and many of the various writers in Peeters (2000); it will become clearer in the following sections and in later chapters. Boas (2003: 168ff.) gives a useful overview of the issue.

Referential or naming meaning has not usually been regarded as a type of meaning. Works that treat it much as I do include Coates (2000), Anderson (2003) and Bauer (2004). Cruse (2004) regards it as I do, but does not list it in his 'types' of meaning.

ii   Descriptive meaning

Descriptive meaning includes most of what is usually called 'meaning'. It is the sort of meaning that determines whether a statement can be judged true or false, and whether it can be negated or questioned. It is objective in being not simply an expression of the speaker's state, and is 'displaced' in having relevance outside the immediate speech situation. It enables a hearer to make inferences (for example, the meaning of *conscious* implies LIVING), whereas from referential meaning it is our knowledge of the world that enables inference, as when being 'in London' implies being at a certain latitude and longitude. (These points are all from Cruse 2004: 44–5; cf. Lyons 1977: 50–1.)

I distinguish two types of descriptive meaning. (a) Perceptual meaning: meaning that is maximally close to perception, either to sense perception (as in 'broken stick', 'heavy stone', and 'red balloon'), or to perception of the mind's own state (as in *anger* or *conscious*). 'Perceptual' is roughly equivalent to 'concrete'. (Perceptual meaning corresponds to Cruse's 'basic meaning' and the meaning of 'observation vocabulary', see Cruse 2004: 50.) (b) Conceptual meaning: meaning that is general and abstract, being relatively remote from perception, as in *elementary*, *capable* and *correct*. (This use is therefore distinct from the broad Cognitive Linguistics use of 'conceptual', which covers all meaning.)

The distinction between perceptual and conceptual meaning is not absolute, since perceptual meaning must be partly conceptualised to be stored mentally and to be integrated with the rest of meaning. Descriptive meaning thus corresponds to 'ception' (Talmy 2001): knowledge that relates perception and conception. Its nature is expanded in the section 'Dimensions of descriptive meaning', §3.1.2.3 below.

Some works that distinguish descriptive meaning from others are Leech (1974: 26 – 'conceptual meaning'), and Lyons (1977: 50 – 'descriptive function'). Some other works distinguish perceptual and conceptual meaning within descriptive meaning, as follows: Adamson (1999: 573), distinguishing meaning that is from 'physical experience' and meaning that is 'abstract and ideational'; and some of the psycholinguistic works to be cited in chapter 9.

iii Expressive meaning

Expressive meaning is what speakers express about themselves; it is what the hearer understands of the speaker's emotive state. I emphasise 'express': *bloody*, for example, commonly expresses anger, but *anger* denotes it. (I use 'denote', here and later, for symbolising a descriptive meaning.)

I take expressive meaning to consist of two types; (a) emotive meaning – emotions or feelings such as anger, fear and irritation – as in *disgusting* and *horrible*; and (b) attitudinal meaning – attitude of either approval or disapproval: *tight-fisted* and *economical* can be used of the same behaviour to convey disapproving or approving attitude. Although we make finer distinctions among emotions and attitudes in everyday life, I do not make them here. As argued by Fillenbaum and Rapoport (1971: 209), there are too many possible criteria for the distinctions to be reliable.

Expressive meaning has been largely ignored in traditional linguistics, but I accord it considerable importance. That is supported not only by Cruse (2004), but by Fillenbaum and Rapoport (1971), Leech (1974: 26 – 'affective meaning'), Lyons (1977: 50 – 'expressive meaning'), Adamson (1999: 573 – the encoding of 'emotions and evaluations'), and Tucker (2002: 53 – 'Verbal semantics rests on a foundation of affective evaluation').

iv   Social meaning

Social meaning is what a word expresses of the social situation in which it is being used. I distinguish two types: (a) dialect meaning, including geographic, historical and social class variation in language; and (b) register, including field (the subject of the utterance), mode (spoken or written language) and style (degree of formality, and individually chosen variation in language). (Register is social to the extent that it depends on the relationship that the speaker or writer is setting up with the audience.) For example, *bach* ('cottage') has geographic meaning ('from New Zealand'); *eftsoons* ('soon') has historical meaning. The following advertisement for a brand of car has formality as part of its meaning: 'It runs on the aroma of a textile offcut soaked in petroleum derivative lubricant' ('It runs on the smell of an oily rag').

This sort of meaning is what Cruse (2004) calls 'evoked' meaning – a term which is not wholly clear, and which is potentially misleading. It has been less recognised than expressive meaning. Works that acknowledge it include Leech (1974: 26 – 'stylistic meaning'), Lyons (1977: 50 – 'social meaning'), and Halliday (1977: 200–1).

v   Grammatical meaning

Grammatical meaning is what words convey of how they are to be related to other words. It is in effect an instruction to hearers, guiding them in how to interpret the utterance; for example, a past tense inflection, as in *walked*, instructs the hearer to interpret the event as occurring in the past. (Eckardt 2006: 249, and Bybee 2002: 11, describe grammatical meaning similarly; see also Lyons 1975: 79, on demonstratives.) At clause level, it includes subject and object relations; in 'police dog bites toddler' and #'toddler bites police dog', grammatical meaning instructs the reader which noun to take as denoting the actor. In a prepositional phrase, it requires the hearer to relate the preposition and the following nominal phrase. Since at both levels the meaning is carried by a construction, I call that sort of grammatical meaning 'constructional meaning', since a construction is a syntactic structure which itself contributes meaning in addition to the meanings contributed by the words; see Croft (1999: 64), Goldberg (1995) and Traugott (2006), for example.

At modifier level, grammatical meaning has two lexical (i.e. non-constructional) forms. (a) Its main form is illustrated in 'clean water': *clean* instructs the reader to relate the concept CLEAN to the referent of the headword *water*; that meaning is entailed in being a modifier – 'modificational meaning'. (b) Its other common form in modifiers is intensification – an instruction to intensify the quality denoted by another word (just as in '<u>very</u> big', the sub-modifier *very* intensifies *big*): for example, '<u>utter</u> fool' instructs the hearer to intensify FOLLY. (Since this lexical form of grammatical meaning will be our main concern, I will usually shorten 'lexical grammatical meaning' to 'grammatical meaning'.)

This grammatical function of words has often not been regarded as 'meaning'; but purely grammatical words such as *the* are not meaningless, and the grammatical function is part of the contribution words make to the hearer's interpretation of the utterance. It often escapes notice, because it is generally below the hearer's full consciousness – as noted by Bybee (2002: 111), for example. But it is increasingly widely recognised, especially in work that accepts that the meaning of utterances is constructed by the hearer rather than being transferred complete from the speaker's mind; see, for example, Barsalou (1987: 101), Geeraerts (1993: 259) and Harder (1996). (Cruse 2004 treats grammatical meaning as an area of semantics, rather than as a <u>type</u> of meaning.)

To summarise: in grammatical meaning, we will be concerned with two lexical forms – modificational meaning (which all modifiers have), and intensifying meaning – and with constructional meaning.

vi Discussion

As noted in the introduction to this section, some meaning is carried by phonology. But the phonology of the whole phrase is independent of the zone structure, and the phonology of particular words does not seem to control their order; so phonological meaning will be given little attention in the book.

Cruse's three ways of designating referents form a scale of generality: (a) naming designates specific referents; (b) pointing is very general, since pointing words, like pointing gestures, can be used for any referent; (c) describing comes between them, being moderately general. (I use 'designate' for having referential meaning – naming an entity. It contrasts with expressing – for emotive and attitudinal meaning, with denoting – for symbolising descriptive meaning, and also with referring, as a speech act). There is a gradient, then: naming (most specific) → describing → pointing (most general). These are semantic 'functions', in being different ways in which words operate to convey meaning. We should distinguish two others: (a) the expressive function, which uses social and expressive meaning, and (b) the reinforcing function, which uses intensifying meaning. They differ from naming and describing, not on the generality scale, but on an objectivity scale, since they are subjective – dependent on the feeling and opinion of the speaker.

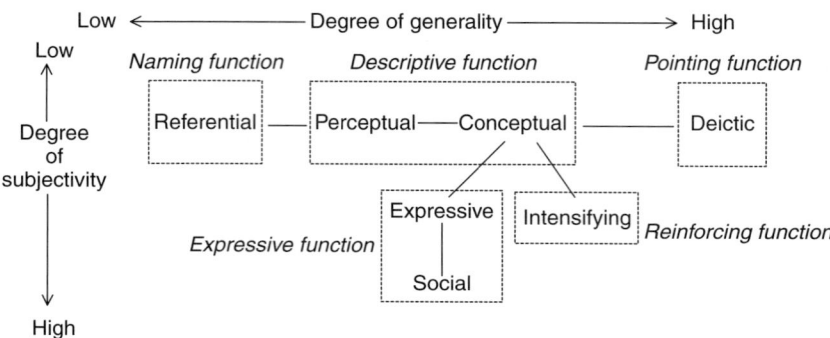

Figure 3.1 Map of semantic functions and meaning types in English

The relationships among the semantic functions and types of meaning may be illustrated in the semantic map shown as figure 3.1. It serves two purposes: summarising what has been said so far, and forming a basis for development of the argument in the rest of this chapter and in later chapters. (In particular, the horizontal scale – generality – and the vertical scale – subjectivity – anticipate later explanation.) It is to be read as follows. The position of the types of meaning (in roman type) relate to the horizontal and vertical scales. The meaning types linked by rules may occur together, synchronically; for example, conceptual and intensifying meaning may constitute the sense of a word, but not referential and intensifying meaning (unless linked by perceptual and conceptual meaning). The italicised words label the dotted boxes, indicating semantic functions (which are carried out by the meaning types).

The map is intended to make explicit and clear the conceptual structure beneath the semantic analysis to be given; the meaning types are essential to the explanations that follow, but the semantic functions and the mapped relationships are not essential. The analysis which the map represents has been documented only from premodification, but the map is presented tentatively as a map for English as a whole, since it builds on Cruse's general analysis (2004). It will be argued in chapter 8 that historical development follows the rules in the map – usually left to right, and top to bottom.

3.1.2.3 Dimensions of descriptive meaning

There are two types of dimension: intrinsic and relative. Intrinsic dimensions of descriptive meaning are those which elements of meaning have in themselves, not as part of their relation to other elements of meaning. They are as follows, with explanation by illustration rather than by definition.

(a) Quality: what makes the difference between *blue* and *yellow*, *big* and *heavy*, *honest* and *intelligent*.

(b) Intensity: what makes the difference between *small*, *tiny* and *minute*, and between *sore*, *painful* and *excruciating*.
(c) Specificity: what makes the difference between *collie*, *dog* and *animal*, and between *chaste* and *virtuous* (instances of type specificity); between *toe*, *foot* and *leg* (part specificity) and between *small*, *tiny* and *microscopic* (specificity of intensity). The opposite of being specific is being general.
(d) Vagueness includes two types, as follows: (i) being ill-defined (for example, if *chair* is defined as 'seat having legs and a back', then it is ill-defined or vague as to having arms); (ii) having lax application (for example, *line* is lax in application, or vague, in being applied to an uneven row of people, as well as to a geometric line). The opposite of being vague is being precise.
(e) Basicness: being primary in the mind's system of meaning: a word's meaning is basic if other words are understood by it; children normally learn more basic concepts before less basic ones. DOG is more basic than both COLLIE and ANIMAL; RED is more basic than MAROON. (I emphasise 'understood'; how words are defined is a separate issue.) However, I regard basicness as being important psycholinguistically, rather than linguistically, and will deal with it in §9.2.

The scale from *chair* through *furniture* to *object* is a variation in both specificity and vagueness; the two qualities are correlates, in both being ways in which words apply widely, and in commonly occurring together – 'that object' is both more general and more vague than 'that chair' (although 'the Milky Way galaxy' is both general and precise).

Relative dimensions relate different elements of a complex word meaning.

(a) Necessity and expectedness. Cruse (2004: 54) says that in the full meaning of *dog* (when used descriptively), ANIMAL is a necessary feature, ABLE TO BARK is an expected feature, BROWN is possible, ABLE TO SING is unexpected, and OF THE FISH FAMILY is impossible. An example from premodifiers is that SILENT is necessary in *still* <2> (in SOED: 'Espec. of a person: silent…'); it is merely possible in *still* <4> ('Free from commotion…'); and it is impossible in *still* <3> ('Of a voice: …not loud'). Necessary and expected meaning elements are usually salient. Expected and possible elements may be excluded by the context, or simply not evoked; they include concepts from 'frames' and 'scenarios' evoked by a word. These distinctions are also made (in different terms) by Burnley (1992: 466). Schwanenflugel (1991: 246) says that there has been a 'general movement' in recent studies towards such a view of meaning.
(b) Sufficiency. For *mammalian*, ANIMAL is a necessary but not sufficient feature of meaning; the addition of SUCKLING ITS YOUNG would make a sufficient combination.
(c) Salience. Salience is the degree to which the feature of meaning stands out from the mental background, or is 'foregrounded'. Elements of

meaning are salient if they are contrasted with another element, if they are in focus in some way, or if we are very conscious of them. In 'He walked with <u>leaden</u> feet', lead's weight is salient; in 'under a <u>leaden</u> sky', it is the colour that is salient.

These dimensions may distinguish among synonyms. (I regard synonyms as 'words whose semantic similarities are more salient than their differences' – Cruse 2004: 154; they are not identical in meaning, and their differences will be important in what follows.) The dimensions may also distinguish among different senses of a word and among different uses of what a dictionary would regard as the same sense of a word.

3.1.2.4   Conclusion: types and dimensions of meaning

In summary, I distinguish five types of meaning: referential, descriptive, expressive, social and grammatical; and I see descriptive meaning as varying along intrinsic and relative dimensions. Those terms and concepts are fundamental to much of the book. Accordingly, I here adumbrate their importance. I will analyse in terms of types and dimensions of meaning: the four zones (this chapter), different senses of the same word, and different uses of what a dictionary might regard as the same sense (most chapters), relations between synonyms (see chapter 6, 'Free order'), and changes in the meaning of a word (see chapter 7, 'Marked order', and chapter 8, Historical explanation).

It will be evident that I do not see words' meaning elements as being units unique to each word, but as parts of a network, each part being shared to some degree by other words: 'bounded sense units are not a property of lexical items as such; rather they are construed at the moment of use' (Croft and Cruse 2004: 109). Lamb (1999, 2004), for example, develops that view.

It will be evident also that in discussing semantics I am concerned not so much with word content as with the way in which words go about conveying content and making reference. (I am certainly not concerned with things in the real world that words may be taken to refer to.) For example, *red* and *green* are semantically the same, for my concerns, since they go about relating language to our experience in the same way – by evoking perceptual experience; but 'of the colour that mixes yellow and blue' is semantically quite different from 'green', since it works conceptually, not perceptually. The term 'semantic structure' relies on this understanding of semantics. (Grimshaw 2005, e.g. 76–7, develops a similar concept, in which *cat* and *dog* are semantically alike, and *melt* and *freeze*.)

Thus, for example, synonyms such as *tight-fisted* and *economical* differ in semantic structure, as follows. *Economical*$_1$ (a subsense of SOED sense <4>) is a neutral sense, with the descriptive meaning '...careful of resources'; *economical*$_2$ (another subsense of SOED <4>, stated there as '...thrifty') has the same descriptive meaning, but it also has an attitudinal meaning of approval,

Table 3.1 *Sample Epithets and Descriptors*

Det.	Epithet	Descriptor	Classifier	Head
a	*splendid*	*silver*	*plastic*	*suitcase*
the	*corrupt*	*local*	*music*	*scene*
a	*mammoth*	*three-tiered*	*wedding*	*cake*

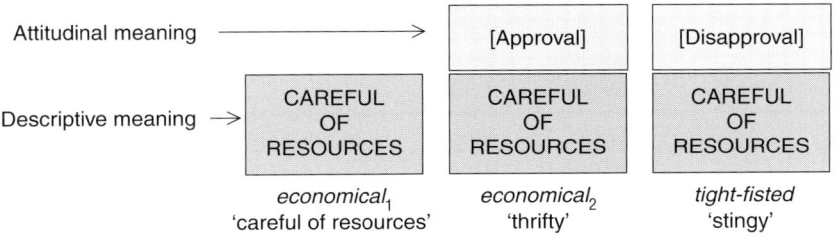

Figure 3.2 Example of semantic structure

as well; *tight-fisted* (SOED '…stingy') has the same descriptive meaning, but has an attitudinal meaning of disapproval. The three senses may be represented graphically, in figure 3.2. The types of meaning are labelled on the left, and are represented by the sections of the vertical bars which make up each sense's semantic structure.

3.1.3 Data

The rest of this chapter (§3.2 onwards) begins the discussion of the first issue set for the book, in §1.1: why there are rules or patterns for the normal order, and what their nature is. This section makes that issue concrete by giving samples of the data to be explained.

Consider the phrases in table 3.1. What is it about the meaning of the Epithets *splendid*, *corrupt* and *mammoth* that makes them precede the other premodifiers? Why do *silver, local* and *three-tiered* come next? In those examples, the words in the different zones have different core meanings; but we must also account for the fact that words occur in different zones with the same core meaning – often in three of the zones, and even in all four zones. The point was made in previous chapters; *pure* and *triangular* provide further examples. What is it about the different uses of *pure*, in table 3.2, that makes them occur in different zones? In the uses of *triangular* in table 3.3, the differences in meaning are slighter still: why are they in different zones?

In a 2006 cartoon, the figure representing Iran says 'We have enriched uranium… and depleted scruples…'; George Bush, president of the USA,

Table 3.2 Pure *used in different zones*

Det.	Reinforcer	Epithet	Descriptor	Classifier	Head
	pure	undiluted	[*modern*]		*hypocrisy*
		pure	white-skinned	[*Irish*]	*colleens*
a		[*legitimate*]	new and *pure*	German	*identity*
		[*attractive*]	[*new*]	Shetland *pure*	*wool*

Table 3.3 Triangular *used in different zones*

Det.	Epithet	Descriptor	Classifier	Head
a	*triangular*	yellow	[*glass*]	bottle
	short	*triangular*	pelvic	fins
	[*strange*]	broken	*triangular*	pediments

responds, '... join the club...'. The humour relies on two different uses of *enriched* (and similarly of *depleted*). How can you pun on a single word? Those examples, and the questions, indicate the scope of this chapter.

3.1.4 Word histories

Understanding words' historical changes of meaning helps in understanding the semantic relationships between the zones; so, although I devote a chapter later in the book to historical explanation, I give some incidental historical explanation in this chapter. I provide a basis for that in this section, by giving three brief word histories that will illustrate the historical connections between the zones, and the main issues. *Byzantine* is given first, as a straightforward and fairly typical history; *bloody* illustrates clearly the development of social and expressive meaning; *positive* illustrates development through all four zones.

The first recorded use of *Byzantine* was in the late eighteenth century. It meant: <1> 'Of or pertaining to Byzantium, the Eastern Roman Empire, or the Orthodox Church'. It had referential meaning (identifying a referent, Byzantium) and grammatical meaning (that of being a modifier, indicated by 'Of or pertaining to'); it had no descriptive meaning. Through frequent application of the word to artistic work, a new sense developed by the mid nineteenth century: <2> 'Spec. Characteristic of the artistic (esp. architectural) style developed in the Eastern Roman Empire'; that has descriptive meaning – partly conceptual (expressed by 'characteristic' and 'style'), but partly perceptual (the physical characteristics concerned). A parallel development occurred from applying the meaning 'of Byzantium' to politics – the first part of sense <3> 'Like Byzantine politics'. That was extended and abstracted, to produce (by the mid twentieth century) the second and third subsenses of <3>, '...complicated; inflexible'; the meaning is wholly conceptual. The last stage has been the development of a new conceptual element and the addition of expressive meaning (disapproving attitude) in the last subsense of <3>, '...underhand'. Although the reference to Byzantium survived in sense <2>, it is now lost – and the OED citations from 1965 and 1966 spell the word *byzantine* with a lower case *b*, accordingly.

The development of *bloody* is similar to that of *Byzantine*. Its first sense (in use in Old English, now obsolete) identified a referent – referential meaning: <1> 'Of the nature of, ... composed of ... blood'; for example, 'bloody drops'. Before the end of that period, it had developed a sense which added descriptive meaning: <2> 'Covered, smeared, or stained with blood'. In Middle English, sense <3> developed: 'Accompanied by, or involving bloodshed' – a more complex sense, with conceptual meaning along with the descriptive and referential elements. From these uses, sense <4> developed in Middle English: 'Of thoughts, words, etc.: concerned with, portending, or decreeing bloodshed', presumably with a possible element of condemnation. By the sixteenth century, sense <6> had developed – 'Bloodthirsty, blood-guilty': the disapproval has become salient, and the sense thus includes expressive meaning. By the mid seventeenth century, a new usage had developed: <8> 'Used vaguely as a strong imprecation or intensive'; being vague, it has lost most of its descriptive meaning ('covered with...' and 'bloodthirsty' have gone); it has either expressive meaning (as 'imprecation') or grammatical meaning of intensification (as 'intensive'). By the eighteenth century, it had social meaning – that of social context: the word was 'on a par with obscene language' (SOED, on the adverbial use); it had the social function of establishing that speaker and hearer were lower-class equals. By the twentieth century, disapproval was no longer a necessary meaning – the word could be used of something the speaker admired.

Figure 3.3 presents the changes in types of meaning as the word gained new senses. The figure reads from the bottom left: it shows new senses developing through time, left to right (with SOED's sense number and period of origin across the bottom); and it shows the layers of meaning being added, on the vertical axis. The wording of the senses (in the columns) is paraphrased from the SOED definitions. The first two columns may be paraphrased as follows: *bloody*, in its first recorded sense, i.e. <1>, (in Old English), had only referential meaning – '...of blood', as in 'bloody drops'; in the same period, it gained perceptual meaning in sense <2> '...covered in [blood]' – something you perceive by sight. (The figure omits modificational meaning, since all of the senses have it.)

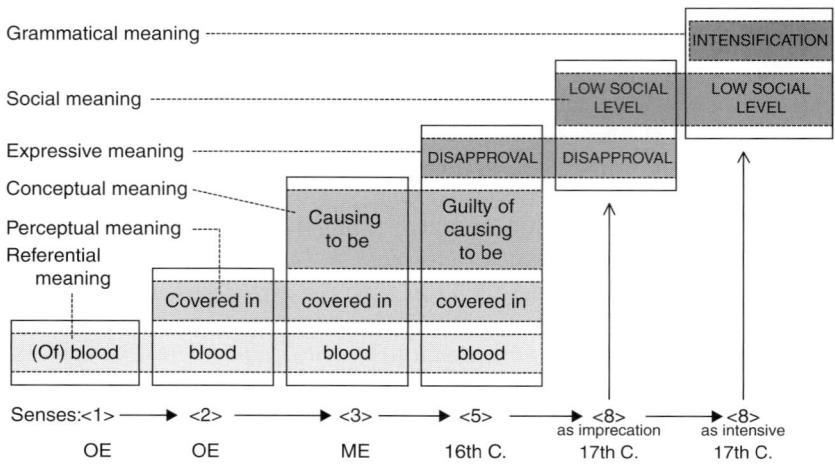

Figure 3.3 *Bloody*: changes in types of meaning, in new senses

Positive has been similar in acquiring abstract and expressive meaning elements (though different in developing a number of technical senses); I include it to illustrate the development of a purely grammatical sense. By the seventeenth century, it had developed a quite abstract sense <5a>, 'Having no relation to or comparison with other things; not relative; absolute…'. By the early nineteenth century, that had led to <5b>, 'That is absolutely what is expressed by the noun; …downright, out-and-out', which SOED illustrates by 'a positive eyesore'. That has the grammatical meaning of intensification.

In those three histories, there are regularities and irregularities in patterns of change, and very gradual changes in meaning. Similarly, in studying the semantic nature of the premodification zones, we should expect to meet both regularities and irregularities in patterns of meaning, both fine distinctions and great differences in the various uses of the same word, and senses that are close to the border between zones. Keeping this historical perspective in mind should aid the following discussion.

3.1.5 Conclusion to the introduction

In this long introduction, I have set out the concepts I will use in this semantic explanation, some data that provide a challenge and stimulus to explanation, and the historical perspective, which will be a useful background. I now turn to the semantic explanation itself, taking the zones in turn and beginning with the Classifier zone. The discussion will be a little discursive, because it will be used in later chapters as well as for the immediate purpose of explaining order semantically.

Table 3.4 *Sample Classifiers*

Det.	Epithet	Descriptor	Classifier	Head
Holland's	*premium*	*white*	*clover*	*honey*
a			*British Pakistani*	*taxi-driver*
a	*shabby*	*dark*	*city*	*suit*

3.2   Semantic structure of Classifiers

3.2.1   Introduction

This section explains the semantic structure of Classifiers. Some examples of phrases with Classifiers are given in table 3.4. The argument of this section is as follows. Classifiers as individual words have referential meaning; they name a bare mental referent, a single concept. In use in a phrase, Classifiers evoke a constructional grammatical meaning, which relates that concept to the head. They have no descriptive meaning, as necessary meaning. The combination of bare reference and implicit grammatical meaning makes the Classifier zone semantically unique.

3.2.2   Grammatical meaning in Classifiers

Classifiers have the grammatical meaning of modification: in effect, they instruct the hearer to relate the entity denoted to the meaning of the head-word: in 'clover honey', *clover* instructs the reader to relate the concept CLO-VER to the referent of the headword, *honey*.

  Our main concern in this section, however, is with the other type of grammatical meaning explained in the introduction to the chapter, constructional meaning: an implicit relation between modifier and head. Examples are as follows: 'Clover honey', which designates honey MADE FROM clover; 'British … taxi-driver', which designates a taxi-driver OF British NATIONALITY; and 'city … suit', which designates a suit OF WHAT IS CALLED THE 'city' TYPE. (To simplify exposition, I will in this chapter generalise those relations as TYPE – clover honey will be a type of honey, a British driver will be a type of driver. I will return to the distinctions in the Classifiers chapter.)

  This implicit relation is not part of the meaning of the modifier itself; the hearer takes it from the construction of the phrase (aided by world knowledge). That can be seen clearly from phrases like example (1).

(1)   'Pakistani British Muslims' (Corpus of Contemporary American English)

British identifies the referents' place of residence and *Pakistani* classifies them ethnically; residence and ethnicity would be reversed if the Classifiers were reversed (in #'British Pakistani Muslims'); so the relationship to the head depends on the position of the word. Similarly with example (2).

(2)   'French teacher'

The phrase is ambiguous between referring to a teacher of French and a teacher from France, until we have an order to show us the construction: #'English <u>French</u> teacher' denotes a teacher of French, but #'<u>French</u> English teacher' denotes a teacher from France. The constructional meaning derives from the position or order, not from the word itself.

The nature of the constructional meaning can be seen also from the usual unacceptability of using these premodifiers predicatively. We cannot say *'The honey is clover', or (for 'a criminal lawyer'), *'The lawyer is criminal'. We must add the constructional meaning, and say 'The honey is OF THE clover TYPE', and 'The lawyer is OF THE criminal-LAW TYPE'. To function as premodifiers, words must denote some quality which can be ascribed to a head.[1] Classifiers as individual words do not denote qualities, but constructional meaning and referential meaning combine to provide them: OF THE CLOVER TYPE is a property, parallel to OF RED COLOUR (for *red*). (Some Classifiers, such as *English*, are borderline in acceptability in predicative use; and usage is changing, I believe, toward accepting expressions like #'The range is 110 cm', as well as 'a 110 cm range'.)

The reality of Classifiers' constructional meaning can be seen also from expressions like 'an apparent electrical fire'. It is neither electricity nor the fire that is apparent, but the causation – the fire is apparently caused by electricity; but the concept of causation is not explicit in the phrase, being evoked by the constructional meaning.

3.2.3   *Referential meaning in Classifiers*

3.2.3.1   *Quality dimension*

Classifiers as individual words (distinct from the constructional meaning they invoke) serve the function of naming a mental referent, rather than carrying any qualitative meaning. That is quite clear for some Classifiers, which are arbitrary: for example, '<u>gamma</u> rays'. Others are words whose usual meaning elements are irrelevant or even misleading in this use: for example, '<u>top</u> quark', '<u>crescent</u> spanner'. I am asserting, then, that Classifiers as a group are names, in much the same way: they identify an individual entity or type of entity, without having descriptive elements in their necessary meaning.

---

[1] As we will see later, Reinforcers (§3.5) and modal premodifiers (§4.4) are exceptions to that generalisation.

That can be seen in several other ways.

(a) It is apparent from the importance of referential stability (as explained in the introduction on types of meaning). That is, words such as *passport* and *cat* (as Classifiers, in '<u>passport</u> photo' and '<u>cat</u> door') would retain their meaning in the phrase, and their use would still be valid, if the required size of the photo changed, or if the door was used by other pets.

(b) The role of referential meaning in Classifiers is reflected in the structure of dictionary entries. The SOED, for example, gives Classifier senses by the formula 'Of or pertaining to...' *Oil* as a Classifier, for example, is <1> 'Of, pertaining to...oil'. (As a Descriptor, it is <2> 'Smeared or covered with oil...') The phrase 'Of or pertaining to' expresses grammatical meaning – 'Relate this entity to the headword'; it does not express any qualitative meaning.

(c) Classifiers frequently become head of the phrase (standing on their own, in the place of Classifier + head): 'cashew nuts' becomes 'cashews', 'a television set' becomes 'a television', and so on. That indicates that the head is felt to be redundant, having the same meaning as the Classifier, which is referential, just as the head is.

(d) As noted previously, Classifiers cannot be used predicatively: we cannot say, *'The nut is cashew', *'The photo is passport'.

Nouns, then, have two uses: first, stating qualities, descriptively, and second, identifying an entity, referentially. The point argued so far in this section is that whereas nouns as heads may have either use, nouns as Classifiers occur only in the identifying, referential use; their necessary meaning is a mental referent, without descriptive content. (Possible Classifier exceptions will be discussed below, in §3.2.4.4; nouns used as Descriptors or Epithets do have descriptive meaning – see §§3.3.6 and 3.4.6.)

This emphasis is supported by Anderson (1997), who sees naming as the quintessential function of nouns, and by Coates (2000). The psycholinguistic research cited in §9.2 will support these points further.

The second main point about Classifiers as individual words is that their meaning lacks boundedness and discreteness. Abstract and generic nouns used as Classifiers fairly obviously do not denote discrete entities; but even concrete noun Classifiers, I assert, are not understood as designating discrete entities, delimited in space and time; they are unbounded (§3.1.2.2). They are like mass nouns in English. They are also like all nouns in Thai and Yucatec Maya, as discussed by Rijkhoff (2002: 50–1): on their own, such nouns denote a substance rather than an individual entity; they become bounded and discrete (and therefore countable, for instance) only when used with a Classifier. (My quality, unboundedness, is Rijkhoff's feature, '[−Shape]'). Similarly, count nouns as Classifiers are generic. In 'a <u>student</u> centre' and 'a <u>cat</u> door', the Classifiers do not evoke in our minds any individuals, or any shape, or any countable number of students or cats – and are morphologically singular; accordingly, the entities are not bounded in space. 'A play station' identifies an activity, but evokes no time or duration: the event is unbounded in time. 'Wind conditions' can be used for a situation in which there is no wind. Those examples reinforce the fact that Classifiers' meaning is a bare concept.

Boundedness and discreteness are important issues in the overall structure and functioning of nominal phrases, and will be discussed in §§9.3.4 and 10.2.4.

3.2.3.2   Other dimensions
On the specificity dimension, Classifiers are specific, designating particular things or classes, not general ones. That is clear for Classifiers like *Ford*, *Paris* and *Byzantine*; but it is also true for Classifiers like 'mobile phone', 'bovine animals' and 'canine teeth'. Even closely related senses are commonly expressed by separate words, as in *ferric*, *ferrous* and *ferrosoferric*; Classifiers for SHINING include *fluorescent*, *phosphorescent*, *luminescent* and *luminiferous*. When one word does have different Classifier senses, they are quite different, not expressing shades of meaning: *perfect* means <13> 'Physics: ...obeying mathematical laws exactly'; <14> 'Printing: ...printed on both sides'; <15> 'Mycology: ...in the sexual state'. Those senses of *perfect* are as different in meaning as the homonyms *bank* (of a river) and *bank* (financial institution).

On the vagueness dimension, Classifiers are precise, as illustrated by the examples just given. (Classifiers can seem to be vague: *concrete* perhaps appears vague in its relation to its head – as in 'concrete nail' and 'concrete block', but the Classifiers chapter will show that those two phrases represent separate constructions, each with a specific meaning; those uses are ambiguous, not vague.)

3.2.4   Descriptive meaning in Classifiers

3.2.4.1   Perceptual meaning
As implied in the previous section, Classifiers have no descriptive elements as necessary meaning. The simple, bare nature of that meaning can be further illustrated by several contrasts – beginning with *silver* and *black*, in table 3.5. The meaning of the Classifier *silver*, in 'a tarnished... silver ring', is only the reference to the substance; it does not denote the perceptual qualities of colour and shininess as the Descriptor *silver* does in 'splendid silver plastic suitcase'. In 'amusing black comedy', *black* designates a type of comedy; it denotes no physical quality (as in 'full-length black leather coat' – Descriptor). The nature of the metaphor, here, is to abstract from the perceptual quality.

Table 3.5 Silver *and* black *as Classifier and Descriptor*

Epithet	Descriptor	Classifier	Head
	# *tarnished, old*	*Spanish silver*	*ring*
splendid	*silver*	*plastic*	*suitcase*
	amusing	*black*	*comedy*
full-length	*black*	*leather*	*coat*

3.2.4.2   Conceptual meaning

Classifiers do not denote conceptual qualities, just as they do not denote perceptual ones. That can be seen in several ways, as follows.

(a) The word *silver*, in 'a silver ring' (discussed above), does not denote the abstract qualities by which SOED explains it: malleability, ductility and atomic number 47.

(b) Words that have conceptual meaning in other uses lose it when they are used as Classifiers. The original meaning has been lost from the Classifiers in 'wisdom teeth' and 'canine teeth', just as *molars* no longer means 'grinders'. (The fact that some users may associate conceptual qualities with such words will be discussed below.)

(c) Often, a Classifier + head combination has a single word as an alternative. For example, we can say 'canines' or 'canine teeth', and 'mobile phone' or 'mobile'. In each case, the Classifier designates a subtype of the type of entity designated by its head, and the single noun designates that subclass directly; neither denotes the quality of being dog-like, or movable.

(d) People often do not, in fact, know the apparent descriptive meaning of Classifiers: people questioned about 'Rice Krispies' did not know they are made from rice (Wray 2002: 3).

3.2.4.3   Intensity dimension: gradability

Classifiers cannot be graded. We cannot say *'a very Ford sedan', *'a very London suburb', and so on – since those Classifiers designate entities. But even words that in other uses denote gradable concepts cannot be graded when used as Classifiers. We cannot say *'the most mobile phone'. As Huddleston (1984: 259) points out, it is acceptable to say 'extremely pornographic [Epithet] Swedish films', but not to say *'Swedish extremely pornographic [Classifier] films'; and compare Bauer (2004: 13) and Adamson (2000: 57). Similarly, Giegerich (2005: 574) points out that we cannot modify *feline, equine* or *bovine* in literal use, though we can do so in figurative use: in literal use, they are Classifiers, but in figurative use, they are Epithets, as shown in table 3.6.

Table 3.6 Pornographic *and* bovine *in gradable and non-gradable uses*

	Det.	Epithet	Desc.	Classifier	Head
Gradable		*extremely pornographic*	[*new*]	*Swedish*	*films*
	a	*most blank and bovine*	[*old*]	[*English*]	*nurse*
Not gradable			[*new*]	* *Swedish extremely pornographic*	*films*
			[*old*]	* *rather bovine*	*animals*

The non-gradability of these uses comes from their designating entities –
just as *Ford* and *London* do – types of entity, that is. (Note that we are dealing with what the language treats as entities, not with metaphysical entities.)
The impossibility of grading Classifiers reinforces the conclusion reached
just above, that they do not bear descriptive meaning; but the issue (generalised as scalarity) will be more important for its role in distinguishing
between Descriptors and Epithets.

3.2.4.4   Discussion of descriptive meaning of Classifiers
My assertion that Classifiers lack descriptive meaning needs further explanation, since commonly the words appear to have content meaning, especially
when they are used descriptively, as in advertising; 'Breville cordless ket-
tle', for example, is intended to have associations of convenience, as apparent
content. There are three elements in the explanation.
   The first element is that much of the apparent content is the constructional meaning discussed above. The second element is that nearly all the
remaining apparent content comes from world knowledge – from experience of life and from education – rather than from meaning that is part
of the linguistic system. As hearers, we use that knowledge in two ways.
First, we use it to determine the implicit relation which constitutes the
constructional meaning – whether *silver* will invoke MADE OF (as in 'silver
plate'), or FOR THE PURPOSE OF as with 'silver polish'). Second, we draw
on it for the details about the thing denoted – the apparent content – as
in 'silver plate', as malleable and ductile – and perhaps as having atomic
number 47. This explanation is supported directly by Hawkins (2004). Of
phrases like 'paper factory', 'paper plate', and so on, he says (2004: 47):
'All that the grammar really encodes here is that … *paper* is the syntactic and semantic modifier. These minimal grammatical specifications are
then enriched by language users with whatever meanings match the world
(a factory makes paper …).' Such a meaning is an 'inference' (2004: 48):
'These constructions can mean whatever the world allows them to mean,

as long as this is compatible with their minimally specified conventional meanings' (2004: 48). The explanation is also in line with most of the chapters in Peeters (2000).

The third element in the explanation is that sometimes the apparent content consists of qualities which are part of a word's meaning in other uses, which we associate with the word when we meet it used as a Classifier. (As suggested in §3.1.2 above, they are neighbouring elements of the semantic network, varying parts of which are invoked by different uses.) That works in several ways. First, the qualities are associations from uses of the words as Descriptors or Epithets, or as head nouns. The qualities may be invoked by the user deliberately, as in trade names like 'the <u>Precision</u> Engineering Company'. We may use the associations mnemonically, to help us grasp the reference, as in 'Breville <u>slow</u> cooker' or 'American <u>short</u> story'; it may be a <u>long</u> short story, since *short* is referential, not descriptive. (Compare the discussion in Bauer 1983: 142–3 on mnemonic motivation in word-formation where there is little content.) Second, the qualities may be invoked deliberately from the origin of the use, as in trade names like '<u>Lux</u> toilet soap', or retained by some users in examples like 'the <u>orange</u> revolution', '<u>crescent</u> spanner' and '<u>Ross River</u> fever'. These qualities constitute possible meanings, varying from person to person, not the necessary meaning which defines the use. Note that the usual content may be irrelevant: '<u>bronze</u> beetles' and '<u>brown</u> beetles' designate insects of the same colour.

In these ways, we can recognise the rather counterintuitive fact that as Classifiers, premodifiers do not have descriptive linguistic meaning.

3.2.4.5 *Conclusion: descriptive meaning in Classifiers*
All these instances show that the descriptive meaning of Classifiers as individual words is minimal. They designate percepts – objects of mental perception – which may be concrete (as in 'a <u>silver</u> ring') or abstract (as in '<u>anger</u> management'). They do not denote qualities, either perceptual or conceptual. They are thus monosemous. The descriptive meaning that they often appear to have is world knowledge or possible associated meaning elements, not the necessary or expected meaning.

3.2.5 *Expressive and social meaning in Classifiers*

With quite rare exceptions, Classifiers do not have expressive or social meaning. The exceptions occur when words bring to their use as Classifiers some social meaning from their use as nouns in other contexts. For example, in 'awesome <u>goodie</u> bags', the Classifier has the informality it gained as a noun in expressions like 'a box of doggie <u>goodies</u>'. '<u>Aussie</u> sport climbing malarkey' has an Australasian slang value.

Technical words are common among Classifiers, but they do not generally carry social meaning as technical jargon, as they do not contrast with a synonymous standard word, as in such sailing terms as '<u>mizzen</u> mast' and '<u>crossjack</u> yard'. An exception is 'traction': compare '<u>traction</u> engine' and '<u>draught</u> horse'; 'traction' is a little technical and 'draught' is a little archaic. (Why shouldn't we have 'a <u>draught</u> engine' and 'a <u>traction</u> horse'?)

3.2.6   *Discussion of Classifier meaning*

Nearly all of my instances of Classifiers have been nouns, and in common case; but nouns in genitive case and words other than nouns occur. However, they all identify a subtype of the type named by the head, as in the following: a genitive noun in 'Madame in her <u>men's</u> shoes'; adjectives in 'Australian <u>little</u> penguin', 'Swedish <u>pornographic</u> films' and 'costly <u>social</u> security'; verbal forms in 'British <u>disabled</u> skiers', '<u>eating</u> apples' and 'electric <u>soldering</u> iron'; and numerals in 'lower income black <u>fourth</u> graders' and 'dislocated <u>fourth</u> vertebra'.

Classifiers which are proper nouns clearly have no linguistic sense relations such as hyponymy and synonymy: in 'a <u>Ford</u> sedan', it is only by world knowledge that we know the relationship of *Ford* to *Mazda* and *Toyota*, or of *Holden* to *Commodore*. The same applies to *Byzantine* in 'a <u>Byzantine</u> street'; it is only as an Epithet that *Byzantine* has synonyms such as *devious*. Other noun Classifiers may have sense relations (e.g. hyponymy in '<u>silver</u> ring', '<u>metal</u> ring'), but in general, Classifiers have few sense relations.

Many words seem to be 'borderline' Classifiers. That is to be expected: I showed in §3.1.4 that *Byzantine*, a Classifier at first, gradually became a Descriptor, then an Epithet, gaining descriptive meaning; so it must at some time have been close to the borderline between zones. A word which currently seems to be close to that borderline is *Miltonic*. In expressions like 'the <u>Miltonic</u> period', the word is clearly a Classifier, with the phrase meaning 'the period when John Milton lived'; but we meet statements such as example (3).

(3)   Wordsworth 'was able to avoid <u>Miltonic</u> diction and write true "conversational" poems'. (British National Corpus)

There, the contrast with *conversational* requires *Miltonic* to mean 'formal' or 'literary', which would make the word a Descriptor. According to SOED, the word has no such established meaning; so I take the word to be ambivalent between the contextual meaning, 'formal', and the established meaning, 'of Milton's time'. It is thus, loosely speaking, 'on the borderline' between the Classifier and Descriptor zones. Strictly, however, it has an established Classifier use, and a not-yet-established use as a Descriptor. Moreover, it would have been a Classifier for the writer – having a referential sense – if he had co-ordinated *Miltonic* with a Classifier (e.g. #'<u>Jacobean</u> and <u>Miltonic</u> diction'); but if he had made it precede a Classifier (without coordination, as in #'Miltonic Restoration diction'), it would have been for him a Descriptor or Epithet – a descriptive sense. To give a final, fairly common example: the British National Corpus shows that 'England team' is now often preferred to 'English team'. *English* therefore seems to be 'on the borderline' between referential and descriptive senses; but in a particular utterance, it is intended, and should be understood, with either the referential or the descriptive sense – it cannot straddle a 'borderline'. (I will discuss 'borderline' instances in the sections on other zones, but I will not repeat the argument that they cannot be <u>on</u> a borderline. Chapter 8 will give a historical explanation for these phenomena, applying to all zones.)

As previously noted, I have deferred full treatment of Classifiers to the separate Classifiers chapter. Accordingly, this section has simplified the semantics, by excluding detail and by the generalisation that Classifiers denote types.

3.2.7 Conclusion: the semantic structure of Classifiers

This section on the semantic structure of Classifiers may be summarised as follows. Classifiers as individual words vary a little in type of meaning, the extreme being proper nouns, which have minimal linguistic meaning. But Classifiers are all alike in three ways. Their linguistic meaning is referential, designating entities. They represent the entity as a unit; that is, the meaning does not include related details and concepts, or feelings or social connotations, and they are simple in semantic structure. Finally, their apparent descriptive content is either constructional meaning (a necessary meaning), or world knowledge of the entity referred to, or historical or personal association with other uses of the word (expected or possible meaning, but not <u>necessary</u> meaning). Apart from that lexical meaning, Classifiers in a phrase invoke a constructional meaning, which relates the meaning of the Classifier itself to what the head designates. The zone thus has a dual semantic structure: simple lexical meaning and constructional meaning.

3.3 Semantic structure of Descriptors

3.3.1 Introduction

This section will discuss the semantic structure of Descriptors, as illustrated in table 3.7. The argument is that Descriptors differ from Classifiers in not being referential words, and in having descriptive meaning (which is largely perceptual, with some conceptual element).

3.3.2 Referential meaning in Descriptors

Descriptors contrast with Classifiers in having no referential meaning; that is, they do not name a referent. (They can be used to help the speech act of

Table 3.7 *Sample Descriptors*

Det.	Epithet	Descriptor	Classifier	Head
	little	*black*	*iron*	*fences*
a	*mammoth*	*three-tiered*	*wedding*	*cake*
a	*large*	*growing*	*[English]*	*family*
	immensely gifted	*disabled*	*Irish*	*writers*
her	*long*	*glittering*	*crystal*	*beads*
the	*archaic*	*Byzantine*	*[architectural]*	*style*
	skinny	*frilled*		*dress*

Table 3.8 Byzantine *as Classifier and Descriptor*

Det.	Epithet	Descriptor	Classifier	Head
a	*tiny*	*[old]*	*Byzantine*	*coin*
the		*Byzantine*	*[architectural]*	*style*

referring, by restricting the reference of the head; and they have a connection with external 'reality' through their psychological basis in perception; but neither of those constitutes their meaning as considered here.)

Descriptors such as *black*, *growing* and *disabled* clearly are not names. Even *Byzantine* as a Descriptor is not a naming word. The meaning, as in '...the archaic *Byzantine* [architectural] style' for example, is <2> 'Characteristic of the artistic (esp. architectural) style developed in the Eastern Roman Empire'. As the definition indicates, the name of the city or empire does not constitute its meaning; the reference to Byzantium is part of its possible meaning, as a readily available association, but it is not a necessary part of its meaning, because the style was used in other areas and periods. Compare the uses in table 3.8. In the examples in table 3.8, 'Byzantine coin' necessarily refers to Byzantium, but 'Byzantine [architectural] style' does not do so necessarily.

When *silver* gained a Descriptor use in Late Middle English, it came to denote a perceptual quality, and became detached from the referent (the metal) and from its world-knowledge associations of 'easily worked' and so on, as in 'splendid silver plastic suitcase'. Compare the uses in table 3.9.

Again in contrast with the referential meaning of Classifiers, Descriptor senses are bounded: they are conceived in relation to space or time. Compare the pairs of uses in table 3.10.

In 'permanent red alert', *red* denotes no area, but in 'red silken shirt', we apply it to the area of the shirt. In 'running races', *running* is like *athletic* in designating only a type (not movement or duration), but in 'running cold water' it is conceived with movement in time.

Table 3.9 Silver *as Classifier and Descriptor*

Det.	Epithet	Descriptor	Classifier	Head
#*a*	*splendid*	*old*	*Spanish silver*	*ring*
a	*splendid*	*silver*	*plastic*	*suitcase*

Table 3.10 Red *and* running *as Classifier and Descriptor*

Word	Det.	Descriptor	Classifier	Head
red		*permanent*	*red*	*alert*
		red	*silken*	*shirt*
running		#*recent*	*running*	*races*
		running	*cold*	*water*

3.3.3 *Descriptive meaning in Descriptors*

3.3.3.1 *Perceptual meaning*

Whereas the meaning of Classifiers is an entity, the meaning of Descriptors is a perceptual quality or state which is being ascribed to an entity. It is commonly a sensory quality or state, as in *silver* (just cited), 'full-length black leather coat', 'cold rain showers', 'a mammoth three-tiered wedding cake'; but it may be somewhat more abstract, as with 'my super-duper new pup tent' and 'hard young [British] officer'. Descriptors commonly have the 'direct connection to the visual perceptual system' described by Lamb (1999: 146), but they grade off to more conceptual words, as in #'a tiny old Byzantine coin'.

The point is seen clearly in the contrast between Descriptor and Classifier uses of the same word. We have already seen that with *silver* and *black*. Further examples are given in table 3.11. The Classifier uses designate types, as discussed in §3.2. As to the Descriptor uses: *short* and *distorted* obviously have perceptual descriptive meaning, I believe; *positive* means <6> 'Consisting in ... the presence... of features... rather than their absence' – the meaning consists of the simple perception of presence (of the enjoyment, in this context); *young* is descriptive – it has a strong conceptual element, but is based on concrete fact that is ultimately perceptual.

3.3.3.2 *Conceptual meaning*

When words develop a Descriptor sense, some element of their meaning is generalised, and the structure of its intrinsic dimensions changes. As *Byzantine*, for example, developed its descriptive meaning according to the similarity of certain buildings, their artistic style was generalised and applied across works from different places; the physical style, which had been merely a possible part of the meaning, became the core, expected meaning: '...distinguished by its

Table 3.11 *Other words as Classifier and Descriptor*

Word	Det.	Epithet	Descriptor	Classifier	Head
short	*a*			*Steve Harrison short*	*ball*
	her	*affectionate*	*short*	*[lyric]*	*poem*
distorted	*the*			*Ames distorted*	*room*
	a	*[big]*	*distorted and swollen*		*calyx*
positive				*human positive*	*law*
	the	*greatest*	*positive*		*enjoyment*
young				*English young*	*people*
			young	*American*	*composers*

Table 3.12 *Non-gradable and graded uses of* young *and* black

Word	Use	Epithet	Descriptor	C.	Head
retiring	Descriptor – not gradable		*retiring*	*Russian*	*cavalry*
	Epithet – graded	*[very] retiring*	*young*		*daughter*
black	Descriptor – not gradable	*little*	*black*		*dress*
	Epithet – graded	*very black and negative*	*[depressed]*		*mood*
		wonderful, very black, very witty	*[new]*		*book*

use of the round arch… and rich mosaic ornamentation' (OED). The colour of *silver* was generalised to apply to other substances. There is, then, some conceptual meaning in Descriptors. The conceptual meaning is quite weak, however. That is demonstrated by the difficulty that dictionaries have in stating the meaning of Descriptors – they commonly resort to pointing, rather than defining: *red* is <1> 'Of the colour of blood, a ruby etc'.

3.3.3.3 *Intensity dimension: gradability*

Descriptors are not gradable: we do not place their meaning on a scale. We cannot apply intensifiers such as *very* to 'silver hair', 'smashed chair', 'disabled Irish writers', or 'little black dress'. Some Descriptors appear to be gradable, but it is the Epithet senses of the words that are gradable. Examples are given in table 3.12, with a Descriptor use of the word followed by graded, Epithet uses.

The non-gradability of Descriptors results from their having perceptual meaning. Like most meaning, perceptual meaning is constructed from experience (or 'construed' – Cruse 2004: 262); it is not presented ready-made by the process of perception. When we construe basic perceptions, we do not construe the quality in degrees; we simply construe the quality (for example

RED, PREGNANT, DEPRESSED) as being present, not absent; it is only with greater abstraction that we construe qualities as being present to a certain degree. (This point will be amplified later, in the discussion of gradability in Epithets, in §3.4.2.3.)

Note that 'gradability' here is taken strictly as a matter of degree, distinct from modification for quality (e.g. 'well protected') or quantity (e.g. 'much needed').

3.3.3.4   Other dimensions

Descriptors vary considerably in specificity: there is a range from very specific to relatively general in *umber, brown* and *coloured*. On the vagueness dimension, some Descriptors are like Classifiers in being precise and monosemous, for example *cerise*, which means 'of a light clear red'. On the other hand, even the apparently precise colour words can be somewhat vague (lax in application): *red*, for example, is applied to rather different colours in 'red hair', 'a red horse' and 'a red face'. Some Descriptors, such as *new, old* and *young*, are vague in the second sense (only partly defined): *young* means 'not many [unspecified units] in age'. As we will see in §3.4 on Epithets, that degree of vagueness makes them like Epithets – indeed, those words are often used as Epithets.

3.3.3.5   Conclusion: descriptive meaning

There is some conceptual meaning in Descriptors, therefore (in that even perceptual sense elements are generalised across instances); but they are primarily perceptual. In general, they are less precise and specific than Classifiers.

3.3.4   Expressive and social meaning in Descriptors

Descriptors do not have expressive meaning. As I will show in §3.4.3.3, words must have scalar descriptive meaning to have expressive meaning, and that makes them Epithets. Social meaning occurs only rarely in Descriptors, if at all. The reason is given in §3.4.4. A possible example is in 'desiccated coconut', *desiccated* being a technical or formal equivalent to *dried*.

3.3.5   Grammatical meaning in Descriptors

Descriptors have modificational grammatical meaning, as all modifiers do: they direct the hearer to apply the content of the word to the head. They do not invoke any constructional meaning, as Classifiers do. Consider the uses of *high* in table 3.13, for example: *high* as Classifier must be understood constructionally – 'a street OF THE TYPE DESIGNATED 'high'' – but *high* as Descriptor must not.

3.3.6   Discussion of Descriptor meaning

3.3.6.1   Descriptors' part of speech

Most Descriptors are adjectives: *black, red, young*, and so on. A few are in the form of nouns, as in 'a silver sound' and 'copper hair', but denote qual-

Table 3.13 *Constructional and non-constructional uses of* high

Det.	Epithet	Descriptor	Classifier	Head
	mild	*high*	blood	pressure
a	typical	suburban	*high*	street

Table 3.14 *Nouns as Descriptors*

Det.	Epithet	Descriptor	Classifier	Head
the	finest	20th *century*	British	painters of flowers
an		early *1970s*	Japanese performance	car

ities not entities (hence their being listed as adjectives by SOED). Table 3.14 gives further examples.

Many Descriptors, however, are verbal in form (having a participial ending); for example (from table 3.7), *disabled, glittering* and *frilled*. To the extent that verbs denote events, their presence is anomalous, since we expect premodifiers to denote qualities and verbs to be predicators. They are acceptable here for two reasons. First, they are construed as states rather than events, and the state is in turn construed as a quality. (Representing an event or state as a quality is semantic metaphor, parallel to regular metaphor – which represents an entity of one physical class by another to which it does not belong – and grammatical metaphor – which represents a semantic entity by a grammatical form to which it does not normally belong; see Halliday 2004.) Second, participles (e.g. *glittering* and *frilled*) fit the descriptive zone in being perceptual – rather than conceptual as Epithets are – and descriptive – not referential as Classifiers are.

Occasionally, numerals and quantifiers are used as Descriptors, as in 'an unprecedented <u>fourth</u> gold medal', 'a <u>fourth</u>, spontaneously created echo' and 'the vital <u>few</u> strategic areas'. (It is not only their position that makes those words Descriptors; they provide new, descriptive information, whereas numerals and quantifiers used as determiners rely on given, non-descriptive information.)

3.3.6.2   Sense relations

Descriptors form semantic relations with other words to a much greater extent than Classifiers do, in the following ways:

(a) Hyponymy. *Coloured* has *red* and *blue* as hyponyms; *red* has *scarlet* and *maroon*; but the Descriptors *young, cold, grassy* and *Byzantine* do not appear to have such relationships.

(b) Opposition of meaning. Descriptors do not in general have antonyms (in the sense of polar or other gradable opposites, like *cold/hot*, *large/small*); but they have a complementary term (the two words divide a conceptual area into mutually exclusive compartments) or other incompatible word. (The distinction is from Cruse 2004: ch. 9.) Examples of complementaries are *working/retired*, *living/dead*, *moving/stationary*. Examples of other incompatible related words are: *red/black/silver*, *grassy/stony/sandy*, *Byzantine/Gothic/neo-classical*. (Note that *young*, *old*, *cold* and *hot* also have Epithet uses, and have antonyms in that use; see §3.4, below.)

(c) Synonymy. Some words with Descriptor uses have synonyms; but it is striking that the synonyms commonly are not Descriptors but Epithets (having expressive or social meaning, as discussed in the following section on Epithets): *old-ancient*, *young-juvenile*, *cold-frigid*, *black-inky*. (The second in each pair is an Epithet, when used in the sense in which it is a synonym.)

(d) Semantic fields. A number of Descriptors fit into semantic fields (their place in the field largely defining their meaning), rather than into the patterns listed above. Examples include the colour words (in the field *red*, *orange*, *yellow*, *green*, and so on); and *-ed* and *-ing* participial forms, as in 'her <u>sleeping</u> face' (where *sleeping* goes with alternatives such as *dozing* and associated activities such as *dreaming*). The semantic fields, in which the patterns are irregular and dependent on the facts of the world, are more typical of Descriptors than are the regular and linguistic patterns of synonymy and antonymy.

3.3.6.3 Borderline instances of Descriptors

Some participles which were Descriptors in their first premodifier use are now Epithets (and are rated as adjectives in dictionaries), as with *surprising* in '<u>surprising</u> new catwalk trend'. It is natural, therefore, that Descriptors grade off towards being Epithets. An example is *frilled*, as in 'a skinny <u>frilled</u> dress', where *frilled* is very close in meaning to *frilly* (which is usually an Epithet – 'a <u>frilly</u> pink dress'). *Old* and *new* as Descriptors are also close to the border of that zone, since they have a somewhat vague meaning, and are frequently used as Epithets (examples are given in §3.4.2.3, below).

Conversely, there are instances close to the borderline with the Classifier zone, as participles weaken in event meaning and begin to acquire referential meaning (denoting a type of the head entity). 'Courageous British <u>disabled</u> skiers' has *disabled* as a Classifier but 'gifted <u>disabled</u> Irish writers' has it as a Descriptor; the latter use is very close to having the 'type' meaning of the former use.

3.3.7 Conclusion: the semantic structure of Descriptors

The main points from this section are that Descriptors have descriptive meaning; that they are empty of constructional meaning, of referential,

Table 3.15 *Sample Epithets*

Det.	Epithet	Descriptor	Classifier	Head
a	*bold*	*new*	*internet-based*	*strategy*
an	*epic*	*eight-minute*	*atmospheric*	*adventure*
a	*cushy*	*subsidised*		*existence*
a	*beaut*	*well-behaved*		*stag*
a	*queer*	*white*	*misty*	*patch*
the	*beautiful*	*sunny*	*winter*	*weather*

expressive and social meaning; and that they are not gradable. Secondary points about Descriptors are as follows: they are fairly simple in semantic structure, objective and dominantly perceptual; in comparison with Classifiers, they are more general, have more complexity of relations to other words, and are vaguer; and there is a significant semantic difference between the participial Descriptors and adjectival or nominal Descriptors, although they share the qualities listed in this summary.

3.4 Semantic structure of Epithets

3.4.1 Introduction

This section will discuss the semantic structure of Epithets, which are illustrated in table 3.15. The section does not discuss referential meaning, since it does not occur in this zone, just as it does not occur in the Descriptor zone.

3.4.2 Descriptive meaning in Epithets

3.4.2.1 Perceptual meaning

Many Epithets have perceptual meaning, just as Descriptors do, but it is less important than for Descriptors, as shown in the rest of this section. In table 3.16, *round* illustrates the continuity of perceptual meaning between Descriptor and Epithet uses (both denote shape); *great* illustrates perceptual meaning in a word without a Descriptor use (denoting size). Other examples of Epithets with perceptual meaning are *big*, *delicious* and *slim*.

The reduced importance of perceptual meaning is shown in the frequent loss or weakening of that meaning in the Epithet use of words that are usually Descriptors, as in table 3.17. Here, *black* means <8b>, 'Macabre'; BLACKNESS is not part of the necessary meaning of the Epithet use.

3.4.2.2 Conceptual meaning

The conceptual nature of Epithets can be seen clearly in their contrast with Descriptor uses of the same words. *Byzantine* as Descriptor, we saw, denotes

Table 3.16 *Perceptual meaning*

Det.	Epithet	Descriptor	Classifier	Head
a	prominent	<u>round</u>	classical	building
	<u>round</u>	pink	[female]	face
	<u>great</u>	grey	cylindrical	waves

Table 3.17 *Weakening of perceptual meaning*

Det.	Epithet	Descriptor	Classifier	Head
a	full-length	<u>black</u>	leather	coat
a	spicy, very <u>black</u>	[new]		comedy

Table 3.18 Byzantine *and* backward *as Descriptor and Epithet*

Word	Det.	Epithet	Descriptor	Classifier	Head
Byzantine	an	archaic	<u>Byzantine</u>	[architectural]	style
	Gordon Brown's	<u>Byzantine</u>	[new]	tax	credits
backward	a	regretful	<u>backward</u>		glance
	a	<u>backward</u>, ignorant, illiterate, inward-looking	[native]		people

architecture with round arches (and so on); as an Epithet, it means <3> 'Like Byzantine politics; complicated, inflexible; underhand'. The abstract meaning is sometimes achieved by metaphor: compare 'a regretful <u>backward</u> glance' (literal, a Descriptor) and 'a <u>backward</u>, ignorant, illiterate, inward-looking [native] people' (metaphorical, an Epithet). See table 3.18.

Conceptual meaning often occurs with other types of meaning. In '<u>garish</u> one-piece climbing suit', for example, garish (<1> '...gaudy, over-decorated') has perceptual meaning (DECORATED), conceptual meaning (EXCESSIVE) and expressive meaning (disapproval).

3.4.2.3   *Intensity dimension: gradability and scalarity*
We have seen that Descriptors are not gradable; most Epithets, however, are gradable – that is a crucial difference between them.

In being gradable, Epithets can represent different degrees of the quality denoted, the degree being expressed in different ways. It can be indicated by comparative and superlative forms, as in *big, bigger, biggest*, and in *curious, more curious* and *most curious*; or by intensifying submodifiers such

Table 3.19 *Grading by intensifying adverbs*

Word	Use	Det.	Epithet	Descriptor	Class.	Head
carved	Descriptor	*the*	*great*	*carved*	*stone*	*dragon*
	Epithet–graded	*the*	*heavy, badly carved*	*dark-stained*		*wardrobe*
		the	*beautifully carved, ornate*	*[old]*		*design*
tailored	Descriptor	*a*	*smart*	*tailored*	*trouser*	*suit*
	Epithet–graded	*a*	*finely tailored, top-of-the-line*	*[new]*		*suit*

Table 3.20 *Grading by a derivational suffix*

Word	Det.	Epithet	Descriptor	Class.	Head
blackish	*the*	*blackish*	*central*		*cone*
	a	*blackish*	*smoky*		*violet*
	the only	*blackish*	*long-legged*		*bird*
greenish	*its*	*greenish, powerful*	*[curved]*		*beak*
	a	*dull, greenish*	*[thin]*		*sickle of shadow*

as *very*, *highly* and *extremely*: 'a <u>rather hoarse</u> female voice', 'a <u>thoroughly unitive</u> mystical experience'. In other instances, there are different words for the different degrees in the gradation, as in *small, tiny* and *minute*, paralleling *small, very small* and *extremely small*.

Some adverbs can intensify while being descriptive, thus denoting degree. Such adverbs turn into Epithets words that are otherwise Descriptors, such as the participial forms in table 3.19.

Gradability can also be represented by a derivational suffix. Words inflected with *-ish* denote a gradable quality and are Epithets, although the base forms are Descriptors. Table 3.20 gives examples from colour words (see §3.3).

It is important to note that words such as *carved, tailored, black, old* and *young* are not graded when used as Descriptors, but when used as Epithets they may be graded (by *-er/-est* or submodification), and have a changed meaning. It is also important that it is <u>uses</u> that are gradable or not gradable, rather than words. I illustrated the point in the Descriptors section, but I provide more examples, for reinforcement, in table 3.21.

The distinction between gradable Epithets and non-gradable Descriptors is not obvious, for several reasons. First, as just noted, words often have both Epithet and Descriptor uses. Second, the fact that words are Descriptors is often not apparent, since they commonly occur without another premodifier

Table 3.21 *Non-graded and graded uses*

Word	Use	Det.	Epithet	Descriptor	Classifier	Head
old	Epithet–graded		*a very old*	'new'		*breed*
		a	*very old*	[*black*]	*iron kissing*	*gate*
	Descriptor	*a*	*fat*	*old*		*pig*
young	Epithet–graded		*very young*	*pregnant*		*schoolgirls*
	Descriptor	*a*	*hard*	*young*		*officer*
black	Epithet; graded	*a*	*very black and negative*	[*recent*]		*mood*
		a	*wonderful, very black, very witty*	[*new*]		*book*
	Descriptor	*a*	*full-length*	*black*	*leather*	*coat*
white	Epithet; graded		*whitest, purest*	_		*sand*
	Descriptor	*a*	*feathery*	*white*	*mink*	*hat*

that would make the zoning clear. Third, the distinction depends on the counterintuitive fact that many qualities may be treated as either gradable or non-gradable (compare §3.3.3.3). As Croft and Cruse (2004: 167) say, the difference between gradable and non-gradable modifiers arises from complementary ways of seeing qualities: either as present or absent, or (with presence presupposed) as present more or less. That fits the distinction between Descriptors, which take the present-or-absent view of qualities, and Epithets, which take the present-more-or-less view. To take an example from the table: in 'a fat old pig', OLD is construed simply as present, not absent; in 'a very old "new" breed', it is construed as present to a great degree. In that last phrase, *new* is construed simply as present – the breed either is 'new' or is not – although *new* is often gradable, and an Epithet. Thus we meet 'new old' as well as 'old new', as in 'This is not just going to be another old new year'; the various senses of *new* are not all antonyms of all the senses of *old*. In the terms of Langacker (2006), Descriptors construe qualities as discrete; Epithets construe them as continuous.

A change of meaning goes with the change of viewpoint; or, to put it differently, if we grade a Descriptor, we change the meaning as well as the zone. (Adamson 2000 makes a similar point.) If, for example, we add *very* to *old*, in 'a fat old pig', we get #'a fat, very old pig' (which could also be #'a very old, fat pig'). 'Very old' needs to be co-ordinated with 'fat' by a comma or *and*: it is in the same zone, as an Epithet (table 3.22).

Furthermore, *old* now has not only the factual meaning <1> 'That has lived long…' (shared with the Descriptor use), but has expressive overtones and associations such as impressiveness; its meaning is close to <7a> '…primeval' or <7b> '…familiar from of old'. Similarly, '…a very clean

Table 3.22 Old *as Descriptor and Epithet*

Det.	Epithet	Descriptor	Class.	Head
a	*fat*	<u>*old*</u>		*pig*
a	*fat,* <u>*very old*</u>			*pig*
a	<u>*very old*</u>*, fat*			*pig*

Table 3.23 Smooth *as Descriptor and Epithet*

Det.	Epithet	Descriptor	Class.	Head
a	*very clean*	<u>*smooth*</u>		*shape*
# *a*	*very clean,* <u>*very smooth*</u>	[*moulded*]		*shape*

smooth shape' could have another *very* added, modifying *smooth*; but *smooth* would become an Epithet, co-ordinated with *clean* and having expressive meaning. See table 3.23.

We conclude tentatively that Epithets are gradable, but Classifiers and Descriptors are not.[2] However, there are some Epithets that are commonly regarded as non-gradable, because of the nature of their meaning. *Eternal* and *remorseless*, for example, seem to be Epithets that are in fact not graded: they do not occur with *very* in the British National Corpus, for example. But that corpus has examples of *very* used with *edible, exquisite, possible, viable* and *unique*, which are all not gradable in formal use. Those examples suggest that many users of English regard all Epithets as in some sense gradable. The explanation for that ambivalence as to gradability can be seen when we distinguish, as does Paradis (2001), between being gradable (in the narrower sense, i.e. intensifiable) and being scalar. The words being considered may not be intensifiable (by *-er, very,* etc.), but they are scalar. As with intensifiable words, their meanings are conceived as being on a scale, but they cannot be intensified because they are at the end of the scale – they are 'implicitly superlative' (Paradis 2001: 54). For example, *remorseless* is at the end of the scale 'rigorous' > 'harsh' > 'remorseless'; *unique* is at the end of the scale 'common' > 'uncommon' > 'rare' > 'unique'.

This distinction also applies to expletives (such as *bloody*) and attitudinal Epithets (as in 'the <u>wretched</u> fool' and 'the <u>poor</u> old thing'). Both types of Epithet are not intensifiable – as noted by Halliday and Hasan

---

[2] The fact that it is only Epithets that are gradable explains the apparent oddity that words like *big* and *small* are Epithets. They are perceptual words – we <u>see</u> that things are big or small – so it would be natural for them to be Descriptors; but they are gradable in all three of the ways listed.

(1976: 276) – but they are scalar – semantically situated on a scale, and at its end (e.g. the scale from 'enviable' to 'pitiable' has *poor* at one end).

We conclude that Epithets are scalar in descriptive meaning; they are accordingly gradable, unless their meaning is construed as being at the extreme of the scale. Classifiers and Descriptors are not scalar (and therefore not gradable). Grading a premodifier converts it into an Epithet, while changing its meaning. Considerable attention has been given to this apparently unimportant issue because it highlights the crucial importance of semantic structure – reconstruing a word's meaning as scalar changes the word's zone, even if its core meaning remains – and because it distinguishes Descriptors from Epithets.

3.4.2.4   Other dimensions

On the specificity dimension, the quality denoted by Descriptors has commonly been derived by generalisation over instances of the entity denoted, as with *silver*, for example (see the previous section). Epithets involve still greater generalisation, resulting in either polysemy – a range of relatively specific senses – as with *Byzantine* <3>, 'Like Byzantine politics', '...complicated', '...inflexible', '...underhand', or in a single general sense, as with *big* <3>, 'Of considerable size, amount, extent, intensity, etc.'.

As to the vagueness dimension, Epithets are vaguer than Descriptors, generally speaking: details of meaning are underspecified in their definition. They vary greatly in this, however, from precise *Byzantine* ('Like Byzantine politics'), through *still* and *good* to very vague *awful*. As a result of developing various specific elements within their meaning, Epithets often have a number of sense elements which vary on the dimension of expectedness. For example, *short* as Descriptor (in 'her affectionate short [lyric] poem') invokes only the necessary meaning, SHORT; as Epithet, in 'a short, sexy dress', it is likely to invoke such meanings as MORE THAN SOCIALLY ACCEPTABLE and PROVOCATIVE.

On the quality dimension, Epithets can have senses that differ to the extent that they allow paradoxes such as the following: a nineteenth-century pioneer, leaving Australia, looks back at 'the reef-bound coasts of this old, new world'.

3.4.2.5   Conclusion to descriptive meaning

Epithets are like Descriptors in descriptive meaning, in that both zones have some perceptual meaning and some conceptual meaning. They differ in that Epithets are generally more strongly conceptual, less specific, vaguer and more complex. Those differences, however, are generalisations, all with exceptions; they do not distinguish the zones absolutely. The crucial difference is in the intensity dimension: Epithets are scalar. In that respect, the two zones are semantically distinct.

Table 3.24 *Paradigm of attitudinal meaning*

Approving	Neutral	Disapproving
famous	*well known*	*notorious*
modern	*new*	*newfangled*

3.4.3 *Expressive meaning in Epithets*

3.4.3.1   *Attitudinal meaning*

We saw in §3.4.2 that as words are generalised to other contexts, they are sometimes applied in quite specific situations. When such a situation regularly evokes a particular attitude, the word often acquires that attitude as part of its meaning. In this way, *Byzantine* was commonly applied to things which speakers disapproved of, so it acquired the disapproving sense, 'underhand'.

In a number of instances, there is a paradigm of approving, neutral and disapproving words, as illustrated in table 3.24. The approving and disapproving words are synonymous conceptually, but antonymous attitudinally. In other instances, there are pairs: attitudinal words (*immoral, feminine, childish*) and matching neutral ones (*amoral, female, childlike*). (In a complexity typical of the issues, *childlike* is also sometimes used with favourable attitude.) The attitudinal words quoted here have a clear conceptual meaning; but *good* and *bad*, for instance, have in many uses lost their conceptual meaning (as in '…and a good job, too!'): the expression of attitude constitutes their whole meaning.

3.4.3.2   *Emotive meaning*

The points to be noted for emotive meaning are much the same as for attitudinal meaning, so I will make them briefly. In some instances, there is a pair of words, with opposed feeling based on opposed concepts (*ugly, beautiful*), or opposed feeling for the same concept (*slim, skinny*) – emotive as well as attitudinal meaning. In other instances, the contrast is between emotive and neutral words: 'child behaviour' / 'puerile behaviour'; 'pig behaviour' / 'piggish behaviour'; 'childlike behaviour' / 'childish behaviour'). For emotive Epithets, the Classifier and Descriptor uses of the word are regularly neutral, as illustrated in table 3.25.

3.4.3.3   *Expressive meaning: general*

Expressive meaning sets up patterns where synonyms and antonyms are distinguished by their expressive value: in the sets *slim/thin/skinny* and *plump/fat/obese*, *slim* and *skinny* are synonyms descriptively (both mean THIN), but antonyms expressively (favourable and unfavourable); the reverse applies to *slim* and *plump* (opposite descriptive meaning and

Table 3.25 *Paradigm of emotive meaning*

Word		Det.	Epithet	Descriptor	Classifier	Head
positive	Neutral				*human positive*	*law*
		the	*greatest*	*positive*		*enjoyment*
	Emotive		*powerful, positive and visionary*	*[recent]*		*speeches*
distorted	Neutral	*the*			*Ames distorted*	*room*
		the	*[big]*	*distorted, swollen*		*calyx*
	Emotive	*the*	*most distorted and aggressive*	*[new]*		*band*
poor	Neutral	*#her*	*occasional*	*poor*		*balance*
	Emotive	*the*	*poor*	*dry*		*hide*
infantile	Neutral	*#his*		*recent*	*infantile*	*paralysis*
	Emotive	*#his*	*infantile*	*recent*		*behaviour*

Table 3.26 *Paradigm of antonyms*

	Antonyms in descriptive meaning	
Antonyms in expressive meaning	*skinny* *thin* *slim*	*obese* *fat* *plump*

synonymous expressive meaning). They thus form a paradigm (Lehrer 1974: 29), as shown in table 3.26.

Words such as *nice, lovely, horrible, terrible* and *appalling*, once words with precise and strong conceptual meaning, have become expressive words, and have lost their conceptual meaning (largely or completely). The absence of descriptive meaning is a very distinctive feature of such Epithets. Even more distinctive of Epithets is the fact that they can have expressive meaning (emotive or attitudinal or both), whereas Classifiers and Descriptors do not have it. It is hard to demonstrate a negative claim, but the point can be illustrated in the following ways. First, the typical Classifiers and Descriptors we have seen do not have expressive meaning: *steel, television, 24-inch, economic, American, oil-pressure* (Classifiers); and *red, grassy, vertical, silver, desiccated, braided* (Descriptors). Second, a Descriptor or Classifier becomes an Epithet when used with expressive meaning. That was shown in §3.4.3.2 above, on emotive meaning, but further examples are given in table 3.27.

The reason why only Epithets have expressive meaning is perhaps that abstract qualities generate attitudes and feelings consistent enough across

Table 3.27 *Words with and without expressive meaning*

Word	Det.	Epithet	Descriptor	Classifier	Head
musical	*a*	*floating*	*musical*	*global*	*trip*
	her	*smooth, musical, and utterly feminine*	*[singing]*		*voice*
liquid		*[copious]*	*liquid*	*organic*	*fertiliser*
	her	*liquid*	*[brown]*		*eyes*
arid	*the*	*[vast]*	*arid, brown*	*Tibetan*	*plateau*
	his	*arid and pedantic*	*[old]*		*head*
infantile	*the*	*dreaded*		*infantile*	*paralysis*
	my	*infantile*	*bad*		*behaviour*

society for expressive meaning to attach to words as an established part of their meaning, whereas physical or factual qualities and states do not, as illustrated in the table.

This section has emphasised expressive meaning in Epithets, but I also emphasise that not all Epithets have it (I have instanced *well-known*). Similarly, some Epithets (such as *soft*) have it in some uses, but not in others.

Finally, expressive meaning is scalar, just as Epithets' descriptive meaning is. We grade it by phonological stress and intonation (for example, 'What a lousy boss!') as much as by intensifiers such as *absolutely* ('They're getting an absolutely lousy deal'). (*Lousy*, having lost its descriptive meaning <1> 'Infested with lice', has in those uses the purely expressive meaning <2> 'Vile, contemptible...')

3.4.4   Social meaning in Epithets

As with emotive meaning, social meaning is conveyed almost exclusively by Epithets (§3.2.5 gave exceptions). Again, it is hard to demonstrate the negative, and I illustrate it in the same ways as before. First, the typical Classifiers and Descriptors we have seen do not have social meaning: *steel, television, 24-inch, economic, American, oil-pressure* (Classifiers); and *red, grassy, vertical, silver, desiccated, braided* (Descriptors). Second, the premodifiers that are typical of those with social meaning are all Epithets: *beaut, swell, cool* (slang); *bonny, bonzer* (dialect); *unspeakable, bestarred* (literary); *rotten, awful* (informal); *ripping* (*ripping* has period meaning; the word was slightly obsolete as slang in 1930, but very obsolete by 1945, according to Partridge 1970). Third, words with social meaning as Epithets do not have it as Descriptors or Classifiers, as illustrated in table 3.28.

As with expressive meaning, social meaning sets up patterns of semantic relationships. Some Epithets form pairs – a word with social meaning and a standard English alternative: colloquial *comfy* and standard *comfortable*;

Table 3.28 *Words with and without social meaning*

Word	Det.	Epithet	Descriptor	Classifier	Head
cool	*a*	<u>*cool*</u>, *trendy* Slang			*dude*
	a	*nice*	<u>*cool*</u> Standard	*pasta*	*salad*
bloody	*a*	*years-long*	<u>*bloody*</u> Standard	*civil*	*war*
	this	<u>*bloody*</u> *great big* Slang			*nutshell*

Table 3.29 *Paradigm of social meaning*

Formal	Standard	Informal
appealing	*attractive*	*sexy*
courageous	*brave*	*staunch*
voluble	*talkative*	*chatty*
praiseworthy	*good*	*cool*

slang *easy-peasy* and standard *easy*; literary *bestarred* and standard *starry*; dialect *wee* and standard *small*. A second pattern is in the double contrast between standard and formal use, and standard and <u>in</u>formal use, illustrated in table 3.29 (the ratings are for current New Zealand usage, from my own experience of it).

The patterns form multiple dimensions: words such as *beaut, ripping, cool, bonny* and *bonzer* are placed on the slang–formal dimension, on the dialect dimension, and on the time dimension (e.g. *ripping* and *bonzer* became old-fashioned before the twenty-first century); they form complex and fairly tight paradigms.

We conclude that social meaning contributes to the distinctiveness of Epithets and increases the semantic relationships that the words form. The reason why this type of meaning is characteristic of Epithets is evidently similar to the reason for expressive meaning's being so. It is only words with attitudinal meaning that can embody the values of a social class: there are social attitudes to being *voluble/chatty* and being *courageous/staunch* (Epithets, in the table above), but not to being *brown, smoky* or *central* (Descriptors, from the tables in §3.4.2.3).

3.4.5   Grammatical meaning in Epithets

Like Descriptors and Classifiers, Epithets have the grammatical meaning of instructing the hearer how to apply the word's content (its descriptive,

Table 3.30 *Participle as Epithet, Descriptor and Classifier*

Det.	Epithet	Descriptor	Classifier	Head
a	*moving*	new	[*English*]	*book*
	[*powerful*]	*moving*	magnetic	*fields*
a	beat-up	white	*moving*	van

expressive and social meaning). For example, in 'sexy new, restyled Ford Mondeo', *sexy* instructs the hearer to apply the descriptive meaning ATTRACTIVE, and approving attitude, to 'new, restyled Ford Mondeo'. However, some Epithets have other kinds of grammatical meaning. Since they involve interaction with other words, I deal with them in chapter 4, on syntactic explanation; but the point can be seen in an example: in 'beautiful warm weather', the hearer will in many contexts feel instructed to intensify *warm*, as well as to apply BEAUTY to the weather.

Epithets thus have several kinds of grammatical meaning; it is a more important part of their semantic structure than it is for Descriptors and Classifiers.

3.4.6   Discussion of Epithet meaning

3.4.6.1   Epithets' part of speech

Most Epithets are adjectives, but a few are participial in form, denoting an abstract quality (*daring*, *gifted*), which may be graded or intensified ('very daring [modern] clothes', 'immensely gifted disabled Irish writers'). They have lost the event meaning they had as Descriptors, and represent qualities directly, whereas participles as Descriptors represent qualities only indirectly (see §3.3.6), and participles as Classifiers have the event meaning nominalised. Compare the uses of *moving* in table 3.30.

Some Epithet uses are nouns – often figurative in origin, and sometimes idiomatic, as shown in table 3.31. Most of those Epithet nouns have Classifier uses – usually with their literal sense: 'A Mickey Mouse outfit' (as attested, meaning 'a badly run company') has a figurative Epithet; but it could be read as having a literal Classifier – and a different sense of *outfit*.

Superlatives are treated by some writers as modifiers, but as postdeterminers by other writers. It follows from the analysis given in this chapter, and from the distinction between premodification and determination in chapter 2, that they can be used both ways – as either Epithet or postdeterminer. Compare examples (4) to (6), and their structure as shown in table 3.32.

(4)   'The newest major new antibiotics' (Corpus of Contemporary American English)

Table 3.31 *Nouns as Epithet*

Det.	Epithet	Descriptor	Classifier	Head
a	*long, <u>quality</u>*	*[new]*	*rock*	*route*
a	*<u>blockbuster</u>*	*[new]*		*novel*
this	*<u>high-tech</u>, covert*	*[recent]*		*battle*
	<u>monster</u>	*[temporary]*	*15%-off, store wide, no deposit*	*lay-by*
	overzealous, misguided, <u>Mickey Mouse</u>	*[local]*	*law*	*enforcement*
a	*false, <u>schoolgirl</u>*	*[suppressed]*		*giggle*
	<u>idiot</u>	*[recent]*	*driving*	*behaviour*
the Darran Mountains'	*most <u>consumer</u>*			*crag*
my	*<u>2008</u>*	*visiting*	*climbing*	*partner*

Table 3.32 *Superlative as determiner and Epithet*

Det.	Epithet	Desc.	Classifier	Head
the <u>newest</u>	*major*	*new*		*antibiotics*
the <u>newest</u>	*tiny*	*fresh*		*perceptions*
the	*<u>newest</u>, largest, and most expensive*		*highway*	*interchange*

(5)   'The <u>newest</u> tiny fresh perceptions' (Corpus of Contemporary American English)

(6)   'The <u>newest</u>, largest, and most expensive highway interchange' (Corpus of Contemporary American English)

In (4) and (5), *newest* is a determiner, using given information (given in the Descriptors *new* and *fresh*) to delimit the reference, not to describe the referent. In (6), it is a modifier, adding new information intended descriptively. *Newest* as determiner is subordinated to the following Epithet (there is no comma), and *newest* as modifier is co-ordinated with the following Epithet (with a comma).

We saw in chapter 2 (§2.2.2.1), that Descriptors, Epithets and so on are phrases, sometimes with headword and (sub)modifier, and sometimes with a single word. We should note that they can also be hyphenated combinations of words. For example, 'up-to-date' can be either Epithet or Descriptor, as shown in table 3.33. (The last example is one of the rare phrases with all four positions filled.) 'Top-of-the-line' and 'run-of-the-mill' also occur as Epithet and Descriptor. Thus, rank shifted (or 'embedded') phrases (which

Table 3.33 *Hyphenated word-combinations as Epithet and Descriptor*

Words	Det.	Reinf.	Epithet	Descriptor	Classifier	Head
up-to-date			*pertinent*	*up-to-date*	*course*	*material*
	the		*most up-to-date*	*new*		*movie*	*houses*
down-the-line	*a*		*good*	*down-the-line*		*pursuit*
		straight	*down-the-line*	*uninteresting*	*Billy Idol rock*	*music*

Table 3.34 Old *as borderline Epithet*

Det.	Epithet	Descriptor	Classifier	Head
	old	*forbidden*	*[British]*	*books*
	curious	*old*	*[British]*	*writers*

are generally not used as examples in this book) are in fact zoned as if they were single-word premodifiers.

3.4.6.2   Sense relations of Epithets

This section on Epithets has shown that they are rich in synonyms: their gradability, their having many sense elements, and their having expressive and social meaning as well as conceptual meaning, all provide the basis for multiple synonymy. In contrast with Descriptors (see §3.3.6.2), they have antonyms (in the strict sense of polar opposites): *courageous/cowardly*, *beautiful/ugly*, and so on.

Whereas Descriptors' sense relations are often dominated by the contrast with other words in their semantic field (see §3.3.6.2), Epithets often have synonyms within the same area of the field. Thus we have *ancient* and *antiquated* as Epithet synonyms for *old*, and *novel* and *newfangled* as Epithet synonyms for *new*. Speakers choose among synonyms almost entirely by their knowledge of the language, rather than their knowledge of the world (which is needed for choosing among Classifiers); compare *ancient, antiquated* and *old, cool, ripping* and *bonzer, bestarred* and *starry, alien, strange* and *foreign*, for example.

3.4.6.3   Borderline instances of Epithets

Epithets may be close to either the Reinforcer or the Descriptor zone. In 'old forbidden books' and 'curious old writers', *old* is used in very similar ways (having the same necessary and possible concepts), but in different zones; see table 3.34. *New* and *young* have very similar uses. (The difference between them is that in the Epithet uses the concepts are construed as scalar; see §3.4.2.3.)

Some other Epithets are very close to the borderline with Reinforcers. Although 'great fool' has *great* as a Reinforcer (it intensifies), 'great eater' seems to have it as an Epithet ('he eats greatly'). *Raving* is similar: in 'raving idiot,' hearers may take it as equivalent to *utter* (Reinforcer) or as meaning 'wild in speech' (Epithet).

There are two small groups of words that I am rating as Epithets, although they are not co-ordinated with other Epithets: diminutive words, as in 'dear little thing', 'good old Joe'; and intensifying words, as in 'nice warm room', 'beautiful big house'. They are not co-ordinated with the other Epithet because in most uses they are submodifying it, as well as modifying the head. As I imply by the term 'intensifying', words of the second type strengthen the meaning of the following word. Words of the 'diminutive' type have a variety of meanings: they are used 'to convey emotional overtones, as affection, amusement, condescension, disparagement, etc.' (SOED, *little* <7>); the overtones apply to the previous word. For example, a 698 cc car was described in a motoring magazine as in example (7).

(7)   'the nippy wee beast' *(AA Torque*, Summer 2006, p. 33)

Wee conveys overtones of admiration for the nippiness (and the car in general), as well as denoting small size. (Huddleston and Pullum 2002: 561 call these uses 'intensificatory tautology'.) I include these words as Epithets because: (a) they are exactly like Epithets in semantic structure; (b) their subordination is not to the rest of the phrase, but to a single word, so they belong in the same zone as that word; (c) they have not become so subordinate as to be submodifying 'adverbs' like *very*. They will be considered further in the 'Syntactic explanation' chapter (chapter 4, §§4.2 and 4.3).

3.4.7   Conclusion: Epithet semantic structure

The characteristics of Epithet semantic structure are as follows. In some respects, they differ from Descriptors in degree: they are more vague and general; they vary more in those dimensions, as in the expectedness of their elements; they have other types of grammatical meaning. However, they are distinct from Descriptors in being scalar and in being able to take expressive and social meaning. They are distinct from Classifiers in all those ways.

3.5   Semantic structure of Reinforcers

3.5.1   Introduction

Examples of Reinforcers are given in table 3.35. It is relatively uncommon for Reinforcers to be used with other modifiers, as they are in the examples in the table; commoner examples are as follows: 'sheer arrogance', 'outright

Table 3.35 *Sample Reinforcers*

Det.	Reinforcer	Epithet	Descriptor	Classifier	Head
a	<u>*complete*</u>	*bloody*			*idiot*
	<u>*pure*</u>	*unmitigated*		*driving*	*pleasure*
	<u>*sheer*</u>	*infinite*		*adrenaline*	*rush*
	<u>*absolute*</u>	*manic*		*basket*	*case*

lie', '<u>pure</u> fabrication' (from Quirk *et al.* 1985: 49); and '<u>utter</u> disgrace' and '<u>perfect</u> stranger' (from Huddleston and Pullum 2002: 555).

3.5.2   Descriptive meaning in Reinforcers

The examples just given (such as *sheer, absolute, outright*) clearly do not have perceptual meaning; they do not even have conceptual meaning. Reinforcers are words with grammatical meaning, not descriptive meaning; they differ radically from Epithets and Descriptors in that respect.

That can be seen in several ways. Apart from *mere*, they are synonymous. In the phrase '<u>sheer</u> arrogance', for example, *sheer* could adequately be replaced by *complete, absolute, pure, outright, utter* or *perfect*, so they must be synonymous (as previously defined, §3.1.2.3). But as Epithets, they are not synonymous: '<u>complete</u> understanding' (there are no gaps in the understanding) is not the same as '<u>perfect</u> understanding' (there are no flaws in it). Second, they do not have antonyms: we cannot say **'<u>incomplete</u> fool', or **'<u>imperfect</u> stranger'. As Epithets, they <u>do</u> have antonyms, as in '<u>imperfect</u> understanding' and #'<u>incomplete</u> understanding'. Third, they are not gradable, or otherwise scalar. For example, we cannot say **'<u>very utter</u> disgrace' or **'<u>very pure</u> unmitigated driving pleasure'; but in Epithet use, the same words <u>can</u> be graded: '<u>very pure</u> natural water'.[3] In these respects, Reinforcers contrast strongly with the same words as Epithets.

Since Reinforcers have no descriptive meaning (merely serving to reinforce meaning given by the head), they are totally vague. For example, in '<u>sheer</u> folly', *sheer* reinforces FOLLY, but in 'sheer arrogance', it reinforces ARROGANCE.

3.5.3   Expressive meaning in Reinforcers

Reinforcers seem to express feeling, but the feeling is generally weak and rather vague, and in fact it depends on the context. Some examples will make

---

[3] The examples show that Paradis is wrong in asserting that Reinforcers are gradable (2000: 251).

the point clear. In 'For <u>sheer</u> daintiness, "Hawera" is hard to beat' (applied to flowers), *sheer* evokes admiration. In 'Absence paralysed her in <u>sheer</u> aching agony' (from fiction), *sheer* evokes empathetic pain. In 'It was a <u>sheer</u> fluke that he began his career with Manchester Collieries Ltd.', *sheer* is used neutrally. The same examples show that the attitudinal meaning of Reinforcers is also generally context-dependent: *sheer* in '<u>sheer</u> daintiness' reinforces the favourable attitude expressed in *daintiness*, but in 'a <u>sheer</u> fluke' it evokes neither favourable nor unfavourable attitude. *Mere*, however, regularly evokes unfavourable attitude: compare #'a <u>mere</u> fluke' with 'a <u>sheer</u> fluke'.

I conclude that few Reinforcers have any expressive meaning in themselves, and that their expressive meaning is contextual, as with their apparent conceptual meaning. Indeed, most discussions of them, such as Quirk *et al.* (1985) and Paradis (2000), do not indicate that they have any such meaning.

3.5.4 Social meaning in Reinforcers

Reinforcers occur in various social contexts, so they evidently lack inherent social meaning and take any social value from context, as with other types of meaning.

3.5.5 Grammatical meaning in Reinforcers

The grammatical meaning of Reinforcers is different from that of other premodifiers. They do instruct the hearer or reader to adjust the meaning of the rest of the phrase, but the instruction is not to relate the word's content to the head entity, as they have no content.

There are three main ways in which they adjust meaning, as follows (this is partly as in Quirk *et al.* 1985: 1338, as discussed below). First, they may instruct hearers to intensify, or maximise, the qualities suggested by the head and by other premodifiers: SOED's 'Having the maximum extent or degree' (*complete* <5>). For example, in '<u>complete</u> idiot', hearers are intended to maximise the degree to which the person is an idiot. That is the meaning of most Reinforcers. Uses with this function may be called 'maximisers'. Second, they may instruct hearers to minimise the head quality: SOED's 'That is barely or only what it is said to be' (*mere* <4>), for example, 'used as <u>mere</u> decoration'. Uses with this function may be called 'minimisers'. (These are the Reinforcers which have unfavourable attitudinal meaning.) Third, the meaning may be intermediate between those two: SOED's 'As an intensive emphasising identity ... [or] significance' (*very* <7>), as in 'under our <u>very</u> eyes', or SOED's '...no more nor less than' (*sheer* <5>). (*Sheer* and *absolute* have this use, as well as a maximiser one.) Since they limit the sense to being 'neither more nor less than', uses with this function may be called 'limiters'. I group together the three forms above as 'reinforcing'.

Reinforcing meaning is dominant in Reinforcers, since they have no descriptive meaning and no inherent social or expressive meaning. A few Reinforcers have other forms of grammatical meaning, as discourse particles, which will be discussed in the following chapter, on syntax (§4.6.1), and in chapter 9 (§9.3).

3.5.6   Discussion of Reinforcers

Reinforcers are distinctive in some other types and dimensions of meaning, as well as in those discussed so far. First, they are totally vague: any content they can be considered to have changes completely, according to context. Second, they are 'pointing' words. Just as Classifiers function by pointing (in naming a referent), so do Reinforcers function by pointing (to the head word, by deixis not naming); and neither Classifiers nor Reinforcers carry descriptive meaning. Surprisingly, Reinforcers are thus like Classifiers.

Reinforcers constitute a simple paradigm of sense relations, in one respect. We have seen that there are three types of Reinforcer: maximisers, minimisers and limiters. Their relationship is thus a paradigm of alternative functions (rather like the favourable/neutral/unfavourable pattern of expressive meaning). Otherwise, Reinforcers have few sense relations: they are not linked with synonyms or antonyms in clear patterns of social, attitudinal or emotive meaning; nor do they form such relations through descriptive meaning, since they have none.

As with the other zones, there are borderline instances. Some uses are ambivalent between Reinforcer and Epithet: 'pure fantasy' would normally be read as having a Reinforcer – <3a> '…with intensive force', but in 'a mixture of recycled gossip and pure fantasy' (said by a spokesman for the British prime minister, in a news report about the prime minister's wife), the balance with *recycled* gives *pure* weight, inviting an Epithet reading – <2a> '…homogeneous'. Some uses seem indeterminate between Reinforcer and determiner: 'This is one strange novel, and this John Buck… is one strange character.' Some words function as Reinforcers in certain rather idiomatic phrases, but do not seem to be established in the language as Reinforcers: for example, 'blithering idiot', 'crashing bore' and 'rank injustice'.

3.5.7   Conclusion: Reinforcers

Reinforcers are semantically very different from other modifiers: they have no descriptive meaning; they have much more grammatical meaning than words in other zones; the grammatical meaning, reinforcement, is quite different from that of other premodifiers; and they are very simple in meaning, and wholly subjective (in relying on the hearer's interpretation). Having only grammatical meaning makes the zone different from all others.

3.6   Discussion of premodifier semantic structure

3.6.1   General discussion

This section makes several diverse points that will be used in later chapters, but will not lead to the conclusion in §3.7.

3.6.1.1   Part of speech and semantics

We have seen that there is a rough correlation between premodification position and part of speech: most noun premodifiers are Classifiers, and vice versa; most participial premodifiers are Descriptors; most Epithets and Reinforcers are adjectives. But we have seen in the previous sections that all three of those parts of speech occur in Classifier, Descriptor and Epithet zones. We have seen also that numerals and quantifiers occur as Descriptors, and that numerals occur also as Classifiers.

Important conclusions follow from that, and the semantic characteristics of the zones. In their various premodifier uses, the various parts of speech function semantically according to their zone, rather than according to any semantic characteristics of their part of speech: as Classifiers, all three forms are treated as designating entities (§3.2.6); as Descriptors, they denote relatively concrete qualities, in a strict or approximate sense (§3.3.6); as Epithets, they all are treated as denoting abstract qualities (§3.4.6). For use in different zones, we construe them differently, making salient different relations in the complex network of meaning elements associated with the word. The distinctions among entities, states and qualities are here semantic, not metaphysical or epistemological: how we use modifiers depends on their semantic structure, not on the part of speech. Other conclusions, secondary to the argument here, are that the 'notional' types (or 'semantic classes' as I will call them) of object, action and property belong in English to zones, not to parts of speech; and that a word's 'part of speech' ('adjective', 'noun' and so on) is of no direct importance to order.

3.6.1.2   Complexity of meaning in different zones

The zones vary greatly in the complexity of their semantic structure. Classifiers are very simple, having only referential meaning (as individual words, apart from the constructional meaning they gain from their construction), and consisting of a single unit of meaning. Descriptors are also fairly simple, having only descriptive meaning – but that may have several elements. Epithets are very complex, as follows. First, they have descriptive meaning, and many have expressive and social meaning, as well. Second, an apparently unitary descriptive meaning may be complex. (Even *bloody*, as 'blood-thirsty' can be analysed as 'likely to cause the shedding of blood'.) Third, the full meaning of a sense may include various elements with different degrees of intensity and expectedness. Finally, part of their meaning resides in their complex network of sense relations. Reinforcers are simple: they have reinforcing meaning. Complexity will become important in chapter 10 (§10.3 on grammaticalisation), in particular.

3.6.1.3   Subjectivity

The zones form a scale of subjectivity, if we take *subjectivity* without strict definition. Classifiers' meaning is objective: naming meaning is quite independent of speaker and hearer; and names are given either to physical entities that are partitioned naturally by perception (Gentner and Boroditsky 2001), such as wire and hair, or to entities strictly defined by convention, such as London. Descriptors are slightly subjective, since perceptual qualities allow some variation according to speaker (as with *maroon/crimson/puce*). Epithet meaning elements are subjective in various ways. Social and expressive meanings are subjective in being 'tied to the here-and-now of the current speech situation' (Cruse 2004: 45, on subjectivity) – expressing feeling, and calling for personal response. Even conceptual meaning is subjective, to the extent that it requires judgement rather than perception – judgement that other people might not accept: for example, '<u>handsome</u> bony face', '<u>steady</u> old eyes' and '<u>hard</u> young officer'. On the other hand, Epithets represent content, which is an objective function, to the extent that assertion of content may be verified. Reinforcers can be subjective in having social and expressive meaning (contextually), and they are wholly subjective in replacing assertion of content with indicating the speaker's intention (that the hearer reinforce the content of the head). This issue will also become important in chapter 10 (§10.3).

3.6.1.4   World knowledge and linguistic knowledge

We can choose among alternative Classifiers only on the basis of world knowledge (*steel/iron/bronze*, or *32-inch/42-inch*, for example); but we must choose among such Epithets as *good/swell/neat* by linguistic knowledge – although we need world knowledge as well for *small/large/huge*. Conversely, it is linguistic relations that constitute Epithets' complex paradigms of sense relations. Reinforcers, being without content, are wholly linguistic in their significance for us. From Classifiers to Reinforcers, then, there is a cline from world knowledge to linguistic knowledge, or 'cognitive dominance' to 'linguistic dominance'. This issue will recur in chapter 9 (§§9.2, 9.4) and chapter 10 (§§10.2, 10.3).

3.6.1.5   Semantic structure and language functions

I follow Halliday (2004) in identifying three underlying functions (or 'metafunctions') in language. They are as follows (this exposition is from 2004: 29–30). (a) 'Every message is both about something and addressing someone.' In being about something, what we say and write communicates our construal of experience: it serves an experiential function. In this function, we offer information about the world, but do not try to change it.[4] (b) In addressing someone, we are 'enacting our personal and social relations with the other people around us'. For example, we ask for a reply, demand action, or share feelings; we try to make something happen in our social world, or at least to keep it as we want it. That constitutes the interpersonal function. (c) To help carry out those functions, we 'build up sequences of discourse, organising the discursive flow and creating cohesion and continuity'. That constitutes the textual function. I am citing Halliday, but other writers give similar functions; for example, the two functions given by Langacker (2003: 14) and the three functions given by Lyons (1977: 50) match the first two above.

The main elements of language we have been examining are correlated with those metafunctions. The semantic functions noted in §3.1.2.2 serve them, working through the premodifiers' semantic structure. Referential and descriptive meaning serve the experiential function; expressive and social meaning serve the interpersonal function; grammatical meaning (in both the modifying and intensifying forms) serves the textual function of building cohesion and continuity. Since the zones are correlated with types of meaning, they too are correlated with the functions. So too is the scale of subjectivity discussed earlier in this section: the experiential function is relatively objective; and the interpersonal function is relatively subjective. The language functions will accordingly recur in the explanations in other chapters.

3.6.1.6   Semantic 'weight'

We have seen that on the whole, zones further 'forward' have more expressive meaning, have a greater range and depth of meaning, and serve a wider range of language functions: they have greater semantic 'weight'. That pattern of differing semantic structure in the zones makes it natural for the earliest premodifier to be the most important communicatively.

3.6.2   Semantic structure as characteristic of the zones

The body of the chapter has considered the zones in turn, discussing their semantic features. To make clear the chapter's conclusions, I must briefly consider the semantic features in turn, assessing the extent to which each one characterises the semantics of the zones. That discussion will form the basis for the conclusions in §3.7. Table 3.36 can serve as illustrative underpinning for the discussion and for the conclusions to follow. In the table, *positive* occurs in all four zones; and, although the precise sense differs, all

---

[4] I am simplifying Halliday's account: I am setting aside the logical function, because it applies only in structures of two or more clauses; the logical and experiential functions together make up the 'ideational' function.

Table 3.36 Positive *in all four zones*

Det.	Reinf.	Epithet	Descr.	Classifier	Head
		[*traditional*]	*human*	*positive*	*law*
the		*greatest*	*positive*	[*musical*]	*enjoyment*
		powerful, positive and visionary	[*recent*]	[*political*]	*speeches*
a	*positive*	[*bloody*]		*dust*	*bowl*

four uses are based on the core meaning of DEFINITE; so we must wonder why the word occurs in all four zones.

We consider first the types of meaning that individual words may have. Referential meaning occurs only in Classifiers, and Classifiers as individual words have no other (linguistic) meaning: they are names, in effect, designating individuals or types of entity (see §3.2). For example, 'positive law' designates a type of law: SOED <1> '...formally laid down.... Opp. *natural*'. (In descriptive terms, such a law may be 'negative', not 'positive'.) The Classifier *positive* has lost the descriptive meaning it had in the source language; the conceptual qualities associated with it (the distinction between natural and adjudicated law) are part of our world knowledge, not of meaning. Descriptive meaning occurs in the Descriptor and Epithet zones. 'The greatest positive enjoyment' has a Descriptor: <2> '...definite', which is descriptive meaning that is only slightly conceptualised (see §3.3.3). 'Powerful, positive ... speeches' has an Epithet: <6> '...characterised by constructive... attitudes', which is fully conceptualised, quite abstract descriptive meaning (see §3.4.2). Expressive and social meaning occur only in Epithets: the Epithet in 'Powerful, positive ... speeches' expresses approval. That makes the zone distinctive, but not all Epithets have those types of meaning (see §§3.4.3 and 3.4.4). Grammatical meaning with a reinforcing function characterises the Reinforcer zone, since that is its sole non-contextual meaning, and since no other premodifiers have it. In 'a positive bloody dustbowl', *positive* has lost the conceptual meaning it had, and simply reinforces 'dust bowl' (see §3.5). When we consider constructional meaning, we see that the Classifier zone is quite distinctive, because Classifiers invoke a constructional meaning such as TYPE OF, and only words in that zone do so. The conclusion is that the types of meaning distinguish the Classifier and Reinforcer zones from the others, but do not distinguish between Descriptor and Epithet zones, since both have descriptive meaning.

We consider next the dimensions and other aspects of meaning. On the intensity dimension, Epithets are scalar but Descriptors are not. In 'positive [Descriptor] enjoyment' (<2> '...definite'), DEFINITENESS simply is present, not absent. But in 'positive [Epithet] speeches' (<6> '...characterised

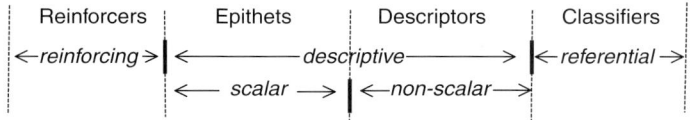

Figure 3.4 Distinctions between meaning types and dimensions that distinguish the zones

by constructive… attitudes'), CONSTRUCTIVENESS is present to a certain degree and may be graded, as in #'very positive speeches'. Thus the remaining demarcation, between Descriptor and Epithet zones, is made by their difference on the intensity dimension.

Thus semantic structure (the pattern of meaning types, and of scalarity) makes clear-cut distinctions between the zones (other dimensions and aspects of meaning are related to the distinctions, but do not constitute them): (a) reinforcing meaning type distinguishes the Reinforcer zone; (b) referentiality (correlated with constructional meaning) distinguishes the Classifier zone; (c) scalarity (in the intensity dimension of descriptive meaning) distinguishes Descriptor and Epithet zones from each other. The distinctions may be illustrated in figure 3.4.

We conclude that semantic structure provides a semantic explanation of premodifier order. That will be set out formally as the conclusion of this chapter, in the next section.

There are two further consequences which should be noted. First, it follows from the correlation between meaning type and zone that each premodifier is occupying a zone, even if it is the only premodifier, and that we can identify its zone from its semantic structure, without relying on other premodifiers to show order. Second, the conclusions given just above show why it is normal for one word to be used in different zones: the different senses of the word can have different semantic structures even when the content is largely the same in the different senses. In comparison with linguistic explanations that treat meaning as simply conceptual, this explanation from meaning types may seem odd or nebulous, and therefore unconvincing; but it will be supported strongly in later chapters.

In the explanation of premodifier order just given, two details are anomalous. First, social and expressive meanings do not appear in that simple explanation. The reason for that is that they are different in nature from other meaning: they are expressed rather than symbolised, and it is symbolic meaning that characterises the zone; but they conform to the explanation, because they depend on Epithets' scalar abstract meaning (§3.4.2.3) and because the expressive and social meaning they express is scalar (§3.4.3.3). The second anomaly is that some Epithets have expressive meaning without the descriptive meaning which is normally the basis for it. The explanation is that they have lost it during their history – see chapter 8 (§8.5.5).

3.7   Conclusion: semantic explanation of unmarked order

3.7.1   The semantic explanation

The discussion in the preceding section, based on the analysis in the whole of this chapter, shows that there is a gradient from the Classifier zone to the Reinforcer zone, from referential and concrete meaning through descriptive meaning and increasing abstractness to grammatical meaning. That explains premodifiers' relation to the other elements of the phrase: Classifiers come next to heads, since they share their referential nature; and Reinforcers come next to determiners because they share their abstract and grammatical nature. There is a single semantic gradient through nominal phrases, from heads through four premodification zones to determiners.

But the zones are distinct, as strict categories, not indistinct areas in a gradient. It was shown in chapter 2 that they are distinct syntactically, having words within the zone co-ordinated with each other, but subordinated as a group to the later zones and the head. We now see that they are also distinct semantically, although it is characteristics arising from the gradient that establish the distinctions, as follows.

- The Classifier zone has referential meaning and constructional meaning.
- The Descriptor zone has nonscalar descriptive meaning.
- The Epithet zone has scalar descriptive or expressive meaning.
- The Reinforcer zone has reinforcing meaning.

There are four zones because there are four types of meaning (in premodification, at least).

The book began (§1.1) by setting the nature of unmarked order of premodifiers in English nominal phrases as the first thing to be explained. Chapter 2 showed that the order is one of zones. This chapter has shown that semantic structure (combination of meaning types and dimensions) explains the number of zones, and their order. To my knowledge, semantic structure has not previously been seen as explaining premodifier order – or any other element of language apart from word meaning; I suggest that it is an important addition to linguistic explanation.

3.7.2   Prospect: later chapters

Some facts that have arisen in this chapter have not been fully explained so far. Anomalies in the Epithet zone were explained in §3.6.2, but only partly. We have seen that the zone order is often but not always a part-of-speech order – paralleling the semantic order: adjectives (as Reinforcers and Epithets) + participles (as Descriptors) + nouns (as Classifiers). There are in each zone instances of modifier use that seem to be at or 'on' the borderline between zones. Those facts will be explained historically in chapter 8, specifically in §§8.3.6 and 8.4.5.

Later chapters will complement, but also build on, the semantic explanation given here. The next chapter will give a syntactic explanation, but will argue that semantic structure underlies syntactic structure. Chapter 6 'Free order' and chapter 7 'Marked order' will rely on this chapter directly; chapter 8 'Historical explanation of premodifier order' will show how the semantics evolved; still later chapters will use this chapter indirectly.

4   Syntactic explanation of unmarked order across the zones

4.1   Introduction

The purpose of this chapter is to provide a syntactic explanation of the zone structure set out in chapter 2, parallel to the semantic explanation set out in the last chapter. The starting point is the basic syntactic fact, set out in chapter 2, that premodifiers modify the following part of the phrase. For example, in 'the [large [public [nature reserves]]]', *nature* modifies 'reserves', *public* modifies 'nature reserves', and *large* modifies the still larger unit, 'public nature reserves'. The chapter explores what is entailed in the relation of modifying.

The argument is that premodifiers do more than modify the following part of the phrase. In general, the further from the head a premodifier is: (a) the wider is its scope of modification – for example, it can relate to other modifiers individually, and to participants in the discourse situation other than the entity denoted by the head; (b) the more types of modification it has; (c) the looser is its bond to the head. Those generalisations, and the exceptions to them, are explained by the semantic structure of the modifiers concerned. These facts lead to the conclusion that syntactic structure makes a partial explanation of premodifier order, but that semantic structure explains the syntactic structure.

Several concepts need amplification. 'Modification' has been understood so far as in Quirk *et al.* (1985: 65): modifiers 'add "descriptive" information to the head, often restricting the reference of the head'. That relation to the head entails dependency, as defined by Hawkins (2004). In 'rock concert', for example, *rock* is dependent on *concert*, because the hearer must use *concert* to know whether the ambiguous word *rock* refers to stone or to a type of music (to know what the reference of the whole phrase is). Stated formally, dependency exists when interpretation 'requires access' to another word 'for assignment of syntactic or semantic properties with respect to which [the word] is zero specified or ambiguously or polysemously specified' (Hawkins 2004: 22). In being dependent on *concert*, *rock* is a modifier. However, *concert* depends on *rock* for specification of the type of concert. Semantically, the words are interdependent, and modify each other; I will use 'modify' to mean 'affect the meaning of'. 'Syntactic modification' (which sets up phrase structure) depends on that 'semantic modification'; but semantic modification may occur without syntactic modification (as when *concert* modifies *rock*). To put the point differently, 'syntax has its basis in a codification of semantic relationships' (Matthews 1981: 124); Givón (1988: 278) and Harder (1996: 95) make similar points. This chapter, then, considers the compositional meaning of premodifiers, whereas chapter 3 studied their meaning individually. Both semantic and syntactic modification will be included in the term 'scope'.

The chapter uses the concept of ascription – a speaker's act of applying a word to a mental entity, implicitly asserting that the word is appropriate; that includes predicative uses like #'the reserves are <u>large</u>', attributive uses like 'the <u>large</u> reserves', and also the use of *reserves* itself, in those phrases – implying that the areas really are reserves, not farms. A distinction made previously will become more important: premodifiers may function restrictively (to restrict the reference of the head), or descriptively (to add information about the head entity, whose reference is clear by deixis or from context, for example).

I repeat the caution I have given earlier, that I am deferring full consideration of the Classifier zone to chapter 5; so this chapter excludes relations between words within the Classifier zone. Also, it excludes relations between words within any of the other zones, which are discussed in chapter 6, on free order.

Sections 4.2 to 4.6 discuss scope of modification, taking different forms of modification in turn: modification of a previous word, of a later modifier, and so on; §4.7 discusses how closely premodifiers in different zones are bound to the head; §4.8 provides more general discussion; and §4.9 summarises and draws conclusions.

4.2 Modification of a preceding modifier

This section shows that although modification is usually of a following word, sometimes a word modifies a previous word.

4.2.1 *Types of previous-word modification*

4.2.1.1 *Relative modifiers*

Cruse (2004: 66–7) says of the phrase 'a large mouse' that '*large* must be interpreted relative to the norm of size for the class of mice'. He comments: 'Here we have a two-way interaction, because *mouse* determines how *large* is to be interpreted, and *large* limits the application of *mouse*.' (He calls modifiers such as *large* 'relative descriptors': they are relative to the head.) Similar treatment is given by Katz (1972: 254), Dixon (1982: 16), Jackendoff (1997: 64 – who makes the interesting suggestion that these modifiers 'semantically subordinate the noun') and Taylor (2002: 450).

4.2.1.2   Explanatory modifiers

Relativity extends beyond the head's setting a norm of size, however – to other properties, and to dependence of one premodifier on another. Example (1) was spoken by a three-year-old child:

(1)   'Those splendid old electric trains' (quoted in Halliday 2004: 311)

The age we assign to the trains (from *old*) is dependent on *electric* as well as *trains* (old electric trains are younger than old steam trains), so *electric* partly modifies the previous word, *old*. Similarly, *old* and *electric* help specify the splendour vaguely denoted by the previous word, *splendid*.

(2)   'Such attractive, fruit-filled big red wines' (*New Zealand Herald*, entertainment section)

In example (2), *wines* indicates the shade of red, which is otherwise indeterminate; *red* and *wines* likewise indicate the kind of 'bigness'; *big* and *fruit-filled* make good the underspecification of *attractive* – a vague word, like so many Epithets. Other examples follow, with the underlined premodifiers modified by a later word: 'Ugly trailing overhead wires' (fiction), 'vibrant green gum trees' (travel journalism), 'a shy and possibly rather dangerous bird' (fiction).

This explanatory relationship resolves Vendler's puzzle with *brave* and *considerate* (1968: 132–3): 'a brave young man' and 'a brave old man' are acceptable, but *'brave blond man' is not. Both *young* and *old* help specify the meaning of *brave* ('brave young...' suggests 'taking risks', and 'brave old...' suggests 'enduring', perhaps), but 'brave blond...' is odd because it has no appropriate meaning elements to specify the sense of *brave*.

Various authors make this point about explanatory modifiers: Bache (1978: 74) about 'a nasty cold wind', Hetzron (1978: 177) about 'a comfortable wide sofa' and Dixon (1982: 26) about 'a good strong box'.

4.2.1.3   Intensifying and weakening modifiers

In phrases like 'good old George' (from SOED entry for *old*, <6>), *old* is an '...intensifier, now rare, exc[ept] after *good, grand*, etc.'; *old* intensifies the modifier *good*. In 'They think that these guys ought to be treated like any old street criminals' (Taylor 1992: 31), *old* modifies the determiner *any*. *Old*'s dependence on the previous word is reflected in the pronunciation, since it is run on closely with that word, and reduced in stress. The converse effect, weakening of a previous word, occurs with *little* and similar words, as an example (3).

(3)   'Oh dear! My poor little brain is giving way' (SOED example)

Little does not describe the size of the brain; it expresses feeling, and makes the mockery expressed by *poor* gentle and humorous. It is used, as SOED

Table 4.1 *Relative modifiers*

Det.	Epithet	Descriptor	Classifier	Head
	huge		*feather*	*diadems*
a	*safe*		*west coast*	*beach*
	ugly	*trailing*	*overhead*	*wires*

says in its entry for *little*, <7>, '...to convey emotional overtones, as affection, amusement, condescension, disparagement, etc.'.

Other examples were given in §3.4.6, which also argued that these words are Epithets, even though they follow Epithets without coordination, as Descriptors do. This use is commonly called 'diminutive'; but the SOED is accurate in its description, just quoted: the key element is emotion, not a concept of size.

4.2.1.4   Other forms of specification of a previous modifier

In 'a <u>safe</u> west coast beach', *safe* means for most New Zealanders that the beach is without unpredictable waves or very big and rough waves (for which our west coast is notorious) – not just without rips. Here, the explanatory specification comes from world knowledge, associated with 'west coast', not from linguistic meaning. (We saw in §3.2.3, that Classifiers rely on world knowledge.)

4.2.2   Discussion: modification of a preceding modifier

Borderline instances occur. In some, it is likely that some readers will interpret a word as modifying a previous one, while other readers do not, because there is an overlap in meaning between the modifiers. Take (4), for example:

(4)   'two <u>hot new</u> game shows' (*New Zealand Herald*, entertainment section)

Here, *new* seems to add the idea of novelty to *hot*; but SOED includes the concept in *hot* <12a> '...completely new; esp. novel and exciting'. Other ambivalent examples with potentially overlapping meaning are '<u>surprising new</u> catwalk trend' and '<u>quaint old</u> chrome-steel statues'.

In the examples of relative modifiers, the modifying word has been variously the head, a Classifier and a Descriptor; but in most instances, the modified word has been an Epithet. That is illustrated in table 4.1, in which the modifying word is underlined, and the modified word has double underlining.

The fact that Epithets are readily modified by following words, whereas other premodifiers apparently are not, is related to various elements of their semantic structure, as follows. (These elements were set out in §3.4.)

- They are gradable, so a later word can grade them, as in relative modifiers.
- Epithets such as *huge* and *safe* are vague (underspecified) in descriptive meaning; so a following word can make the meaning more specific (in combination with our world knowledge).
- Epithets' expressive meaning can be given a factual basis by a later modifier, as for the disapproval meaning in *ugly*: '<u>ugly</u> trailing overhead wires'.
- Some Epithets are rich in possible sense elements (the expectedness dimension); the later word guides the reader in selecting among the possible meanings, as in the *brave* examples.
- Finally, Epithets are often complex. For *safe*, Taylor (2002: 452) says that the word entails a 'scenario' involving value, danger and protection. Commonly, the context provides these details; in the example given above, 'west coast' provides the nature of the danger.

Descriptors are open to this modification because they are partly conceptual and accordingly a little vague or polysemous; for example, in 'ugly trailing overhead wires', the sense of the Descriptor *trailing* is determined by the Classifier *overhead*, as being <1> '...hanging down', not <2b> '...forming a trail'. However, Descriptors are less open to such modification than Epithets, because they are more concrete and not scalar. Reinforcers cannot be modified at all, simply because they have no content to modify. Classifiers likewise have no descriptive content to be explained or graded.

4.2.3   Conclusion: modification of a previous word

The words that modify earlier ones can be in any zone, and can be the head; so there is no significance for order in the zone of the modifying word. The words modified are mostly Epithets, which can be modified in various ways and to a great degree; a few Descriptors can be modified, but only by selection between conventionalised meanings, not by addition of nuances, it seems; Classifiers are apparently not modified by later words and nor are Reinforcers. We conclude that whether modifiers can be modified by following words depends on their semantic structure, according to their zone, and that there is a pattern: words closest to the head are least modifiable, and the furthest away are most modifiable, except for Reinforcers.

4.3   Modification of a later modifier

Several writers assert that premodifiers sometimes modify a following modifier, while also modifying the head. Such modification is natural, since generally each modifier modifies the rest of the phrase, which includes the later modifiers. The issues here are whether it can modify individual words rather than the group as a whole, and whether it can do both at once.

4.3.1   Types of later-modifier modification

Some modifiers grade a later modifier. Quirk *et al.* (1985: 1339) say that 'emotionally tinged adjectives often have an adverbial, subordinated relation', such that 'beautiful warm weather' is equivalent to 'beautifully warm weather' – warm to a beautiful degree. Bache (1978: 74–5) gives '<u>nice</u> cosy house' and '<u>good</u> hard knot' as premodifiers that 'function semi-adverbially': 'nice cosy' means 'cosy to a nice degree'. I accept those assertions. (However, 'nice cosy house' can be read as having *cosy* explain why the house is nice, and thus as having modification of a previous word, discussed in §4.2.) In approximating adverbs of degree, these words have a grammatical meaning – that of intensifying the word they modify. I emphasise that the modification of the later modifier is additional to the regular modification of the head, with the result that the phrases are ambivalent: in many contexts, 'nice cosy house' will mean both 'a [[nice cosy] house]' and 'a [nice [cosy house]]'. The effect of these uses is shown in the contrast with 'a nice, quiet bed' (= a [[nice] [quiet] bed]), in which *nice* modifies *bed* ('nice bed') without modifying *quiet* ('quiet to a nice degree'). The semi-adverbial uses grade off to purely adverbial (submodifying) uses: '<u>nice</u> cosy house' seems more adverbial than '<u>good</u> hard knot'; '<u>pure</u> academic interests' seems still more adverbial ('purely academic', but possibly 'pure interests' as well); '<u>pure</u> jet aircraft' seems completely so (it means 'pure jet' and cannot mean 'pure aircraft').

A modifier sometimes contributes a cause or reason to a later modifier. Quirk *et al.* (1972: 1064) cite 'long slow strides' (of a person walking), explaining that the strides are slow because they are long. In 'that typical, ordered, middle-class, "responsible" life', the life is 'responsible' because it is middle-class and ordered.

A third form of this modification is contributing evaluation to the concept expressed by the later modifier. For example, a reviewer, having said that a book was a welcome antidote to attacks on popular culture, qualified his approval as in example (5).

(5)   It has an '<u>unfortunate</u> narrow focus on America' *(Economist,* 28 May 2005, p. 84)

The context shows that it was the narrowness that was regarded as unfortunate rather than the focus itself; so semantically, *unfortunate* modifies the following modifier, *narrow*. (Syntactically, it primarily modifies *focus*, the head of the phrase.)

(6)   '<u>magnificent</u> prancing stallions' *(New Zealand Herald,* travel section)

In (6), we take it that the prancing in particular is magnificent, as well as the stallions generally.

Finally, Reinforcers semantically modify the descriptive meaning of each of the following premodifiers, as in (7).

(7)   'a <u>mere</u> useless gibbering stop-the-war-at-any-price pacifist' (cited in Fries 2000: 312, without context)

Here, *mere* reinforces *useless* and *gibbering*. Because Classifiers have referential not descriptive meaning, it does not reinforce the *stop-the-war-at-any-price*, although we expect the Reinforcer to modify each following word. (That awkwardness explains why phrases with all four zones filled are rare – a point noted in §2.2.1.1.)

Example (8) confirms the general point negatively.

(8)   'It [i.e. a Turgenev play] was a high class and cultural performance' (Doris Lessing, *The Summer Before the Dark*, p. 150)

The word *and* has been inserted to <u>prevent</u> us from reading *high class* as modifying *cultural*. We conclude that premodifiers may modify a following modifier and the head ('a <u>nice</u> warm room'), or a following modifier but not the head ('<u>unfortunate</u> narrow focus'), or all following modifiers and the head ('<u>mere</u> useless gibbering…').

4.3.2   Discussion: modification of a later modifier

Again, there are borderline examples. In 'beautiful long hair', there is a suggestion that the length is beautiful, but that interpretation is not a required one.

I have said that in 'a nice warm room' *nice* modifies *warm* and *room* simultaneously. I suggest that the parallel modification is made possible by the semi-independence of the meaning types which were discussed in chapter 3: words like *big* and *low* usually have conceptual meaning alone; words like *terrible* can have expressive meaning alone; words like *utter* can have grammatical meaning alone. In modification of a later premodifier, those meaning types work independently, as follows. *Nice* has in most contexts a descriptive (conceptual) meaning, ATTRACTIVE, and an expressive meaning, the emotion of APPROVAL; in this context, it also has a grammatical meaning, the requirement to apply INTENSIFICATION to another word. The three types of meaning work rather independently: the INTENSIFICATION meaning modifies *warm* (= 'very warm'); the ATTRACTIVE meaning modifies *room* (= 'the room is nice'); APPROVAL modifies the rest of the phrase, in the normal syntax (= 'I approve of the room's being warm'). Figure 4.1 will perhaps make the structure clearer. Arrows represent modification; boxes delimit the modifier (*nice*) and its meaning, and the elements modified. I suggest that modification of later modifiers occurs because, as hearers, we tend to take successive words together, making 'nice warm' a constituent, rather than *nice* and its

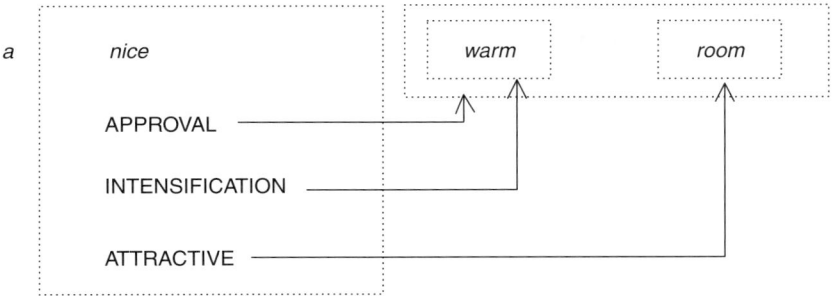

Figure 4.1 Structure of semantic relations, in modification of different words at once

distant head, *room*. (This is the principle of minimising domains, which I will discuss in section §9.2.)

This modification is a characteristic of the Reinforcer and Epithet zones. Reinforcers regularly modify following premodifiers, as in 'a <u>mere</u> useless gibbering stop-the-war-at-any-price pacifist', cited previously. Another example is '<u>sheer</u> desperate necessity': the phrase entails both sheer desperation and sheer necessity. All the other examples given have been of Epithets, as shown in table 4.2. But Epithets modify later premodifiers only sometimes: in the phrase in table 4.3, *classic* does not modify *snowy* or *volcanic* individually. I have found no examples in the Descriptor zone or in the Classifier zone.

The fact that Epithets readily modify following words is related to various elements of their semantic structure, in much the same way as we saw in the last section. First, words such as *magnificent* are fairly general, with the result that the hearer can interpret them as applying to quite different things: movement (in 'prancing'), physique (in 'horses') – or stance, and so on. Second, Epithets are often complex. In 'that typical, ordered, middle-class, "responsible" life', both *ordered* and *middle-class* have complex meanings including elements like 'planning for the future' that provide the causal link to *responsible*, while other elements (such as 'living by conventional moral standards', for *middle-class*) relate directly to the head, *life*. Finally, the expressive meaning of Epithets such as *lovely* (in 'lovely soft hands') makes it easy for hearers to apply the approving feeling to abstract softness (in the following modifier), while applying the descriptive meaning (attractive in appearance) to the physical entities denoted by the head (*hands*). I attribute my finding no Descriptors or Classifiers as examples to their lacking those features of Epithets – to their being precise, simple and neutral.

These modifiers are of a specifying type of modification: they serve to specify degree, causation, evaluation and so on, that are not (fully) specified

Table 4.2 *Epithets modifying a later modifier*

Epithet	Descriptor	Classifier	Head
beautiful	*warm*		*weather*
nice cosy			*house*
long	*slow*		*strides*
unfortunate	*narrow*		*focus*
magnificent	*prancing*		*stallions*

Table 4.3 *Epithets not modifying a later modifier*

Epithet	Descriptor	Classifier	Head
Classic	*snowy*	*volcanic*	*cone*

in the meaning of the word modified. (Other types of modification will be noted in later sections of this chapter, and summarised in §4.8.2.3.)

4.3.3   Conclusion: modification of a later modifier

Classifiers and Descriptors do not modify later premodifiers; Epithets do so sometimes; Reinforcers do so regularly. Zones further from the head have wider scope in this respect: they can modify more words other than the head. This modification is made possible by the words' semantic structure. To the extent that they are not modifying the head, Epithets and Reinforcers are bound to those other words, and bound more loosely to the head.

4.4   Modification of the act of ascribing properties

4.4.1   Introduction

In using the phrase 'aged whisky', a speaker ascribes to the liquid both the property of being aged and the property of being whisky. Syntactically, *aged* modifies the word *whisky*; semantically, it modifies the entity, whisky – the liquid. But in 'fake whisky', the modifier applies to the very act of ascribing to the liquid the property of being whisky, asserting that it is wrong to use *whisky* of that liquid. The word *fake* does not apply to the entity itself: it is not fake liquid. This section deals with the use of premodifiers to modify the act of ascription in such a way.

This use has been studied before: see Cruse (2004: 67) on 'negational descriptors' such as *fake*, *imitation* and *reproduction*; see also Jackendoff (1997), Sweetser (1999: 150–4), Dalrymple (2001), Löbner (2002: 108), for example. Fries (1986: 129) aptly calls them 'meta-linguistic directives on how to interpret the head term'.

Modifying the ascription of a property, rather than adding to the meaning of a constituent, is 'modality'. Stubbs (1996: 200) defines it as 'speakers' or writers' expression of attitude towards propositional information'; one such attitude is confidence in the truth of the information, as in sentence adverbials such as *probably* and *certainly*. Accordingly, this type of modification is modal modification. That view is supported by Huddleston and Pullum (2002: 557), who describe these words as 'modals', and list many more. Warren (1984: 231) also calls them modals, giving *actual*, *potential* and *literal* as examples. See also Partington (1993: 178) and Löbner (2002: 108). Van de Velde (2007: §3.2.2) discusses 'epistemic modification' of nouns or adjectives, which is modification of a 'descriptive sub-act', whereas most modification is of a 'referential sub-act'.

4.4.2   Modal modification

This section lists some types of modal premodification, and offers brief discussion.

Truth of the ascription. The example given above, 'fake whisky', illustrates the use of a modifier to modify the truth of an ascription. Other examples are 'a <u>bogus</u> English heiress' and 'a <u>possible</u> last stand'. Other words sometimes used this way are *imitation*, *replica*, *genuine* and *reproduction*. Sometimes, the headword is duplicated as a modifier of this type: 'In spite of his age, he's a <u>student</u> student' (the headword, *student*, truly is ascribable to him); 'It's not a <u>problem</u> problem' (it is not something to which *problem* can be validly ascribed). (Both examples are from Jim Miller, forthcoming.)

Value of the evidence for the ascription. Similarly, premodifiers sometimes apply to the nature or trustworthiness of the evidence for the ascription. Examples include '<u>purported</u> rape', 'a <u>suspected</u> heart attack' and '<u>feared</u> swansong'. Other words sometimes used this way are *accused*, *alleged*, *reported*, *self-styled*, *apparent*, and *putative*. An interesting example is 'an <u>apparent</u> electrical fire', where *apparent* does not modify any stated ascription (it was not apparent fire or apparent electricity), but the implicitly ascribed meaning 'caused by'.

Time when the ascription applies. A third group of words modifying the ascription indicate the time when the ascription is or was true, for example '<u>former</u> glamour model'. Other words that may be used this way include *potential*, *present*, *wartime*, *ex* (now sometimes used as a separate word), and *then* (as in 'the <u>then</u> president'). These uses are discussed by Huddleston and Pullum (2002: 556–7) as 'temporal attributives'.

Other examples, which I will not try to classify, are as follows: 'his two <u>rela-</u><u>tive</u> failures', 'a <u>threatened</u> massacre', 'his beloved <u>only</u> son' and 'his <u>only</u> beloved son'. (In modifying the following word or phrase, the modal-pre-modifier use of *only* is like its adverbial use, as in '<u>Only</u> *I* could see her', #'I could <u>only</u> *see* her' and #'I could see <u>only</u> *her*'; in its restrictive use, *only* modifies the preceding word not the following one: 'a lesbian <u>only</u> book group', 'Arab <u>only</u> cities'.)

We noted in §3.4.6.1 that phrases as well as words could act as modifiers. In the following, a whole clause acts as a modal modifier: 'It's not just the polls with their, <u>as the White House would argue</u>, loaded questions, that are drooping.' (The clause qualifies the truth of ascribing 'loaded questions' to the polls.)

The scope of modification of these words varies. Although they syntactic-ally modify all of the following part of the phrase, it is possible for them to semantically modify no more than another modifier. They therefore resem-ble submodifiers. *Then*, in 'my <u>then</u> young family' (meaning 'then young', not 'then a family'), seems to be a submodifier (as an 'adverb'), but in 'a <u>probable</u> new route' (which in context asserted that an actual mountaineer-ing route was probably new), *probable* is an 'adjective', and seems intended as a modifier.

4.4.3   Reinforcement

Reinforcers, such as *utter* and *sheer*, are usually treated in the literature as intensifying the denotation of the headword, which is thought to be a matter of degree; for example, Paradis (2000: 238) cites 'absolute bliss' and 'a perfect idiot' thus. Treating these as intensifying the degree of the quality denoted by the head makes a generally adequate account (and one I use myself, in section §3.5.5); but a more precise explanation of what is happening in the utterance is that the speaker is reinforcing the act of ascribing the headword to the entity. For example, in 'utter nonsense' (Paradis 2000: 238) and 'It weighs an <u>absolute</u> ton!' (spoken of a sewing machine), being nonsense and weighing a ton are not matters of degree; the speakers use such phrases to emphasise that using the words *nonsense* and *ton* is justified – adding expres-sive force, not adjusting an abstract concept: the Reinforcer is modifying the act of ascription. Some other examples are as follows: 'That's <u>absolute</u> unmitigated garbage!', spoken of a political accusation; '<u>sheer</u> infinite adren-aline rush', of an exciting experience; 'an <u>absolute</u> manic basket case', of a person.

4.4.4   Discussion: modification of the act of ascription

There are borderline examples. In 'absolute <u>unmitigated</u> garbage', it is not clear whether *unmitigated* has more meaning than its disapproval. If it does,

Table 4.4 Former *as modal*

	Det.	Epithet	Descriptor	Classifier	Head
(a)	*the*		*former*	*British welterweight*	*champion*
(b)	*his*			*British former*	*wife*

Table 4.5 Replica *as modal*

	Det.	Descriptor	Classifier	Head
(a)	*a*	*replica*	*Tomkin long-case*	*clock*
(b)	*a*	*beautifully crafted*	*Swilken 19th-century replica*	*putter*

perhaps it is a truth modal, *unmitigated* being equivalent to 'it is certain...' (that the accusation referred to is garbage); otherwise, it is a non-modal expressive word.

There does not seem to be a definable set of modal modification types (or of particular words that can modify modally); but the groups I have given fit quite well with general classifications of modality into probability, obligation and so on, as in Halliday (2004: 147).

The relationship of modifying the act of ascription to the zone structure is a little complex. Reinforcing modification occurs in the Reinforcer zone. The modal premodifiers occur in various zones. In table 4.4, *former* in example (a) is placed as a Descriptor to modify 'British welterweight champion', but in (b), it is placed as a Classifier, and after *British*, to modify 'wife'. In table 4.5, *replica* varies in position similarly. (Both sets of examples are from the British National Corpus.)

The use of *fake* shows the issue to be more complex, however. Consider (9), for example:

(9)   'Purple fake Indian feathers' (Corpus of Contemporary American English)

Purple is a Descriptor and *Indian* is a Classifier, as shown in table 4.6. It would be grammatically acceptable to vary 'purple fake Indian feathers' to #'purple Indian fake feathers' or #'fake purple Indian feathers'. The lack of coordination implies that all of the premodifiers are in separate zones, but there are no zones for *fake* to be in, as suggested by table 4.7. In (a), *fake* modifies all of 'purple Indian feathers'; nothing positive is ascribed to the feathers. In (b), *fake* modifies only 'Indian feathers'; the fake feathers are asserted to be purple. In (c), *fake* modifies only 'feathers'; the fake feathers are asserted to be purple and Indian.

Table 4.6 *Zoning of* purple *and* Indian

Epithet	Descriptor	Classifier	Head
[big]	*purple*	*Indian*	*feathers*

Table 4.7 Fake *as modal*

	Epithet	?	Descriptor	?	Classifier	?	Head
(a)	*[big]*	*fake*	*purple*		*Indian*		*feathers*
(b)			*purple*	*fake*	*Indian*		*feathers*
(c)			*purple*		*Indian*	*fake*	*feathers*

Those examples show, then, that modal premodifiers have a definite scope, but not a definite zone: they are placed immediately before the word or group of words to be modified. Nor do they have a set semantic structure. *Potential* and *relative*, for example, are quite abstract, gradable ('wholly relative'), and subjective (in depending on speaker opinion), so they are like Epithets; but *then, alleged, suspected* and even *fake* are fairly objective, and are not scalar, so they are like Descriptors – we do not say **'very fake'. (For scalarity, see §3.4.2.3.) Moreover, they are used in different positions without a change of meaning, as just shown. Those facts are significant exceptions to the general correlation of semantic structure and zone.

We conclude, then, that modal premodifiers are zoneless; they are outside the zone system, which ties position to semantic structure. The reason lies in their very nature. They modify an act of ascription (not the head entity, as other premodifiers do basically), so they do not follow the rule for other premodifiers, but stand immediately before the word or words whose ascription they modify.

4.4.5   *Conclusion: modification of the act of ascription*

Reinforcers, using one form of modifying the act of ascription, do so regularly, and by their nature. Modal premodifiers, using the other type, are an exception to the principle for all other premodifers: a single sense – with constant semantic structure – can occur in different positions; they are outside the zone system.

4.5   Modification of a discourse element other than the head entity

We have seen that normally a premodifier gives information about the entity denoted by the head. In some uses, however, a premodifier gives information about something else in the discourse, modifying it semantically, though not syntactically modifying the word that denotes it. (That will be explained and illustrated in the following subsections.)

4.5.1 Types of other-element modification

Two types of modifying another participant will be distinguished. In the first, premodifiers give information about other participants in the discourse, as follows.

(a) They can inform us about an explicit participant, denoted by the determiner. When a tramper wrote that the boulders in the riverbed 'began disappearing behind <u>our</u> <u><u>happy</u></u> feet' (*New Zealand Alpine Journal*), it is the tramper and her companion that were happy, not their feet. (In this section, I use double underlining to mark the word denoting the element modified.) Other examples (from Huddleston and Pullum 2002: 558) are '<u><u>Leslie Nielsen's</u></u> <u>astonished</u> face', '<u>my</u> <u><u>naive</u></u> freshman days', '<u>your</u> own <u>stupid</u> fault'. Sometimes, the modifier is relational, so can be seen as modifying both terms of the relation: '<u>his</u> <u>older</u> <u><u>brother</u></u>' ('<u><u>he</u></u> was <u>younger</u> than <u>his brother</u>'), '<u>his</u> <u>favourite</u> <u><u>music</u></u>' ('<u><u>he</u></u> <u>favoured</u> that <u><u>music</u></u>').

(b) Premodifiers can inform us about a more distant participant. The participant may be explicit as the subject of the clause: '<u><u>Matt</u></u> emitted <u>happy</u> little squawks' *(Climber 53*, Spring 2005, p. 9), '<u>a naturalist</u> [would see a rare bird] besport itself before his <u>amazed</u> eyes, or appear... to his <u>appreciative</u> gaze' (British National Corpus). In phrases like this, the syntactic modification remains, leaving the reader in an imaginative tension between *naturalist* and *eyes* as the target of *amazed*. The participant may alternatively be represented in a subordinate prepositional phrase: 'a <u>naked</u> photo of the <u><u>mayor</u></u>' (Huddleston and Pullum 2002: 558). The participant may also be only implicit: in 'an <u>indiscriminate</u> massacre of commuters' (British National Corpus), 'indiscriminate' gives information about the unidentified people who committed the massacre.

(c) Finally, premodifiers can inform us about a participant in the speech event, not the reported event. To the extent that modifying something entails giving information about it, expressive modifiers can modify the hearer ('you'): 'How the hell could <u><u>you</u></u> give away half the <u>fucking</u> company?' (Kurt Eichenwald, *Conspiracy of Fools*, p. 228); the anger expressed in *fucking* was directed at the hearer, and implied that the hearer was foolish. Similarly, the speaker can be modified. When a book reviewer refers to a book as 'a <u>slim</u> volume', *slim* informs us (unintentionally) of the reviewer's condescension. The various forms of social meaning inform us of the speaker's social background or help create the speaker's relation to the hearer: by regionalism – 'the nippy <u>wee</u>

beast', by informality – 'your own stupid fault', by formal use – 'Leslie Nielsen's astonished face', or by obscenity – 'the fucking company'. (The examples have graded off in the relevance to the head of their descriptive meaning; the last one does not modify the head semantically at all.) Huddleston and Pullum (2002: 556–9) discuss two types of such usage, as 'associative attributives' and 'transferred attributives' (which they note as being the traditional figure of transferred epithet or 'hypallage'.[1]

In the second type of other-element modification, heads denote an event (rather than an object)[2], or include an event in their denotation, as in 'a big eater', 'hard worker', 'his frank admission', 'an indiscriminate massacre', and the much-discussed 'a beautiful dancer'.[3] But the event modified is sometimes denoted by a word other than the syntactic head, as follows. It may be denoted by the verb in the clause: a pianist 'played a heavy first note and a curtained second one', meaning 'played the first note heavily'. 'Laos threatens to attack new village' (Ferris (1993)), meaning 'attack for the first time'. The event may be entailed by the modifier itself: the KGB 'employed a younger Mr Putin' (*Economist*, 15 December 2007, p. 11), meaning 'employed Mr Putin when he was younger'. The event may be wholly implicit: linguistic nativists are said to 'use performance factors and the maturation of universal grammar as unprincipled fudge factors for recalcitrant data' (Tomasello 2003a: 289), meaning 'the nativists explain the data with great difficulty'. This use seems to grade off into modifying another participant, as discussed just above. For example, 'Matt emitted happy little squawks', could be taken to mean 'Matt emitted little squawks happily' or 'Matt emitted happy little squawks'.

4.5.2   Discussion: modification of another discourse element

This modification occurs in the Epithet and Reinforcer zones. The examples given have all been Epithets, with the possible exception of 'a naked photo of the mayor' (which seems to have a Descriptor), as shown in table 4.8.

Reinforcers regularly use this form of modification: being emphatic, and expressing intention, they convey something about the speaker, as illustrated in table 4.9 – a political exclamation cited previously. The modification structure here relies on the semantic structure of the modifying words. Nearly all

---

[1] They regard expressions like 'criminal lawyer' as modifying an entity 'associated with' the head. That seems to be wrong. 'Criminal lawyer', 'nuclear scientist' and so on are like 'political party', 'social comment' and so on: they all denote a type of the entity denoted by the head. I explain the issues fully in chapter 5, on Classifiers. (I suggest that this resolves the long debate in the literature about 'criminal lawyer'.)

[2] 'Event' and 'object' are used here rather loosely; I will refine the use of such terms in the introduction to chapter 5.

[3] Huddleston and Pullum (2002: 557) give a list of such uses, as 'process-oriented attributives'. Warren (1984: 239) analyses 'hard worker' as '[hard work]-[er]'. Quirk *et al.* (1985: §7.73) describe them as corresponding to construction with an adverb.

Table 4.8 *Epithets modifying another discourse element*

Det.	Epithet	Descriptor	Classifier	Head
our	*happy*			*feet*
the	*fucking*			*company*
	good			*shot*
	happy	*little*		*squawks*
a	*heavy*	*first*		*note*

Table 4.9 *Reinforcers modifying another discourse element*

Reinforcer	Epithet	Descriptor	Classifier	Head
complete	*unmitigated*			*garbage*

of these expressions rely on the expressive meaning of Epithets. In 'good shot', the descriptive meaning ('skilful' in the context of cricket) relates to the head entity (the shot); it is only the attitudinal meaning (approval) that relates to the speaker. In other instances, it is Reinforcers' and Epithets' abstract meaning that controls the effect: in 'happy feet' and 'happy squawks', the hearer transfers HAPPINESS to the other participant because *feet* and *squawks* cannot take abstract descriptors. Classifiers and Descriptors do not modify other discourse elements because they have no expressive or abstract meaning (the Descriptor in 'nude photo of the mayor' modifies another participant only by figure of speech – transferred epithet).

4.5.3 *Conclusions : modification of another discourse element*

From this section, we draw the following conclusions. Modifiers can modify a discourse element other than the participant denoted by the head. The element modified is outside the scope of normal modification, which is the denotation of the remainder of the phrase. Neither Classifiers nor Descriptors appear to be used in this way; Epithets are often so used; Reinforcers are so used routinely. This modification of another element is dependent on the modifier's semantic structure. This is a subjective use of modification, since it expresses personal attitudes and feelings rather than objective facts or impersonal concepts.

4.6 Modification of the discourse situation

This section shows that a modifier may relate semantically to part of the discourse situation: a whole state of affairs in the external world, the social situation of the participants' relationship, or the linguistic situation – the text.

4.6.1   Types of situation modification

Sometimes modifiers adjust or maintain the social relationship between speaker and hearer, or give the hearer information about the social situation. Slang, for example, establishes group membership and identity (Eble 2000), creating or modifying the social situation – some language has 'the power … of actually creating a situation' (Cruse 2004: 59). 'Awesome goodie bags' (give-aways), for example, was part of the publicity for a major sports event (appealing primarily to the young), using young people's slang to create rapport with its readers. Similarly, informal modifiers establish a relationship of social equality. 'Bloody great stupid game' has three such modifiers; other examples include *nice* and *cosy*, as in 'nice cosy house' cited above. All of these modifiers reflect the informality of the social situation, and help to create it.

In another type of this modification, a word modifies the whole situation being referred to. A passenger in a plane which crash-landed expressed his feeling as in (10):

(10)   'Get those bloody doors open and get out of the bloody thing.'
            (*New Zealand Herald*, 19 June 2007, p. A5)

Here, the modifier *bloody* expresses anxiety, not with the doors or the plane (the 'thing'), but with the situation of being in such a landing. The speaker seems to have been attaching the expletive to every available noun. Examples (11) and (12) are similar.

(11)   'I have moved five-fucking-thousand miles to be a public-relations jerk!' (Kurt Eichenwald, *Conspiracy of Fools*, p. 219)
(12)   'When you are sitting up front driving, you can neither see nor hear a damned thing.' (British National Corpus)

In this usage, modifiers are placed for emphasis – typically, near the end of the clause: they can be placed well away from the word denoting what they modify (if any); and (as shown just above), they can in colloquial English even interrupt another word or phrase. Vandelanotte (2002: §3.2) describes these attitudinal adjectives as having scope over an entire situation, which may be expressed by a whole clause. (In these examples, *bloody* and *damned* also modify the relation between speaker and hearer, as discussed just above.)

In a third type of discourse-situation modification, a word modifies the textual situation, as discourse marker. The word *actual* is sometimes used straightforwardly as an Epithet or Descriptor: 'the actual words of Jesus' has OED's meaning <2>, '…existing in act or fact'. It is sometimes a Reinforcer, emphasising the meaning of the head: 'hatred and persecution, later to be transformed into <u>actual</u> genocide' – although this Reinforcer use is not recorded in SOED. In other uses, however, *actual* serves a discourse function, and semantically does not modify the rest of the phrase, the ascription, or the participants, as in (13).

(13)   'A man came who was the bishop of Durham, but whose <u>actual</u> name I don't know.' (spontaneous remark by an anonymous speaker at a public meeting, 14 November 2005)

Actual focuses the hearer's attention on the name, to make it contrast with the man's position (bishop). If the speaker had said, #'A man came who was Bishop of Durham but I don't know his name', she would presumably not have used *actual* at all, since the hearers' attention would have been focused on *name* by its position at the end of the sentence. *Actual* here does not give us information about the head entity (the bishop's name); nor does it modify any participant, or the speaker's situation: it is purely a discourse marker, with the function of focusing attention. (Tognini-Bonelli 1993 discusses this use of *actual*.)

   A second discourse function of *actual* is marking a change of topic, which is illustrated in (14) and (15) (the emphasis is in the originals; they are treated there as illustrating the 'focusing' use of *actual*).

(14)   '... women's magazines that matter get grottier and grottier if Claire will forgive my saying so. *The actual problems* that people are allowed to ask advice about have become disgusting beyond belief...' (Tognini-Bonelli 1993: 195–6)

(15)   'I don't want to read a book that is about *psycho-analysis* but I think *the actual presentation of Freud himself* is amazingly successful...' (Tognini-Bonelli 1993: 197)

In both of these examples, *actual* focuses attention, but the purpose of the focusing is to help the unexpected change of topic: in the first example, the hearer would have expected the topic of the new sentence to be either women's magazines or grottiness; in the second example, the hearer would have expected the 'but...' clause to be about the speaker's wants or about psychoanalysis, not about Freud.

   Single has a similar discourse use, as in 'the country's <u>single</u> largest computer system' and 'GM's <u>single</u> biggest investment'. In this use, *single* seems to have moved from postdeterminer position to Reinforcer position, with the discourse-marker function of emphasis, since its postdeterminer meaning of SINGLENESS is already expressed by a specific word (the superlatives 'largest' and 'biggest') and by the singular form of the head ('system', 'investment'). In phrases like 'a <u>sort of</u> vast, unfurnished house' (Aijmer 2002: 181), *sort of* acts as a one-word discourse particle in adjusting the speaker–hearer interaction, but it acts like a regular minimising Reinforcer in downplaying following descriptive words. Other words seem to be acquiring this use; for example, in 'a whacking great ugly wind farm' (from a columnist in the *New Zealand Herald*), both *whacking* and *great* seem to be general emphasisers, as much as regular modifiers.

These uses modify the head syntactically, but they can hardly be said to modify any one word semantically, since they do not affect any particular word's interpretation.

4.6.2   Discussion: modification of the discourse situation

Almost all examples of modifying the speaker–hearer relationship and of modifying the social situation have been Epithets ('a <u>useless</u>... pacifist', 'a <u>damned</u> thing'). One example was a Classifier: 'awesome <u>goodie</u> bags'. The two premodifiers modifying the textual situation (as discourse marker) were Reinforcers.

As in other forms of non-canonical modification (§4.2 to §4.5), modification of the discourse structure is controlled by semantic structure and occurs only with Epithets and Reinforcers. Effect on social situation is achieved by social meaning: 'awesome <u>goodie</u> bags' relies on its social meaning as young people's language (their social dialect, in the terms of Cruse 2004: 59); '<u>bloody great stupid</u> game' relies on its informality. So, as in §4.3.3, the ability of Epithets to serve two modification functions at once rests on their semantic structure: the descriptive meaning of *great* and *stupid* can modify the head (*game*), while their social meaning modifies the discourse situation. As we saw in §4.4.4, Reinforcers *(actual* in this case) can readily modify something other than the head because they have no inherent descriptive meaning linking them to the head entity. *Goodie*, in 'awesome <u>goodie</u> bags', is exceptional as a Classifier; it has the semantic structure and powers of an Epithet because it has carried them through its migration from slang inter-jection (as 'oh goodie!') to Epithet, to noun (as plural, *goodies*), and back to Classifier.

4.6.3   Conclusion: modification of the discourse situation

We draw the following conclusions. Premodifiers are sometimes used to modify the situation of use – either the situation referred to, or the speaker–hearer relation, or the textual situation. In this use, their scope is wider than the rest of the phrase (which is the scope of normal premodification), and wider even than modification of other participants, as discussed in §4.5. They rely for this structure on the complexity of their semantics, and on social and expressive meaning, in particular. They are strongly subjective, in serving the speaker's feelings and discourse intentions rather than supplying information about entities. The further from the head a zone is, the more frequently do its members modify the discourse situation.

4.7   Modification of the head: closeness of the syntactic bond

This section discusses how closely premodifiers in the different zones are bound to the head (with incidental comment on how closely they are bound to each other). It draws on the previous sections, but also on new material.

4.7.1   Closeness to the head of modifiers in the different zones

Classifiers are syntactically and semantically very close to the head. First, Classifiers can have no other type of modifier intervene before the head, as is entailed in the zone structure set out in chapter 2. Next, Classifiers take almost no part in the forms of modification studied above, in §4.2 to §4.6. (Exceptions were '<u>goodie</u> bags', §4.6.2, and 'ugly trailing <u>overhead</u> wires', §4.2.2.) Finally, Classifiers and their heads are often replaced by a single word. Sometimes the modifier stands alone, for both words; for example, '<u>macadamia</u> nuts' becomes 'macadamias'; '<u>TV</u> set' becomes 'TV'. Sometimes the head stands alone, for both words; for example, 'lawn mower' becomes 'mower'. Sometimes another word replaces both words; for example, 'novel writer' becomes 'novelist', '<u>ambulance</u> man' and '<u>St John's</u> man' became 'zambuck' (in Australia and New Zealand). In these examples, the Classifier has lost its descriptive meaning and is referential, serving the same function as the head.

Descriptors are a little more loosely bound to the head. In one way, they are close to the head: '<u>young</u> man' is close to functioning as a lexical unit, like 'youth' (hence the frequent use of *young* as a Classifier, e.g. 'American <u>young</u> men') and '<u>retired</u> person' is like 'retiree'. On the other hand, they are distant from the head in several ways. By definition, Descriptors may have other modifiers (Classifiers) intervene between them and the head. Their bond is not so much to the head as to succeeding premodifiers and head, as a group; *black*, in '<u>black</u> iron fence' modifies 'iron fence', not 'fence' alone. Some are relative modifiers, as in 'beautiful <u>young</u> Kuwaiti girls' and 'beautiful <u>young</u> Kuwaiti women'; the contextual adjustment of the meaning on the scale of age is a syntactic operation that can occur only between elements that are distinct.

Epithets have a much looser bond to their syntactic head, in a number of ways. They are separated from the head by two zones of modification; and, since there may be several modifiers in each of those zones, Epithets can grammatically be separated from the head by a number of other premodifiers. Epithets can take part in all the non-canonical forms of modification studied in this chapter, though not all Epithets do. We have seen that expletives like *bloody* modify the situation, not being semantically bound to any particular word ('The army must be paying you more than the <u>bloody</u> colonel', for example.) Finally, an Epithet is sometimes inserted into another word: 'amalga-bloody-mated' (OED example). Since Epithets can modify in so many ways, and can vary in position so greatly, they are quite loosely bound to the head.

Reinforcers are bound more loosely still. They routinely take part in the non-standard forms of modification studied in this chapter. In general, Reinforcers modify each of the other premodifiers in the phrase in turn, rather than having a single modifying relation (to the rest of the phrase). For example, 'sheer desperate necessity' signifies both 'utterly desperate' and 'utter necessity', not simply 'utter [desperate necessity]'. Further, their very nature as reinforcing words is to modify the act of ascription of words (the head and other modifiers), rather than to modify the head entity, in the sense of adding information to it. That is reflected in the fact that we cannot use Reinforcers predicatively: 'the complete idiot' is grammatical, but not *'The idiot is complete'. Finally, some Reinforcers (such as *actual*) can modify the situation, not particular words at all. Reinforcers, then, are the most loosely bound of premodifiers.

4.7.2   Conclusion: modification of the head

There is a cline in the syntactic bonding of premodifiers with the head, from Classifiers (the most tightly bound) to Reinforcers (the most loosely bound). It can be represented as in (16):

(16)   Reinforcer < Epithet < Descriptor < Classifier

where the sign '<' means 'is less tightly bound than' or 'is more autonomous than'. The variation in bonding is another syntactic difference between the zones.

4.8   Discussion: syntactic explanation of unmarked order

4.8.1   Other syntactic features of the zones

This section discusses syntactic features which explain premodifier order only partially or indirectly. The first feature is that the zones vary in subjectivity. Standard premodification (where the word simply modifies the rest of the phrase) is relatively conventionalised and objective. Producing and interpreting the other forms of modification are more reliant on users' judgement, and allow them some freedom (as to when to use it and as to what the modifier may relate to); it is therefore more subjective. It often entails what Traugott (1995: 32) identifies as 'subjectification': 'the development of a grammatically identifiable expression of speaker belief or speaker attitude to what is said'. The earlier sections of this chapter have shown that the degree of subjectivity increases with distance from the head. This subjectivity parallels the subjectivity noted in the last chapter (§3.6.1.3); it will likewise have some importance later (especially for grammaticalisation, in §10.3).

Another feature of the zones is that their syntax serves different metafunctions. (For the metafunctions, see §3.6.1.5, based on Halliday 2004.) Premodification by means of referential and descriptive meaning, characteristic of the Classifier and Descriptor zones, serves the experiential metafunction. Modifying the speaker and hearer and the discourse situation is characteristic of the Epithet zone, and serves the interpersonal function. Modifying the act of ascription, characteristic of the Reinforcer zone, serves the textual function.

Finally, the zones differ in whether they allow submodification. Although the other zones allow it, the Reinforcer zone does not, because its words have no content to be modified. (We will see in chapter 5 that the Classifier zone differs in the nature of its submodification, as in other features.)

4.8.2　Other syntactic features of premodification

4.8.2.1　Sentential adjectives
We have seen in §4.6 that adjectives (and potentially other premodifiers) sometimes act on the whole assertion rather than on the rest of the nominal phrase. For example, in the advertising slogan 'The best damned coffee in the civilised world', 'damned' emphasises the whole assertion, not simply 'coffee', which it modifies syntactically. ('Civilised' presumably acts almost as widely, since the slogan suggests that drinking that brand of coffee is very civilised.) Since expressions like '*frankly*' and '*hopefully*' are 'sentential adverbials' when modifying the whole sentence, these adjectives should perhaps be regarded as 'sentential adjectives'. (Vandelanotte 2007: 247 notes the parallel with sentential adverbs.)

4.8.2.2　Parts of speech
We saw in the previous chapter that 'nouns' and 'participles' can act as 'adjectives', in that they can be used descriptively: their semantic structure is reconstrued. We should now note that 'adverbs', 'numerals' and 'quantifiers' can also function as premodifiers, as if they were 'adjectives'. We can have 'an up beat', 'a down train' (with 'adverbs'). 'They grew a remarkable eight metres in a year' has a 'numeral' as a Descriptor; 'The Animal Welfare (Dogs) Code of Welfare fourth draft' has a 'numeral' as a Classifier. 'I spent a pleasant few hours' has a quantifier as a Descriptor. These words do not need to have their semantic structure reconstrued, since it is already appropriate: the concepts UP, DOWN, EIGHT and FEW are relatively concrete and nonscalar, so may be expressed in Descriptors. Rather, their syntactic function is reconstrued. The 'adverbs' now modify the head of a nominal phrase, instead of the whole or part of a verbal phrase, relating semantically to the movement which is a part of the noun's descriptive meaning. The 'quantifiers' and 'numerals' now modify, not determine, the head: they are used to present descriptive information about the head entity, not to limit the reference of the head.

4.8.2.3   Types of modification

In the literature on modification, on adjectives, and on noun phrase structure, there seems to be no consensus on what modification consists of, and (in my observation) no clear outline of it. For that reason, and because this chapter has set out considerable variety and complexity in noun phrase modification, it seems worthwhile to suggest an analysis of modification, briefly. I suggest that there are the following types in nominal phrase premodification. (I mark the modifying word with double underlining, and the location modified with single underlining.)

(a) Modifying the information given in the phrase. (i) Amplifying modification. The modifier amplifies the reader's interpretation of the phrase; that is, it adds information to it; for example, in 'thick slow hug of the bush', *thick* amplifies *slow* by adding its causation; in 'a nice warm room', WARMTH is added to ROOM. (See §4.3.2, on cause and evaluation, and §4.5.2.) (ii) Specifying modification. The modifier makes specific some information that is given vaguely elsewhere; for example, 'a good thick layer'. (See §4.2.) (iii) Intensifying and weakening modification. The modifier affects the degree of information given elsewhere; that is, it instructs the hearer to interpret another word more strongly (for example, 'a nice warm room'), or more weakly (for example, 'mere decoration', and the patronising use of 'a dear little thing'. (See §§4.2.1, 4.3.2, and 4.4.3.)

(b) Modifying the situation. The modifier does not relate to the informational content at all, but affects the discourse situation – the relation between speaker and hearer; for example, 'awesome goodie bags' (both modifiers modify the situation towards informality). (See §4.6.)

(c) Modifying the act of ascribing information; for example, 'his former Labour-voting parents'.

Words are sometimes ambivalent, carrying two types at once: *nice* is intensifying in 'a nice warm room', but is also amplifying – 'a nice warm room'. Also, the classification applies to submodification within a noun phrase: 'a badly carved wooden chair' has amplifying modification; 'the highly carved, soaring Gothic look' has intensifying modification.

The types do not characterise the zones: intensifying modification occurs in both Reinforcer and Epithet zones, for example. Nor do they characterise the scope of modification: intensifying modification takes scope over both preceding and following words, and previous-word modification may be either specifying or intensifying, for example. Therefore, the types of modification do not determine or characterise premodifier order.

The list of types does not include 'referent modification' and 'reference modification', discussed by Bolinger (1967), Taylor (1992) and Hengeveld (2008: §3.3.3), for example. That distinction turns on the semantic function of the head, not on the type of modification in this sense. For example, 'a poor doctor' ('with little money') is an example of referent modification: in it, *doctor* is in referential use, designating a person. 'A poor doctor' ('incompetent') is an example of reference modification: in it, *doctor* is in descriptive use, denoting a professional quality of the person already designated. (The examples are from Hengeveld 2008; another example is the much-discussed 'old man' / 'old friend', with 'relational nouns'.) In both phrases, *poor* amplifies information given in the head, so the type of modification is the same. The same point applies to 'intersective' and 'subsective' modification, as in Kamp and Partee (1995), for example.

That distinction between modifying a descriptive meaning of the head and modifying its referential meaning has a little relevance to the order of premodifiers, however, to the extent that it is part of the distinction between Reinforcers and other premodifiers. Reinforcers reinforce the descriptive meaning of the head, operating on its intensity dimension, and cannot reinforce referential meaning; that explains why they virtually never occur with Classifiers. That is clear with heads like *fool* and *nonsense*, where Reinforcers such as *utter* and *complete* can modify the descriptive meaning, FOLLY. But it applies also to more concrete heads like *mist* (<1> 'A diffuse cloud…') and *fog* (<1> 'A thick cloud…'). A Reinforcer can modify *fog*, as in 'complete fog', because *fog* has meaning on the intensity dimension (THICK); but we do not meet *'complete mist' (in the British National Corpus or the Corpus of Contemporary American English), because *mist* lacks an intensity dimension. But the other zones may express modification of either descriptive or referential meaning in the head – and accordingly either 'referent modification' or 'reference modification', and likewise 'intersective' or 'subsective' modification). See the examples in table 4.10.

4.8.2.4   *Marked syntax*
I do not have properly attested examples of this marked use of syntax, although I believe it is reasonably common in informal speech. I construct one, beginning from example (17):

(17)   'a black large sofa' (Huddleston and Pullum 2002: 452)

The authors assert that the order is acceptable (instead of the normal 'large [black [sofa]]') when a speaker is distinguishing among large sofas: 'a [black [large sofa]]'. I believe that that reordering is so rare as to be unacceptable, and that we use other devices for that sort of contrast.[4] For example, we use contrastive stress, as in (18):

(18)   #'a large **black** sofa'

---

[4] I discuss the acceptability in the 'other theories' section of chapter 10 (§10.4.3.5), giving evidence from the British National Corpus for a number of such phrases.

Table 4.10 *Modification of the head's referential or descriptive meaning*

Zone	Head with referential meaning	Head with descriptive meaning
Epithet	*an eager <u>boy</u>*	*an eager <u>student</u>*
Descriptor	*a red <u>ball</u>*	*a retired <u>officer</u>*
Classifier	*a British <u>lawyer</u>*	*a criminal <u>lawyer</u>*

There, *black* is contrasting one sort of large sofa with others, so that the concept BLACK modifies the concept LARGE SOFA, and the word *black* modifies the words 'large...sofa'. *Black*, then, occurs in the middle of the word group it modifies, not before it, as in regular (that is, unmarked) syntax. The structure is 'a [large {black} sofa]', where {....} indicates a constituent occurring <u>within</u> the constituent it modifies. That is a marked use, with the contrastive stress carrying out the marking.

A real example of dubious attestation occurred earlier in this chapter (§4.2.1.2), where I wrote example (19):

(19)   'Old electric trains are younger than old <u>steam</u> trains.'

That contrasts the meaning 'old trains powered by electricity' with 'old trains powered by steam', with the concept OLD TRAINS modified by ELECTRICITY and by STEAM; so the last phrase of the quotation is structured: '[old {steam}trains]'.

4.8.2.5   Semantic implications of the chapter

Section 4.6.2 illustrated general emphasis as a form of reinforcing, as in the discourse-marker use of the Reinforcers *single* and *actual*. It is more subjective than the intensifying form of reinforcement (which characterises Reinforcers), since it is underspecified as to what is to be reinforced and the nature of the reinforcement, relying on the hearer's contextual interpretation. We did not have occasion to observe it in chapter 3, the 'Semantic explanation' chapter, as it is not characteristic of any zone. Accordingly, I note it here as a type of meaning; emphasising and intensifying are two meaning types serving the reinforcing function. In figure 4.2, it is added to the semantic map (figure 3.1), where the semantic functions and meaning types were set out. (The addition is in bold type.)

4.8.2.6   Support from other writers

I have already cited support for specific points. General support for my treatment of modification comes from several writers who view the interpretation of nominal phrases as being more than adding the effect of successive words and applying straightforward compositional rules. Cruse (2004), Taylor (2002) and Pustejovsky (1995), from their different points of view, all

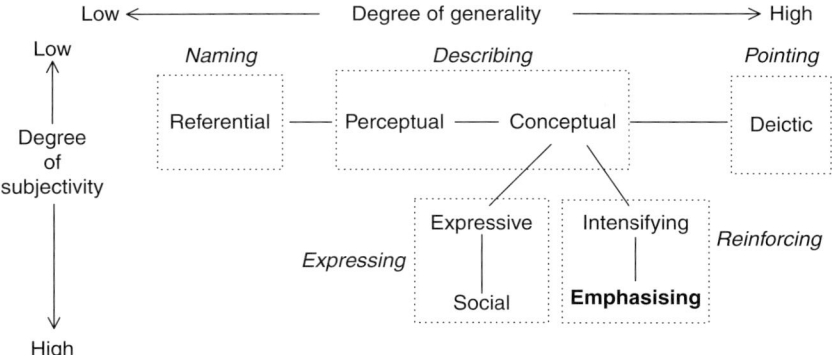

Figure 4.2 Map of semantic functions and meaning types in English

describe meaning as being built by a complex interaction of the word meanings, which varies with the syntax and the context to develop a total meaning that is far from being the sum of straightforward and linear modification. Support from psycholinguistics will be given in chapter 9 (§9.2).

4.9   Conclusion: syntactic explanation of unmarked order

4.9.1   *Summary*

The first main issue dealt with in this chapter has been scope of modification. Modal premodifiers such as *alleged* and *former* (discussed in §4.4.2) occur in different positions, being placed so as to immediately precede the word or words they have scope over. They thus appear to change zones, even though they have the same content and semantic structure in the different positions. In that, they differ from other premodifiers. They differ also in having a single syntactic power (the regular one, of modifying the following part of the phrase), not the wider powers that other conceptual premodifiers do.

For other premodifiers, the scope is as follows. The syntactic scope is the following zones and the head. The semantic scope is (a) the same as for syntactic scope, and (b) occasional additional scope, which is in general as follows:

- modification of previous words, by some Epithets, and a few Descriptors, in a relative or explanatory relation, for example (§4.2);
- modification of later premodifiers, by Reinforcers and Epithets, as to degree or evaluation, for example (§4.3);
- modification of the speaker's act of ascribing properties to the head, by Reinforcers and modal premodifiers (§4.4);
- modification of some element other than the head entity (the speaker, for example), by some Epithets, and a few Descriptors (§4.5);

- modification of the discourse situation, by Epithets, and by Reinforcers
  (to a small degree), making the situation informal, for example (§4.6).

There are a few particular words which are exceptions to those generalisations; for example, the Reinforcer *actual*, as discourse marker, does not modify the following part of the phrase. In general, however, the further forward a zone is, the wider its power: its syntactic scope is necessarily wider; its members have more potential forms of modification, and they use those potential forms more often.

The second main issue has been the relation of syntax to semantic structure. The generalisations in the previous paragraphs show that premodifiers derive their varying additional scope from the semantic structure characteristic of the zones (e.g. Epithets like *bloody* modify the social situation because of their social meaning); the exceptions derive from the structure of particular words (e.g. the Epithet *big* does <u>not</u> modify the social situation because it does not have social meaning).

The final issue has been the closeness of premodifiers' bond to the head. We have seen (§4.7) that the further forward a zone is, the looser are its members' bonds to the head.

4.9.2   *Conclusions drawn*

4.9.2.1   *Syntactic nature of the zones*

Chapter 2, on the zones, asserted that the premodifier zones are syntactic units, in that words within one zone are syntactically co-ordinate with each other and subordinate to those in later zones; this chapter has confirmed the zones' syntactic status: zones are in order of increasingly wide syntactic scope, further from the head. The chapter has also shown that the zone order is one of increasingly wide and varied semantic scope, and that the zones are in order of increasingly loose bonding to the head. Finally, the modal premodifiers are syntactically different from other premodifiers, being placed purely syntactically, not by zone; the generalisations just above do not apply to them.

From those specific conclusions follows the general one, that the order of premodifiers in English nominal phrases has a syntactic explanation as well as the semantic explanation set out in the previous chapter. It is a further answer to the question with which the book began: what is the nature of unmarked premodifier order?

4.9.2   *Relationship between syntax and semantics*

The general conclusion just reached suggests that syntax and semantics are parallel and equal, in nominal phrases; but the conclusion reached in §4.9.1, that the syntax of premodifiers is based on their semantic structure, shows that that is not so. This section works out more fully the relation between syntactic structure and semantic structure. It argues that the relation is complex: explanatorily, semantics is dominant; functionally, the two work mostly together as co-operating equals; when they conflict, however, semantics overrules syntax.

We consider first how we may understand the relation conceptually. The position of modal premodifiers (such as *fake* and *supposed*) is explained wholly by syntax: they can occur in different positions according to what they modify syntactically, without change of meaning. For other premodifiers, however, the scope and type of modification is determined by their semantic structure; that is obviously so for semantic modification, but it is true for syntactic modification also. The gradation in syntactic closeness to the head is controlled by the gradation from referential to abstract and expressive-social meaning, as shown in §4.7.

The basic structure – Reinforcer [Epithet [Descriptor [Classifier head]]] – also depends on the semantic structure, as example (20) shows.

(20)   'a [splendid [silver [plastic suitcase]]]' (British National Corpus)

In this phrase (whose modification is wholly descriptive, in its context), the Classifier *plastic* modifies 'suitcase': the referential word and the constructional meaning, 'made of', add factual meaning to the referential head. The Descriptor *silver* modifies 'plastic suitcase': being perceptual, it gives physical detail of both the entities denoted by the referential words, *suitcase* and *plastic*. The Epithet *splendid* modifies 'silver plastic suitcase': being a conceptual and expressive word, it conveys the writer's judgement and attitude (admiration of the suitcase, the plastic, and the silveriness). Descriptors by their concrete and usually perceptual nature aptly modify referential Classifiers, as well as the head; and Epithets by their abstract and expressive nature aptly modify other description, as well as the head. Reinforcers can modify all of the words in the phrase because all the other types of meaning can be reinforced. Semantically, the structure is: reinforcement [conceptual-and-expressive description [perceptual-description [referential-detail [head]. Thus, for these non-modal premodifiers (the vast majority), syntax does provide some explanation of the order, but semantics explains the syntax. (Note that these semantic relationships between the zones, underlying the syntactic relationships, are a potential that the language provides but which is not always realised – as in a fish having 'short triangular pelvic fins' (British National Corpus), where the fins simply are short, and are triangular, and are located on the pelvis.)

We turn next to how syntax and semantics are related in operation. As we have just seen, their relationship is simple, in basic modification: they operate in parallel, with each premodifier modifying the following part of the phrase both semantically and syntactically. Normally, syntax and semantics operate in unison.

Semantic and syntactic considerations sometimes conflict, however. Occasionally, syntax dominates semantics, but generally semantics overrules syntax. Syntax is dominant in three situations, as follows. (a) In modal premodification, as we have seen (§4.4.2), the modal, e.g. *fake* and *alleged*, can be placed in any zonal position, retaining the same simple semantic structure, although the semantic rule specifies that semantic structure must change with zone (chapter 3). (b) When numerals and quantifiers are used as modifiers (§4.8.2.2), syntax is again dominant. In phrases like 'his <u>third</u> American wife' (British National Corpus) and #'his American <u>third</u> wife', the numeral has the same semantic structure; its different positions simply provide different scope – modifying 'American wife' and modifying 'wife' alone. (c) Certain phrases have a marked punctuation of the premodification (to be discussed more fully in chapter 7, §7.1.2). For example, the phrase 'other minor diseases' usually has no comma; it is structured as 'other [minor diseases]', with *other* subordinated to 'minor diseases', and the two modifiers in separate zones (determiner and Epithet). But in '[other,] [minor] diseases' (which allows the previously mentioned diseases to be major ones), the marked use of the comma changes the syntax, co-ordinating the modifiers into a single zone, although they are semantically quite different.

Semantics dominates syntax in the following more numerous, and more important, situations. (a) In marked syntax (§4.8.2.4 above), a semantic rule is followed, at the cost of breaking a syntactic one. In #'a large **black** sofa' (with contrastive stress on *black*), the premodifiers stay in their semantically established zones (*large* as Epithet + *black* as Descriptor). But the phrase contrasts large sofas that are black with large sofas of some other colour, so BLACK modifies LARGE SOFA, for which the syntactic rule would require 'a [black [large sofa]]', with the premodifier order reversed.

(b) In many phrases, there is no practical significance in the syntactic order, but the order is fixed – by semantics. Consider (21):

(21)   'I stepped through the <u>thick red velvet</u> curtains of the Royal Opera House.' (New Zealand Opera Society's *Opera News*, 2007)[5]

The curtains are identified by the postmodifier ('of the Royal Opera House'), so the premodifiers are wholly descriptive, adding separate facts about the curtains. So for the reader's interpretation, there would be no difference if the order were *'red thick velvet curtains' or *'red velvet thick curtains', and so on. If the phrase were used restrictively with all premodifiers stressed (#'No, I want **thick red velvet** curtains!'), the order would make no <u>practical</u> difference, since what matters is presence of all the properties, not the order in which they are specified. Nor does different order affect the truth value. Thus the order is determined by the semantic structure, as set out

---

[5] I am treating *red* as modifying *curtains*, not *velvet*.

above in the discussion of 'a splendid silver plastic suitcase'; the syntactic structure is of no practical effect in either of those uses. (It is only when one premodifier is contrastive and the other is not that the syntax is of practical importance, e.g. #'No, I want red velvet curtains, not blue velvet ones!')

(c) The number of zones is set semantically, outweighing syntactic considerations. Consider the restrictive phrases in (22) and (23), built from examples (17) and (18):

(22)   #'I want a <u>large, soft, comfortable</u> sofa.' (Epithet + Epithet + Epithet)

(23)   #'I want a <u>large black leather</u> sofa.' (Epithet + Descriptor + Classifier)

There is no evident difference between the two in the conceptual relation of premodifiers and *sofa;* each lists three properties the sofa must have. But the first phrase has co-ordinated modifiers, all in one zone (as Epithets), and the syntax is 'I want a [large, soft, comfortable sofa]'; but the second phrase has subordinated modifiers, in separate zones: 'I want a [large [black [leather sofa]]]'. (The fact that we interpret them with the same semantic structure of the phrase is reflected by what I believe to be the normal pronunciation of restrictive phrases: they are run on without pause, even if there are commas.) In the first phrase, the modifiers are all in the Epithet zone because they are all conceptual; in the second phrase, they are in different zones because they are conceptual, perceptual and referential respectively. The semantic structure of each word, not any underlying structure of the phrase, sets the zones; there are four zones because we distinguish four semantic structures in premodifiers. To make a similar argument: if 'a large black leather sofa' made three zones because of the syntax ('a [large [black [leather sofa]]]'), then we could have ? 'I want a [fashionable [large [soft [comfortable [new [black [Italian-made [leather sofa]]]]]]]]', with eight zones; but English semantics specifies only three zones for that phrase: #'a [fashionable, large, soft, comfortable] [new, black [Italian-made leather sofa]]]'.[6]

Since syntax determines the number of zones and determines unmarked order, and since breach of the semantic rule makes a use marked (marked syntax), we must conclude that semantics outweighs syntax in premodifier order.

4.9.3   *Prospect*

Some things arising from the chapter remain to be explained in later chapters: why there are borderline instances (to be explained historically in

---

[6] For why *Italian-made* and *leather* go together in one zone, without punctuation, see chapter 5.

§8.4.5); and why semantics and syntax have such a complex and asymmetrical relationship (to be explained similarly in §8.4.5).

Two issues that have arisen in this chapter need to be considered further. The importance of descriptive and restrictive modification in premodifier order will be discussed in §9.3.2 (on discourse explanation); and the scales of increasing power of modification and decreasing closeness to the head will be discussed in §10.3.3 (on grammaticalisation).

This chapter and the previous chapter have together given most of the synchronic explanation for unmarked order; the exception is that unmarked order within the Classifier zones remains to be considered – this will be explored next, in chapter 5. The free and marked orders are discussed in chapters 6 and 7.

5   Unmarked order within the Classifier zone

5.1   Introduction

5.1.1 General introduction

In the previous chapters, I have generally treated the Classifier zone as if it always contained only a single word; but, as I noted in the chapter on zones, that is a simplification: the Classifier zone not only often has several words, but it has a structure of its own. This chapter sets out and explains that internal structure, which is complex and quite different from the structure of the other zones; its discussion of semantics parallels chapter 3, expanding §3.2 in particular, and its discussion of syntax parallels chapter 4.

The chapter starts afresh from the discussion of zones in chapter 2, because there are fresh facts to be explained, as follows. First, there are subzones within the Classifier zone, which show coordination within the subzone and subordination of the subzones to following ones, as in examples (1) and (2).

(1)   'This [[<u>brick</u> and <u>tile</u>] [<u>three-bedroom</u>, <u>single-level</u>] townhouse]' (advertising brochure)

Since the premodifiers are all Classifiers (according to the semantic rules given in §3.7.1), and since coordination of premodifiers occurs only within zones (see §2.2.1), the structure of example (1) must be as in table 5.1.

(2)   #'Residential alcohol services'

That is a reduced form of an attested example, from a publicity brochure, given in table 5.2.

The second main fact to be explained is that semantic relations between Classifiers and their heads vary from those of Descriptors and Epithets, and vary from subzone to subzone, in a number of ways. The modifiers denote entities, rather than denoting properties as other premodifiers do (see §3.2.3). Sometimes, the semantic relation does resemble that of an entity (expressed by the head) and one of its properties (expressed by the modifier), as in 'honing his voice to a <u>steel</u> edge'. (The relation there is very like that of the Epithet

Table 5.1 *Co-ordinated Classifiers in two subzones*

Det.	Classifier subzone	Classifier subzone	Head
this	*brick and tile*	*three-bedroom, single-level*	*townhouse*

Table 5.2 *Co-ordinated Classifiers in three subzones*

Classifier subzone	Classifier subzone	Classifier subzone	Head
Residential and outpatient	*alcohol and drug*	*assessment, education, treatment, counselling and rehabilitation*	*services*

in '[he applied] a <u>steely</u> edge to his questions'; both quotations are from the British National Corpus.) With some other Classifiers, the entity–property relation seems to occur, but with the syntactic roles reversed, as in 'public road safety', the modifier (*public*) denotes an entity, and the head (*safety*) denotes the property, SAFETY. For some Classifiers, the relations are those of an event and its arguments, as in 'Israeli arms sales': 'Israel [Actor argument] arms [Goal argument] sales [Event of selling]', which parallels 'Israel [Actor] sold [Event] arms [Goal]'.

The third main fact to be explained is that Classifiers are ambiguous in a systematic way. For example, '<u>English</u> teacher', '<u>Japanese</u> teacher' and so on mean either 'from [that country]' or 'teacher of [that language]'; in '<u>Iraqi</u> invasion', '<u>Iranian</u> attack', 'the <u>Smith</u> murder' and so on, the named participant may be either culprit or victim.

There are several potential sources of confusion in explaining order within the Classifier zone, as well as the usual problem with borderline examples. An important part of the meaning of the phrase is inexplicit and therefore particularly liable to ambiguity. In 'British exports', for example, *British* may be taken to denote the source of the exports, or a category of exports, or the agent of the action of exporting. As a consequence of such indefiniteness, it is sometimes very hard to determine the subzone of a Classifier on its own, just as it is hard to know whether '<u>tailored</u> suit' has a Classifier, a Descriptor or an Epithet (see §3.4.2.3). The syntactic role may be ambiguous; for example, in 'Pioneer award-winning plasma tv', *Pioneer* is ambiguous between 'Pioneer [determiner = *Pioneer's*] award-winning [Descriptor] plasma tv' and 'Pioneer [Classifier] award-winning [Classifier] plasma tv'. Again, there can be ambiguity between being a modifier and being a submodifier; 'Effluent holding tank', for example, may be read as either 'effluent [holding tank]' (*effluent* as modifier), or '[effluent holding] tank' (*effluent* as submodifier) – or as '[effluent-holding] tank' (a compound single modifier).

Finally, there is often ambiguity as to whether the words form a phrasal structure or a single lexical item. 'Sand dune', for example, can be read as a phrase, but can be read as 'sand-dune' – a compound. I will avoid such problematic examples in the exposition, but will deal with the problems in the subsequent discussion.

5.1.2 Outline of the argument

There are five types of order within the Classifier zone. Each has its own combination of constituents; in each, the syntactic relation of head to premodifier carries a meaning of its own. Each thus constitutes a construction. There is a sixth use, in which Classifiers occur singly and in which the hearer infers the relation to the head from context: a constructionless use.

As with the overall order of premodifiers, there is a syntactic explanation and a semantic one. In syntax, the explanation is the same as for the overall order (as set out in chapter 4): each premodifier modifies the group comprising the following premodifiers and the head. The semantic explanation for the order of Classifiers lies in their relationship to the head. (It does not lie in their semantic structure as single words, as the overall order does – see chapter 3.) The principle here can be stated in two ways. First, the positions are in order of expectedness (which we saw as a dimension of meaning, in chapter 3): Classifiers with relations that are necessary to the meaning of the head (that is, wholly expected, and so most salient in the head) come closest to it (in the position of least prominence in the modifying group); those with relations least necessary to the meaning of the head come furthest from it (in the position of greatest prominence). The other way of stating the order is that the words which fill the positions are in order of generality and abstractness: the most general words fill the slot of greatest expectedness; the most particular words fill the position of least expectedness. There is a stepped gradient between the two extremes.

The nature of the expectedness – varying with the five constructions – will be explained in the main sections of the chapter, which deal with the five constructions in turn.

5.1.3 Introduction to Classifier semantics

The purpose of this section is to explain the concepts and terms to be used in the body of the chapter. The concepts are useful as a means of explanation, but the argument does not depend on them; so the section is not a complete treatment, and it uses description and illustration, rather than strict definition. I use terms from Croft and from Halliday, but most of the concepts are used by many scholars. (Because it contains background and is long, the reader may wish to read the section after the main sections of the chapter.)

It was emphasised in §§3.2.3 and 3.2.4 that Classifiers as single words designate simple concepts. I follow Croft (1991) in postulating that simple concepts fall into three basic semantic classes: objects, actions and properties.
Those classes have an 'unmarked correlation' (Croft 1991: 53) with certain
parts of speech: objects are correlated with nouns e.g. *vehicle*; actions are
correlated with verbs e.g. *destroy*, and properties with adjectives e.g. *white*.
They may, however, be realised differently. (The term 'realised' is from
Halliday 2004.) The action DESTROY may be realised in the noun *destruction*, as well as in the verb *destroy*, or in the adjective *destructive*. (DESTROY
remains an action while its expression changes syntactic function: these are
<u>semantic</u> entities.)

The semantic classes are used as constituents of larger semantic structures, that is, processes. I follow Halliday (2004) in identifying three kinds
of process. Material processes are those of the outer, material world, as
expressed in #'Smith scored six runs', or #'The boat sank'. Mental processes are those of the inner world of our experience, as in #'He felt sick'.
Relational processes are those of our reflections on those two worlds, and
are a construal of our experience rather than the direct representation of
it, as in #'Six runs is a pitiful score' or 'The boat was leaky'.

The constituents of the processes (which realise the semantic classes) are
'roles': either Process (an unfolding through time), or Participant (what is directly involved in the process) or Circumstance (what is associated with the
process).[1] Examples are: #'He [Participant] won [Process] the 100 metres
[Participant] in 9.8 seconds [Circumstance]'. The distinctions between these
constituents are not absolute; (for an explanation, see Halliday 2004: 259–63;
compare Cruse 2004: 293).[2] There are several types of Participant, according
to the type of process. Those relevant to Classifier order are Actor and Goal[3] in
material processes, e.g. 'He [Actor] won the 100 metres [Goal]', and Carrier and
Attribute in relational processes, e.g. 'The boat [Carrier] was leaky [Attribute]'.

Semantic processes are realised in a syntactic structure – commonly, a
clause; for example, a material process may be realised in a transitive clause:
'He [Actor] won [Process] the 100 metres [Goal]'. But just as the semantic classes are realised in varying ways (as shown with DESTROY, above),

---

[1] These are semantic concepts, not metaphysical or even epistemological ones; Process is
what is construed as temporally extended experience, rather than a temporally extended
piece of external reality (Kemmer, 2003: 94); so relational Processes such as 'is a...' and
'has a...' are natural. I use capitals for 'Process', 'Participant' and 'Circumstance' in this
use, to distinguish them as technical terms from other uses, such as 'discourse <u>partici-
pant</u>' and 'material <u>process</u>'.

[2] Croft (2001, ch. 7) makes the same point for 'argument' versus 'adjunct', and Matthews
(1981: ch. 6) makes it for 'complement' versus 'peripheral element'.

[3] Actor and Goal are general terms, here: I do not distinguish between 'actor' and 'agent',
for example, or between 'goal' and 'patient'. The analysis to follow does not need such
distinctions.

so are the processes and their constituent roles. DESTROY may be realised in a Participant role, as in #'The destruction was severe', or in Process role, as in #'The suicide bomber destroyed the police headquarters', or as Circumstance, as in #'The bomb exploded with great destruction'. The process realised in 'He [Actor] won [Process] the 100 metres [Goal]', may be realised in a nominal phrase, #'the 100 m [Goal] winner [Actor]'; the process of selling arms may be realised in the clause, #'Israel [Actor] sold [Process] a lot of weapons [Goal]', or in the nominal phrase, #'Israeli [Actor] weapons [Goal] sales [Process]'. The underlined words are Classifiers: Classifiers represent roles in a process, not qualities ascribed to an object; they are radically different from other premodifiers.

A final and more complex example follows, to prefigure the less common Classifier constructions. The Participant GAS, the Process EXIT and the Circumstance WITH SPEED may be realised in a material process clause, #'The gas exited quickly', or in a relational process clause, #'the gas's exit was quick'. Alternatively, the process may be realised in the nominal phrase, #'fast exiting gas' (with the Participant GAS expressed in the head), or in #'fast gas exit' (with the Process EXIT in the head), or as 'gas exit velocity' (with the Circumstance WITH SPEED in the head).

The facts that nominal phrases realise processes, and are accordingly semantically equivalent to clauses, are essential for understanding Classifier order; they are fundamental to the rest of the chapter. The next section (§5.1.4) introduces the types of order by means of clause types, and §§5.2 to 5.6 present the types in detail.

5.1.4   Introduction to the types of Classifier order

As noted previously, there are five types of order within the Classifier zone, each of which constitutes a construction, and a sixth, constructionless class of Classifier. (I will explain the claim that they are constructions more fully in §5.2.3.)

The nature of the types of order can be shown most clearly in terms of Process, Participant and Circumstance, and through the parallel between Classifier structures and clause structures, as follows.

(a) The commonest type of order is illustrated by 'Panasonic 32 inch plasma tv'. It parallels the clause, 'The tv is made by Panasonic, 32 inches in diameter, and of the plasma type', structured as shown in table 5.3. In this table, the nominal phrase ('Panasonic 32 inch plasma tv'), the Circumstances are expressed as premodifiers, and the Participant (the tv) is expressed as the head; but the relationships expressed in the clause by prepositional phrases are expressed only implicitly, as shown in table 5.4. Since the head denotes a Participant, I will call this structure 'Participant-head construction'. (The parallel clause is relational, of the circumstantial type.)

Table 5.3 *Structure of the parallel clause*

Participant	Process	Circumstance	Circumstance	Circumstance
The tv	*is*	*made by Panasonic,*	*32" in diameter,*	*of the plasma type*

Table 5.4 *Structure of the sample phrase*

Circumstance (modifier)	Circumstance (modifier)	Circumstance (modifier)	Participant (head)
Panasonic MADE BY	*32 inch* IN DIAMETER	*plasma* OF.... TYPE	*tv*

Table 5.5 *Structure of the parallel clause*

Participant (Actor)	Process	Participant (Goal)	Circumstance
Israel	*sold*	*arms*	*in 2006*

Table 5.6 *Structure of the sample phrase*

Circumstance (modifier)	Participant (modifier)	Participant (modifier)	Process (head)
2006	*Israeli*	*arms*	*sales*

(b) The second most common type of order is illustrated by '[2006] Israeli arms sales'. It parallels the clause, 'Israel sold arms in 2006' (a material-process clause), as shown in table 5.5.

In the nominal phrase ('2006 Israeli arms sales'), the Process SELL is expressed as head ('sales'); and both of the Participants, and the Circumstance, are expressed as modifiers, as shown in table 5.6. I will call this structure 'Process-head construction'.

(c) A much less common type is illustrated by 'flue gas exit velocity' (from Varantola 1984: 122). The parallel here is the material-process clause, 'The flue gas exits [at a certain] velocity', as shown in table 5.7. In the nominal phrase ('flue gas exit velocity'), the Participant and the Process are expressed as modifiers, and the Circumstance is expressed as the head, as shown in table 5.8. I will call this structure 'Circumstance-head construction'.

Table 5.7 *Structure of the parallel clause*

Participant	Process	Circumstance
The flue gas	*exits*	*at a certain velocity*

Table 5.8 *Structure of the sample phrase*

Participant (modifier)	Process (modifier)	Circumstance (head)
flue gas	*exit*	*velocity*

Table 5.9 *Structure of the parallel clause*

Participant (Carrier)	Process	Participant (Attribute)	Circumstance
The public	*is*	*safe*	*on the roads*

Table 5.10 *Structure of the sample phrase*

Participant (Carrier) (modifier)	Circumstance (modifier)	Participant (Attribute) (head)
public	*road*	*safety*

(d) Another order is illustrated by 'public road safety'. That is paralleled by the clause, 'the public is safe on the roads' (a relational clause of the intensive type), as shown in table 5.9. In the nominal phrase ('public road safety'), the Attribute Participant SAFE is expressed as head, and the Carrier Participant and the Circumstance are expressed as modifiers, as shown in table 5.10. I will call this structure 'Intensive-Attribute-head construction'. ('Intensive', and the matching term 'Possessed', will be explained when the constructions are discussed.)

(e) The last order of Classifiers is illustrated by '28 GB external disk [storage] capacity'. That is paralleled by the clause, 'the external disk has capacity for storage, to the extent of 28 gigabytes'; (a relational clause of the possessive type), as shown in table 5.11. In the nominal phrase, the Attribute CAPACITY is expressed as head, and the Carrier and the Circumstances

Table 5.11 *Structure of the parallel clause*

Participant (Carrier)	Process	Participant (Attribute)	Circumstance	Circumstance
The external disk	*has*	*capacity*	*for storage*	*to the extent of 28 GB*

Table 5.12 *Structure of the sample phrase*

Circumstance (modifier)	Participant (Carrier) (modifier)	Circumstance (modifier)	Participant (Attribute) (head)
28 GB	*external disk*	*[storage]*	*capacity*

are expressed as modifiers, as shown in table 5.12. I will call this structure 'Possessed-Attribute-head construction'.

(f) Classifiers also occur singly, with semantic relations to the head that do not fit into any of the types just listed. Examples are 'charcoal burger' (cooked over charcoal), 'Fiennes hostess' (the hostess who had an affair with Ralph Fiennes), 'crash victim', 'glory days' and 'sleep inertia'. I will call them 'constructionless uses', since they have no conventionalised pattern of relationship, and since they have no meaning contributed by the structure – the relation of head and modifier is inferred from context, or is idiomatic to specific phrases.

I emphasise that the clausal forms are given here only as an explanatory parallel (compare Langacker 2004: 77); I am not asserting that the phrasal form is derived from the clausal form. I see the two forms as alternative expressions of the same underlying meaning.

5.2   Participant-head construction

5.2.1   *The order of Classifiers in Participant-head constructions*

5.2.1.1   *The basic construction*

As noted in §5.1.4, the Participant-head construction consists of a head expressing a Participant, and modifiers expressing Circumstances. The example given was, 'Panasonic 32 inch plasma tv'. Again as noted in the introduction, the modifiers are related to the head by implicit relations. For example, '[British] 2 inch [brass] electronic oil-pressure gauge' can be paraphrased as: 'a gauge *of* British *origin*, 2 inches *in size*, *made of* brass, *of the* electronic *type*, and *for the purpose of* (*measuring*) oil-pressure' – where the italicised words make the implicit relationships explicit. There are five such relations, as in table 5.13.

Table 5.13 *Relation of modifiers and head, in the Participant-head construction*

	Nominal modifier	Relation	Head
1	*British*	IS THE SOURCE OR ORIGIN OF	
2	*2 inch*	IS THE SIZE OF	
3	*brass*	IS THE MATERIAL OF	*gauge*
4	*electronic*	IS THE TYPE OF	
5	*oil-pressure*	IS THE FUNCTION OF	

Table 5.14 *The qualia*

Position:	Class. 1	Class. 2	Class. 3	Class. 4	Class. 5	Head
Example:	*British*	*2 inch*	*brass*	*electronic*	*oil-pressure*	*gauge*
Relation expressed:	origin or source	size or dimension	what constitutes it	type	function or purpose	–
Name:	Origin	Dimension	Constituency	Type	Function	–

I will call those five implicit relations 'qualia' (and 'quale' in the singular), following Pustejovsky (1995). They are constructional meanings – meanings not expressed by a specific word – discussed above in chapter 3, §3.1.2.2.

Table 5.14 sets out the order of these Classifiers; for each position, it gives an example, a statement of the relation the quale consists of, and the name by which I will refer to it.

Table 5.15 gives examples of phrases invoking the various qualia, from a range of contexts.

The exact nature of the subzones varies a little. For example, the Origin quale basically represents the place of origin (as I will show in chapter 8); but that has been extended to time of origin (e.g. *1990's*), manufacturer *(Sony)*, brand (*Elite*), and even to destination not origin ('Japanese-market-only 2.4 litre GDI engine'). Dimension was originally spatial dimension, but has been extended to any measurable attribute, such as voltage (and even to time of origin, as with '16th century' in the last example in the table). Type varies also, as the table shows.[4] There is thus some freedom for reconstruing a constituent with a different grammatical relation (and in a different position accordingly), even though it represents the same real-life relation (e.g. time of origin).

---

[4] Type Classifiers include 'a criminal lawyer': 'a lawyer of the type who deals with criminal law, not family law etc'. The phrase has been discussed by Coates (1971: 164), Levi (1978), Bauer (1978: §4.4.3), (Warren 1984: 96), Adamson (2000: 60), and perhaps by others. I have shown its semantics here and in §3.2.2, and its syntax in §4.8.2; perhaps the phrase may rest in peace now.

Table 5.15 *Examples of the qualia*

Modifier: Origin quale	Modifier: Dimension quale	Modifier: Constituency quale	Modifier: Type quale	Modifier: Function quale	Head: Participant
Jayline Classic	*17 kw*	*black enamel*	*clean-air*	*wood*	*fire*
Elite	*110 cm*	*stainless*	*double oven*		*range*
Kingston	*3-piece*		*recliner*	*lounge*	*suite*
Uniden	*2.4 GHz*		*cordless phone*		*combo*
Orlando	*9 drawer*		*Scotch*		*chest*
Roman			*winter*	*fertility*	*festival*
Aboriginal			*rock*		*art*
Neath	*15-man*		*handling*		*movements*
1990's	*2 litre*		*Nissan*		*Primera*
	high denier	*nylon*		*lining*	*fabric*
	high thread-count	*nylon*	*oxford*		*weave*
	6 litre	*alloy*	*V8*		*engine*
	60 cm	*stainless steel*	*gas*		*cook-top*
	5 ton	*granite*			*statue*
		leather	*sports*	*steering*	*wheel*
		diamond	*double leaf*		*ear-rings*
		white chocolate	*raspberry*		*cheesecake*
	60 w		*electric*	*soldering*	*iron*
	6 zone		*remote control*	*alarm*	*kit*
	[6 kg]	*weigh shaft lever*	*[fixed]*	*balance*	*weight*
Iranian	*16th century*	*brass*	*boat shaped*		*vessel*

The subzones are thus like the main zones in being elements of syntactic structure, with identity through position, coordination and subordination (as in 'This <u>brick and tile</u> [Constituency] <u>three-bedroom, single-level</u> [Type] townhouse'); and like the main zones in having a semantic identity which is no longer simple. Consequently, the names I have given are used as technical terms, naming the subzone, not describing it.

The positions and relations in this construction are grammatical realities, just as those of subject, predicator and object are. That can be seen in several ways (which I list at some length, since the claim seems to be a new one). First, it can be seen from the disambiguation of ambiguous phrases by the presence of other premodifiers. In '<u>brick</u> kiln', *brick* is ambiguous between the kiln's being made of brick and having the function of baking bricks; but in #'reinforced-concrete <u>brick</u> kiln' it is not ambiguous. The presence of a preceding modifier ('reinforced-concrete') filling the 'what it consists of' position makes it clear that *brick* is in the

Table 5.16 *Regularity of the qualia pattern*

Constituency	Type	Function	Head
		water	*board*
		wire	*gauge*
		hair	*net*
	water		*bat*
	wire		*birch*
	hair		*moss*
water			*cushion*
wire			*basket*
hair			*bag*

'purpose' position. A headline writer used such ambiguity for a pun, as in example (3):

(3)   'Illegal <u>pigsty</u> flats cost farmer \$22,500.' (*New Zealand Herald*, 4 July 2007, p. A7)

The flats were at once pigsty in type and pigsty in origin: *pigsty* is ambiguous in position. (There was perhaps a third meaning – taking *pigsty* as Epithet, 'dirty' – the flats were a health risk.) Compare '<u>American</u> football' with #'American Rugby football'; in the former, *American* is ambiguous between Type – a variety of football – and Origin – all football played in America. (Other examples were given in §3.2.2.) That position-dependent ambiguity is like that of digits in numbers: in '222', the meaning of each '2' depends on its position; empty subzones are place-holders, like the zero in '202'.

Second, the reality of the subzones can be seen from the fact that some of these Classifiers can be repeated, with successive Classifiers invoking different relationships: #'a brick brick kiln', #'an English English teacher' (a teacher of English from England).

Third, there are many Classifier phrases that seem random and vague, but that actually pattern regularly, with consistent qualia meaning; examples are 'water board', 'water bat', 'water cushion', 'wire gauge', 'wire birch', and so on. The regularity is shown in table 5.16. The patterning shows that there are various 'slots' where Classifiers fit, and that the Classifiers in each column evoke a common meaning. ('Hair net' and 'hair bag' can each be read with another interpretation.)

Finally, the reality of the subzones can be seen from the range of examples in table 5.15 above; the consistency with which Classifiers pattern in the order shown and the freedom with which people now write such long phrases show that present-day users of English accept this construction as part of the language.

I have so far written as if hearers simply interpret the relations from the positions. That needs justification, for two reasons. First, previous studies have almost all treated these relations as purely semantic (not syntactic), as

Table 5.17 *Taxonomic construction*

Det.	Type Classifiers				Head
the			*Australian*	*little*	*penguin*
			compound	*mitre*	*saws*
the			*marketing*	*general*	*manager*
the		*bleached*	*lesser*	*earless*	*lizard*
the		*Revised*	*Extended*	*Standard*	*Theory*
	acting	*principal*	*deputy*	*assistant*	*secretary*
two	*12-gauge*	*single barrel*	*Greener*	*pump-action*	*shotguns*
a	*hydrated*	*calcite*	*magnesium*	*uranyl*	*carbonate*

unpredictable (see 'Other theories', §10.4), and accordingly as inferred from context or learned for particular phrases. Second, the relation to the head sometimes is in fact unpredictable; for example, the newspaper headline's phrase, 'coma baby', relied on the relation, '*x* [baby, in this example] that was born while the mother was in a state of *y* [coma]'; but another headline had 'beer baby' – '*x* found lying in *y*'. In the unpredictable uses, the reader infers the relation wholly from the context. In other instances, the reader must use world knowledge as well: for example, in interpreting 'steel band' with *steel* as a Type of musical group, not as Constituency – 'strip of metal'. But the previous discussion shows, I believe, that for such phrases, hearers can draw on the grammatically established relations, using context and world knowledge to resolve ambiguity; hearers need not create the relations afresh for each phrase they meet. In using the established qualia, they use a strictly linguistic source of information.

5.2.1.2   *Recursive constructions*
The phrases given so far have used different qualia. There are two types of phrase, however, where successive Classifiers invoke the same quale, constituting subtypes of the Participant-head construction.

i   Taxonomic construction
Some phrases use the Type quale recursively; each Classifier denotes a type or subtype of what is denoted by the following parts of the phrase – hence my name, 'taxonomic' construction. Examples are given in table 5.17. (In the table, 'Australian little penguin' has *little* as a Classifier, although it is usually an Epithet; 'acting principal deputy assistant secretary' – from *Economist*, 2 February 2008, p. 43 – refers to a 'lavishly titled' official in the US Department of Energy.)

The taxonomic construction is sometimes used to postmodify a premodifier, just as 'Henry <u>VIII</u>' has a postmodifier of the head. Consider example (4):

Table 5.18 *Meronymic construction*

	Whole–part Classifiers		Head
	locomotive	*boiler*	*barrel*
	appendage	*boom*	*arms*
	express-train	*coach*	*body*
U.C.	*Davis*	*biology department*	*committee*
Arab	*Muslim*	*janjaweed*	*militias*

Table 5.19 *Part–whole words as Constituency Classifiers*

Modifier: Dimension quale	Modifier: Constituency quale	Modifier: Type quale	Modifier: Function quale	Head: Participant
[6 kg]	*weigh shaft lever*	*[fixed]*	*balance*	*weight*

(4)   'Genuity Roundup Ready 2 Yield soya beans' (*Economist*, 21 November 2009, p. 72)

Genuity is a brand name for all Monsanto genetically modified seeds; *Roundup Ready 2* designates a type of those seeds (able to withstand Roundup weedkiller), and postmodifies *Genuity*; *Yield* is a strain of that type, and postmodifies it. The syntax, then, is: '[[Genuity [[Roundup Ready] 2]] Yield] [soya beans]'. It seems likely that this postmodifying use of the construction explains some puzzling phrases in advertising, of which '[[Shimano Hyperloop] 6000] [8–12 kg [6 inch [rod set]]]' is a simple example.

ii   Meronymic construction

A much less common construction consists of recursive Constituency Classifiers, invoking the part–whole relation – hence the name 'meronymic' (following Cruse 2004). Simple examples of part–whole phrases are 'a body part' and 'sonata movement'. More complex examples are given in table 5.18. (In the table, 'U.C. Davis' refers to the University of California Davis campus, and the last phrase given is not obviously whole–part, but I can find no better analysis for it.)

I rate these part–whole Classifiers as invoking the Constituency quale, although nearly all Constituency Classifiers denote the substance constituting the referent; that is because, when they do occur with other qualia Classifiers (which is very rare in my observation), they occur in the constituency position. That is illustrated by 'weigh shaft lever', in an example given above and repeated in table 5.19.

5.2.2   Explanation of the order in Participant-head constructions

5.2.2.1   Syntactic explanation

Nominal phrases in the Participant-head construction have the same syntactic structure as nominal phrases with Epithets and Descriptors (as set out in chapters 2 and 4): each modifier modifies the group of words that follows. Examples include: 'optical [digital [audio output]]' and 'Fisher & Paykel [7.5 kg [Excellence [washing machine]]]'. The fact that each Classifier modifies the rest of the phrase can be seen in contrastive phrases: '<u>optical</u> [digital audio output]' versus #'<u>electrical</u> [digital audio output]', and '<u>digital</u> [audio output], versus #'<u>analogue</u> [audio output]'.

5.2.2.2   Semantic explanation

The order of the Classifiers follows the general principle given in the introduction to the chapter: Classifiers with relations most necessary to the concept denoted by the head come closest to it. (I use 'Elite 110 cm stainless double oven range' as an example for all but the first point.)

(a) Function quale. Examples are 'electric <u>soldering</u> iron', 'remote control <u>alarm</u> kit'. These Classifiers come closest to the head, since function is part of the definition of the entity denoted by the phrase. The Function quale is absent from 'Elite 110 cm stainless double-oven range' – for that very reason: '<u>cooking</u> range' is tautologous. The Function quale is also tautologous as Classifier where it is expressed morphologically in the head – *refrigerator, beater*. Being an expected part of the meaning, the function is often omitted; when expressed, it is placed next to the head – a non-salient position – since its expectedness gives it some salience of its own.

(b) Type quale (e.g. '<u>double oven</u> range') comes next closest to the head. The type of range is less necessary to RANGE than COOKING is; the fact that it is nevertheless expected in the head concept is shown by the fact that a Type word and its head are often equivalent to a single word ('<u>morocco</u> leather' can be stated as 'morocco', and '<u>prime</u> minister' as 'premier').

(c) Constituency quale (e.g. '<u>stainless</u>... range') comes next. The material is not a necessary element in RANGE, and is less expected than DOUBLE-OVEN and COOKING are; it is much less dependent on the head than Function or Type. Other examples are '<u>nylon</u> fabric', '<u>granite</u> statue'.

(d) Dimension quale (e.g. '<u>110 cm</u>... range') comes next. The head entity must have dimensions, but dimensionality is extrinsic to the definition; the size of the range is less expected than its constituency, so it is nearer the salient first position.

(e) Origin quale (e.g. '<u>Elite</u>.... range') comes first. Whether a range originates from Elite or from Baumatic is quite extrinsic to its nature; the origin is not an expected element in the head. Being least predictable, it is placed first.

Table 5.20 *Collocation of qualia with* knife

Quale	Collocation	Frequency
Origin	*American knife*	2
Dimension	*....-inch knife*	3
Constituency	*steel knife*	15
Type	*carving knife*	94

The concept of collocation provides another view of that explanation: words more necessary to the concept of the head should collocate with it more frequently. (See Halliday 2004: 576; Croft 2001: 272; Matthews 1981: 124–5.) For example, for #'American 6 inch steel carving knife', *carving* should collocate with *knife* most often; *steel* less often and so on. That is in fact the case, as shown in table 5.20, with data from the Corpus of Contemporary American English, as at January 2010. (For '... inch', phrases with any number of inches were counted.)

We conclude that in this construction, the order of Classifiers is determined by the nature of the qualia: the most expected and semantically salient quale is closest to the head; the merely possible and therefore semantically non-salient is furthest from it, being given syntactic salience. The relation between successive position and the scale of expectedness may be visualised in figure 5.1, using '[American] 60 watt [brass] electrical soldering iron' as the example. The word order is one of decreasing syntactic salience; the qualia are listed below the head in a scale of semantic expectedness and salience; arrows lead from the listed qualia to their positions.

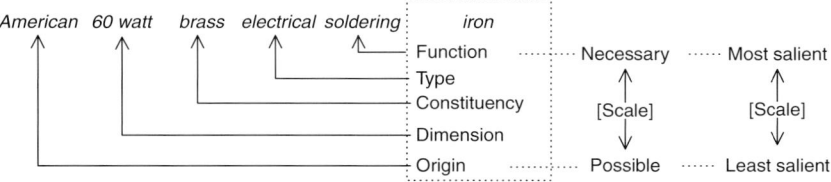

Figure 5.1 Position, expectedness and salience in the Participant-head construction

5.2.3   *Discussion of the Participant-head construction*

In accordance with the definition of 'construction' given in §3.1.2.2, each quale position is part of a construction, because there is a structure of categories of words (not of particular words) – a modifier of a specific semantic category and a head; and because the structure contributes to the expression a meaning of its own (the quale). Three perspectives reinforce that. The first is the difficulty of making Classifiers predicative (as noted in §3.2.2): 'the locomotive boiler barrel' is acceptable; but *'the barrel is boiler' and *'the boiler barrel is locomotive' are unacceptable.[5] The reason is that the predicative form lacks the meaning which the Participant-head construction supplies through the qualia; the predicative forms become acceptable when that relation is made explicit lexically: #'the barrel is *part of* a boiler'.

Another perspective is semantic. First, we have seen that the quale position carries the meaning that disambiguates ambiguous Classifiers; for example, 'brick kiln' as 'made of bricks' and 'for baking bricks'. Second, we saw in chapter 3, (§3.2.3), that the word meaning of Classifiers is a bare, unbounded concept. The constructional meaning (a relation) complements that: the bare concept and its relation to the head constitute the full meaning. That is why Classifiers sometimes seem to have a property meaning, like other premodifiers, as noted in §5.1.1; the example there was 'Honing his voice to a <u>steel</u> [Classifier] edge' – like having 'a <u>steely</u> [Epithet] edge to his questions'. Since each quale Classifier forms a specific construction, the Participant-head construction as a whole is a general one – a construction of five constructions. It is high on the generality taxonomy of constructions (Croft and Cruse 2004: 262).

The final perspective on Classifiers constituting constructions is morphological. The premodifying function of adjectives is signalled by their adjectival inflection, e.g. *-ous, -ary*. The function of nominal Classifiers is not signalled morphologically, but only by their position; and adjectival Classifiers are now increasingly being morphologically reduced to nouns – 'California oranges' not 'California<u>n</u> oranges'. The structures to be discussed in the next four sections are constructions just as this one is; I will not repeat the explanation.

I have acknowledged above my debt to Pustejovsky (1995, 2001) for the concept of the qualia, and for the term. However, my account differs from Pustejovsky's: my qualia are broader (especially Origin – his 'Agentive' – see 2001: 56); I identify five qualia, not four (Dimension is added); and I describe them as relations between modifier and head, not as constituents of the head noun's meaning, as Pustejovsky does. Johnston and Busa (1999) discuss this construction (as 'nominal compound construction'), relying on the qualia; their account has the same limitations as I have noted for Pustejovsky, and they do not explain order, being concerned only with constructions having a single premodifier. Croft and Cruse (2004) recast the concept of qualia as 'ways-of-seeing' (2004: 137), which is closer to my concept. Sussex (1974)

---

[5] Judgements differ here; for example, some people find 'The set is 24 piece(s)' acceptable (from '24 piece dinner set'). I will show in §8.5.2 that these constructions have developed quickly, and are presumably still changing; difference in judgement of acceptability is normal in periods of change. I believe that the predicative form is the newer, spreading variant.

Table 5.21 Self launching

	Det.	Epithet	Descriptor	Classifier	Head
(a)		*ultra light*	*affordable, self launching*		*gliders*
(b)	*the*			*TeST 14 m … self launching 40:1*	*glider*
(c)		*ultra light*	*affordable*	*self launching*	*gliders*

prefigured the point, noting the implicit meaning of noun modifiers and the dependence of meaning on order.

Classifiers in each of the positions can be submodified. Examples follow, with single underlining marking the quale modifiers and double underlining marking the submodifiers. 'A 4 storey (over-height by 3.9m), 74 unit apartment block' has co-ordinated Dimension qualia, each submodified by a numeral (and with '4 storey' post-modified by appositional 'overheight by 3.9m'). 'The S-series Bravia LCD tv' has the Origin quale submodified by a Type-quale Classifier. 'Asynchronous Transfer Mode call switching functions' has the Function quale submodified by a Goal (see the next section). There is still more complex Type submodification in this phrase from the Corpus of Contemporary American English: 'the [second [annual [[Kingwood College] [[[[single parent] scholarship] fund] [benefit tournament]]]]]'.

As noted earlier in this section, these Classifiers and their qualia relations are semantically equivalent to postmodifying phrases, and to full clauses: 'apartment block' is equivalent to 'block of apartments' and to 'the block consists of apartments'. Just as the Classifier can be seen as a syntactically reduced form (having lost the clause's verb and the postmodifying phrase's preposition), so it is morphologically reduced, having lost the plural -*s*. That relates to the semantic nature of Classifiers as bare concepts, as noted in §3.2: they are semantically reduced, as well as syntactically and morphologically reduced. (The point will apply correspondingly to the Classifiers in other constructions, discussed in the following sections; it will be expanded in §9.3.4.)

Borderline examples occur in the Classifier subzones, as in the main zones. For example, many adjectival Classifiers also have a descriptive use as Epithet or Descriptor, as in 'the Supreme [Classifier] Court' and 'the supreme [Epithet] sacrifice'; so their Classifier uses naturally often seem to be on the borderline. Example (5), written with a comma in the original, has all its adjectives used descriptively – and *self launching* is a Descriptor, as in table 5.21(a). Example (6) has *self launching* used to define a type – as a Classifier, as in table 5.21(b); and example (5) would also have it as a Classifier if the comma were omitted, as in table 5.21(c).

(5)   'ultra light affordable, <u>self launching</u> gliders' (*Gliding Kiwi 29:1*, 2005, p. 13)
(6)   'the TeST 14 m ... <u>self launching</u> 40:1 glider' (also from *Gliding Kiwi 29:1*, 2005, p. 13)

5.3   Process-head construction

5.3.1   *The order of Classifiers in the Process-head construction*

As noted in §5.1.4, the Classifiers and head in Process-head constructions are linked semantically by a material–process relationship. The head represents the Process role; the premodifiers represent the Participants (Actor and Goal) and Circumstances. '2006 [Circumstance] Israeli [Actor] arms [Goal] sales [Process]' is semantically equivalent to 'Israel [Actor] sold [Process] arms [Goal] in 2006 [Circumstance]'. As with the Participant-head construction, some relationships are implicit, in the sense that some of the meaning may be naturally expressed lexically by the addition of a preposition: *2006* (in the example given) can be paraphrased as '<u>in</u> 2006'. Other relationships here, however, do not invoke such semi-descriptive meaning: they are purely grammatical, as in the relation of *Israeli* and *arms* to *sales* – the relation of Actor and Goal to Process. The meanings that this construction adds to the meaning of the whole phrase are thus either semi-descriptive or fully grammatical.

Those relationships, and the difference from Participant-head constructions, can be seen from the nature of ambiguity in these constructions. In the headline, 'DNA test for <u>dog kiwi</u> killer', the Classifiers could be reversed ('a kiwi dog killer'): the kiwi would then be the killer, and the dog would be the victim. 'The Armenian massacre' is ambiguous between the Armenians (Actor) killing others, and others killing them (Goal). 'Lexical diffusion' is ambiguous between words ('lexis' – Goal) being diffused, and something (such as sound changes) being diffused through the lexicon (an indirect participant). 'Holiday sale' is ambiguous between holidays being sold (Goal), and a holiday being the occasion (Circumstance). Resolution of the ambiguities requires relations of Actor and Goal and so on, not qualia relations.

The full order is shown in table 5.22. 'Extent' is the distance in space, or the duration in time, over which the Process unfolds; 'Location' is the point at which it occurs, again in either space or time. (The concepts and terms are from Halliday, 2004: 263–5.) Note that in table 5.22: (a) 'plastic catfood cover retail manufacturer rebate offer' meant that a retail manufacturer offered a rebate on plastic catfood covers; it is cited in Al-Kharabsheh (2005: 165); (b) 'student job search' meant that someone searched for jobs for students – although we say 'searched <u>for</u> jobs', I take *job* as Goal; (c) 'cab mob hit' meant that the mob (i.e. the Mafia) killed someone, in a cab.

Table 5.22 *Process-head construction*

Modifiers: Circumstances		Modifiers: Participants			Head: Process
		Indirect Participant	Direct Participants:		
Extent	Location		Actor	Goal	
			Israeli	arms	sales
			government	farms	buy-up
			municipal	solid waste	generation
		plastic catfood cover	retail manufacturer	rebate	offer
		student		job	search
		business		broadband	offerings
		leaky homes	court		ruling
	Texas	chain saw			massacre
	in-cache	scalar			processing
	real-time	mother-foetal		heart	monitors
	ante-natal			foetal	surveillance
	nasal	oxygen			therapy
	cab		mob		hit
NZ$2.5m	pre-tax		currency hedge		cost
global	atmospheric			OH	concentration
overnight	on-site			explosives	storage
NE Pacific	millennial		deep-water		change
world-wide	annual			fisheries	harvest
coast-wide			[whiting]	pinniped	consumption[6]

The distinction between Extent and Location is not common in linguistics, but it is needed here. When time and place are both expressed as Circumstances, time regularly precedes place; as in '24 hour roadside assistance' and 'overnight on-site storage'. However, the positions can not be characterised through those concepts, because many phrases have two time Classifiers ('five minute pre-heat countdown'), or two place Classifiers ('wrong-way motorway drive'). Moreover, in the examples above where time and place occur together, the first Classifier designates extent, e.g. '24 hour' (time), and the second designates location, e.g. 'roadside' (space).

As with the qualia, there is some variation in the relationships denoted here. The Indirect Participant position, which is used relatively seldom, has participants in a range of semantic relationships, as the following

---

[6] The attested phrase read, 'the total annual coast-wide pinniped consumption of coastal Pacific whiting'.

partial paraphrases of three examples show: 'therapy *by means of* oxygen', 'a rebate *for* plastic catfood covers' and 'court ruling *on the subject of* leaky homes'. The position therefore accommodates participants in 'Beneficiary' and 'Instrument' roles, and so on. Classifiers in the Circumstance position denote entities which are participants in the broad sense, but not Participants in my narrower sense; for example, the globe and the atmosphere in 'global atmospheric OH concentration': the distinction between Participant and Circumstance is not clear-cut, but evidently subject to construal. Two participants may appear as joint Actors: 'parent child interaction', 'peer peer group interaction'.

My interpretation of the Classifiers in 'government farms buy-up' (for example) as Actor and Goal, often expressed as subject and object of a clause, is supported by many writers: Coates (1971: 166), Levi (1978: 172 ff.), Mitchell (1985 §1266) on Old English, Mel'cuk (1988: 63–4), Nevalainen (1999: 408), Radford (1993: 79) and Du Bois (2003: 56).

5.3.2 *Explanation of the order in the Process-head construction*

As with the Participant-head construction, the main explanation of the order is semantic. The order of the modifiers follows the general principle given in the introduction to the chapter: Classifiers with the most expected relation to the head come closest to it, as follows (I use '2006 Israeli arms sales' as the main example).

(a) The Goal Classifier comes closest to the head. The fact that the Goal is necessary to the Process can be seen in two ways. (i) As argued by Seuren (1975), the concept of a generic goal is entailed in the concept of the transitive event itself; BREW entails BEER, in Seuren's example (1975: 84). The word stating the Goal makes it more specific or merely makes it explicit. 'Israeli arms sales' makes more specific the generic goal entailed by *sales*. An ergative interpretation of events (see Halliday 2004: §5.7.2) shows the point effectively: the arms are the 'Medium' or locus of the event, as in 'those arms sell well'. (ii) Analysis of event structure (e.g. Croft 1998) shows that SELL, for example, as in 'Israeli arms sales', has at least two successive subevents, an offer of goods and an acceptance; the goods (instantiating the Goal) are involved in the first subevent, and must be invoked for the second subevent to be conceived: they are necessary to the event as a whole.

(b) The Actor Participant ('Israeli arms sales') is slightly less necessary: selling can be defined without reference to a buyer (as transferring ownership of goods for money).

(c) Circumstances, such as time ('2006') and place, are not salient in the concept of selling, and not expected in every expression of it. They add content, as shown by the paraphrases '...in the Middle East [place] in

2006 [time]'. They are thus more extrinsic than the Actor and Goal relations, which are purely grammatical and without content.[7]

(d) Extent precedes Location, when they both occur, because it is still less necessary: an event must have a time, but need not have duration.

Like the Participant-head construction, then, this construction has the most expected element next to the head and the least predictable element furthest from it, in the position of most syntactic prominence.

The order can also be explained usefully as depending on degree of 'affectedness'. The Goal (the arms) is most affected (the arms change in ownership and location), and is placed closest to the head; the Actor (Israel) is affected to a lesser extent; the Circumstance (the year 2006), is not affected at all, and is placed furthest from the head. But that does not make clear why the most affected should be closest.

As with the previous construction, the order is also syntactic. Each premodifier modifies the remainder of the nominal phrase: '2006 [Israeli [arms sales]]', 'student [job search]'.

5.3.3 Discussion of the Process-head construction

Table 5.22 shows that most of the zones in this construction may be submodified, since most of the modifier columns have submodifiers. The construction also may be submodified recursively, as in (7).

(7)   '[Serotonin reuptake] inhibitor' (British National Corpus)

This phrase has *reuptake* stating the Goal of the Process INHIBIT, and *serotonin* stating the Goal of the Process TAKE UP AGAIN. *Reuptake* is thus both modifier in one construction and head of another; and it is at once 'noun-like' in denoting a Goal (what is inhibited) and 'verb-like' in denoting a Process (taking up).[8] The title of a doctoral thesis in applied linguistics was '[[Language teacher] educator] learning'; the modifier ('educator') denotes an Agent and a Process, and the two submodifiers denote further Goals and Processes. The Process-head construction is used to submodify other constructions, as in example (8).

(8)   'On-site employee health testing clinic' (sign on an Auckland bus)

The basic structure is a Participant-head construction, 'testing [Function quale] clinic [head]'. *Testing* is submodified in a Process-head construction,

---

[7] The point was suggested by a remark in Brinton and Traugott (2005:15), to the effect that grammatical cases such as nominative are purely grammatical whereas oblique cases such as the dative have some content.

[8] Such words perhaps are 'dot-objects' (Pustejovsky 1995), or have 'facets' (Cruse 2004: 112ff.), as in 'Put this book back on the shelf: it's quite unreadable' (Cruse's example), where *book* denotes the physical object and the content, at once.

with *health* giving the Goal for the Process TEST and *on-site* giving a Circumstance. (*Employee* submodifies *health*, in the construction to be discussed in §5.6.) A final example (from the Corpus of Contemporary American English) is: 'a [single [small [[[primary coolant] [hollow core] outlet] temperature] redistribution]]'.

There is a parallel between the order of Participants in this construction and Givón's hierarchy of semantic case-roles and hierarchy of pragmatic case-roles (1984: 364), and the Accessibility Hierarchy of Keenan and Comrie (1977): all are affected by some form of accessibility, and all present indirect participants as less accessible than direct participants, and circumstances as less accessible still. But in this order, as table 5.22 shows, the Actor/subject is apparently less accessible than the Goal/object, although the other hierarchies reverse that order.

There is a striking ambivalence in the way words function in this construction. As I noted of *reuptake* in 'serotonin reuptake', heads here are 'noun-like' in designating a measurable, nameable object (the reuptake), and 'verb-like' in denoting an event (taking up) – *reuptake* is an 'event nominal'. Its syntax is dominated by the event part of its semantics, not the object part, since it takes a Goal (serotonin) in its modifier. The same ambivalence can occur with the participant-head construction. In #'a stainless steel potato masher', *masher* designates an object, but we also construe the expression to mean that potatoes are the Goal of the event MASH. Here, the syntax is dominated by the object part of the semantics not the event, since *masher* takes *stainless steel* as Constituent quale, and *potato* must accordingly be read with the Type-quale as denoting a type of MASHER, not a Goal of MASH. Note that with the object and event elements of *reuptake*, and with the object concept SALE and the event concept SELL, both members of the pair represent the same item of knowledge – and presumably the same outer-world reality. In §5.1.3, I set out the concepts of two semantic 'levels' (object/event/property, and Process/Participant/Circumstance), and the syntactic 'level' (modifier/head). I suggest that those concepts, with that of construal, provide a simple and coherent analysis, without the problematic 'prototype' concepts of being 'noun-like' and of degrees of 'nouniness'; and that the syntactic and semantic structures are independent of metaphysics and epistemology.

The order in the Process-head construction may be summarised visually (as for the Participant-head construction) in figure 5.2.

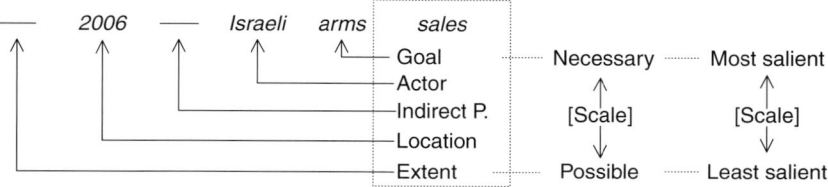

Figure 5.2 Position, expectedness and salience in the Process-head construction

Table 5.23 *Circumstance-head construction*

Modifier: Circumstance (Extent)	Modifier: Circumstance (Location)	Modifier: Participant (Actor)	Modifier: Process	Head: Circumstance
		instrument	*operating*	*cycles*
		flue gas	*exit*	*velocity*
		plant	*water-use*	*efficiency*
		sound	*travel*	*time*
	straight-through	*[machine]*	*wash and dry*	*cycle*
	winter	*air*	*[flow]*	*speed*
	air	*[passenger]*	*travel*	*time*
20%		*product*	*hit*	*rate*
vertical and horizontal	*target*		*[distribution]*	*efficiency*
3 or 4 week		*menu*	*[succession]*	*cycle*
64-bit		*[computer]*	*data transfer*	*rate*
400 knot	*air*	*[plane]*	*[flight]*	*speed*
twenty-five hours			*flight*	*time*
20 minute	*one-way*	*light*	*[travel]*	*time*
5 m/sec		*freestream*	*[flow]*	*velocity*
excess		*black*	*death*	*rate*

5.4 Circumstance-head construction

5.4.1   *The order of Classifiers in the Circumstance-head construction*

As stated in §5.1.4, the Circumstance-head construction parallels a material-process clause, with a Circumstance as head. For example, 'instrument operating cycles' parallels 'the instruments [Actor] operate [Process] in cycles [Circumstance]'; so we have 'instrument [Actor; modifier] operating [Process; modifier] cycles [Circumstance; head]'. Also as before, the nature of the relationships is highlighted by the possibilities for ambiguity. In '64-bit data transfer rate', *data* is ambiguous between representing the Actor of an intransitive event (the data transfer elsewhere) and the Goal of a transitive event (the computer transfers the data). That shows that *transfer* is to be interpreted as Participant-related, not as quale-related (with *transfer* as a Type of rate, and *data* denoting a subtype of *transfer*). Again as before, we have some of the content not stated explicitly: *cycles* evokes a manner relation, as shown by the paraphrase, 'the instruments operate <u>in</u> cycles'.

The full order is shown in table 5.23. I have supplied extra words fairly freely, because I believe the relations in this construction are often confusing.

Some of the Classifiers given in the Location column could be taken as Indirect Participants (e.g. *target*); but I have no example that suggests that a separate position exists for Indirect Participants.

5.4.2   Explanation of the order in the Circumstance-head construction

The order of the modifiers follows the general principle given in §5.1.2: those with the most expected relations come closest to the head, as follows (I use '20 minute one-way light [travel] time' as the main example). (a) The Process modifier (*travel*) comes closest to the head (*time*, Circumstance), because it is necessary to it: time is by its nature the duration of some Process. (That is reflected in *travel*'s omission from the attested example.) (b) The Actor (*light*) comes next. It is next to the Process (*travel*), since an Actor is highly expected in any Process concept (as argued in §5.3.2, on the Process-head construction). It is further from the head (*time*), since the connection between light and time is only through the concept of TRAVEL. (c) The other Circumstances come further from the head (*time*), being still less expected. These Circumstances – direction *(one-way)* and duration *(20 minute)* – are related to time only through the whole process – through both *light* and *travel*. (d) Extent comes further from the head than Location, if both occur, because it is still less necessary: an event must have a time, but need not have duration.

As with the previous constructions, the order is also syntactic: '20 minute [one-way [light [time]]]', '1962 [Beethoven [cycle]]'.

5.4.3   Discussion of the Circumstance-head construction

Classifiers in the Circumstance-head construction can be submodified, like those in other constructions. In 'flue gas exit velocity', the Actor (*gas*) is sub-modified by a Type-quale Classifier (*flue*). In 'data transfer rate', the Process (*transfer*) is submodified by a Goal Classifier (*data*) in a Process-head construction (the computer transfers data).

5.5   Intensive-Attribute-head construction

5.5.1   The order of Classifiers in the Intensive-Attribute-head construction

As stated in §5.1.4, the Intensive-Attribute-head construction parallels a relational-process clause of the intensive type, with the Attribute as head. (An intensive relational clause is one whose Attribute 'intensifies', or expands, our information about the Carrier Participant, which is in Subject position: e.g. 'Mary [Carrier] is wise [Attribute]'; see Halliday 2004.) For example, 'public road safety' parallels 'the public [Carrier] is safe [Attribute] on the roads'. 'Road' expresses a Circumstance. The Process (equivalent to 'is') is

Table 5.24 *Intensive-Attribute-head construction*

Modifier: Circumstance	Modifier: Carrier Participant	Modifier: Circumstance	Head: Attribute Participant
64%	*[child]*	*word reading*	*accuracy*
NFL career	*[player]*	*field-goal*	*accuracy*
	public	*risk*	*aversion*
	military	*nuclear*	*capability*
	home	*energy*	*efficiency*
heating value	*plant*	*[fuel]*	*efficiency*
	visage	*UV*	*protection*
	prison inmate	*probation*	*readiness*
	public	*road*	*safety*
	youth	*internet*	*safety*
top level	*corporation*	*[fraud]*	*security*
six month	*job*	*[redundancy]*	*security*

implicit. So is the nature of the Circumstantial relation, which is explicit in 'the public is safe <u>on the</u> roads'. Examples are shown in table 5.24.

5.5.2   *Explanation of the order in the Intensive-Attribute-head construction*

The order of the modifiers here follows the general principle given in §5.1.2: those with the most expected relations come closest to the head, as follows (I use 'public road safety' as the main example). (a) SAFETY entails a danger that you are safe <u>from</u>; so the danger (expressed by *road*) is necessary to it: it comes closest. Similarly with 'home energy efficiency': EFFICIENCY is the waste-free use of <u>something</u>: an entity used (expressed in *energy*) is intrinsic to the head concept (*efficiency*). (b) The Carrier Participant ('<u>public</u> road safety', '<u>home</u> energy efficiency') is necessary to the relation, but not intrinsic to the concept denoted by the head, just as in 'That book was interesting', the subject, book, is necessary for the existence of a predicate, but the concept of the interesting thing is not intrinsic to INTERESTING. (c) The other Circumstance is Extent or Location, as in '<u>six month</u> job security'. Conceptually, SIX MONTHS is independent of SECURITY, just as the Circumstance WINTER is independent of the head SPEED in 'Winter air speed', as is discussed in §5.4.1.

As with the previous constructions, the order is also syntactic: 'public [road [safety]]', 'home [energy [efficiency]]'.

5.5.3   *Discussion of Intensive-Attribute-head construction*

The table 5.24 shows examples of submodification in each of the subzones. The construction appears to be little used, and to occur with a very limited range of heads: I have found examples with only half a dozen different words as heads, and they express an even smaller number of concepts, since *safety*, *protection* and *security* are roughly synonymous.

5.6   Possessed-Attribute-head construction

5.6.1   *The order of Classifiers in the Possessed-Attribute-head construction*

The Possessed-Attribute-head construction is illustrated in '[28 GB] magnetic disk storage capacity'; it parallels the clause 'The magnetic disk has capacity for storage to the extent of 28 GB'. It is like the Intensive-Attribute-head construction, just discussed, in that both parallel a relational-process clause; and both have the structure of Participant + Circumstance + Participant. But they differ in two ways. First, the relational Process here is of the possessive type. (A possessive relational clause is one whose Attribute denotes another participant, which is possessed by the Carrier Participant; it commonly uses the relation HAVE; see Halliday 2004.) For example, 'magnetic disk storage capacity' parallels the clause 'the magnetic disk [Carrier] has [possessive relational Process] capacity [Attribute] for storage [Circumstance]'. Second, the Circumstance is an action, e.g. 'disk storage capacity', not a location as in 'public road safety'. The action is not Process; the Process is relational – 'the disk has....'.

The full order, and examples, are set out in table 5.25. Note that in context, 'wetland treatment ability' referred to the ability of wetland to treat water, i.e. filter it.

5.6.2   *Explanation of the order in the Possessed-Attribute-head construction*

The order of the modifiers follows the same general principle as before: those with the most necessary relations come closest to the head, as follows (I use '28 GB external disk [storage] capacity' as the main example; the argument parallels points made about the other constructions, especially the Intensive-Attribute-head construction). (a) These heads denote an ability to perform; a Process is intrinsic to the Attribute itself. So a Process such as STORE or WRITE is intrinsic to CAPACITY. (b) As with the previous Attribute construction, the Carrier Participant ('28 GB external disk [storage] capacity') is not intrinsic to the concept (though necessary to the relation); so it precedes the Process. (c) As with the Process-head construction, other Circumstances come further from the head (and with Extent further than Location, if both occur), being extrinsic to the concept of the Process.

As with the previous constructions, the order is also syntactic: '28 GB [external disk [capacity]]', 'dual layer [write [capabilities]]'.

Table 5.25 *Possessed–Attribute-head construction*

Modifier: Circumstance (Location)	Modifier: Carrier Participant	Modifier: Circumstance (Action)	Head: Attribute Participant
	soil	*absorption*	*ability*
	wetland	*treatment*	*ability*
28 GB	*external disk*	*[storage]*	*capacity*
	magnetic disk	*storage*	*capacity*
	system	*storage*	*capacity*
dual layer		*write*	*capabilities*
	anal sphincter	*contractile*	*capacity*
	transducer	*production*	*capacity*
summer	*snow*	*[coverage]*	*extent*

5.6.3   *Discussion of the Possessed–Attribute-head construction*

Modifiers in the construction may be submodified, as in example (9).

(9)   'Apollo block II fuel system storage capacity'. (Sears 1971: 52).

The basic structure is 'system [Carrier] storage [Process] capacity [Attribute head]'. *Block II* and *fuel* submodify *system*, through Origin (i.e. place) and Function qualia in a Participant-head construction: 'block II [fuel system]'. *Apollo* submodifies *block II*, through the Origin quale in a lower-level Participant-head construction: 'Apollo [block II]'.

The Possessed-Attribute-head construction seems to be even less productive than the Intensive-Attribute-head construction. The difference in productivity among the constructions calls for an explanation, which will be given in §8.5.5; it is historical.

5.7   Constructionless uses of Classifiers

5.7.1   *Introduction*

There are many occurrences where a Classifier is not used in any construction (in the sense employed by this chapter). Some examples are: 'bed cuts', 'death rate' and 'avian carnage' (the killing of many birds). On the other hand, phrases such as 'Sony tv', '32 inch tv' and 'plasma tv' may seem to be constructionless, but must be rated as constructional, since phrases such as 'Sony 32 inch plasma tvs' are established (using the Participant-head construction). Phrases such as 'shareholder activist' and 'propeller shaft' are well established, but it is not clear whether they represent constructions. This section seeks to resolve those issues.

When we examine phrases like the above, with a single Classifier, we find that they meet the criteria for constructions to varying extents. They may accordingly be divided into types (to be considered in the next section), as follows. (a) Some have no characteristics of constructions at all, being evidently used on a single occasion, with a semantic relation between modifier and noun that is not to any degree established in the language; I will call them 'nonce uses'. (b) Some meet a first, low-level criterion (i): they have a semantic relation that hearers can recognise without a context, and which occurs with a few modifiers and a still more sharply limited range of heads; I will call them 'slightly conventionalised uses'. (c) Some meet that criterion and a higher one (ii): they have a simple relation that occurs freely in many premodifiers and with many heads but is not part of a larger relation (as qualia are, and Actor and Goal are); accordingly the premodifiers do not occur (in that relation) with other premodifiers. I will call them 'partly conventionalised uses'. (d) Others meet the higher, additional criterion (iii): the relation is part of a larger one, so the Classifiers occur (in other phrases) with other Classifiers; they are constructional uses, e.g. 'Sony tv' and '32 inch tv', as discussed in the previous sections.

5.7.2   Types of constructionless Classifier

5.7.2.1   Nonce uses

Nonce uses meet none of the criteria; they are evidently invented for some occasion (such as a brief headline), but have too little generality of use to be kept and conventionalised. Examples include the following: 'nude email' (email containing photos of nudes), 'charcoal burgers' (burgers cooked over charcoal – not made of charcoal!), 'Megan and Jessica's holiday toes' (Megan and Jessica's toes photographed while the girls were on holiday), 'water-cooler status' (referring to a topic of conversation: status of such celebrity that people talk about the topic when they meet while getting a drink at the water-cooler). Readers of the phrase can only infer the relationship from context, with help from analogy perhaps; the speaker and the hearer assign the meaning independently. (Some writers focus on these uses: Downing (1977), who sees 'no constraints' (1977: 841) on the process of combining nouns, and Ryder (1994), who describes the linguistic situation as being frequently 'chaos'.)

5.7.2.2   Slightly conventionalised uses

These meet only criterion (i): they have a semantic relation that hearers can recognise without a context; they occur with only a few modifiers and a still more sharply limited range of heads; the relation is generally simpler than in nonce uses. Examples follow. In 'red alert', the relation seems to be DEGREE OF DANGER. We meet that phrase often, 'yellow alert' sometimes, and 'black alert' rarely, but (according to the British National Corpus) not 'green alert', or 'orange alert'. That relation is used with *zone* as head – 'red zone' – but the British National Corpus does not have 'black zone' in this sense, or 'yellow zone'. 'A people person' is (approximately stated) a person ENTHUSIASTIC ABOUT people. We also meet 'a morning person' and 'a night person', but not 'a week person', or 'a December person', or 'a people man'; we meet 'a bags person', but not 'a bags woman' (and 'a bag lady' is something else). The relation is used (at the time of writing) with only a few modifiers, and a sharply limited number of heads. (Phrases such as 'rain date' have a semantic relation that hearers can recognise without a context, but seem to be learned and used as units; so they are structured as lexical items rather than phrases.)

5.7.2.3   *Partly conventionalised uses*

These meet criterion (ii): they have a simple relation that recurs freely with many modifiers and heads, but is not part of a larger relation (as quale and Goal relations are). Examples follow. The phrase 'boy hero' has the appositional IS relation: the boy is a hero, and the hero is a boy. We also meet 'boxer hero', 'rebel hero', 'rabbit hero', and so on. Apposition is used with other heads: 'shareholder activists', 'Nazi activist' and 'Tory activist'. 'Helicopter blade' seems to use the possessive HAS A relation, as do 'helicopter rotor', 'propeller blade', and 'propeller shaft'. The ABOUT/CONCERNING relation occurs in such phrases as 'human rights protester' and 'peace protester', 'disease breakthrough' and 'FM breakthrough', 'pay formula' and 'fragrance formula'. These relations do not in my observation occur with other relations linking another nominal modifier to the same head. (They can have a nominal submodifying the modifier, as in '[executive pay] formula'.) They are fairly fully conventionalised in being common, understood out of context, and used with many different modifiers and heads; but they have not (yet) combined with other relations into a construction in the sense used here; they are specific constructions that belong to no schematic construction.

5.7.3   *Discussion of constructionless Classifiers*

Constructionless Classifiers can be submodified. For example, in 'rape prevention educator Kylie Tippett' *'prevention'* is a constructionless modifier of *'educator'*; it is in turn modified by *'rape'* as Goal to the Process PREVENT, in a Process-head construction. The submodification can be recursive: 'hero [pilot [Captain ['Sully' Sullenberger]]]', with several appositional relations. These uses sometimes result in considerable complexity: 'mountain [death [safety call]]' and '[[Dome Valley] [death crash]] teen' (both *New Zealand Herald* headlines); 'its [complicated [[[telephone directory] [1–7–4–10–2–8–6–12–3–9–5]] [firing order]]]' (*AA Torque* magazine).[9]

---

[9] I take the phrase to have 'telephone directory 1–7–4–10–2–8–6–12–3–9–5' as Dimension Classifier with complex constructionless submodification, and 'firing' as Type Classifier.

There is support from other writers for my assertion that some Classifiers fit into no established structure, other than the general structure of modification. Few writers have discussed the order of Classifiers, but among those who do, Downing (1977) and Warren (1978, 1984) find no established structure. Levi (1978) claims that there is an order (based on the transformational derivation of the phrase), but even she concedes that some Classifier uses are constructionless (1978: 253).

In these uses, the Classifier often seems close to the borderline of the Descriptor zone: *horse* in '<u>horse</u> face' is close to the adjective *horsy*; *wine* is close to *winy* in '<u>wine</u> smell'. Some Classifier uses are close to the borderline between constructionless and constructional Classifiers: 'fresh Family Homogenised Milk nutrition information' (from a milk carton) can be matched with 'internet nutrition information', 'consumer nutrition information', and so on. They seem to belong to a partly developed construction that is different from those I have analysed (using other relations – 'information ABOUT nutrition', 'FOUND ON the internet', FOR consumers'); but they occur too rarely, and in too limited a range of situations, to be adjudged as forming an established construction. On the other hand, in 'the inverse square force law', ABOUT can be read as using a new quale ('law ABOUT force', with 'inverse square' read as using the Constituency quale). Finally, some of these Classifiers are close to the borderline with elements of a compound – '<u>bag</u> lady', perhaps.

Ghomeshi and others (2004/2010) discuss as 'contrastive reduplication' expressions such as, 'I'll make the tuna salad, and you make the <u>SALAD-salad</u>', and 'That's not <u>AUCKLAND-Auckland</u>, is it?' (I consider those spoken expressions to be Classifier + head constructions not compounds, as asserted by Ghomeshi and others 2004/2010: 343.) Those examples seem constructionless; but they match constructions with the Type and Origin qualia. One could say, #'It's a French [Origin] parmesan [Type] cheese, not a Parmesan [Origin] parmesan [Type] cheese'; so #'a Parmesan parmesan' would be well constructed. These expressions rely on the contrast between descriptive and referential usage: the Classifier describes the entity referred to by the head. They thus are effectively modal qualifiers like *alleged*, *fake* and *real*, as discussed in chapter 4 (§4.4.2): a '<u>salad</u> salad' is a '<u>real</u> salad'.

5.8   Discussion of Classifier order

5.8.1   Relation between Classifier phrases and compounds

Some of the regular semantic relations between Classifiers and their heads also appear in many expressions written as one-word compounds or as hyphenated compounds. Table 5.26 illustrates that, giving forms which are all taken from the SOED section on combination forms for the word *sand*. In the first two columns, the table lists constructions and relations for them;

Table 5.26 *Equivalence of compounds and Classifier phrases*

Construction	Relation	One-word compound	Hyphenated compound	Words written as a phrase
Participant-head construction	Origin		*sand-fish*	*sand dollar*
	Constituency	*sandcastle*	*sand-dune*	*sand filter*
	Type	*sandfly*	*sand-bur*	*sand boa*
	Function	*sandman*	*sand-trap*	
Process-head construction	Goal		*sand-binder*	*sand blow*
	Circumstance	*sandstock*	*sand-casting*	*sand culture*

then, for most of the relations, it gives a one-word compound, a hyphenated compound, and an expression written as a phrase, all using the form *sand*. The line for Constituency, for example, means that the single word *sandcas-tle*, the hyphenated form *sand-dune*, and the phrasally expressed 'sand filter' all have their elements related by the implicit grammatical meaning MADE OF – the Constituency quale relation. (In the table, *sandstock* designates a brick made with a dusting of sand on the surface.)

'Sand dollar' (denoting a type of shellfish) will be regarded as a compound by many people, I believe; but *dollar* is a metaphor for the shellfish (from its round shape and silvery colour), and *sand* modifies it. The other expressions in that column should also be regarded as phrases, since they have the same semantic and syntactic relation as 'steel knife' (Constituency quale), 'double-oven range' (Type quale), and so on – none of which phrases would to my knowledge ever be regarded as compounds. We see, then, that many 'compounds' have exactly the same semantic structure as many phrases, and that their semantic relations involve modification. That reinforces the view that there is no absolute distinction between compounds and phrases – see Quirk *et al.* (1985: 1567) and Giegerich (2005: 588–90), for example.

Linguists often use stress to distinguish compounds from phrases: compounds have a single stress; see Bauer (1998) and Giegerich (2005: 589), for example. However, whether the head of a Classifier phrase is stressed varies with the Classifier's position: 'French teacher' as 'teacher from France' (with *teacher* in Origin position) has relatively strong stress on *teacher* – 'French **teach**-er', approximately; but 'French teacher' as 'teacher of French' (*teacher* in Type position) has relatively weak stress on *teacher* – '**French** teacher'. (That variation accords with the varying semantic and syntactic closeness, as expectedness, noted in §5.1.2.) Table 5.27 illustrates the point further, from expressions given by SOED as phrases. For the *toy* examples there, and the *French* examples above, the difference in stress is the hearer's only perceptible clue to the difference in meaning. It follows that the stress is

Table 5.27 *Stress in Classifiers*

Classifier		Constituency	Type	Function	Head	Meaning
slate	(a)		*slate*		*quarry*	'quarry for slate'
	(b)	*slate*			*roof*	'roof made of slate'
toy	(a)		*toy*		*factory*	'factory for toys'
	(b)	*toy*			*factory*	'factory that is a toy'

Table 5.28 *ISRAEL – SELL – ARMAMENT in a Process-head construction*

Participant (modifier)	Participant (modifier)	Process (head)
Israeli	*arms*	*sales*

differentiating between different phrasal constructions, not between phrases and compounds.

I will not develop fully the implications of this chapter for the extensive literature on 'compounds', 'complex nominals', 'noun + noun compounds'. I conclude by noting that further comment will be made in the history and discussion chapters (8 and 10), and by emphasising what seems to me the crucial fact that discussion of 'compounds' has failed to allow for Classifiers' constructional meanings.

5.8.2   *Relation of Classifier constructions to each other*

We have seen alternative construals of a word invoking one quale as invoking another, in section 5.2.1.1, for example. Alternative construals also underlie the parallel between the five Classifier constructions – reconstrual of the process. For example, the ISRAEL – SELL – ARMAMENT concepts may be construed with a material process, in a Process-head construction, as shown in table 5.28. Alternatively, those concepts may be construed with a possessive relational process, in a Possessed-Attribute-head construction, as in table 5.29. They may be reconstrued again in the Participant-head construction, in qualia relations, as in table 5.30.

The examples just given show variation in the construal of the semantic classes, as well as in the construal of the processes. SELL, which is an action at that level, may be construed as Process ('Israeli arms <u>sales</u>'), or as Participant (#'their 2005 <u>sales</u> success'), or as Circumstance (#'the company <u>sales</u> pitch' or #'company pitch <u>for sales</u>'). At the syntactic level, SELL can be expressed

Table 5.29 *ISRAEL – SELL – ARMAMENT in an Attribute-head construction*

Circumstance (modifier)	Participant (Carrier) (modifier)	Circumstance (modifier)	Participant (Attribute) (head)
# *Israeli*		*arms sales*	*capacity*

Table 5.30 *ISRAEL – SELL – ARMAMENT in a Participant-head construction*

Circumstance Origin quale	Circumstance Dimension quale	Circumstance Type quale	Participant (head)
# *Israeli*	*multi-million pound*	*armament*	*sales*

as modifier ('<u>sales</u> capacity') or as head ('arms <u>sales</u>)'. Expressing SELL as *selling* would allow still more construals.

My treating each Classifier as having its own relation with the head, thereby forming a construction, suggests that each of the five main constructions is a group of constructions, rather than a single construction. There is, nevertheless, a semantic unity in each of the five. That should be clear from the fact that each construction represents a single process; it has the same unity as a clause. The unity goes further: the main constructions are never mixed – no qualia-related Classifier occurs with Classifiers from the other constructions, for example; and, perhaps most strikingly, constructionless Classifiers are not combined (although one can submodify another).

Following Croft (1999: 65), Traugott (2006), and others such as Bergs and Diewald (2008), who argue that constructions are schematic (or abstract) in varying degrees, we can say that there are different levels of Classifier construction. The five main constructions are relatively schematic. The Participant-head construction (whose constructional meaning is the relation of Circumstances to Participant in a relational process) is a schematic one, made up of the specific qualia constructions (whose constructional meaning is the quale relation).

5.8.3   Relation of Classifier constructions to the overall premodification structure

There is a significant overlap in meaning between the Participant-head construction and the overall construction of the premodification zones. Consider examples (10) and (11):

(10)   'A Sony 36 inch plasma television'
(11)   #'Sony's big plasma television'

Table 5.31 *Overlap of Classifiers and overall premodification*

Det.	Epithet	Descriptor		Classifiers		Head
a			*Sony*	*36 inch*	*plasma*	*television*
Sony's	*big*				*plasma*	*television*

The two expressions are approximately synonymous; and until you analyse them, they seem to have much the same syntax, as well; but analysis shows them to be different, as shown in table 5.31. In these phrases, a determiner (*Sony's*) and an Origin Classifier (*Sony*) are equivalent; so are an Epithet (*big*) and a Dimension Classifier (*36 inch*). Since determiners and the various types of premodifier are semantically and syntactically distinct, that overlap may seem odd. A partial historical explanation will be given in §8.5.4, and some further comment in §10.2; but the fundamental explanation lies in the fact we have met repeatedly, that linguistic structure, in nominal phrases at least, is controlled not by underlying content but by the linguistic meaning into which we construe it, and the purposes for which we then use the meaning.

5.8.4   Relation of Classifiers to genitives

Most work in the extensive literature on genitives in English takes -*s* expressions and *of-* expressions as alternative forms of the genitive – 'the dog's tail', 'the tail of the dog'. What unites the forms is semantic: they express the same set of semantic relations, such as possession. If we accept that understanding, then we must accept that many Classifiers are genitive: in 'some battalions of the army', 'some of the army's battalions' and 'some army battalions', the three forms express the same relation, and are alternatives semantically. That is confirmed by the exact parallel between many of the Classifier implicit relations, as set out in this chapter, and semantic relations set out in the genitives literature, ranging from Mitchell (1985) on Old English to Stefanowitsch (2003) on Present-Day English, such as 'the genitive of measure' and the 'subjective genitive'.

Subjective and objective genitives, for example, fill the main two positions in the Process-head construction. In the Participant-head construction, possessive genitives occur in the Origin position ('the new Ford 2 litre Mondeo'; cf. 'Ford's new Mondeo'); measure genitives occur in the Dimension position ('a ton weight'); genitives of substance or 'descriptive genitives' occur in the Constituency position ('a Minoan bronze dagger', cf. 'a dagger of bronze'); possessive genitives occur in the Type position ('fresh pasteurised goats' milk' and 'fresh goat milk', cf. 'a goat's fresh milk'). Genitives thus run right through Classifier constructions.

Because they fill specific positions in well-defined constructions, constructional Classifier genitives render systematically and precisely meanings that -s and of- genitives leave vague. Constructionless Classifiers, on the other hand, are very vague, as noted in §5.7 above; they seem to be taking over the role of the of- genitives: they act as a catchall default construction, as phrases with of have done in the past (Brinton and Traugott 2005: 15).

The literature on premodifiers generally omits discussion of genitives; the inflected forms, such as 'goats' milk' and 'men's shoes' – sometimes called 'the descriptive genitive' – are a partial exception, being discussed by Rosenbach (2006) and Huddleston and Pullum (2002), for example. The literature on genitives seems to omit the uninflected form altogether.

5.8.5   Completeness of the account of Classifier constructions

My account lists five constructions, and the constructionless uses of Classifiers. But there are many Classifier phrases that may seem to be outside those six groups and to cast doubt on the completeness of the account. This section discusses such phrases, and argues that they do not in fact falsify my account.

Some phrases may represent inchoate constructions. I have already noted (§5.7.3) that one new construction seems to be partly formed but not established; there may be others. That fits the account to be given (§8.5.4) of the recent and probably continuing development of Classifier constructions.

Some apparent exceptions to my account of the qualia structure are reconstruals of Classifiers from their usual qualia position to another. Pairs of examples are given as (12) and (13).

(12)   'Heart native timber' and 'native heart timber' (Both are from the internet.)

The first has *native* as the Type, because the context was native versus exotic timber; the second has *heart* as the Type, because the context was heartwood versus sapwood. (The other Classifier in each phrase is construed as Subtype.)

(13)   'Glass '41 coupe' [a fibreglass coupe car made in 1941] and ''38 four door sedan' (Both are from *Hot Rod*, October 2006, p. 18.)

The first construes *'41* (the year) as Type (with *glass* as Constituency); the second construes *'38* (the year) as Origin, with 'four door' as Type.

Some of the apparent exceptions to my categorisation are due, I believe, simply to the writer's confusion about the structure: the phrases are exceptions to grammaticality, not to my account. Consider example (14):

(14)   'Novelty race shock wire game' (catalogue for Jaycar electronic products)

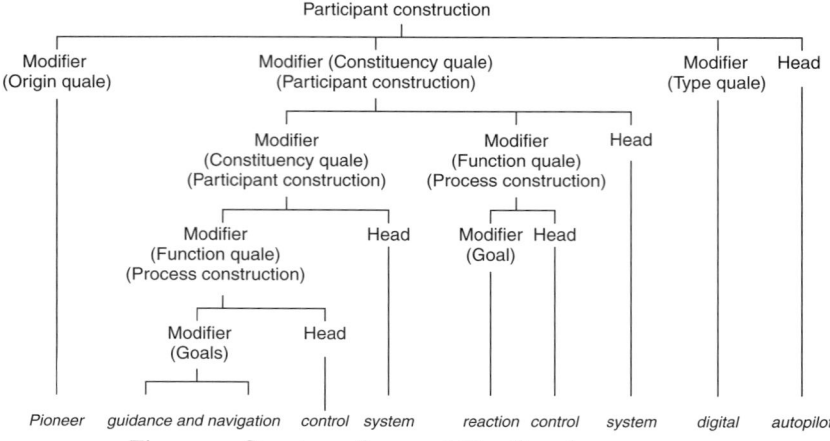

Figure 5.3 Structure of 11-word Classifier phrase

That was intended to mean 'a novel game which is a race, played using wires, and giving a shock when a player fails'. All four modifiers seem to be intended as Type Classifiers; but several do not give a Subtype for later words, which makes them ungrammatical in construction; and *wire* does not seem to have an acceptable Type interpretation anyway (**'wire game'*).

Some Classifiers that are apparently premodifiers are postmodifiers, in fact:

(15)   'Sanyo 3100 <u>Pinkilicious Go</u> prepaid mobile' (advertising brochure for 'FlyBuys' loyalty scheme)

Here, 'Pinkilicious Go' is not a premodifier of *mobile*, but a postmodifier of the model number, *3100*. Other apparent premodification structures are appositive, as in (16)

(16)   'Packard Bell <u>C3–244</u> Notebook' (*New Zealand Herald* display advertisement)

C3–244 identifies the referent uniquely; *Notebook* is in apposition to it.

Some of what may seem to be modifiers are submodifiers. An example follows. (I give considerable space to this analysis, for a further purpose: demonstrating that my analysis of Classifier constructions can give a convincing account of even the most complex and potentially confusing Classifier phrases.)

(17)   'Pioneer guidance and navigation control system reaction control system digital autopilot' (cited in Varantola 1984: 33)[10]

---

[10]   I regard this aerospace jargon from the 1970s as outdated, especially in its use of the Constituency quale for the whole–part relation, and the analysis seems open to dispute.

Table 5.32 *Participant-head construction*

Modifier: Circumstance: Origin quale	Modifier: Circumstance: Dimension quale	Modifier: Circumstance: Constituency quale	Modifier: Circumstance: Type quale	Modifier: Circumstance: Function quale	Head: Participant
Elite	*110 cm*	*stainless*	*double oven*		*range*
[Wyndham]	*high denier*	*nylon*	*[Oxford weave]*	*lining*	*fabric*

The structure is shown in figure 5.3. The top line indicates that the whole phrase is a Participant-head construction. The next two lines indicate that the phrase has four main parts (three modifiers related by various qualia, and the head), and that the second modifier is itself a construction.

We conclude that there is much less variability in Classifier constructions than there may appear to be, which suggests that the account of Classifiers given here is complete.

5.9   Conclusion: order within the Classifier zone

5.9.1   Summary

The order of the Classifiers is not so much an order of word senses (as with the order of Reinforcer → Epithet → Descriptor), as an order of constructions. Each Classifier position constitutes a construction, consisting of the meaning of the Classifier itself and the constructional meaning (the relation of the Classifier's lexical meaning to that of the head). Those specific constructions constitute more schematic constructions, each of which has a single unifying relation which controls the order.

There are five constructions, as follows.

(i) The Participant-head construction has its modifiers in the Circumstance role, in the order: first Origin, then Dimension, Constituency, Type, and Function, as in table 5.32. (Those five Circumstantial relations have been called 'qualia'.)

(ii) The Process-head construction has its modifiers in the order: first Circumstances (Extent, then Location), then Indirect Participant, Actor Participant, and Goal Participant, as in table 5.33.

(iii) The Circumstance-head construction has its modifiers in the order: first Circumstance (Extent, then Location), then Actor Participant, and Process, as in table 5.34.

(iv) The Intensive-Attribute-head construction has its modifiers in the order: first Carrier Participant, then Circumstance, as in table 5.35.

Table 5.33 *Process-head construction*

Modifiers: Circumstances		Modifiers: Participants			Head: Process
		Indirect Participant	Direct Participants		
Extent	Location		Actor	Goal	
overnight	*on-site*		[*contractor*]	*explosives*	*storage*
	[*2005*]	*leaky homes*	*court*		*ruling*

Table 5.34 *Circumstance-head construction*

Modifier: Extent Circumstance	Modifier: Location Circumstance	Modifier: Actor Participant	Modifier: Process	Head: Circumstance
5 m/sec	[*surface*]	*freestream*	[*flow*]	*velocity*

Table 5.35 *Intensive-Attribute-head construction*

Modifier: Carrier Participant	Modifier: Circumstance	Head: Attribute Participant
public	*transport*	*safety*

Table 5.36 *Possessive-Attribute-head construction*

Modifier: Circumstance	Modifier: Carrier Participant	Modifier: Process	Head: Attribute Participant
28 GB	*external disk*	[*storage*]	*capacity*

(v) The Possessive-Attribute-head construction has its modifiers in the order: first Circumstance, then Carrier Participant, and Process, as in table 5.36.

There are also constructionless uses of Classifiers, which take only a single Classifier, and are therefore without internal order.

The semantic explanation of the order is that the Classifier whose constructional meaning is most expected in the conceptual meaning of the head comes closest to it; the least expected comes furthest from the head; the nature of being expected varies with the construction. The syntactic explanation is that Classifiers conform to the same syntactic structure as do other premodifiers: they modify the following part of the phrase as in, 'Wyndham [high denier [nylon [Oxford weave [lining fabric]]]]'. The relation between semantics and syntax is that semantics controls syntax, fundamentally. Furthermore, no subzone has different or wider powers of modification, as Reinforcer and Epithet zones do (chapter 4); so syntax does not have the extended role that it does in the other zones.

We now have explanations of the facts with which the chapter began (§5.1.1). The positions (or specific constructions) in the constructions (i) to (v) in the summary above explain the first fact, the existence of subzones. The variation in the nature of the constructions explains the second, the variation in relations between Classifier and head. The difficulty of knowing which position a Classifier is occupying when only some positions are filled explains the third, the systematic ambiguity.

This chapter, on Classifiers, complements chapters 3 and 4, on the semantics and syntax of the zones overall, to answer the original question of the book (§1.1): what is the nature of unmarked premodifier order?

5.9.2 *Prospect: the following chapters*

The preceding sections have explained the order of Classifiers and many other features, but there are a number of features noted in the discussion that need further explanation. They include the great differences between Classifiers on the one hand and Reinforcers, Epithets and Descriptors on the other; the number of constructionless uses; the range of relations invoked by some of the positions, especially the qualia positions; the amount of ambivalence and ambiguity that occur; the great differences in complexity and productivity of the different constructions; and the existence of borderline instances. Chapter 8 will offer an historical explanation for those features, in §8.5.5. Two features will be explained psycholinguistically, in §9.2: the complexity of the Classifier zone, which is much greater than that of the other zones, and Classifiers' frequency of use.

Chapters 3 and 4 and this one have explained the unmarked order of nominal phrase premodifiers. The next two chapters explain free order (chapter 6) and marked order (chapter 7).

6   Free order

6.1   Introduction

This chapter explains free order (order within one zone), complementing the previous three chapters, which explain unmarked order (grammatically set order across zones). It starts from two points made in chapter 2: order within a zone is not bound by grammatical rule, and multiple premodifiers within one zone are co-ordinated (phonologically, or by commas or conjunctions such as *and* and *but*).

Premodifiers within the same zone are sequential in utterance, but not sequential in syntactic structure: they modify the group made up of words in later zones and the head; they do not modify later words in the same zone (§2.2.1.2). They are structured paratactically, not hypotactically. The phrase, 'its full-bodied, soft, sweet lingering dark cherry flavours', can be represented in Figure 6.1, which has arrows added to the bracketed analysis of constituency, to make the modification structure more explicit.

The lack of structural sequence gives the speaker freedom to vary 'full-bodied, soft, sweet…' to 'soft, sweet, full-bodied…', or 'sweet, soft, full-bodied…'. This chapter examines that freedom.

Previous work on premodifier order does not account for free order. Sussex (1974: 111–12) notes that it can be used for 'stylistic markedness', but does not explain it further. Vandelanotte (2002: §1) discusses co-ordinated adjectives, but does not grasp the nature of their freedom. Neither work relates the freedom to zoning.

The chapter argues as follows. Although the order is free grammatically, there are some constraints that limit speakers' freedom, arising from content and from convention (§6.2). In other situations, speakers set the order

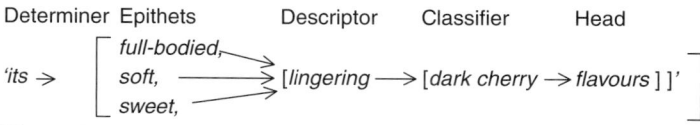

Figure 6.1: Modification structure of co-ordinated premodifiers

by a stylistic principle, accepting a constraint on their grammatical freedom voluntarily: the most important of the modifiers is put first (§6.3), or it is put last (§6.4) – first and last both being positions of prominence in language. Otherwise, the order is a random one (§6.5). Discussion follows (§6.6), and conclusions (§6.7).

6.2   Constraints on the order within a zone

6.2.1   Conventionalised order

With some groups of premodifiers, the order has been conventionalised to some degree. For example, we regularly prefer 'black and white' to 'white and black', as in 'black and white photography'. (The OED gives 'black and white' as a combination, but not 'white and black'.) Other examples of conventionalised order are 'black and tan terriers' and 'men's and women's foot-wear'. Sometimes, conventionalisation is taken further, to the point where different orders carry different meanings. For example, the British flag is regularly a 'red, white and blue flag'; the order has connotations of British patriotism, as in '… the professional patrioteer … who waves a red-white-&-blue handkerchief'. The expression 'blue, white and red flag' is commonly taken to refer to the French tricolour.

6.2.2   Time order

When two premodifiers refer to successive events, they are normally written in the order in which the events occurred – iconic order – as in 'I came, I saw, I conquered.' Consider, for example, the common phrase, 'dead and gone'; the Corpus of Contemporary American English has over a hundred examples of it, but has only two examples of 'gone and dead': people die before they disappear from memory. We say 'second and final' (over fifty entries in the Corpus of Contemporary American English), not 'final and second' (no entries in that corpus) for much the same reason. A recipe instructs the cook to fry some fish, marinate it, then 'put the fried, marinated fish in a bowl'; if you bought some fried fish and marinated it, you would presumably have #'marinated fried fish'.

6.2.3   Order of experience

Modifiers may be given in the order in which the qualities are experienced. In example (1), emigrants from England are approaching Australia by ship, early one spring morning:

(1)   'The faint, new, spicy smell of land wafted across the water.'
          (H.H. Richardson, *The Fortunes of Richard Mahoney*, p. 421)

Here, the smell is experienced first as faint, then (when more distinct, as the ship sails closer) as new, and finally as spicy.

6.2.4   Explanatory order

Section 4.2.2 shows that an Epithet can be explained by a following word (a Descriptor). Speakers who want to use two Epithets, with one explaining the other, seem to be under a strong constraint to put the explaining word after the one explained. Examples include 'a nice, warm prison' *(warm* explains why prison is nice) and 'a good, strong boat'. The force of the constraint is shown by the oddity of the reversed order: #'a warm, nice prison', #'a strong, good boat'.[1] Sometimes the explanatory word is appositive: 'a large, red (i.e. <u>risky</u>) area' (on a map), 'the so-called "gray" (<u>questionable</u>) sayings' of Jesus.

The phrases discussed in this section would be grammatical with the order reversed, but would not be fully idiomatic English: ?'white and black photography', ?'a risky (i.e. red) area'. We are constrained in the order we use, with limited freedom to vary it. The following sections deal with situations where there is great freedom.

6.3   Order with the most important modifier first

This section illustrates the fact that speakers often rate one premodifier as more important, and place it first accordingly. Three reasons are suggested for speakers' choice, but they are not fully independent. (The relative importance of underlined words is shown by type size.)

6.3.1   Thematic meaning first

Example (2) comes from a review of a biography:

(2)   '[In 1986] Vesua Bjelogrlic............ decided to leave her <u>stagnant</u> but <u>peaceful Yugoslav homeland,</u> and move with her English fiancé to London.' (*Economist*, 26 March 2005, p. 77)

Here, *stagnant* provided the motivation for Vesua's move, so was vital to the biographical theme. *Peaceful* had secondary importance. *Yugoslav* was unimportant in the book – outweighed by personal interest – and *homeland* was already given in the context. The order is that of thematic importance, in relating to a recurrent topic in the text. These uses sometimes operate on the principle (noted in §4.3) that premodifiers can modify a following word; thus expressive Epithets are commonly put first to colour following Epithets:

---

[1] However, we also expect the 'nice warm' order because of submodification – 'nicely warm'; see chapter 4, §4.3.2.

'A <u>bloody</u>, great, stupid game', 'an <u>irate</u>, <u>steely</u> black steeple'. This thematic use enhances the cohesion of the text (as discussed by Halliday and Hasan 1976), that is, the structure of text as a unit greater than the clause.

6.3.2   New or attention-worthy information first

Example (3) comes from an Automobile Association review of a new Mazda sports car.

(3)   'The outgoing car's been hailed for its fine balance for some 16 years, and fans were concerned the recipe would be lost in the model change.
          They needn't have worried. The iconic sports car may be bigger, but not by much; and the <u>light weight</u>, <u>fine-handling</u>, <u>nicely-balanced</u> and <u>affordable</u> sports recipe appears to have been retained.' (*AA Autofocus*, Autumn 2005, p. 7)

The concept of the head word, *recipe*, is given in the previous paragraph, and *affordable* is inferrable from the fact that the car is a Mazda, so their information is not new. The concept of *nicely balanced* is also given in the previous paragraph (as *fine balance*), but has importance for the sports-car theme. The new information in the phrase, therefore, comes from the first two modifiers, *light weight* and *fine-handling*, which are also attention-worthy for an 'iconic sports car'. The phrase, then, has its new and important information placed first. Similarly, a European news report on AIBO, a household robotic dog, said: 'Most Japanese consumers.... like AIBO because it is a <u>clean, safe and predictable</u> pet.'

The issue of newsworthiness will return, with greater importance, in the discourse explanation of order (§9.3).

6.3.3   Emotion first

Emotive words are often put first. A newspaper headline has, 'It's a <u>cruel</u>, <u>cool</u> summer.' An opinion article has, 'Africa is a continent of breathtaking beauty and diversity with an <u>extraordinary</u>, <u>energetic</u> and <u>resilient</u> people.' This order is frequent in everyday phrases, such as '<u>nice</u>, <u>polite</u> little kid' and '<u>nasty</u>, <u>cold</u> wind', and is often reinforced by the explanatory principle given in §6.2 above. The existence of the order is supported by Bache (1978: 73ff.), in his principle of 'emotional load', and by Quirk *et al.* (1985: 1337).

6.3.4   Conclusion

We conclude that writers and speakers sometimes use their freedom to arrange same-zone premodifiers as they wish by putting first what they consider to be most important. That importance may consist of the word's being emotive, being new or being thematic. The order here has the same pattern as the overall order of premodifiers, where emotive and otherwise forceful words (Epithets) precede less forceful ones.

6.4 Order with the most important modifier last

6.4.1 Emotion last

A frequent motive for arranging words in free order is to have the most emotive word come last, climactically, as in example (4):

(4)   'I tell you, this <u>quiet</u>, <u>bowed</u>, <u>bandy-legged</u>, almost <u>deformed</u> little man was immense in the singleness of his idea, and in his placid ignorance of our agitation.' (Joseph Conrad, *Youth*, p. 25)

Quiet is vague and weak; *bowed* and *bandy-legged* are more precise and convey an image; *deformed*, being based on the previous imagery, is vivid and emotive. Other examples are, 'the biggest, most complex, <u>most audacious</u> thrill of the film' and 'the sharp, rather arrogant, and even <u>offensive</u> tone'.

6.4.2 Most significant concept last

A political report on Iraq commented on the formation of a government, as in (5).

(5)   '[Wrangling over a new government] is what democracy is bound to be about, in a <u>multi-ethnic</u>, <u>multi-confessional</u>, <u>artificially constructed</u>, <u>war- and dictator-blighted</u> country.' (*Economist*, 16 April 2005)

The modifiers in that example are conceptually climactic in the scale of the issues they represent, each issue being more damaging to Iraq than the one before.

Sometimes the last modifier is a logical conclusion from the others, as in, 'an extraordinary, celestial, divine, and therefore <u>all powerful</u> being', and 'the sly, evasive, <u>untrustworthy</u> smile'.

6.4.3 Most evocative word last

Consider example (6), which comes near the end of a novel:

(6)   '... a large, bright, brilliant, buoyant, <u>tumultuous</u> sun' (Doris Lessing, *The Summer Before the Dark*, p. 235)

The phrase, reporting a dream, creates a symbolic image which expresses the climactic change in the main character's life; and *tumultuous* is a climactic word in the phrase. The evocative effect relies on the transfer of concepts and imagery from literal *large, bright* and *brilliant* to metaphorical *buoyant,* and from all of those to almost paradoxical *tumultuous*. Further examples include the description of George Bush's house in Texas as 'a <u>small</u>, <u>very modern</u>, even <u>spare</u> ranch-style house', and 'good, penetrating, <u>X-rayish</u> phrases' (Aldous Huxley, *Brave New World*, p. 145).

6.4.4   Conclusion: order with the important last

The conclusion is that writers (and possibly speakers) sometimes arrange free-order premodifiers by putting what they consider to be most important last, climactically. That importance may consist of the word's being thematic, or most emotive, or most conceptually significant, or most evocative.

6.5   Discussion of free order

6.5.1   Rhythm

Quirk *et al.* (1985: 1341) include rhythm as an influence on the order of modifiers within the same zone. Other influences given in the literature include words with fewer syllables preceding those with more syllables (Bache 1978), morphologically derived words following nonderived words (Bache 1978), and 'common items' preceding 'rare ones' (Quirk *et al.* 1985: 1341). Where they do apply, those principles work together, since derived and uncommon words regularly have more length, and affect rhythm. Their influence is weak, however. Bache (1978) and Quirk *et al.* (1985) both accept that they are tendencies not rules; and the alternative orders give alternative rhythms, not a rhythmical phrase and an arhythmic one – compare 'black and yellow' and 'yellow and black'.

6.5.2   The basis for free order

This section discusses what underlies the constraints and the stylistic choice of order outlined in the previous sections.

   One basis is the semantic structure of premodifiers. If we examine the zone membership of the modifiers involved in the choice of order within a zone, as illustrated by the examples in the preceding sections, we find striking results. First, we find that the premodifiers constrained by convention, time or experience are all Descriptors, which are perceptual words (expressing experience, including time), simple in semantic structure, and easily conventionalised because they <u>are</u> simple. Those constrained by explanation are Epithets, which express abstract concepts, the stuff of explanation. Second, the premodifiers subject to placement by importance are all Epithets, which are words that by their nature have expressive meaning and depth of possible meaning; that makes gradation in importance possible, and makes thematic linking possible. The conclusion is that whether co-ordinated premodifiers can form a significant order depends on their semantic structure, which confirms the latter's importance – as shown in §3.6.2, §4.9.2 and §5.9.1.

Syntax, as well as semantics, is sometimes the basis for free order. In particular, the climactic structures sometimes rely on the power of Epithets to modify other premodifiers, as with '... a large, bright, brilliant, buoyant, tumultuous sun', cited above.

Where a phrase allows either of the significant orders (important-first or important-last), the choice seems to depend on the genre in which it is used. The climactic, important-last examples given above come from fiction and news-reporting articles: climactic order fits the narrative build-up to a culminating event, which can aptly be mirrored in a climactic structure of premodifiers. The important-first examples come from book reviews or editorials. Those genres expound a theme, so they use theme-related linking words to help show the development of thought and to keep the text cohesive; those thematic words are highlighted by prominence in first position. (Chapter 3, §3.6.1.6, shows that coming first is the default position for prominence.)

The last basis for free order is language function, just as function underlies unmarked order (§3.6.1.5). The forms constrained by experience or time are controlled by the experiential function. Putting thematic or new information first serves the textual function, since it develops the structure of the passage as text. Putting emotive, significant or evocative information last serves the interpersonal function, since it builds a climax, whose effect lies in the hearer's personal response.

6.5.3   *Marked use of coordination, in free order*

The unmarked form of premodifier coordination uses *and* – as in '..., ..., ... and...'; it signifies that the premodifiers occupy the same structural position (see §6.1, especially figure 6.1); any of the later premodifiers could replace an earlier one – syntactically, at least. Omission of *and* is a marked form, giving the coordination a different significance. In 'good, penetrating, X-rayish phrases', for example, *X-rayish* denotes a way of being penetrating, and *penetrating* denotes a way of being good; each later modifier elaborates the earlier one, and could not replace it – semantically, that is. That reading is forced by the meaning of the words, but it is also signalled by the marked omission of *and* before *X-rayish*. (Compare Halliday's distinction, at 2004: §7.4, between extending, enhancing and elaborating.)

Example (7) comes from a novel, when the main character is leaving nineteenth-century Australia, and reflects on the people he has known.

(7)   '... all those boisterous, kindly, vulgar people' (Henry Handel Richardson, *The Fortunes of Richard Mahoney*, p. 346)

The marked omission of *and* leads the reader to take *boisterous, kindly* and *vulgar* as not additive but overlapping: the Australians are kindly in a boisterous way; and perhaps their 'vulgarity' was merely their boisterousness as well – perhaps the character was snobbish in his superior outlook, it is suggested. Shortly before, he had looked back from his ship at 'the reef-bound coasts of this <u>old, new</u> world' (cited in chapter 3); the absence of *and* facilitates the paradox – #'old and new world' would be unacceptable. That is the last phrase in volume 1 of the novel: the marked use allows a pithy phrase that sums up the book thematically.[2]

Just as the replacement of the final *and* with a comma is marked usage, so is the replacement of the medial commas with *and*. Example (8) quotes the American senator, Ted Kennedy, reflecting on an incident much earlier in his life, in which he reportedly escaped from a car in which his young woman companion drowned, without reporting the incident to the police until the car and dead body were discovered hours later.

(8)   'His "irrational and indefensible and inexcusable and inexplicable" behaviour' (reporter quoting Kennedy, *Economist*, 29 August 2009, p. 34)

Using *and* throughout emphasises the additive implication, suggesting that there were four things wrong with the behaviour – not just one, and making the remark much more forceful.

6.6   Conclusion: free order

When speakers and writers use two or more premodifiers in the same zone, they may use them in any order: the order is not set grammatically, and may be arbitrary, as with 'We pray for all peoples separated from one another because of <u>religious</u>, <u>social</u>, <u>ethnic</u> or <u>political</u> differences.' However, there are some external constraints (namely convention, time order and experience) which limit speakers' freedom. Speakers often choose a stylistic order: either they put first, in a position of prominence, what is new or what relates to the theme of the whole text (for example); or they put the most emphatic or emotive (for example) last, to form a climax. That summary explains the second phenomenon noted in §1.1 of chapter 1 – why the order can sometimes be varied freely – and the nature of the variations.

The chapter leaves two matters unexplained: how the mind can use principles for premodification within a zone that are quite different from the principles it uses for premodifiers in different zones, even while processing a single phrase; and why the principles discussed as constraints (in §6.2) do not allow freedom, whereas those discussed in later sections do allow it. A

---

[2] In these phrases, the full meaning is not <u>decoded</u>; it is created, using linguistic skill and imagination; the English language is not a code.

psycholinguistic explanation is suggested in §9.2. The language functions and the principle of importance discussed in §6.5.2 will gain further significance in the discussion of discourse explanation (§9.3).

We have been considering speakers' freedom to arrange words within a zone; we turn in the next chapter to a more powerful freedom: that of flouting the grammatically prescribed order across zones, in marked order.

7 Marked order

7.1 Introduction

7.1.1 General introduction

This chapter completes the exposition of the three types of order: chapters 3, 4 and 5 presented unmarked order; chapter 6 presented free order; this presents the last type, marked order.

Like the last four, the chapter starts from the outline of zones and types of order given in chapter 2. Specifically, it starts from the assertion there that premodifiers are sometimes used in an apparently ungrammatical order (but one established by usage), in which the unmarked order is changed for a special purpose. For example, *ruby* has a Classifier sense, as in 'sweet-tasting [E] [old] [D] ruby [C] port', and it has a Descriptor sense, as in '[beautiful] [E] ruby [D] lustre [C] tiles'. (Here, and often in this chapter, the zones are abbreviated to their initials.) But it is used in Epithet position in example (1).

(1)   'ruby [E], sweet-tasting [E] Parma [C] ham' (*Economist*, 20 January 2007, p. 73)

The word has no established Epithet sense: its anomalous position in co-ordination with an Epithet forces us to ascribe to it a new Epithet-type sense combining the colour element from the Descriptor sense and other elements inferred from the context, such as 'rich, attractive'. See table 7.1.

The argument of the chapter is primarily that marked order is an established device in English; that it has two different and important functions; and that the marking is carried out in a variety of ways. Some more general conclusions will be drawn, as well. The next section, §7.2, deals with the function of changing modification structure, and §7.3 deals with the function of changing meaning; §7.4 gives general discussion; and §7.5 concludes.

'Marked order' here means both (a) an order that is used less frequently, and (b) an order that carries special significance. (These two senses correspond to Croft's 'frequency' sense of *unmarked*, and his 'neutral value' sense, respectively; Croft 1991: 57.) The markedness of the use is commonly

Table 7.1 *Uses of* ruby

	Epithet	Descriptor	Classifier	Head
Unmarked order (established senses):	*sweet-tasting*	[*old*]	*ruby*	*port*
	beautiful	*ruby*	lustre	tiles
Marked order (new, marked sense):	*ruby, sweet-tasting*		Parma	ham

shown by the sequence; for example, a word with no Epithet sense precedes an Epithet, as in example (1) above; but in some situations, as we will see, sequence alone will not show that a marked use is intended, so speakers use some other linguistic device (such as submodification): they 'mark' the use. We thus have a third sense of *marked* (corresponding to Croft's 'structural' sense of *unmarked* – Croft 1991: 57).

Two other points need introductory comment. As shown in chapter 3 (§3.6.2), zone membership can be determined from semantic structure (taking context into account if necessary to determine meaning), so it can be determined even when there is only one premodifier. Consequently, I will in this chapter often rely on semantic structure for determining zone membership, without demonstrating it from relation to other premodifiers. Second, as in chapter 2, the concept of order is taken broadly, as equivalent to zoning and position; so that marked order and marked position are equivalent, and can apply even to phrases with a single premodifier.

7.1.2   Cautions

I repeat two points made in the 'zones' chapter, §2.2.1.2, that are crucial to this chapter: premodifiers co-ordinated by commas or conjunctions (for example 'red[D], white[D] and blue[D] stripes') belong in the same zone; and conversely, premodifiers that are not co-ordinated belong in different zones – for example, 'trendy [E] new [D] cigarette [C] tins'. The rest of this chapter relies on those points. Not keeping them in mind would cause confusion.

It is possible for speakers and writers to make errors in punctuation, so apparent exceptions to the analysis may not be real ones. Where there is doubt, I use semantic structure and context as well as punctuation, to determine the speaker's intention.

Marked order can easily be confused with marked punctuation. Consider example (2):

(2)   'Virtually all the state's counties [i.e. North Dakota's counties] have been losing well educated young people to other states.

Only Iowa retains fewer of its <u>young home-grown college-edu-cated</u> residents.' (*Economist*, 7 May 2005, p. 33)

Since the modifiers are not co-ordinated, they should, when taken at face value, be read as belonging in different zones, as shown in table 7.2.

Table 7.2 *Possible zones for example (2)*

Epithet	Descriptor	Classifier	Head
? young	*home-grown*	*? college-educated*	*residents*

But the results are anomalous. *Young* cannot be an Epithet, and *college-educated* cannot be a Classifier; they must be interpreted as Descriptors, because of the semantic structure required in the context.[1] The explanation is that they have been written without coordination to signal to readers that the phrase must be taken restrictively: 'its [young [home-grown [college-educated residents]]]'. Inserting the commas normal for co-ordinated pre-modifiers ('its [young,] [home-grown,] [college-educated] [residents]') makes the phrase read descriptively (that is, nonrestrictively), implying that all residents in the state are young, all are home-grown, and all are college-educated. In fact, then, the order is not significant, and is not marked: the words have their normal senses, and are in a normal order (i.e. free order). Rather, the <u>punctuation</u> is marked (in the sense that it is the exceptional use, not the regular one); the punctuation is used to switch from descriptive syntactic structure – [...] [...] [...] – to restrictive structure – [... [... [...]]].

Example (3) illustrates the converse use of marked punctuation: it forces a descriptive reading on what would otherwise be a restrictive reading.

(3)   '... the results of syphilis, gonorrhoea, or other, minor sexually transmitted diseases' (British National Corpus)

That reads as '[other,] [minor] [sexually transmitted diseases]'; with normal punctuation, it would be 'other [minor [sexually transmitted diseases]]', implying that syphilis and gonorrhoea are minor diseases. These are two marked uses of punctuation, then, not marked premodifier order: the words retain their usual sense, and there is none of the salience that marking brings.

Care must be taken with combinations of words that have varied or uncommon senses. In examples (4), (5) and (6), *smooth* and *dark* are used as Epithet + Descriptor, Descriptor + Epithet, and Epithet + Epithet;

---

[1] *Young* is often an Epithet in other contexts, with a different sense, as illustrated in chapter 3, §3.3.3.4.

Table 7.3 *Varied zones for* smooth *and* dark, *in unmarked order*

Epithet	Descriptor	Class.	Head
smooth <6b> 'Soft or pleasing to the taste'	*dark* <3> 'Having... intensity of colour'.		*rum*
dark <5> 'Gloomy, dismal'),	*smooth* <10> 'Of... the sea etc.: not broken'):		*hollows*
smooth, dark smooth: <1> 'Presenting no roughness' dark: <3> 'Approaching black in hue'.	*lanceolate*		*area*

nevertheless they are all unmarked uses, because the senses are among the words' varied, established Epithet and Descriptor senses.

(4)   '... smooth [E] dark [D] rum' (British National Corpus)
(5)   '[The ship] pitched headlong into <u>dark</u> [E] <u>smooth</u> [D] hollows' (Joseph Conrad, *Nigger of the Narcissus*, p. 49)
(6)   'The ventral surface of the yolk-sac ... is visible as a <u>smooth</u>, [E] <u>dark</u>, [E] olive-greenish [E] lanceolate [D] area.' (British National Corpus)

Table 7.3 shows how the senses fit the Epithet and Descriptor zones.

7.2   Marked order used to change modification structure

The use of marked order to change modification structure is well shown in the experimental results of Oller and Sales (1969). Their subjects were shown squares that were small and coloured. The unmarked order for describing such a square is illustrated in 'small red square': *small* modifies 'red square' (i.e. 'small [red square]'), making a contrast with red squares of other sizes. However, when most of the squares on display were green and small, and only one of them was red and small, a majority of the subjects said 'red small square' (= 'red [small square]'); the modification structure is marked, the contrast being with small squares of other colours.[2] (Oller and Sales explained the change as *red* being moved forward into a position of prominence.)

The existence of such an order is asserted by several scholars: Dixon (1982: 24), Vendler (1968: 126, 130), Martin (1969b: 704, and 1970), Danks and Glucksberg (1971: 66), Bache (1978); but they do not show its markedness.

---

[2] It is noteworthy that many of the subjects were (according to Oller and Sales) inhibited from using that marked order by the strength of the unmarked order, 'small red square', which they felt to be required as the grammatical order.

Quirk *et al.* (1985: 1341) and Huddleston and Pullum (2002: 452) are closer to my view, acknowledging that the use constitutes an exception to a rule.

Although this use is so widely supported, it appears to be quite uncommon in normal usage, the examples given in the literature having been obtained in experiments (Oller and Sales 1969), or apparently invented (e.g. 'Swiss red chair' – Danks and Glucksberg 1971: 66). I deal with its frequency and acceptability in discussing other theories, in §10.4.3. The only example I have recorded comes from a short story in which the characters are awed into reverence by the sight of a 'one-hundred-dollar pure white vanilla ice-cream summer suit'; see example (7):

(7)   'We only see the <u>reflected pure white, holy</u> light of the suit. A church-organ chord rings out.' (Ray Bradbury, 'The wonderful ice-cream suit', cited in the Corpus of Contemporary American English)

In semantic structure, 'reflected' is a Descriptor, and 'pure white' and 'holy' are Epithets. Putting them in the usual order (as 'the pure white, holy reflected light of the suit') would suggest that the light was pure and holy only when reflected; Bradbury reversed the order to prevent that implication, evidently. I conclude that marked order can be used to change the modification structure, usually to highlight a contrast, but that the usage is rare – which is not surprising, given how abstruse the effect is, in example (7).

7.3   Marked order used to change meaning

7.3.1   *Introduction*

The most frequent function for marked order is changing the meaning of the word which is moved into marked position: the non-standard position requires the hearer to take a non-standard meaning from it, since it has no established meaning for that position. For example, when the word is moved forward into Epithet position, hearers will construct a new meaning of the Epithet type; that is, one that is abstract, or with richer connotations, or with attitudinal or emotive meaning (see chapter 3).

There must be some feature that prompts the hearer to reinterpret the word – something to mark the use. The examples so far have relied on position relative to other premodifiers; when there is only one premodifier, the speaker must mark the usage in some other way. The following sections discuss marked uses classified by the different methods of marking.

7.3.2   *Marked by position relative to other premodifiers*

Marked order for changing the meaning of the word most often involves changing the word to an Epithet. In example (8), *young* is used twice – in

Table 7.4 *Zones for 'young woman'*

Epithet	Descriptor	Classifier	Head
	young 'not yet old'		*woman*

Table 7.5 *Zones for example (8)*

Epithets			Descriptor	Class.	Head
young *impulsive* 'youthfully foolish' + [disapproval]		*over-curious*	*young* 'not yet old'		*woman*

its usual position as a Descriptor, and as an Epithet. The sentence describes a character in a novel, and is written from the point of view of another character.

(8)   'Here was a <u>young</u>, impulsive, over-curious <u>young</u> woman.' (P. D. James, cited in Adamson 2000: 58)

The second *young* has SOED's meaning <1>, 'Not yet old…'; it is shown in table 7.4.

The first *young* must have a meaning different from 'not yet old'. That is required pragmatically, since we presume a good novelist to be not repeating herself; but it is also required linguistically, because *young* is in Epithet position (since it precedes two Epithets), and is contextually linked to *impulsive* and *over-curious*. The nearest SOED meaning for *young* here is <2> '… having or showing the freshness or vigour of youth', which suggests approval. But in the phrase being considered the word is disapproving, through its link with the negative words *over-curious* and *impulsive*; so its meaning in this use is approximately 'youthfully foolish', as shown in table 7.5. The word *young* has a different sense primarily because of its position (as an Epithet); but the meaning relies partly on other words in the context. It is forceful, because of the markedness of the usage, and because of its prominent position.

Other examples follow, with less analysis. The words are marked as Epithets by position in front of Epithets.

(9)   [The Civil Unions Bill is] 'just <u>Labour Government</u> [E], vote-buying [E], we're-nice-to-gays [E] garbage'. (Deborah Coddington, reported in *New Zealand Herald*, 9 December 2004, p. A6)

Labour government is normally an emotionally neutral Classifier. It has become a sarcastic Epithet.

(10)   'A strange[E], <u>chemical</u>[E], putrid[E] smell' (Graeme Eades, reported in *New Zealand Herald*, 23 July 2005, p. A1)

Chemical is normally a factual Classifier, but here it is an expressive Epithet. The phrase was spoken spontaneously, and punctuated by the reporter, so that presumably intonation and pausing carried the marking which in print is carried by the commas; position marks the use also. (I have not attempted to document phonological marking formally. Another example of it – marked chiefly by stress – is 'I was going to make some <u>coffee</u> coffee', a spontaneous spoken apology for making instant coffee.)

Rarely, a word is given a marked use as a Reinforcer, as in example (11):

(11)   'There was worse than slackness: there was <u>black</u>[R] downright [R] treachery by men in the king's pay.' (Arthur Bryant, *Samuel Pepys: the Saviour of the Navy*, p. 211)

The Epithet use of *black* (<7> 'Foul.... atrocious') has been converted to Reinforcer use, equivalent to *utter*, augmenting another Reinforcer, but carrying some of its Epithet meaning and perhaps some Descriptor meaning of colour, by metaphor.

Occasionally, the marked use is as a Classifier, as in (12):

(12)   'He has a mean[E], unbroken[E] <u>sheer</u>[C] bastard in his outfit.' (From the Brown Corpus, cited by Fries 2000: 314)

Sheer, normally a Reinforcer, must be read as a Classifier, since it follows Epithets and since the only plausible interpretation (I believe) is that of the Type quale (§5.2.1), implying 'There are various types of bastard, and he was a member of the worst type!'

7.3.3   *Marked by coordination*

This section illustrates marking by coordination.

(13)   'These were celebrated[E], <u>American</u>[E] breasts, engineered by silicon to be as broad and bountiful as the prairie.' (*Economist*, 17 February 2007, p. 87; the phrase refers to Anna Nicole Smith.)

Without the co-ordinating comma, the phrase would read, 'celebrated[E] <u>American</u>[C] breasts'. Here, since *American* is co-ordinated with the Epithet *celebrated*, it must be read as an Epithet, taking favourable associations like those of *broad* and *bountiful*. It contrasts with example (14):

(14)   '....one of those bland[E], wishy-washy[E], <u>American</u>[E] kind of statements' (David Clark, public discussion in Auckland, 14 October 2005)

The same process has occurred, but the context produces negative associations – contrasting with those in the previous example. (The remark was spoken and spontaneous; the coordination was conveyed by pauses and intonation.)

A climber complained of:

(15)   'rotten[E], <u>Weetbix</u>[E] rock' (*New Zealand Alpine Journal*, 2005, p. 127)

Marked uses quite often use metaphor; in this example, *Weetbix*, which in literal use is a Classifier designating a notoriously fragile breakfast cereal in biscuit form, becomes a metaphorical Epithet use, expressing the climber's horror.

In (16), a determiner has become an Epithet. The sentence refers to a law that would reserve 33 per cent of parliamentary seats for women:

(16)   'This would be momentous, especially for India's <u>half a billion</u>, badly served women.' (*Economist*, 13 March 2010, p. 29)

Co-ordination, by the comma, with the emotive and evocative Epithet expression 'badly served' requires the reader to take 'half a billion' as Epithet instead of postdeterminer, evoking associations of vastness and feelings of concern.

7.3.4   Marked by being graded

As we saw in the 'semantic explanation' chapter (chapter 3), Classifiers and Descriptors cannot be graded, either by *-er/-est* or by intensifying sub-modifiers like *very, rather, fairly* and so on – only Epithets can be graded. For example, in 'Swedish <u>pornographic</u> films', *pornographic* designates a type of film, and is a Classifier and not gradable; but in 'extremely <u>porno-graphic</u> Swedish films', it is a disapproving and emotive Epithet, and grad-able. Position before *Swedish* signals to the hearer that *pornographic* is an Epithet, but so does *extremely*. The Epithet use is an established one, so is not a marked use; but grading a normally non-gradable word will constitute a marked use.

While the Reserve Bank of New Zealand was planning to abolish the five-cent coin and replace most of the country's other coins, a spokesman ended a radio interview with (17).

(17)   'Yes, it's <u>quite a</u> <u>logistical</u>[E] matter.' (Radio New Zealand, National Programme news, 11 November 2004)

Logistical is normally a Classifier (meaning 'concerned with the detailed organisation of a plan') and cannot be graded. The grading submodifying expression, *quite a*, marks it as an Epithet; the context showed that it was to mean approximately 'complex, difficult, and time-consuming'.

In example (18), the referential Classifier, *real time*, has become a praising Epithet:

(18)   'very, very real time[E] intelligence' (British National Corpus; attributed to Oliver North, testifying to the US Senate, as quoted in Ann Wroe, *Lives, Lies and the Iran-contra Affair*)

The grading can also be carried out by affixes (see §3.4.2.3), as in 'good[E], penetrating[E], X-rayish[E] phrases', cited in the last chapter, where the Classifier *X-ray* has become an Epithet, meaning 'brilliantly penetrating'.

7.3.5   *Marked by semantic clash*

A man out walking in London was said to be under:

(19)   'an Italian[E] sky' (Arthur Bryant, 1938, *Samuel Pepys: the Saviour of the Navy*, p. 67)

The clash between locations – England and Italy – forces the reader to reinterpret *Italian* as meaning approximately 'rich, deep blue'. (The literary and artistic associations of *Italian* affect the reading, too.) A Classifier is marked as an Epithet by the semantic clash between its usual meaning and the context. Other examples follow.

The praise that is integral to *superb* clashes with the bitter blame expressed by other words in (20).

(20)   '…for pure vacillating stupidity, for superb[R] incompetence to command…' (George MacDonald Fraser, *Flashman*, p. 98)

The Epithet *superb* is marked as an ironic Reinforcer, meaning 'utter'. In the description of Chinese-style dried pork as having 'an oriental[E] taste of New Zealand', the Descriptor *oriental* has become an Epithet, for its New Zealand readers, through its clash with the name of the country. In a climber's complaint that a certain peak has become 'the Darran Mountains' most consumer crag', the Classifier *consumer* has become an Epithet through its clash with *crag* (and through the superlative, *most*).

Marked position is common in poetry. Matthew Arnold ends a poem lamenting separation with the line given in (21).

(21)   'The unplumb'd[E], salt[E], estranging[E] sea.' ('To Marguerite')

All three premodifiers would normally be Descriptors. But *estranging* applies only to human behaviour, so clashes with inanimate *sea*; so it is read as an Epithet (by personification). Since *salt* and *unplumb'd* are co-ordinated with it, they become Epithets too; as such, they cannot be read as perceptual words ('containing salt' and 'not measured'); they are taken figuratively, also. All three words now signify estrangement, loss and grief – because *estranging* is marked by its semantic clash.

7.3.6   Discussion: marked order used for change of meaning

Metaphors rely for their effectiveness on the contrast between the literal and metaphorical meanings. Similarly, marked use relies on the contrast between the established meaning and the nonce meaning. For example, the effect of 'just <u>Labour Government</u>, vote-buying, we're-nice-to-gays garbage', in example (9), relies on the pungent contrast between the established referential meaning and the abusive meaning it is given here, with its implication that to be a Labour government is to be corrupt and hypocritical. Marked use is thus unlike outright neologism, which it otherwise resembles. Compare the expression of the concept YOUNG in 'a <u>young</u>, impulsive, over-curious young woman' and 'the hard and <u>unyoung</u> look her face assumed when she spoke of her stepmother'; both are neologistic in creating a new pairing of form and meaning, but the former has an imaginative vividness that the latter lacks.

We have seen *Italian* used to mean 'rich, deep blue', and *American* used to mean 'broad and bountiful' and to mean 'wishy-washy' – descriptive senses quite different from their established referential senses. *English* and *French* also have descriptive senses different from their referential ones, but those senses are established; for example, SOED gives *French* <2> 'Having... (a) refinement [or] (b) impropriety'. I suggest that whereas Bryant's marked use of *Italian*, seventy years ago, to mean 'rich, deep blue', has not been taken up into the language, we have the established descriptive senses of *French* and *English* because marked uses <u>were</u> taken up and conventionalised – and that the senses of *Byzantine* developed in the same way (see §3.1.4). I will argue later that marked use has been important historically in the development of new word senses (see §8.4.5 and §8.5.4).

7.4   Discussion of marked order

7.4.1   Borderline instances

Some uses of premodifiers seem close to the borderline between marked and established use, just as there were borderline instances noted in previous chapters. *Red* (in literal use for colour) is a Descriptor; but it is often used as an Epithet, retaining the literal meaning but adding elements of being bright, unusual or dangerous, and of expressive meaning, which shifts with context. I have found so many instances of that use, as in (22) to (25), that I believe it is now an accepted one, although it has not reached SOED.

(22)   'A large[E], <u>red</u>[E], hairy[E] monster' (British National Corpus)

(23)   'The red[E], curvaceous[E], 1950's[E] double-decker' [i.e. London bus] (*Economist*, 10 December 2005, p. 59)[3]

(24)   'His rather red[E], slightly over-full[E], countryish[E] cheeks' (Doris Lessing, *The Summer Before the Dark*, p. 186)

(25)   'A large[E], red[E] (i.e. risky) area' [on a map] (*Economist*, 21 May 2005, p. 77)

Similarly, *American* is now so often used with intensifiers such as *particularly*, *truly* and *peculiarly* (see the Corpus of Contemporary American English) that it is close to being established as an Epithet, and its use in examples (13) and (14) is close to being unmarked, accordingly.

There are many uses of words of size or quantity with a marked quality but without significant change of meaning. Consider examples (26) and (27):

(26)   [The Rio Grande flows] 'between pleasant sandy banks, complex rock formations, and 1,500-foot[E] sheer[D] rock[C] walls.' (Corpus of Contemporary American English)

(27)   'Police said Patterson stole the A$1 million[E] black[D] ex-British Army[C] tank from his former employer.' (*New Zealand Herald*, 17 July 2007, p. B2)

Such size words are normally Classifiers (see §5.2.1); and #'sheer[D] 1,500-foot[C] rock[C] walls' and #'the black[D] A$1 million[C] tank' seem normal. But the size words are in Epithet position here, with no evident change of meaning. They seem to have been put in marked position primarily to give the word prominence, but with the suggestion that the size specified is extreme, and that the word is therefore scalar, and consequently an Epithet.

7.4.2   Other discussion

There are interesting connections between the generation of new meanings in marked order and the discussion of lexical generativity in Pustejovsky (1995), Bouillon and Busa (2001), and related work – the study of means of ' "shifting" meaning in ways and across domains that are not random' (Bouillon and Busa 2001: xiv). There is also a connection with the literature on polysemy; see Ruhl (1989) and Cuyckens (2001), for example. The implication of this chapter is that words are more monosemous than has generally been thought: since placing a modifier in a new position produces a new sense within the range of polysemous senses, there is perhaps a mechanism that can produce most polysemous senses according to context and construction, without their being stored separately.

---

[3] *1950's* is also in marked use, here, since it is normally a Classifier.

The concept of a marked order in premodification has provided powerful explanation in this chapter, and will recur in the historical explanation in the next chapter. As far as I am aware, it is new in the literature on premodifiers.[4] Most explanations of premodifier order have not resolved the order fully, relying on qualifying expressions such as 'tendency' and 'preferred order', with inadequate explanation of what controls the tendencies and preferences. The account of marked order in this chapter, and of free order in the last chapter, explain the variations in premodifier order simply and tightly, without unexplained qualifications. That, I suggest, is an important advance on previous work.

7.5   Conclusion: marked order

In summary, the main point made has been that just as nominal phrases can have a marked stress pattern (e.g. 'a large **black** sofa', with primary stress on *black*), so can they have a marked order of premodifiers, in which words are used in a position for which they have no established sense. Although the marked use breaks the 'rule' (that position is set by the word's established sense), it is (again like marked stress) an established pattern in English. Its main function is nearly always to require hearers to construct a nonce meaning (using context and world knowledge, as well as one of the word's established senses) which is vivid or emphatic; and sometimes it changes the modification structure. The order can be marked in different ways: inherently, by the word sequence (e.g. 'red big' as against 'big red'); or syntactically, by coordination or submodification; or morphologically, by inflection; or phonologically, by stress or intonation.

Several conclusions follow from the previous sections. First, marked order generally makes the word more prominent by putting it in a zone further forward; that reinforces the general principle that the important word comes first, seen in unmarked order (in §3.6.1), and in much free order (in §6.3). Second, it serves the linguistic metafunctions discussed in previous chapters: to the extent that it controls prominence, it serves the textual function; and in being used for its special impact on the hearer, it serves the interpersonal function. Finally, since the new meaning is forced upon the word merely by use in a new zone (it is not acquired by gradual development), that meaning must be constructional. That suggests that <u>all</u> zones are constructions – not just the Classifier zone (chapter 5); we return to the issue in §10.2.

---

[4] Vandelanotte (2002: 246) notes the fact that 'swear words will often turn up in "marked", emphatic places rather than "expected" places'; but there is no recognition of change of meaning correlated with change of position. The concern is with scope, as in the syntactic discussion in chapter 4. Davies (2007) comes close to the issue in discussing *rich* in 'a canal barge dwelling white Rasta rich bitch', but misses the point that *rich* (normally an Epithet) is in marked use (as Type Classifier) making the sarcastic implication that there is a whole type of such people, not just an individual.

This chapter has explained the last of the three main phenomena noted in chapter 1: the acceptability and effect of flouting the rules for unmarked order. It leaves unexplained the fact that marked order is rather incongruous with unmarked order, in working on different principles and in being salient to the hearer – like the purposeful choice of free order discussed in the last chapter. A psycholinguistic explanation for that will be offered in §9.2. Some wider issues that have arisen here will be developed further in chapters 10 and 11. First, however, we turn to the historical explanation of all three pre-modifier orders, the exposition of substantive synchronic explanations being now complete.

8   Historical explanation
        of premodifier order

8.1   Introduction

This chapter sets out to explain premodifier order generally, and to explain specific features which have not been explained previously. It complements the previous chapters: they explained premodifier order synchronically; this chapter explains diachronically both the basic structure of zones (chapter 2) and the types of order (chapters 3 to 7).

Taking in turn the periods in the development of English (taken from Hogg 1992–1999), the chapter argues as follows. The unmarked order of premodifiers has evolved (from Old English times onward) gradually, and in stages. In Old English, the order was by part of speech: [adjective] [participle] [genitive noun] [head]. By late Middle English, the part-of-speech order had been reinterpreted as a syntactic one: premodifier [premodifier [premodifier [head]]]. By the sixteenth century, the order had its present structure, by the reanalysis of the syntactic pattern as embodying a semantic pattern: Epithet [Descriptor [Classifier [head]]]. Free order has always existed, but has changed in use. Marked order has evolved in the last century or so. The later changes depended on changes in what semantic structure was possible for premodifiers, and involved individual words changing in zone membership (as they developed new senses). That evolution helps explain general features of premodifier order that also have a synchronic explanation, and explains some specific features that have no good synchronic explanation at all.

The chapter gives 'snapshots' of the order at particular times and in the work of particular authors, which shows that the various features of one stage of development did occur together, and that they were available as a system to individual users of the language.

Although general explanation of the causes of change is outside the purpose of the chapter, I am arguing for certain elements of causation, so some explanation is needed here. I follow the 'invisible hand' explanation of Keller (1994). In competitive business, merchants set out to make money for themselves; but, through better goods and lower prices, everyone benefits – as a result of an 'invisible hand'. (See also Haspelmath 1999;

Table 8.1   *Order of premodifiers in Old English (as in Mitchell 1985)*

6th position *eall, sum, manig* 'all, some, many'	5th position (pronoun)	4th position (numeral)	3rd position *oþer* 'other'	2nd position (adjective or participle)	1st position (noun in genitive case)	Headword (noun)
	þære 'that/the'			*geættradan* 'poisoned'	*deofles* 'devil's/of the devil'	*lare* 'teaching'
		an 'an'	*oþer* 'other'	*healf* 'half'		*gear* 'year'
		ænne 'a/one'		*blacne* 'black'		*stedan* 'stallion'

Bybee, Perkins and Pagliuca 1994: 300). Functional value may cause changes to be retained, although it does not initiate them. I also assume the mechanisms of word change accepted in such historical linguistics literature as Croft (2000), Bybee and Hopper (2001) and Traugott and Dasher (2002) – mechanisms (or 'processes') such as metaphor, analogy and incorporation of contextual meaning. They are dealt with only briefly, near the end of the chapter (§8.7.3).

The account here is rather sketchy, and the conclusions rather tentative; more detail is given in Feist (2008) – sources, and discussion of apparent exceptions, for example.

8.2   Old English period

This section argues that in the period up to about 1066, premodifiers were ordered by part of speech, and shows the semantic and syntactic structures from which modern premodifier order evolved. The section does not deal with changes within the period, and generally excludes the poetry from consideration, since it differs greatly from the prose in both syntax and semantics (see Mitchell 1985; Strang 1970). I emphasise that we are dealing with premodifiers, since the authorities cited deal with 'adjectives', 'participles' and 'nouns', not 'premodifiers'.

8.2.1   Order of premodifiers in Old English

According to Mitchell (1985: §143), nominal phrases in prose followed 'basic rules' of order for 'qualifying elements' preceding the noun. Table 8.1 reproduces part of his table, taken from Carlton (1963: 780), with translations added.

Table 8.2 *Order of premodifiers in Old English (amended)*

4th position: determiners	3rd position: adjectives	2nd position: participles	1st position: nouns (genitive)	Headword
þæs 'that/the'		*acænnedan* 'begotten'	*godes* 'of god/god's'	*sunu* 'son'
	fule 'foul'	*forlegene* 'having committed fornication or adultery'		*horingas* 'adulterers'
	hwitum 'white'	*scinendum* 'shining'		*reafe* 'clothes'
þære 'that/the'	*mæran* 'great'	*behatenan* 'promised'		*sige* 'victory'
þa 'that/the'	*scenan* 'beautiful'	*scinendan* 'shining'		*ricu* 'kingdom'

Both Mitchell (1985: §173) and Carlton (1963: 779) accept that their findings may need revision. That is indeed so: the '2nd position' in the table (adjectives and participles) should be divided into two positions, since adjectives and participles occurred in the same phrase, with adjectives regularly preceding participles. Accordingly, the situation is more accurately represented in table 8.2, with adjectives and participles in separate positions. It condenses Carlton's 3rd to 6th positions into one (since they are all for determiners not premodifiers).

The rules for premodifier order in Old English nominal phrases thus appear to be as follows. (a) Adjectives precede participles; participles precede genitive nouns. (b) Two or more words of the same class may be co-ordinated with each other, by a conjunction such as *and* or *but*. An example of co-ordinated adjectives is 'swetum and wynsumum wyrtum', ('sweet and pleasant plants/herbs'), and an example of co-ordinated genitive nouns is 'Godes and mædenes bearn', ('God's and maiden's child'). (I have not found any co-ordinated participles as premodifiers.) (c) A word from one of the three premodifier classes may not be co-ordinated with a word from another class. (I have found none myself, and neither Mitchell nor Carlton seems to cite any.)

The order of premodifiers as set out in table 8.2 is clearly grammatical in the sense that it is an order of word class (or 'part of speech'). That was natural for a form of the language in which word-class morphology (derivational and inflectional) showed the relations among word, phrase and clause elements. But since that kind of order can be determined by an underlying syntactic or semantic order, as in Present-Day English (see chapter 3, especially §3.6.1, and chapter 4), we should consider whether that was so for Old English.

It is clear that the order was not based on semantic structure of the type discussed in chapter 3. Different kinds of meaning occur in the same position: adjectives were abstract or concrete (*mæran* 'great', and *hwit* 'white', in the table); they were descriptive or ordinal or emotive (*scenan* 'beautiful', *forman* 'first/former', *ful* 'foul'). The same kind of meaning occurs in different positions: size meaning occurs in determiners (*micel* 'big') and adjectives (*lytel* 'little'); expressive meaning of disapproval was expressed in genitive nouns (*deofles*, 'of-the-devil/devilish'), and in adjectives (*ful*, 'foul'). The underlying reason for the order not being semantic is that there was in Old English not enough differentiation in the semantic structure of premodifiers to support such an ordering. In descriptive meaning, premodifiers in Old English were generally like *good* in Present-Day English, in that their established meaning was broad; hearers inferred any more specific meaning from the context, or took it from world knowledge.[1] That accords with the syntax, since modifiers and headwords were not well differentiated (adjectives and nouns could both be modifiers or heads, and adjectives were denominal and sometimes effectively compound nouns e.g. *manlic* 'manly'); the attributive, predicative and appositive uses of modifiers could not always be distinguished (Mitchell 1985: §99); and adjectives were like numerals and demonstratives in being 'really pronouns' (Strang 1970: 300–1). It accords also with lexical relations: English had a very much smaller lexicon than now, and did not have regular sets of synonyms that could set up contrasts in expressive and social meaning (see chapter 3, §3.4), or minor elements of meaning. Specifically, then: referential meaning was not distinct from descriptive meaning; social meaning was not at all developed; and expressive meaning, although it existed for a few words, was contextual and not a part of the semantic system, as noted by Stein (1995: 131).

The order is not syntactic, either; that is, multiple premodifiers modified the head independently, not the rest of the phrase as in Present-Day English, e.g. 'the [finest and fastest [light [GT car]]]'. Consider the phrases in table 8.2, and example (1) in particular, (cited from Richard Morris, *Legends of the Holy Rood; Symbols of the Passion and Cross-Poems*, p. 5):

(1)   Þæs acænnedan godes sunu
         the [begotten] [God's] son

That cannot be read as 'the [begotten [god's son]]', because there is no other son of God to distinguish the begotten son from. Also, the phrase as a whole denotes the referent in modern English; but in Old English, all elements of the nominal phrase were referential to some extent – demonstratives, modifiers and head (Mitchell 1985).[2] Moreover, syntax was in general not signalled by order, but by morphology (although that was changing).

---

[1] The role and importance of world knowledge in words' significance has been shown in chapter 3, and will become clearer in §9.4 ('Language acquisition').

[2] They were thus somewhat like nominal expressions in the languages discussed by Rijkhoff (2002: §1.5.4.1) which have nominals in parallel, rather than nominal phrases.

Table 8.3 *Old English antecedents of modern zones*

OE structure:	Determiner	Adjective	Participle	Noun	Head
Examples:	*the*	*great*	*promised*		*victory*
	the	*beautiful*	*shining*		*kingdom*
	a	*pleasant*		*wine*	*smell*
Modern structure:	Determiner	Epithet	Descriptor	Classifier	Head

8.2.2   *Discussion and conclusion: the Old English period*

There are many expressions in which a genitive noun precedes an adjective; as in example (2) (cited from Mitchell 1985: §56).

(2)   N̲o̲e̲s̲ eltstan sunu
           Noah's oldest son

Phrases such as that come from the end of the Old English period, when the order set out in table 8.1 and table 8.2 was giving way to the modern structure in which genitives were either determiners ('Noah's') or postposed phrases ('of Noah'). Since the genitive noun is functioning as a determiner, such phrases are not exceptions to the rule for premodifier order given above.

Table 8.3 suggests that the Old English positions were antecedents for the modern zones – which the rest of this chapter will demonstrate – since the words fit both the Old English positions (shown in the top line) and the modern English zones (in the bottom line). The table reformats phrases from table 8.2, and adds a genitive noun premodifier (from Mitchell 1985: §1288).

The conclusion must be that in Old English, the order of premodifiers in nominal phrases was determined by the modifiers' part of speech: adjectives preceded participles, which preceded genitive nouns.[3]

8.3   Middle English period

8.3.1   *Introduction*

In the transition to Middle English (about 1066 to about 1476), there were several general changes important for premodifiers and their order. In the period 1170 to 1370, definite and indefinite articles, which are not

---

[3] I have not tried to explain why adjectives preceded participles, not vice versa, and so on, because that is not needed for the argument, and I am not sure why they did. I suggest, however, that the explanation goes like this. The demonstratives and other premodifying elements were all partly referential and (approximately speaking) nominals, and their relationships resembled case relationships between nominals, as set out by Jacobson

referential, became fully established (as determiners, that is), distinct from demonstratives, which are referential (Strang 1970: 271). Most genitives came to be either inflected determiners (e.g. 'John's book'), or uninflected postposed *of-* phrases, although some remained as uninflected premodifiers (including both words that took no -*s* inflection in Old English, e.g. 'mother tongue', 'precious heart blood', and others).[4] The articles, adjectives and premodifying nouns lost their grammatical inflections, adjectives becoming more distinct from nouns. Speakers had much less freedom to place adjectives, participles and genitive nouns after the head.

The overall structure of nominal phrases had thus changed radically: they had been a series of semi-independent words, each being at least partly referential; now they were unified and tightly structured, with all words before the head clearly dependent on it. Syntactically, the structure must be represented as: determiners [modifiers [head]]. ('Determiners' includes articles and demonstratives, and 'modifiers' includes adjectives, participles and uninflected nouns.) Semantically, the structure is as follows: (a) determining words, serving to specify or determine an entity; (b) words serving to describe the entity, being abstract or perceptual in varying degrees (modifiers); (c) a referential word (head).

The last general change to be mentioned is that there was a great influx of new words (borrowed and derived), affecting lexical relations and semantics.

The section will argue that by the end of the fourteenth century, individual premodifiers commonly modified the following part of the phrase – modifier [modifier head] – just as determiners did, as noted just above. Premodifiers had by then developed most of their modern semantic features, but the order was nevertheless controlled by the syntax. The argument will be made directly from usage, since there seems to have been no discussion of premodifier order in the standard works on Middle English such as Mossé (1952) and Mustanoja (1960), or elsewhere.

8.3.2 Syntax in Middle English

The main syntactic change was in scope of modification. As noted in §8.2, Old English premodifiers modified the headword directly – as in 'the [holy]

(1936/1990). They were ordered by the closeness of their semantic relation to the head nominal: genitives, e.g. 'England's king', were placed closest to the head, being most closely related; adjectives, e.g. 'English king', were more distantly related; demonstratives, being empty of content, were furthest from the head; participles, being like both adjectives and nouns, were intermediate between adjectives and genitives. (The relations of these semi-nominals resembled those of the nominals in the modern Classifier zone.) The discussion in §10.2.4, gives some background.

4 This survival of genitives as uninflected noun premodifiers in Middle English and on into Present-Day English seems to be omitted from recent discussion of the history of the genitive in English, from Altenberg (1980) to Rosenbach (2006), although it is recorded by more general works, such as Curme (1931: 70 ff.). It deserves investigation, I believe.

[Christ's] [cross]'. (Modern spelling is used here for Middle English words and phrases, and for Old English phrases cited for comparison.) In Middle English, premodifiers came to commonly modify the group consisting of any following premodifiers and the headword. Feist (2008) shows that in Wyclyf's work (written from about 1360 to 1384) the majority of nominal phrases with more than one premodifier are clearly structured that way, as in 'little [poor priests]', where *poor* is restrictive, setting up a contrast with well-off priests. Moreover, premodifiers alternate in position, according to the syntax, as in 'thy <u>poor</u> [wretched priests]' and 'little [<u>poor</u> priests]'. 'The [holy] [Christ's] [cross]' became ungrammatical; it would have been written as 'Christ's [holy cross]' or 'the [holy [cross of Christ]]'. It seems likely that the new structure developed as part of the overall development of nominal phrases discussed in §8.3.1.

That subordinating structure was not universal. Examples are 'these [[uncunning] [worldly] priests]' and '[open] [cursed] traitors' (Feist 2008: ch. 9, §3.2), whose contexts show them to have two descriptive modifiers and no restrictive sense in the order. The lack of commas suggests to modern readers that the first modifier is subordinated, but it seems clear that the punctuation of English has changed, along with its syntax. It is instructive that Ross (1940), an anthology of Middle English sermons with the texts edited for punctuation, has commas in 'rich, hard men' and 'a false, feigned love' (for example), making it clear that the modifiers are co-ordinated; and by contrast it has no commas in 'this false worldly friendship', making subordination clear.

Two of the forms of wide scope noted in chapter 4 had developed by late Middle English. Premodifiers occasionally related semantically to some entity other than the head (§4.5), as in Mary Magdalen's '<u>meek</u> sitting'; and modal premodification occurred (§4.4), as in Mandeville's '<u>very</u> diamond' and Wyclyf's '<u>open</u> wicked deeds', meaning 'deeds that are obviously wicked' (Feist 2008: ch. 9, §3.2).

8.3.3   Semantics in Middle English

During the Middle English period, there were gradual changes in semantics on which the development of modern premodification depended. Referential meaning became fairly distinct from descriptive meaning; that is, some premodifiers denoted a type or subtype of entity, while others gave descriptive information. That parallels the distinction between determiners and demonstratives, and is shown in several other ways: the frequent use of nouns as modifiers, expressing minimal descriptive meaning but denoting a subclass – 'kitchen clerks', 'altar stones', 'church yards', for example; the similar restrictive use of participles and adjectives – *fried* and *roasted* to designate types of meat or fish, and *contemplative*, in 'feigned <u>contemplative</u> life' ('monastic life') contrasted with '<u>active</u> life' ('in a parish'); and the distinction between modifiers and elements of a compound, as distinct roles for the same word-form – *seaboard* and *riverside* were compounds, but '<u>sea</u> fish' and '<u>river</u> fish' were phrases, used contrastively.

Descriptive meaning of premodifiers became much more precise, in such ways as the resolution of one vague word meaning into several more precise ones. For example, in Old English, *worldly* ('woruldlic') had a vague meaning that shifted contextually, but Wyclyf uses it in three distinct senses: 'physical' (versus 'mental or inward'), 'secular' and 'over concerned with physical or secular things' (Feist 2008: ch. 9, §3.3).

Other types of meaning developed also. Some word uses were purely expressive, having lost their original descriptive meaning, for example *rotten*, *cursed* and *stinking*; and expressive meaning is sometimes clearly one element of meaning, along with conceptual meaning, as in Wyclyf's use of *worldly* in the sense 'over-concerned with physical or secular things'. With the slow development towards a standard form of the language, users became more sensitive to dialectal and technical use, as words spread from one variety to others (Burnley 1992); and there were social restrictions – in the fifteenth century, members of the Mercers' Company were fined several pounds for calling people *carl* or *harlot* (Burnley 1992: 458). Grammatical meaning developed a great deal: in Old English nominal phrases, only demonstratives and adverbial submodifiers such as *swithe* were predominantly grammatical, but in Middle English, several premodifiers gained use as intensifiers – *perfect, pure, utter, horrible, extreme* (see OED) – Reinforcers, in effect.

Various types of meaning were being used in premodifiers, then, but normally separate types of meaning needed separate words. For example, in '<u>little poor</u> priests' and 'such <u>wretched worldly</u> life', the first premodifier was expressive and the second descriptive (Feist 2008: ch. 9, §3.3) The distinction between expressive and descriptive uses of words like *little* and *poor* was largely contextual, as was the precise feeling and attitude being expressed. The semantic structure of individual words was substantially different from that of today.

8.3.4   *The nature of premodifier order in Middle English*

To some extent at least, Middle English premodifiers seem to follow the Old English structure (adjective + participle + genitive noun), as seen in the examples from Wyclyf in table 8.4.[5]

Since the previous sections show that there was significant syntactic structure and apparently some semantic structure, this section evaluates which of those three structures controlled the unmarked order in Middle English.

---

[5] I have found no phrases with premodifiers in all three positions.

Table 8.4 *Apparent order by part of speech, in Middle English*

Adjective	Participle	Genitive noun	Head
new	*feigned*		*religious* (n.)
precious		*heart*	*blood*

Table 8.5 *Apparent order by semantics in Middle English*

Reinforcer type	Epithet type	Descriptor type	Classifier type	Head
very, perfect	*gentle*			*knight*
	great	*fat*		*horses*
	silly	*little*		*clout*
	precious		*heart*	*blood*

Middle English often breaks the old part-of-speech rules: participles sometimes precede adjectives; modifiers of the same part of speech are often not co-ordinated; and different parts of speech <u>are</u> co-ordinated (Feist 2008: ch. 9, §3.4). So the order was not controlled by part of speech.

We saw, in the syntax section (§8.3.2), that late Middle English had two syntactic structures. In one structure, premodifiers modified the rest of the phrase, restrictively (as in 'feigned [contemplative life]'); the order was set, syntactically. In the other structure, the two modifiers were semantically co-ordinated, and modified the head separately and nonrestrictively; the order of the premodifiers is not set syntactically.[6] That constitutes a simple and consistent system, in which the premodifiers may be restrictive (with subordinated premodifiers in subordinating order), and may be nonrestrictive (with co-ordinated premodifiers in no syntactically set order).

There is some evidence suggesting that Middle English had semantic zones, much as in Present-Day English: table 8.5 shows that when words of different types occurred together, they often occurred in the modern semantic order – grammatical words first, followed by abstract or emotive words, followed by more concrete and descriptive words, and referential words.

However, that pattern is not standard. The Reinforcer type is not often combined with others; nor is the Classifier type. When Epithet and Descriptor types occur together, the order is just as often reversed, as in

---

[6] The distinction between co-ordinated and subordinated modifiers was not fully developed, however. As noted in §8.3.2, commas were not regularly used for this purpose; and co-ordinated words were not always marked with conjunctions. It is my impression that writers used conjunctions when they felt the words to be synonymous – as in '<u>stinking</u> and <u>abominable</u> blasts' – but not otherwise – as in 'thy [[poor] [wretched] priests]'.

'feigned rotten habit'; nor do particular words such as *new* and *poor* change sense as they change position (Feist 2008: ch. 9, §3.4). Moreover, where the order is reversed, it conforms to the syntactic principle, not a semantic one. For example, in 'new [i.e. 'modern'] sinful caitifs', *new* would by semantic order follow *sinful*, being less abstract and less emotive, just as it comes second in 'false <u>new</u> pharisees'; but it precedes *sinful*, because the phrase is distinguishing the 'new' sinful caitifs from the old ones (the heathen philosophers): 'new [sinful caitifs]'.

The conclusions are, first, that where the order of premodifiers was set, it was set by syntax – the syntax of restrictive modification. There are many phrases with premodifiers in part-of-speech order, as in Old English, since there was no general shifting of word classes (apart from possessive genitives); but the part-of-speech order had been reanalysed as a syntactic one. That presumably occurred in stages: first, the parts of speech were treated restrictively – adjective [participle [genitive-noun head]]; and second, the parts of speech became moveable and equivalent (because all were simply modifiers) – modifier [modifier [modifier head]]. Second, since the syntactic order was not regularly matched by a semantic order, we conclude that premodification zones did not yet exist.

8.3.5   *Discussion: the Middle English period*

The development of restrictive syntactic order had important consequences. When one premodifier identified the referent fully, another would necessarily be intended and interpreted as giving extra descriptive information, and that pattern became common. For example, 'these proud [worldly clerks]' identifies the referents as worldly clerks, and makes the extra comment that they were proud. Since the first premodifier is descriptive not restrictive, it could readily acquire wider meaning from context – becoming expressive, for example, especially in phrases like 'poor [needy men]]' and 'little [poor woman]]'. Indeed, it was in this period that *poor* came to mean 'unfortunate'; that *little* came to mean 'trivial', and to be used 'to convey emotional overtones' (SOED); that *cursed* came to mean 'damned, confounded'; and that *new* came to mean 'strange'. Those are distinctively Epithet senses; those changes presumably contributed to the development of expressive and social meaning, and of the Epithet zone.

Further, having a commenting word distinct from the identifying words begins the pattern of topical words and commenting words to be discussed in chapter 9 (§9.3), as information structure. That was aided by the alternation between a preposed word and the corresponding postposed prepositional phrase: Wyclyf has 'ordinal of Salisbury' becoming 'Salisbury use' ['use' = 'ordinal'] a few lines later; 'office of priests' becomes 'priests' office'; 'traitors of God' becomes 'God's traitors' (Feist 2008: ch. 9, §3.5). In each case, Wyclyf uses the postposed phrase when the entity is introduced – New information – and the preposed word when the information is Given. Modifier position was already being used for information structure in Middle English.

The use of Classifier-like premodifiers, noted in Old English, expanded in Middle English. Some uses fitted the Old English genitive pattern, as in 'parish church' (cf. 'parish's church'), assimilating the old masculine and neuter -s forms to the old feminine form which had no -s (as in 'mother tongue'). Some that appear to derive from a genitive noun in fact assimilate a former adjective to the expanding use of nouns, for example 'silver vessel'. Some were conversions from postmodifying phrases, as in 'Salisbury use'. Some broke up former compounds – 'shell fish'; the variation of nominal morphemes between uninflected first element of compounds ('ironbands', 'goldcrown') and genitive noun premodifiers ('of-iron nails', 'of-gold ring') was systematised as uninflected noun premodifiers. (Note that the Old English compounds cannot have been 'lexical units': poetry relied on semantic modification within compounds like 'whaleroad'.) Other uses again appear to have none of those antecedents – 'cathedral church', 'barnacle geese'. Uninflected noun modifiers were presumably much more natural now that adjectives were no longer inflected.

8.3.6   Conclusion: the Middle English period

The development of premodification in the period may be summarised as follows. By the end of the fourteenth century, Reinforcers, Epithets, Descriptors and Classifiers had developed as semantic types, except that Epithets and Descriptors formed a range, without a clear borderline, and social meaning had not yet developed fully. In syntax, premodifiers had come to commonly modify the group consisting of any following modifiers and the head, while sometimes two premodifiers modified the head independently. Where the order was set, it was set by syntax. Since syntax regularly prevailed over semantics, the modern zones were not established; but nearly all of the elements for them were present. The semantic and syntactic principles were a reanalysis of the Old English order.

The fact that the Old English part-of-speech order was not destroyed, but reanalysed, provides the explanation (promised in chapter 3, §3.7.2) for why Present-Day English so often has that part-of-speech order, within the semantic structure: it has survived the intervening thousand years. The facts that premodifier order was syntactic in Middle English and that the semantic order is a later modification imposed on the syntax provide the explanation, promised in chapter 3 (§3.7.2), of why the present-day semantic order is not wholly simple and clear-cut – having descriptive meaning spread over two zones, and having several types of meaning in the Epithet zone: the order did not originally develop as a semantic one.

8.4   Early Modern English period

8.4.1   Introduction

This section covers the years from 1476 to 1776; but it concentrates on the early part of the period, since premodifier structure was already modern then. It argues that by the mid sixteenth century, there were both a syntactic order and a matching order of semantic structure; therefore the modern zonal order of premodification was established.

There are two general changes in the language that concern us, in the transition from Middle English. A standard form of the language developed by about the late fifteenth century, according to Görlach (1999) and Nevalainen (1999). Some dialectal words, for example, were accepted as standard (Görlach 1999), while others came to be regarded as variants within the standard form, rather than as belonging to a different form of the language. The acceptance of a standard made possible the development of distinct social meanings, and therefore of the full Epithet semantic structure. The second important change was the great increase in borrowing from other languages, continuing right through to 1660 – at a rate of up to 6,000 words per twenty years (Nevalainen 1999: 339). That expansion of the vocabulary was very important in the development of lexical relations, and thence of semantic structure.

8.4.2   Syntax in Early Modern English

In Early Modern English, the non-canonical scope of modification set out in chapter 4 developed fairly fully. Premodifiers began to interact semantically, as with 'the very Roman eloquence' (which could be paraphrased as 'the truly Roman eloquence') and 'good thick quilt of cotton' (i.e. 'good because thick'); and premodifiers came to modify other participants in the discourse situation freely – in priests' 'wood [reckless] and raging contention', recklessness applies to the priests, rather than to abstract contention (Feist 2008: ch. 9, §4.2).

As the period began, writers almost never used more than two premodifiers in one phrase. The use of several premodifiers at once is, however, a necessary condition for the development of premodification zones: there can hardly be four clearly distinct zones when there are only two premodifiers. In the Early Modern English period, writers cast off this restraint enthusiastically: 'How many decrepit, hoary, harsh, writhen, bursten-bellied, crooked, toothless, bald, blear-eyed, impotent, rotten old men shall you see flickering still in every place?' (Burton, as cited in Adamson 1999: 556). Such long phrases facilitated, and almost required, zoning.

We saw that in Wyclyf, premodifiers are commonly ambiguous between being co-ordinated and being subordinated: there is no reliable marking of it (by conjunctions or commas). But in Early Modern English, it <u>is</u> marked. With the Renaissance came precision in punctuation, along with new punctuation marks such as semicolons and hyphens (Salmon 1999). In Burton's twelve premodifiers (cited just above), there are commas co-ordinating the first eleven, but no comma before the last (*old*), indicating that it is to be read as being in a separate zone, with the others subordinate to it but co-ordinate with each other.

Since phrases often had many premodifiers, which were clearly co-ordinated or subordinated, and which used varying scope, the syntax of premodification in this period is modern.

8.4.3   Semantics in Early Modern English

SOED shows that the use of Reinforcers flourished. *Open*, *very* and *perfect* continued in use, and *utter*, *mere*, *sheer*, *perfect* gained a Reinforcer use.

Epithets and Descriptors became fairly distinct from each other, in several ways. First, expressive and social meaning both developed fully. In Middle English, words which could have expressive meaning rarely combined expressive and descriptive meaning in a single use, and the hearer or reader inferred the meaning type from context. In Early Modern English, many words came to combine the meaning types clearly (Feist 2008: ch. 9 §4.3). Example (3) illustrates the point well.

(3)   'But now good readers, I have unto these <u>delicate</u> and <u>dainty</u> folk
           that can away with ['get along with'] no long reading, provided
           with mine own pain and labour, as much ease as … [I can].'
           (Thomas More, as cited in Raumolin-Brunberg 1991: 195)

Delicate and *dainty* are to be taken ironically as disapproving words to mock certain readers, but for that to happen, the reader must be aware that they are normally favourable; thus expressive meaning is treated as an established dimension of the words' full meaning, along with descriptive meaning.

Social meaning developed largely because of the development of standard English: learned, dialectal and informal meaning rely on a standard, for contrast. See Nevalainen (1999: 343–4) for the large number of specialist borrowings and the range of colloquial synonyms, at the beginning of the seventeenth century. More wrote 'fruitful ghostly food', where *ghostly* was an archaic and rather literary synonym for *spiritual*; and 'your <u>accustomed benignity</u>', a formal variant on 'your <u>usual kindness</u>'. In Middle English, *big* had half a dozen synonyms (*great*, *giant*, etc.). In this period it acquired more, from the avid borrowing: *monstrous, enormous, vasty, Cyclopean, elephantine, prodigious, gigantic, Brobdingnagian, colossal, whopping* (and others). They were distinguished partly by their expressive meaning – dislike, awe, admiration, and so on – and partly by their social meaning – e.g. learned *Cyclopean*, colloquial *whopping* and *whacking*.

A further element of the clearer distinction between Epithets and Descriptors is that some Descriptors had become simpler and more perceptual, as with some of the colour words, which (in literal use) are typical Descriptors in Present-Day English. *White* lost its use to describe silver, and its senses 'light or pale in colour' and 'colourless' became limited to technical use – as Classifier senses. The remaining senses became more sharply either perceptual Descriptor senses, or figurative Epithet senses.

Classifiers strengthened as a semantic type. Conversion of postposed modifying phrases to noun premodifiers helped establish them as referential uses without descriptive content, as when John Colet's 'other business of the school' became 'school business' later in the sentence:[7] they lost syntactic salience and semantic content. See Sørensen (1980) for detail, and Altenberg (1980) for parallel changes of genitives from postmodification to determiner position. Classifiers were now sometimes used two at a time, with subclassifying effect, as in (4):

(4)   (a) 'diaper table cloths'; (b) 'halfpenny wheat loaf', 'penny wheat loaf' and 'penny white loaf'. (Manuscript of 1505; cited from Frederick J. Furnivall *Early Middle English Meals and Manners*, pp. 362–3. *Diaper* designates a type of fabric.)

Increased technical writing and the borrowing of learned terms helped establish their classifying function further. For example, Burton used them frequently in *Anatomy of Melancholy* (1621), classifying the causes of melancholy as either 'general' or 'particular'; the general causes are either 'natural' or 'supernatural'; and so on; diseases are 'acute' or 'chronic', and 'first' or 'secondary'. Those examples also illustrate the increasing use of adjectives as Classifiers.

The distinction between Classifiers on the one hand and Descriptors and Epithets on the other is complete when the same word is used, not only in different meanings but in different positions. When Mandeville wrote (in the Middle English period) 'great long leaves' (describing the wonderful banana palm), and Mallory wrote 'great black horse' (in the early sixteenth century), both used *great* descriptively, and in first position. But when Fuller wrote example (5) in the mid seventeenth century, the order is different.

(5)   '… like a Spanish great galleon and an English man-of-war'. (Trapp *et al.*, p. 1530)

Here, *great* is primarily referential (designating a type of galleon),[8] comes second, and moreover follows another Classifier, *Spanish*. Similarly, *white* in

---

[7] Cited from J. H. Lupton 1887, *A Life of John Colet*. New York: Burt Franklin Reprints, p. 280.
[8] *Great* had other such uses, such as *great hundred* 'one hundred and twenty', *great raisins/ raisins* 'raisins' / 'currants' (Kurath 1963, on *great*).

example (4) is a classifying word following another Classifier: 'penny white loaf', and 'halfpenny white loaf'.

We have seen, then, that Epithets, Descriptors and Classifiers became distinct semantic types in this period; Reinforcers had become distinct in Middle English. Epithets do not seem to have been distinguished from Descriptors by gradability, as now, but the next section shows that the distinction on which gradability is built was observed – that between factual, concrete words arising from perception, and abstract words arising from judgement.

8.4.4   Zones, as syntactic-semantic structures, in Early Modern English

We have seen that syntax and semantics were almost completely modern by the mid sixteenth century. It remains to be shown that position and semantic structure were correlative, as now.

Table 8.6 (from Feist 2008: §4.4) shows that premodifiers expressing judgement (including emotive and abstract ones) regularly precede perceptual and factual ones, and that referential ones come last – in the modern sequence. Group 1 phrases, identified in the left-hand column, have both premodifiers used restrictively, so it is possible to see them as simply following the old syntactic principle that each premodifier restricts what follows: for example, 'good [Latin authors]]'. Group 2 have a descriptive premodifier followed by a restrictive one; since they are not bound by the syntactic principle, and are in semantic order, they are more telling examples. Group 3 are completely descriptive; there can be no restrictive order, but they are all in semantic order. The last example is the most telling ('Spanish great galleon'), since the other order would change the meaning: in 'great Spanish galleon' great denotes size, not type.

The order is evidently set by the semantic structure.[9] For the structure to be completely modern, phrases with co-ordinated premodifiers should have them co-ordinated with a comma if not a conjunction, but that was not always so; punctuation seems to have been still not fully codified.

We may conclude that the positions did function as zones, and that the modern structure of (unmarked) premodifier order was complete, in its essentials, in Early Modern English. Just as the Old English part-of-speech order persisted into Middle English but was reanalysed as a syntactic order, so that syntactic order continued into Early Modern English, but was reanalysed as embodying a parallel semantic order.

8.4.5   Conclusion: the Early Modern English period

In summary: the semantics and syntax of nominal phrases in unmarked order were now modern in most ways; the semantic order had become established, and it was correlated with the syntactic order. The Present-Day English zone structure was therefore established.

---

[9] Raumolin-Brunberg (1991: 212) notes emotive and evaluative meaning as influencing modifier order in this period.

Table 8.6 *Zone structure in Early Modern English*

Group	Reinforcer	Epithet	Descriptor	Classifier	Head
1		*good* [abstract]		*Latin* [referential]	*authors*
		very ['true'] [abstract] [expressive]		*Roman* [referential]	*eloquence*
2			*old* [factual]	*Latin* [referential]	*speech*
		fruitful [abstract]		*ghostly* [referential]	*food*
		good [abstract]	*lettered and learned* [factual]		*men*
		little [judgement]	*mid* [factual]		*chamber*
		old [judgement]	*burned* [factual]		*chamber*
		great [judgement]		*banqueting* [referential]	*dishes*
3		*little* [judgement]	*white* [perceptual]		*hands*
		malicious [abstract] [expressive]	*revenging* [concrete] [neutral]		*devils*
	very, perfect [grammatical]	*gentle* [abstract] [expressive]			*knight*
4				*Spanish great* [both referential]	*galleon*

Note: 'very, perfect... knight' in its context paralleled the modern #'complete, utter ... gentleman'.

The history of this period provides the explanation for several points not explicable synchronically. Just as the history of Middle English explained why nominal phrases so often have a part-of-speech pattern (adjective + participle + noun), the history of this period provides the explanation (promised in chapter 3, §3.7.2) for why the exceptions occur: the newly formed semantic structure created the exceptions. Taking an adjective or participle as referential (denoting a type) moves it to the 'noun' position as a Classifier (as in Burton's 'acute diseases' and 'chronic diseases', and 'falling sickness'). Reconstruing a participle as conceptual moves it to the 'adjective' position, as an Epithet (as in Burton's 'most unparalleled and consummate industry').

We have seen that expressive and social meaning emerged as a systematic part of word meaning only in the Early Modern English period, and piecemeal, as contextual meanings were integrated with the existing descriptive meaning, word by particular word. That precedence of descriptive meaning partly explains, I suggest, why it so often occurs without the other types, as noted in §3.4.

We see also the explanation for words' being close to the borderline between zones, remarked on many times in previous chapters: it is historical. From the assumption generally made, that word use changes gradually, it follows that some speakers began to say 'a Spanish <u>great</u> galleon', while others were still saying 'a <u>great</u> Spanish galleon' for the same meaning; so for some time 'a <u>great</u> galleon' must have been ambivalent when it had no word that shows the zoning, as *Spanish* does when present. That parallels other apparently anomalous features, such as titles ('<u>Mr</u> Smith') and expressions like '<u>Secretary</u> Smith', which historically clearly had nouns in apposition but now have premodifiers. Proper names such as 'Joe Smith' appear to have changed the other way, from premodified phrases to compounds, by lexicalisation.

Finally, we consider the feature that seems to most need explanation: the existence of parallel semantic and syntactic explanations of premodifier order in a quite complex relationship (see §4.9.2). That explanation also is historical. The syntactic system evolved first, in Middle English, and was simple and consistent. Its provision that the earlier modifier modified the rest of the phrase syntactically came gradually to be equated with the earlier modifier modifying the rest semantically, since abstract and expressive meanings (in Epithets) modify concrete meaning (in Descriptors) naturally, and concrete descriptive meaning modifies referential meaning (in Classifiers) naturally. (See §4.9.2.) Premodifiers' common element (modifying the rest of the phrase) kept syntax and semantics working harmoniously in most circumstances. But with modal premodifiers (§4.4.2), the old preeminence of syntax survived; and in other circumstances – marked order, most clearly – semantics has come to dominate. (§9.2 will give psycholinguistic support for that explanation.)

8.5   Later Modern English period

8.5.1   *Introduction*

This section traces the development, from about 1776 onward, of some features of the Classifier and Epithet zones that were not yet fully formed in Early Modern English.

Throughout this period, society was becoming more egalitarian, democratic, and libertarian; education became universal; and more speakers became familiar with written English. Those changes facilitated linguistic changes already underway: standardisation, nominalisation (dating from Old English – Strang 1970: 330), new varieties of English (notably advertising and technical varieties), increased freedom in use of the varieties, in word-formation, and in use of syntax.

8.5.2 Classifier zone in Later Modern English

This section shows how the two commonest Classifier constructions (chapter 5) have evolved, and how Classifiers' semantic structure has changed.

Until the nineteenth century, Classifiers were used singly, with a few exceptions (§8.4.3), and were therefore constructionless (§5.7). Difference in semantic relation to the head, as with '<u>sea</u> fish' and '<u>sea</u> shore', was resolved contextually. However, some relations were so familiar as to be readily conventionalised: the relation in Old English '<u>Scottish</u> folk', for example, became the Origin quale; the relation in Old English '<u>silver</u> vessel' became the Constituency quale; Middle English '<u>parish</u> church' represents the Type quale, and so on. It became natural for readers to take the contextual meaning as a constructional meaning when two Classifiers were used together in a recognisable set order.

That began with the Participant-head construction, which seems to have become conventionalised in the early nineteenth century, although similar uses had occasionally occurred earlier, as in some examples in §8.4.3, one of which is repeated as example (6).

(6)   '<u>diaper table</u> cloths'

In a modern reading, that has Constituency (*diaper*, a fabric) and Type (*table*) qualia. I presume that to its users it represented a common-sense classification (those cloths were a subtype of table cloth), related to frequency ('table cloth' occurred frequently, 'diaper … cloths' did not); and I presume further that the qualia understanding emerged slowly from the common-sense one. These Classifiers presumably continued to come from the sources given in §§8.3.5 and 8.4.3; Sørensen (1980) shows writers converting postmodifying phrases to one-word premodifiers when new information becomes given, especially from the eighteenth century onward.

Table 8.7, from Feist (2008: ch. 9, §5.2), illustrates the first stage, the conventionalisation of the Origin position, in which an Origin word was used with no more than one other Classifier, of indeterminate relation to the head (inferred in context). The top line shows the structure at that stage, while the bottom line shows the corresponding modern structure. The examples are all from *Nature*, volume 1 (November 1859). Here, and in the next stage, the occurrence of many examples of a quale in a single publication is good evidence that the quale was then established.

By the 1930s, the positions for Dimension and Constituency qualia were also established; a fourth position was indeterminate between Class and Function. Table 8.8, again from Feist (2008), gives examples from display advertisements in the *New Zealand Herald* of 2 March 1935.

Table 8.7 *First stage of the Participant-head construction*

Origin Classifier	Other Classifier				Head
ordnance	*one-inch*				*series [of maps]*
French		*gold*			*coins*
English			*working*		*men*
Oriental				*tooth*	*paste*
Origin	Dimension	Constituency	Class	Function	

Table 8.8 *A later stage of the Participant-head construction*

Origin	Dimension	Constituency	Other Classifier		Head
	5-piece	*solid wood*	*bedroom*		*suite*
	54-inch	*all-wool*			*worsted*
		leatherette	*tip-out*		*seats*
Turkey			*rug*		*wool*
White Heather			*baby*		*wool*
Origin	Dimension	Constituency	Class	Function	

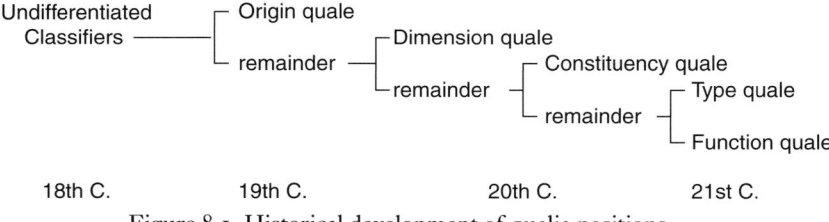

Figure 8.1 Historical development of qualia positions

The last stage in the growth of the Participant-head construction is the distinction between the Class and Function positions, as at the present day, evidently occurring late in the twentieth century.

That successive specialisation of undifferentiated Classifiers into the qualia positions is illustrated in figure 8.1. It represents the passage of time from left to right, with centuries printed across the bottom as an approximate time scale; junctions represent differentiation between a new quale (represented by its name) and the vague, undifferentiated 'remainder', which grew progressively smaller. (The figure hypothesises an intermediate stage, where Origin and Dimension were distinct from the other three positions.)

The qualia developed steadily from leftmost in the phrase to rightmost presumably because (as set out in §5.2.2) the leftmost qualia are most particular, and therefore make those Classifiers most distinct from the head. It seems natural that the Origin quale position developed first for the further reason that words of origin (such as *English* and *Danish*) are very old, and are common from the earliest texts onward.

The Process-head construction (e.g. '2005 Israeli arms sales') developed slightly later, with similar stages, and again conventionalising roles and relationships that had been expressed in single Classifier-type premodifiers for centuries. For example, the Old English subjective genitive, e.g. 'God's love' (of us), had expressed the Actor role, and the objective genitive, e.g. 'God's love' (by us), had expressed the Goal. By Early Modern English, noun modifiers were expressing the Circumstance role, e.g. '<u>midnight</u> murderer' ('the killer murdered someone at midnight'); and adjectival premodifiers were expressing the Actor: '<u>demoniacal</u> possession' ('demons possessed people'). Feist (2008: ch. 9) gives more detail. The other constructions seem to have arisen later.

The Classifiers inherited from previous periods, constructionless in their original use, have thus been converted to constructional use, at an increasing pace. However, speakers have continued to invent constructionless uses, even faster. For example, such Classifiers constitute a large proportion of the neologisms given in the 2005 edition of the *Macquarie Dictionary* (Australian), such as '<u>beer</u> o'clock' ('any time you want a drink'), '<u>dunnie</u> budgie' ('blowfly'), '<u>cappuccino</u> course' ('lightweight academic course') and '<u>hose</u> rage' (like 'road rage'). (From a report in *New Zealand Herald*, 20 October 2005, p. A20.)

The other main development in the Classifier zone has been the differentiation between word meaning and constructional meaning, paralleling the differentiation of words' roles in the construction. The process may be illustrated with 'gold coins', meaning 'coins <u>made of</u> gold', in contrast with 'gold mines', 'mines <u>for</u> gold'. Until the nineteenth century, some speakers will have taken MADE OF as part of the meaning of the word *gold*, while others will have taken it as contextual meaning. But as the Participant-head construction developed, MADE OF came to be understood as constructional meaning – the content of the Constituency quale: the different positions (as in '(1) French (2) gold coins') were clearly correlated with different relationships (<u>from</u> France, <u>made of</u> gold), and therefore suggested different constructions; and so did different uses of the same word (#'<u>gold</u> silk cloth' = 'rich yellow', but 'French <u>gold</u> coin' = 'MADE OF gold'. As that constructional meaning became more sharply defined, and became established as linguistic meaning, associated qualities such as HEAVY and VALUABLE were implicitly construed as world knowledge of gold, not meaning of the word *gold* (aided by the general increase in knowledge, with education). The bare central concept, GOLD, was left as the linguistic meaning of *gold*. That meaning became unbounded, because it now represented a concept in an abstract relationship (Constituency); in not referring directly to reality, it did not denote a bounded physical object or substance. (That loss of bound-edness will be amplified in §9.3, on 'Discourse explanation'.)

8.5.3   Epithet zone in Later Modern English

Social meaning, the last element of modern lexical semantics to appear, developed quite slowly in the seventeenth and eighteenth centuries: dialectal pronunciation of standard vocabulary became acceptable at the end of the eighteenth century (MacMahon 1998: 388), dialectal vocabulary and syntax by about the early nineteenth century (Adamson 1998: 551), and informal vocabulary in the late eighteenth century (Finegan 1998: 553 ff.) or early nineteenth century (Adamson 1998). Since then, the social, educational and literary changes mentioned in §8.5.1 will have speeded up the development, bringing in the present situation where the social meaning of premodifiers like *swell* and *top-hole* will place a speaker by region, social class and age.

The enlargement of scope of modification, begun in Middle English, continued in this period. The power to modify the discourse situation (§4.6) presumably came late in history because of the length of the development from concrete meaning through abstract meaning and attitudinal meaning to social meaning, which is its prerequisite – as illustrated in the semantic map (§4.8.2). *Bloody*, for example (§3.1.4), was used in Old English, but did not gain its social meaning until the eighteenth century.

8.5.4   Discussion: the Later Modern English period

When writers began using several premodifiers at once, they generally used only one or two zones (with two or three words in one of them). The earli-est examples I have observed of three zones used at once are from the late sixteenth century and early seventeenth century: 'above fourteen several sweet-smelling timber trees' (1580s, in Hakluyt's book of voyages, first pub-lished in 1589), 'hard usual English words' (1604, cited in Görlach 1978: 150) and 'their loud up-lifted angel trumpets' (1640s, Milton's poem, 'At a solemn music'). The maturity of the zone structure is marked, perhaps, by the moderately frequent occurrence of this usage in the nineteenth century (Feist 2008: ch. 9, §5.4).

It seems likely that the following current trends in premodification will continue.

(a) Greater structure in the Classifier zone. For example, a third type of Circumstance (Means) could become established in the Process-head con-struction, as in the attested phrase, 'ocean [extent Circumstance] acoustic waveguide [means Circumstance] remote [location Circumstance] sensing'

Table 8.9 *Possible Goal-headed construction*

Modifier: Circumstance (Location)	Modifier: Participant (Actor/s)	Modifier: Process	Head: Participant (Goal)
London	*inter-bank*	*offered*	*rate*

(compare §5.3.1). The pattern of Classifiers with *information* (noted in §5.7.3), could become established as a sixth Classifier construction; and phrases like 'London inter-bank offered rate' (compare 'banks offer the rate in London') could establish a Goal-headed seventh construction, as in table 8.9.

(b) Greater nominalisation. Dating from Old English at least (Strang 1970: 329–30), and continuing at present (Halliday 1978, Leech *et al.* 2009), nominalisation has led to such sentences as example (7), from a city council proposal for changes to a public park. (The underlining marks nominal phrases.)

(7)   '<u>Existing footpaths</u> phased out and <u>a new wide footpath network</u> introduced to allow <u>multi-user access</u> throughout <u>the year</u>.' (Auckland City Council website, on Churchill Park, 2006)

The next stage is presumably as in (8), in which the sentences consist entirely of nominal phrases, and over 80 per cent of the words are nominals:

(8)   'Existing footpath elimination. New wide footpath network introduction. Twelve-month multi-user access potential.'

(c) Decreasing use of compounds. Since Old English times, noun + noun expressions felt to have a semantic relationship but no grammatically acceptable syntactic relationship have been expressed as 'compounds'. Now, with the many Classifier constructions and the very wide use of constructionless Classifiers, virtually any noun + noun expression will be acceptable as a phrase, so compounds are not needed. Hyphenated forms (e.g. 'power-house') will continue to die away. Instead, we will have full modification (e.g. 'power house' meaning 'building for generating power'), or fusion (e.g. 'powerhouse', a modifier with one morpheme, meaning 'dynamic'), or forms combined with a slash signifying 'or' (e.g. 'clock/radio' where SOED has 'clock-radio'). Similarly, using separate words to form a lexical unit will continue to fade, as with 'tidal wave' giving way to 'tsunami'.

(d) Further morphological reduction of Classifiers. We have seen that: adjectival Classifiers become nouns ('<u>geography</u> lecture', '<u>Fiji</u> president'); genitive nouns become uninflected ('<u>doctor</u> parking'); plural nouns become singular ('<u>student</u> centre'); verbal forms reduce to the base form ('swim school'). That seems likely to continue.

(e) Greater orientation to message structure. Halliday (2000) and Du Bois (2003) argue that English has over several centuries been giving 'greater prominence to the structure of the message', and less prominence to 'the structure of the experience' (Halliday, 2000: 229), that is, more prominence to textual function and less to experiential function. Section 9.3 ('Discourse explanation'), will show that the trend has recently spread to the premodification structure of nominal phrases.

8.5.5   Conclusion: the Later Modern English period

The main changes in the unmarked order have been as follows. In the Classifier zone, the modern constructions and subzones developed, with the Participant-head construction developing first. In the Epithet zone, the full extent of social meaning developed gradually, and the last forms of modification developed. The zones came to be used freely, with three and even all four zones used in one phrase.

This period provides the explanation, promised in §5.9.2, for a number of Classifier features not explained in that chapter. The facts that the Classifier patterns have developed quite recently, and that they are still evolving, explain why the Classifier constructions differ in complexity and productivity, why there are many borderline and constructionless uses, and much ambivalence. Those facts also partly explain the overlap between the Classifier constructions and overall premodification (§5.8.3), since there has not been time for the overlap to be resolved; the rest of the explanation is that Classifiers evolved from genitive nouns and the separation of noun + noun compounds, not from adjectives and participles. The origin from genitives also explains Classifiers' overlap with determiners ('a big Sony Bravia set', 'Sony's big Bravia').

The late development of the Classifier zone also seems to explain in part the marked difference from other zones – in using constructional meanings equivalent to content, in allowing extensive recursive submodification, and in having subzones. The four zones were established in one phase of growth, between the fourteenth and sixteenth centuries. The Classifier subzones developed separately, from the nineteenth century onwards; and I suggest that it has had a separate impulse[10] and motivation. (See §10.3.3.4.)

The recent vigorous expansion and popularity of the Classifier zone also seems to explain the recent appearance of nouns as Descriptors, and even Epithets as in 'the worst cowboy cleaning company in the country', 'their low-rent letter boxes' and 'an iconic, breakthrough device'.

---

[10] I find this impulse – to use nouns to modify nouns – reminiscent of the impulse that allowed nouns (in the form of genitives and denominal adjectives) to modify nouns in Old English. The similarity perhaps merits further study.

The conceptual meaning of many Epithets has been lost through exaggeration (compare Partington 1993 and Haspelmath 1999), while the words retained their expressive meaning; for example, *horrible* ('hair-raising'). That explains the anomaly noted in §3.4, that Epithets are characteristically descriptive, but may have no descriptive meaning.

8.6   Free and marked order, through all periods

In Old and Middle English, free order existed, since phrases quite often contained co-ordinated premodifiers, and there is no evident rule for their sequence. But the freedom does not seem to have been used in prose for specific effects such as climax, as it is in modern free order. That remained true even in Early Modern English, although phrases with several co-ordinated premodifiers were common, and many Renaissance writers used premodifiers imaginatively.

Marked order of the type considered here was impossible in Old English and Middle English, since the zones did not exist, but became possible in the Early Modern English period. Examples are two phrases already quoted in §8.4.3. 'A Spanish great galleon' must have been a marked use, because *great* regularly appeared before other premodifiers, including *Spanish*. Its use after *Spanish*, therefore, would have been read, when first used, as an apparent anomaly highlighting the new sense of *great*. (Equally distinct uses had been occurring, as in 'great mile', but with the different sense simply inferred from context.) Contrasting 'penny wheat loaf' and 'penny white loaf' converted *white* from a Descriptor to a Classifier designating a type of loaf. I believe that marked order is now used much more frequently, and more deliberately, although we cannot be sure of that without more evidence of when particular senses began, which requires good evidence of spoken usage throughout both modern periods.

8.7   Discussion of the historical explanation of premodifier order

The chapter so far has demonstrated that the premodification zones have evolved; this section complements that by setting out the role of individual words' evolution through zones. It also draws attention to some other features of how the zones have evolved.

8.7.1   *Words changing zone*

This section sets out to show that words have developed senses in a new zone frequently enough for that zone-changing to have affected the history of premodifier order, as has been assumed so far. ('Changing zone' and 'moving forward' – toward the determiner – are potentially misleading, since the older meaning was usually retained.)

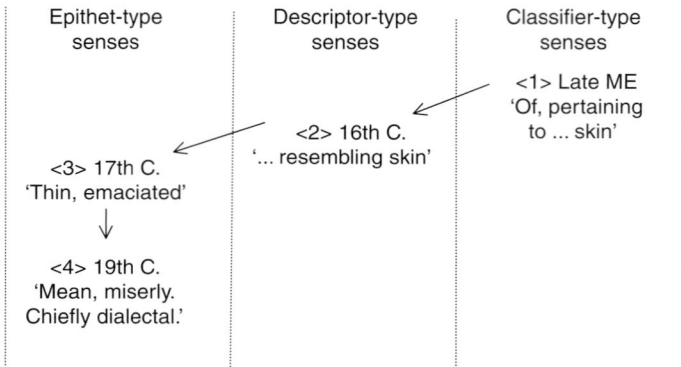

Figure 8.2 *Skinny*: development of senses in new zones

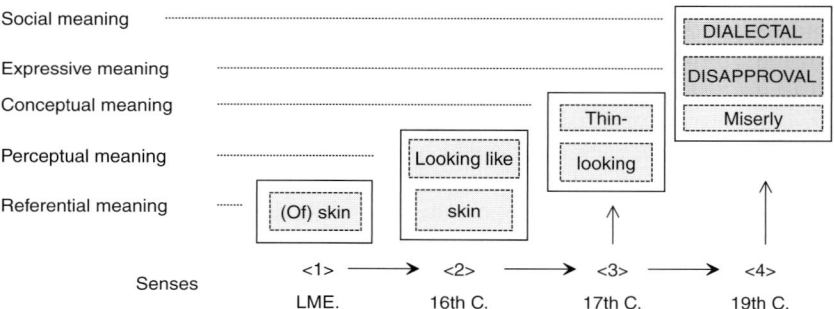

Figure 8.3 *Skinny*: changes in types of meaning, in new senses

Figures 8.2 to 8.4 illustrate the linguistic reality behind the generalisations about movement to be given below, emphasising that the movement is not simply a morpheme's change of position, but change in descriptive meaning and addition of new layers of meaning. Figure 8.2, for *skinny*, illustrates new senses in new zones, in 'moving forward'. The columns across the diagram represent the zones in their order in the phrase – Classifier senses on the right – and the rows downward represent successive historical periods. The linking of senses indicated by arrows is mine, based on their conceptual relationships and SOED's developmental order. Sense <5>, 'Of clothing: tight-fitting', has been omitted.

Figure 8.3 complements figure 8.2, by showing development of the types of meaning in the senses given in figure 8.1, as shaded layers being added. The columns represent word senses, and historical order now reads across the page. The meanings are paraphrases of the SOED meanings. (The expressive meaning of sense <4> is not explicit in SOED.)

Table 8.10: *Half of the sample in Feist (2008: ch. 9, §6.3.7) of words changing zone*

Words from the written sample			Words from the spoken sample	
additional	*free*	*recent*	*bloody*	*long*
average	*ill*	*regulatory*	*bright*	*nice*
basic	*important*	*residential*	*cheapo*	*pedigree*
big	*key*	*secondary*	*compulsory*	*regular*
cheap	*little*	*social*	*disgusting*	*skinny*
defective	*massive*	*tiny*	*extreme*	*special*
economic	*new*	*tough*	*funny*	*top*
familial	*old*	*urgent*	*ginger*	*twin*
fast	*psychological*	*wholesale*	*great*	*white*
financial	*progressive*	*vast*	*goddam*	*wee*

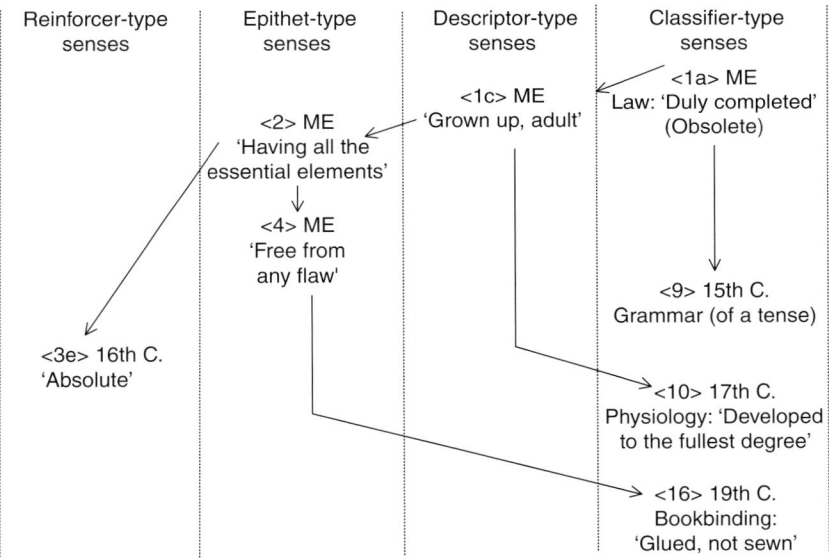

Figure 8.4 *Perfect*: development of senses in new zones

Figure 8.4, which is like figure 8.2, uses *perfect* to illustrate a word moving both forward and back.

Feist (2008: ch. 9, §6.3) gives an analysis of movement between zones for all senses of a hundred premodifiers from a random sample of everyday written and spoken English, with 'senses' taken as what SOED numbers as <1>, <2>, and so on. Table 8.10 lists half of the words in the sample, showing a representative range of concrete and abstract words, formal and informal words, and so on.

The majority of the hundred words (64%) have changed zone, but the scale of the changes is much greater than that, for the following reasons. First, Epithets have virtually no scope to change zone: it is extremely difficult for them to develop a Reinforcer sense, because the Epithet sense must be one of the very few appropriate conceptual types (such as COMPLETENESS and EXTREMITY), and there are existing words for all the possible Reinforcer senses; and Epithets' corresponding Descriptor senses also already exist. Second, since words take a long time to develop new senses, recent borrowings and recently formed senses can hardly have changed zone either. Allowing for those constraints, the proportion of words capable of movement that did move is 96 per cent. (Further, the analysis includes only words that moved in their existing form – not words that changed by derivation, like *steel* > *steely*.) Change of a premodifier's position, then, is so common as to be almost universal; it has certainly been widespread enough to strengthen the zone system, by multiplying the senses in the lexicon and thereby strengthening the structure of lexical relations within zones and across zones.

Some additional points may be made, for their own interest and for their relevance to later chapters.

In general, change of zone takes an appreciable time – about 200 to 250 years, on average, for a forward move – with very variable rates of change. (Figure 8.2, showing *perfect*, is potentially misleading here: it shows Classifier, Descriptor and Epithet senses all recorded in Middle English, as if they developed quickly; but it seems likely that they were simply borrowed from French in the same period, the development having taken place slowly, as the Latin word evolved.) Movement back occurred about once in 200 years in the sample; but the range was so great (from the same period to seven centuries) that the average seems to have little validity.

Movement forward is more common than movement backward: in the sample, 50 per cent of the 64 words that moved had some forward movement, but only 26 had some movement back. (Some had both movements e.g. *perfect*.) Words may traverse all four zones, as with *perfect*; but that is unusual. Words seldom 'jump' zones; they move through the Descriptor zone on their way from Classifier to Epithet. With most words, the number of senses per zone increases with movement to Epithet, reflecting the polysemy of Epithets – see §3.4.2.4; *perfect* is an exception, for its number of Classifier senses. These movements include 'pejoration' and 'amelioration' as words gain or change expressive meaning, 'weakening' as their conceptual meaning becomes more abstract, and 'enrichment' as their conceptual meaning gains more possible but not necessary meanings.

Movements back are more limited. That is presumably mainly because as words move forward the earlier meanings are retained; so that when a word gains a Reinforcer use, it has corresponding Epithet senses, and words with Epithet senses generally have corresponding Descriptor senses; so that apart from the few senses lost by archaism, every sense that is likely to evolve on the route back is already in the lexicon. Words do not (in the sample or in the rest of my observation) move back from the Reinforcer zone: grammatical words do not regain a descriptive meaning. When Classifier senses develop from descriptive senses, it is presumably the Descriptor, not the Epithet, that is the source of the Classifier, since referential senses presumably develop from a concrete and non-gradable sense, not from a scalar one.

Adamson (2000) shows change of zone with change of meaning, which accords with my account. However, that work does not account for all four zones or all of the movements, and does not show how widespread and systematic the changes have been.

8.7.2   Systematisation

In the changes described in this chapter, English has become fairly steadily more systematic, illustrating 'the extraordinarily strong tendency of language to maintain and neaten its patterns' (Aitchison 2001: 181).

Nominal phrases now offer a very wide range of structured choices among modifying elements. For a given concept, speakers can choose postmodification, premodification, or (for 'genitives') determiner; they can choose among the various zones, various constructions within the Classifier zone, and sometimes among various qualia within that construction. The choices are now structured hierarchically in the layers of zone constructions, and also in levels of dependence as heads, modifiers and submodifiers. As those choices developed, gaps that opened have frequently been filled; after *childish* developed its pejorative sense, 'immature', in Late Middle English, the lack of an unambiguously neutral word was filled in the sixteenth century by *childlike*. Irregularities and inconsistencies have frequently been reduced. Modification by nominal elements is a particularly striking example: noun + noun compounds always had semantic modification; now they increasingly have syntactic modification as well (see §5.8.1, and this chapter, §8.3.5); structureless compounds and adjectival Classifiers are being removed (§8.5.4 above); and especially, fluctuating contextual meanings are being replaced with the conventionalised meanings of individual modifiers and the constructional meanings of each modifier position. Premodification has become multidimensional: in syntax, with the layers of submodification (indefinitely deep for Classifiers) and the availability of nominalisation (§8.5.4); in semantics, with the types and dimensions of the meaning; and with the provision for the interpersonal and textual functions, as well as the experiential function (§8.5.4, and earlier discussion of the metafunctions).

The benefits of that increased systematisation are manifold. First, premodification is now more precise, as with the specific qualia replacing the vague *of*- genitive. Second, it is clearer, both in avoiding lexical and syntactic ambiguity much more thoroughly, and in lesser ways such as the following. The hyphenated phrase 'hydraulic stump-grinder', with a general-purpose adjective and a general-purpose compound noun, leaves the relations uncertain (is *hydraulic* descriptive or is it denoting a type? and does it relate to *stump?*); but the modern form, 'hydraulic [Classifier of manner] stump [Classifier as Goal of a Process] grinder [nominal denoting the Process GRIND', specifies the semantics and syntax clearly – 'the machine grinds stumps hydraulically'. Third, premodification is more economical, through its replacement of postmodifier phrases with single words and its multiple positions. Fourth, its consistency makes it easier to learn and to use. Above all, through the qualities just noted, it is very flexible, providing scope for richer, subtler and more complex expression.

8.7.3   Other features of premodification history

8.7.3.1   Mechanisms by which premodifier order evolved

The mechanisms of linguistic change have been mostly taken for granted in this chapter, but a few are worth noting, drawing together points established earlier in the chapter. The role of marked order in the development of meanings (and therefore of zone structure) seems to have remained unnoticed in the literature. Indeed, Traugott (1999: 178) and Bybee, Perkins and Pagliuca (1994, as quoted by Traugott, just cited) explicitly deny that change in syntactic position can cause or even precede change in semantics. Other noteworthy mechanisms include the distinction between restrictive and descriptive use, and the sheer increase in the number of premodifiers, which increased the pressure towards zoning. (The increase was brought about chiefly by borrowing, especially during the Renaissance, but also by the trend from postmodification to premodification.)

In §8.1, reference was made to the 'invisible hand', whereby a functional system results from changes that began without deliberate intention, and for non-functional reasons. The highly systematic and functional system described in §8.7.2 has resulted from such non-functional and disparate causes as the general human tendency to associate ideas (producing expressive and social meaning, and wealth of possible meanings, for example), to emphasise and exaggerate (producing Epithets and Reinforcers), and to save time.

8.7.3.2   History of semantic structure

The chapter has traced the development of premodifiers' internal semantic structure, with descriptive meaning becoming differentiated into scalar and nonscalar types, with grammatical meaning developing, and with expressive and social meaning becoming lexicalised (as a further differentiation of meaning). That history can be visualised by converting the semantic map given earlier (§3.1.2.2, and §4.8.2.5) to a historical version, as in figure 8.5. The details given have all been for premodifiers, but I suggest that the map may be valid for English words in general. The arrows in the figure represent the

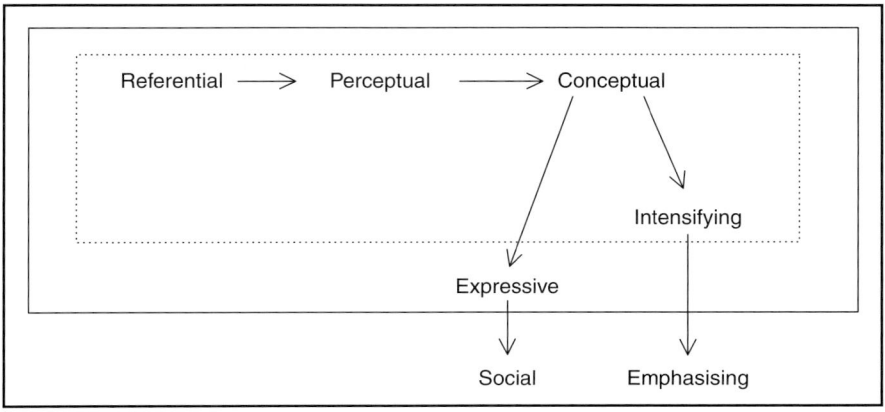

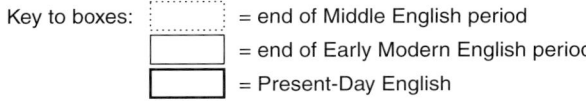

Figure 8.5 Historical semantic map of English

order in which words gain new types of meaning; but they also represent the order in which the types themselves have evolved. The boxes represent the extent of the semantic structure of premodifiers at the end of the periods discussed, showing its gradual expansion. (The horizontal scale is generality, and the vertical scale is subjectivity, as before. The differentiation of scalar from nonscalar meaning is omitted for the sake of simplicity; expressive and intensifying meaning both developed from scalar meaning.)

Many writers have described changes in the meaning of particular words; but, to my knowledge, there has been no recognition that the semantic nature of English itself has changed historically, as illustrated in figure 8.5. It is always assumed that the systems of phonology, morphology and syntax have changed, but that although words have changed in meaning individually, the semantic system itself has not. But we have seen that in Old English, the nature of word meaning was such that speakers simply could not use words with the full semantic structure set out in chapter 3. This account, then, opens up a new field – 'historical semantics' perhaps – distinct from historical lexical semantics, dealing with the system, not particular words. I suggest that further study is likely to produce important results – through comparison of the semantic structure of verbal and nominal expressions with that of premodifiers, for example.[11]

---

[11] A typological study of the semantic structure of different languages should also be profitable.

8.7.3.3   New word classes

We saw in chapters 3, 4 and 5 that each of the groups of words (word senses, strictly) that can occupy the zones and subzones have semantic and syntactic characteristics of their own: they are 'word classes', according to common linguistic usage. Common linguistic opinion holds that the only word classes to have developed since the Old English period are determiners and auxiliaries – that new word classes are rare, and develop very slowly; see Denison (2010: 124), for example. But this chapter has shown that the four zones and the many Classifier subzones have evolved in that time; and chapter 5 showed that there are between 17 and 24 word classes, depending on how you count; the majority have appeared since about 1800. Word classes develop much faster and more often than they are thought to.

8.7.3.4   Nominal phrases as restructured clauses

We have seen that the Classifier zone has been greatly expanded in recent times, as elements from elsewhere in the phrase or clause have been moved into premodifier position. From scholars' reconstruction of Germanic and Proto-Indo-European (see Lehmann 1974, in particular), it seems that the other zones are also the result of movement in position. I suggest that the overall development of English nominal phrases may be outlined schematically as follows: (1) in pre-historic times, predicative nonderived adjectives became prenominal adjectives; (2) nouns used predicatively, in prepositional phrases, became derived prenominal adjectives; (3) participles moved from Predicator position to be Old English prenominal participles; (4) nouns used as complements or adjuncts became Old English preposed genitive nouns; (5) in more modern times, some verbs were nominalised to become Classifiers; (6) some initial elements of compound heads separated to become Classifiers. That outline is speculative, and the schematisation blurs such things as the overlap of step (4) with others.

Those processes may be represented in figure 8.6. The top line represents the basics of Old English clause structure; the bottom line represents the corresponding Present-Day English structure. The numbers at the left represent the stages given just above. The arrows represent the movements; the bracketed numbers refer to the notes on processes other than change of position. The figure portrays only subject phrases as being affected, but in fact the expanded nominal phrases occur more often elsewhere in the clause, because subjects are often simple, since they commonly denote given information.

Note also that the role of participles in Old English and earlier structure is obscure and controversial, and that there are more routes to the Classifier position than are shown. Further, the different positions of the arrows in the Genitive-Classifier column are significant: elements from later in the clause generally move to subzones further from the head, and elements of compound heads remain immediately next to the head.

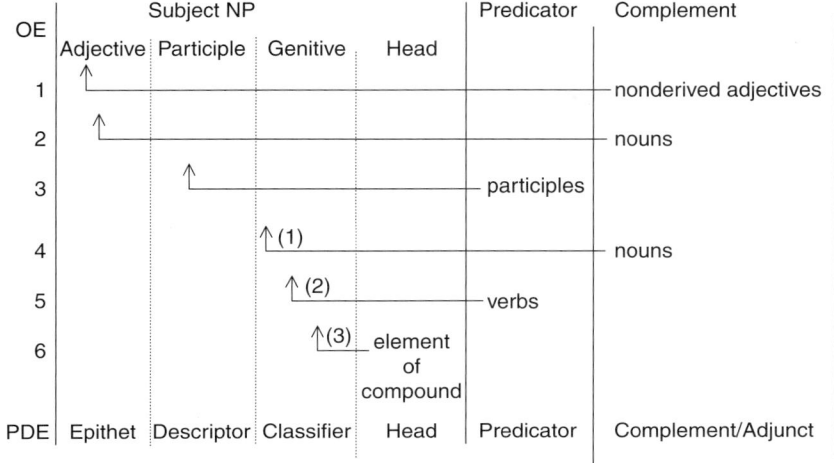

Figure 8.6 Restructuring of clauses into nominal phrases
Notes: Processes: (1) = derivation of adjectives from nouns; (2) = nominalisation of verbs; (3) decompounding.

We conclude that the expansion of nominal phrases in English has been in part the rearrangement and condensation of clause structure, just as the expansion of sentence structure is correlated with reduction of multiple sentences to a single sentence. We see also that in general, the earlier a clause element moved to the nominal phrase, the further from the subject was the position it moved from and the further from the head of the phrase was the position it moved into. That is because phrase elements further from the head are less closely bound to it semantically and syntactically, as we have seen in previous chapters, and clause elements further from the subject are less closely bound to it: in each structure, the less closely bound are further away, and move more easily. Control of discourse prominence is perhaps the motivation.

8.8   Conclusion: historical explanation of premodifier order

In summary, the chapter has shown that in Old English (up to the eleventh century), the order of premodifiers in nominal phrases was determined by the modifiers' part of speech: [adjective] + [participle] + [genitive noun] + [head]. By the end of the fourteenth century, premodifiers still commonly occurred in that order, but the order had been reanalysed: [premodifier [premodifier [premodifier head]]]. That is, premodifiers were seen as ordered by restrictive syntax, as in modern English, and premodifiers could be placed in different positions (for the sake of syntax), without change in meaning.

The semantic structure characteristic of modern Reinforcers, Epithets and so on was fairly well developed, but it did not control order; so the modern zones were not established, although nearly all of the elements for them were present. By the sixteenth century, in the Early Modern English period, premodifiers were still in syntactic order, but their semantic structure was felt to constitute a semantic order correlated with the syntactic one (premodifiers could not be moved simply for the syntax); since most of the characteristics of modern semantics and syntax had become established, the Present-Day English zones and unmarked order were established: Reinforcer [Epithet [Descriptor [Classifier head]]]. In the Later Modern English period, the unmarked order of premodifiers became complete, as the Epithet zone developed further, and the Classifier zone developed its constructions; the marked and free orders came to be used freely and purposefully. While premodifier structure has been changing, the meaning of particular words has also been changing, in semantic structure and zone position; the majority of premodifiers have changed zone, in fact.

Historical development explains many features of English premodifier order, both general (such as the parallel of semantic and syntactic orders), and specific (such as the existence of borderline uses). Some of those features have a partial explanation elsewhere (in semantic structure especially), but some (such as the part-of-speech pattern, borderline uses, and the close but imperfect fit of semantics and syntax) have no explanation other than the historical one. This chapter also helps explain why there has been so much difference of opinion on the order of premodifiers: first, the history has made premodifier semantics and syntax quite complex, so that difference between understandings is natural; second, some features of premodification, having arisen for historical reasons, have no good synchronic explanation, as Bauer notes (1998: 84).

We conclude that the unmarked order of premodifiers has evolved, gradually and in stages, from a part-of-speech order through a syntactic order to the present semantic and syntactic order of zones; and that a good understanding of the modern structure requires an understanding of its history. We also conclude that as well as the meaning of particular words, semantic structure of English as discussed in chapter 3 has changed – at least that of premodifiers.

This chapter completes the basic explanation of premodifier order: the chapters so far are intended to show that all features of premodification zones are adequately explained by the semantic and syntactic analyses, both synchronic and diachronic. The next chapter offers supporting explanation – that is, discussion which gives further insight without being explanatorily necessary, and which comes from fields wider than the core of linguistics. Chapter 10 gives still wider discussion.

9 Supporting explanations of premodifier order

9.1 Introduction

The argument in the book so far, from synchronic and diachronic semantics and syntax, leaves several areas of language not discussed. This chapter argues that scholars' knowledge of those areas supports the explanations given previously, completing and integrating the argument of the book as a whole.

Section 9.2 deals with psycholinguistics, §9.3 with discourse structure, §9.4 with language acquisition, and §9.5 with morphology and phonology.

9.2 Psycholinguistic explanation

Since I have assumed so far that language is integral with other mental activity, the explanations given in previous chapters should be credible psychologically. In this section, I set out to show in outline that they are. I deal with the main features of the synchronic and diachronic explanations given in the previous chapters, and in the same order.

9.2.1 Types of order

Unmarked order – the standard, routine order – fits processing by automatic control (e.g. Barsalou 1992: ch. 4, and 1999), which is fast and unconscious and therefore operating under binding grammatical rules. Free and marked orders, which have been portrayed as relatively uncommon, and as chosen stylistically, fit Barsalou's processing by 'strategic' control, which has some degree of conscious intention. (However, the constraints on free order given in §6.2, presumably operate under automatic control.) Increasing skill in strategically controlled processing can convert it to automatic control (Barsalou 1992: ch. 4); that would enable historically new uses to become embedded in regular use and in linguistic structure, and would enable some speakers to manage free and marked order spontaneously.

9.2.2   Semantics

The semantic structure described in chapter 3 is supported strongly by psycholinguistic research. We consider the zones in turn, and then the dimensions of meaning.

Hawkins (2004: 40) states as the first of the mind's three main principles in processing: 'Minimise forms; that is minimise the number of morphemes, words and so on to be processed'; specifically, 'Assign more properties to fewer forms'. That principle explains the nature of Classifiers and their frequency in current usage, as noted in §5.9.2: a single word evokes a complex meaning, by invoking implicit constructional meaning, and by invoking associated knowledge selectively, outside linguistic meaning and below full consciousness; that is like the economy of acronyms, where *radar* needs less linguistic processing than 'RAdio Detection And Range-finding'.

The lexical meaning of Classifiers was described in §3.2 as consisting of a single referential concept, without descriptive content. The psychological reality of that account is supported by Schreuder and Flores D'Arcais (1989). They see the mind's content for *coffee* (their example) as consisting of: (a) a minimal node (COFFEE), (b) 'perceptual elements' (such as colour, smell, and taste – BLACK, LIQUID, etc.), and (c) 'functional elements' (such as coffee's being made from roasted beans, and where it is produced). Those three elements of the network are activated together or independently in different situations (of speech, experience and thinking). I suggest that the minimal node (e.g. COFFEE) provides the meaning of *coffee* as Classifier: the single referential concept, without descriptive content, without spatial and temporal boundaries. (Classifiers in established constructions seem to be truly minimal; constructionless Classifiers, and Classifiers as used in earlier centuries, seem to have varying degrees of perceptual elements attached to them.) McClelland, Rumelhart and Hinton (1986) describe featureless 'instance units' denoting an entity; representing content (i.e. features) requires linkage to neighbouring nodes; the mental network can inhibit links to neighbouring nodes. All of that is supported by Lamb (1999) and Barsalou (1999). Malt *et al.* (1999) show that patterns of naming things often do not match the pattern of understanding; so the referential concept and the descriptive concepts must be distinct. Malt, Sloman and Gennari (2003) give a very similar and more up-to-date account of entities represented as points in mental space, citing other researchers.

Descriptors express the 'perceptual elements' of Schreuder and Flores D'Arcais (1989), just above – BLACK, for instance; they may be specific to one mode of perception, such as auditory or visual imagery (Barsalou 1992: ch. 5), or partly generalised as 'image schemas' (as discussed by Gibbs and Colston 2006). This is the 'observational meaning' described as basic in Cruse (2004: 133–4), and the experientially basic meaning of Barsalou

(1992: ch. 5). (Classifiers, by contrast, are basic semantically.)[1] Other works in the field that make the distinction between perceptual and conceptual elements in both mind and language include Baars (1988), Lamb (1999) and Tomasello (2003). Fortescue (2009) – a neurolinguistic study based on recent neuro-imaging techniques – makes a parallel physical distinction: there are sense-based 'affordances' at the base of the cortical columns that represent each lexical entry, which link the word to sensory images and the mind's representation of objects; and there are 'functional' affordances near or at the surface of the cortex, which process abstract concepts, both semantic and syntactic. The inhibition mentioned for Classifiers, just above, also helps explain how a word can have certain sense elements as an Epithet, but not as a Descriptor: its position and context inhibit them.

The primary element of an Epithet meaning is a relatively abstract concept. Concepts evolve from further processing of perceptual material (Barsalou 1999), and are primarily the 'functional elements' of Schreuder and Flores D'Arcais (1989). That fits my conceptual/perceptual division between Epithet and Descriptors, and the gradation between them. Barsalou (1999: §2.3) also shows that inner perceptions of bodily position and movement, emotion, mood and affect are processed and represented in the same way as sensory perceptions, which supports my account of expressive and social meaning as cognitively and semantically equal to conceptual meaning; it is perhaps only a certain philosophical and scientific predisposition that has prevented their status from being recognised. Fortescue (2009) says that expressive meaning is processed by affordances at the very base of the cortical column, linked to the limbic system in the base of the brain.

Hawkins's principle of minimising processing (stated above for Classifiers) helps explain Epithets' complex and somewhat inconsistent semantic structure. They use vagueness and ambiguity; they are polysemous; they have expressive and social meanings as well as descriptive meaning: that is, they assign many meanings ('properties') to a single word. Although some knowledge is 'logical' in the everyday sense, other knowledge is structured by 'illogical' association (Barsalou 1992: ch. 7). That provides for association of meaning elements within a word, including expressive and social meaning within Epithets.

Reinforcers' purely grammatical (or functional) meaning corresponds to 'procedural' knowledge – one of the three types, along with 'episodic' knowledge (memory of particular episodes in the past) and 'declarative' knowledge (knowing that. ...). (See Barsalou 1992: ch. 7, for example.)

The existence of dimensions of meaning is supported (indirectly) by the writers cited so far in this section, and particularly by McClelland and Rumelhart (1986) and Rumelhart and McClelland (1986), in two ways.

---

[1] Strictly: Classifiers in constructions are semantically basic; constructionless Classifiers are experientially basic.

First, they all regard the meaning of a word as an area of a network, such that varying parts of the whole meaning are activated in varying circumstances. Second, they regard each item of content as being activated to varying degrees, according to the 'weighting' of the connections, and as being more or less closely related to other content. The dimensions, such as degrees of expectedness, are part of those variations.

Barsalou (1999) emphasises the physiological point that concepts, and therefore meanings, do not exist in the static mind, but exist only as varying patterns of activation. Fortescue (2009) emphasises that anatomically words and meanings exist only as nerve fibres. That psycholinguistic understanding supports my portrayal of meaning as function, rather than content – as evoking certain conceptual, emotive and operational responses in the hearer's mind, not as data to be stored at box-like addresses.[2]

All of these writers emphasise that much processing is unconscious, which explains why speakers are unaware of grammatical meaning especially – since it is handled by unconscious and automatic processing – and perhaps helps explain why it has been underrated by linguists.

The variation in the effects of brain injury on concrete and abstract language is well known, e.g. Reboul (2000: 77). Kemmerer (2000) shows from neurolinguistic research that some brain injury affects certain abstract forms of meaning, and thereby disturbs the placing of adjectives in zones; that comes very close to demonstrating that the zones are real in the brain, as well as in the mind.[3]

9.2.3   Syntax

Hawkins's principle of minimising domains requires minimising the size of the structure to which syntactic and semantic properties must be assigned. I suggest that my account does minimise the structure to be processed, and the rules to be followed, for the following reasons. First, there are only four elements in premodification structure, at most – the four zones – and usually fewer. Second, for producing a nominal phrase, the rules are simple: you can use either the semantic rule (the type of meaning determines the zone – chapter 3) or the syntactic rule (put the word before all the words it is to modify – chapter 4) – since they give the same order. For understanding a phrase, corresponding rules apply.

My account, with the zones categorically distinct, allows for processing to be very much simpler and quicker than allowed for in other accounts,

---

[2] The conception of meaning as content, inherited from philosophy, has been reinforced by the misleading analogy with computers, where content does in fact exist – as electrical charges.

[3] The demonstration is not exact; I suspect that the reason lies in Kemmerer's reliance on Bache's inexact understanding of zones; see below, §10.4.

especially those that have an indefinite number of rather arbitrary points on a scale, or probabilities – not rules – for order (see §10.4). The distinction between the zones illustrates Givón's principle (1988: 278) that 'Syntax tends to *discretize* the scalar cognitive dimensions that underlie it.... [into] discrete, Platonic features or structures' (Givón's italics). I accept his assertion (1988: 278): 'Such discretization is an absolute necessity for information processing under real-world time constraints.'

The account of interactive syntax in chapter 4 fits the modern understanding, as in Barsalou (1999: esp. §4) and Fortescue (2009) for example, that neither thinking nor using language is a one-way process, or a process of comparing features, but a back-and-forth process of construal and construction. That interaction is part of premodifiers' being part of a network (see above), which has multiple connections, each of which may operate in either direction. Syntax, like semantics, exists as varying patterns of activation.

9.2.4 Discussion of the psycholinguistic explanation

Chapter 8, §8.4.5, gave an historical explanation for the imperfect match between semantics and syntax – for their working in parallel but with different kinds of 'rule', which seems linguistically strange. It has a psycholinguistic explanation, as well: in the parallel distributed processing of McClelland and Rumelhart (1986) and Rumelhart and McClelland (1986), different modules (such as semantics and syntax, in my application of the parallelism principle) naturally work simultaneously, and there are no abstract or explicit rules (just patterns of behaviour, and constraints on them); any clashing constraints from different modules are resolved according to their weighting.

According to Barsalou (1992: ch. 5), the mind recasts perceptual material gradually (with repeated use) into conceptual form; and it co-ordinates different modules, such as perception, cognition, emotion and control of physical action. That fits the word histories and development of semantic structure given in the chapter on historical explanation, in which, for example, conceptual meanings evolved from perceptual ones, expressive and social meaning (from other modules) became associated with conceptual meaning, and a few conceptual meanings developed into wholly abstract reinforcing meanings.

9.2.5 Conclusion: psycholinguistic explanation

The strictly linguistic explanations of premodifier order given in earlier chapters conform to widely accepted recent psycholinguistic research. If that research is correct, the earlier explanations are psycholinguistically credible. In particular, the research supports the features that distinguish my account from other accounts: it shows that the key types of meaning (referential, perceptual, conceptual and grammatical) are psycholinguistically real, and that the zones which they distinguish are psycholinguistically real, accordingly.

9.3   Discourse explanation

9.3.1   Introduction

The purposes of this section are to show that the order of premodifiers often creates a discourse structure, and to support the syntactic and semantic explanations by showing that they explain the discourse structure as well as the zone structure. By 'discourse', I mean the perspective that sees language through its overall function for the speaker or writer, not 'discourse' in the sense of units of language greater than the sentence (Schiffrin 1987).

Chapter 7 showed that order serves effects like climax, and linking the nominal phrase with the context, which are discourse effects. Chapter 8 showed that marked order increases impact on the reader, which is also a discourse effect. Free and marked order, then, are largely controlled by discourse function; the rest of this section discusses phrases in unmarked order.

The section argues that some nominal phrases have a discourse structure as clauses do: there is sometimes a Topic-Comment structure (§9.3.2), or a Theme-Rheme structure (§9.3.3), or a participant-status structure (§9.3.4).

9.3.2   Structure of Topic and Comment

As understood here, the 'Topic', or 'the Given', in a clause or unit of information is what is treated as already known to the hearer, having later information built on it. 'Comment', or 'the New', is the added information; it includes what is important, as well as what is new in the narrow sense. The added 'information' may be a fact, a quality, a reference to a participant entity, and so on.

9.3.2.1   Head as Topic, and premodifier as Comment

Modifiers are often used descriptively, adding information about the head entity, but sometimes the description serves the deeper discourse purpose of making a comment on the head – which accordingly is in effect a Topic, as in (1).

(1)   'He felt he had made a mistake by hiring the <u>flashy, controversial</u> Carly Fiorina as his successor at Hewlett Packard.' (*Economist*, 29 July 2006, p. 66)

The head, *Carly Fiorina*, identifies the referent; the modifiers, *flashy* and *controversial*, add extra information which is asserted of the head, as if the words were in a nonrestrictive adjectival clause (as in '…hiring Carly Fiorina, who was flashy and controversial'). The overall structure is: 'He [Topic] felt he had made a mistake….. [Comment]', and another structure is embedded in it – 'Carly Fiorina [Topic] was flashy and controversial [Comment]' – giving the reason for the hiring being a mistake. A further example is, 'At the Commons, a clearly emotional Prime Minister Gordon Brown…'. There can even be two Comments on one Topic: '[The mosaics at the street corner in Ellerslie] will be a stunning, and Ellerslie's first, public artwork'.

The status of the Comment is sometimes signalled syntactically, by an article. In 'the flashy, controversial Carly Fiorina', '*the*' signals that the speaker takes 'flashy, controversial' as known to the hearer; and when a cricketer 'was caught behind by a diving Geraint Jones', '*a*' signals that the speaker takes 'diving' as new to the hearer.

We conclude that there is a rule of discourse order (applying when there are both descriptive and restrictive premodifiers), given as (2):

(2)   Descriptive premodifiers precede restrictive ones.

The rule leads to two unusual uses noted previously: marked punctuation (§7.1.2) and conversion of postdeterminers to premodifiers, as in 'a therapeutic few hours' and 'a quiet three decades'. Givón (1990: 470) gives a narrower version of the rule; otherwise it seems to have escaped notice.

This Topic-Comment structure supports the main argument of the book, because it flows from the explanations in previous chapters. Premodifiers further from the head are more general, more complex, more subjective and expressive (chapter 3), so they are semantically suitable for Comment. Premodifiers modify the rest of the phrase syntactically (chapter 4), so they make a 'comment' on it, even when used restrictively.

My assertion that premodification order is often a Topic-Comment order has some limited support in other works: Svoboda (1968: 66), Warren (1978: 40), Altenberg (1980) and Sørensen (1980). Plank (2006) and Szendrói (2006), however, deny that it is even possible.

9.3.2.2 *Premodifier as Topic, and head as Comment*

A second structure, quite rare, is that a head word functions as Comment. In example (3), a climber describes the scene at dawn:

(3)   '… red snow, red rock, red sky'. (*New Zealand Alpine Journal*, 2006, p.15)

A modifier, *red* (in the second and third phrases), represents Given information – given by the first *red* – and comment is made on it by heads: 'Red spread over the rock, and over the sky', in effect.

9.3.3   *Structure of Theme and Rheme*

The Theme (Halliday 2004: ch. 3) is the speaker's point of departure, which locates and orients the information for the hearer; it is always expressed at the beginning of the information unit (usually contained within one clause), whereas Topics may be introduced later. The Rheme traces the speaker's route through the information from the point of departure (Halliday 2004: 93; compare Mel'cuk 1988: 58). The Theme may orient the information by means of stating the Topic (serving the experiential function); or it may serve the textual or interpersonal functions.[4] Ramsey (1987) applies the concepts to whole sentences, showing that *if-* and *when-* clauses are thematic when preposed. This section applies the concepts to phrases; and since §9.3.2 above illustrates structure with Theme as Topic, this one concentrates on the other types of Theme.

Halliday (2004: §6.2.1.1) notes that articles and other deictics can act thematically for a phrase. For example, '<u>a</u> city' and '<u>the</u> city' orient hearers as to whether they can identify the referent city as yet. The beginning of the premodification also can orient hearers, enabling them to interpret the following words or phrases correctly. If we hear a sentence begin, 'He's a <u>mere</u>…', we know that the following information will be derogatory. Reinforcers such as *mere* act as textual Themes, guiding hearers' interpretation of the following words. Epithets can act the same way.

(4)   'There was a <u>queer</u> white misty patch in the sky like a halo of the sun.' (Joseph Conrad, *Typhoon*, p. 89)

Queer orients us as readers to oddities, encouraging us to take *white* and *misty* as odd; that interpretation is confirmed by 'like a halo of the sun' and by following events: the misty patch is the first sign of the coming typhoon.

The beginning of the premodification can also guide the hearer or reader to the intended emotional response, as interpersonal Theme. A humorous anecdote from a hunting story begins as in example (5):

(5)   'Rain fell all night… The water began flowing through the bush. My <u>super-duper new</u> pup tent that was guaranteed "totally weather-proof" began to leak so badly that my sleeping bag became a soggy sponge.' (Peter Harker, *Random Shots*, p. 26)

Super-duper, being colloquial hyperbole, orients us to the tone of the sentence – self-mocking humour – and makes us interpret *new* and *totally weather-proof* as continuations of that humorous tone. Expletives work similarly, coming first to colour following modifiers ('<u>Bloody</u> sober boring

---

4 For an explanation of the functions, see §3.6.1. For discussion of interpersonal and textual Themes in clauses, see Halliday (2004: §3.4).

sincerity'), and even the whole utterance ('<u>Bloody</u> rotten thing to wake up to').

Just as the determiner and first premodifier can act as Theme, so can successive premodifiers act Rhematically, marking the speaker's chosen route through the information. In example (5), the unmarked order of the premodifiers reflects their discourse importance: 'My super-duper (1st) new (2nd) pup (3rd) tent'. Expletives can be moved out of first position, to make them Rhematic: 'Discovery is an incredible <u>bloody</u> thrill, it's un-<u>bloody</u>-believable'. That explains the apparently anomalous shift in position noted in §4.6.1.

I believe that in Present-Day English, Rhematic order is increasingly important, particularly with words denoting size and shape, as in examples (6) to (8), where '*x*-minutes' expressions vary in zone. ('E' = Epithet, and so on.)

(6) 'A <u>15 minute</u>[E] back-of-the-envelope[D] benefit-cost[C] analysis' (Corpus of Contemporary American English)

(7) 'A thrilling[E] <u>14-minute</u>[D] fun[C] ride' (Corpus of Contemporary American English)

(8) 'A new[E] weekly[D] <u>15 minute</u>[C] reading[C] program' (Corpus of Contemporary American English)

Those expressions can be read with the size expression interpreted according to zone; but to me, any difference in meaning with difference in zone seems minimal. I believe that in speech and informal writing such uses are certainly often motivated by discourse importance, rather than semantic structure, as with the position of expletives.

Like Topic-Comment, Theme-Rheme often constitutes an additional layer of structure, building on the semantics and syntax on which it relies.

9.3.4 Structure from participant status

In clauses, position as subject or object makes an entity a central participant in the discourse, and position as oblique object or part of an adjunct makes it increasingly peripheral. In nominal phrases, similarly, position as head makes an entity central; position as modifier (i.e. as a Classifier) makes it peripheral – it is not referential in function.

That reduction in discourse status is marked by morphological reduction, as in the following. When 'on business <u>of the school</u>' became 'on <u>school</u> business' when repeated (§8.4.3), *school* was reconstrued as denoting a type of business, rather than a participant in the discourse, and the definite article disappeared (and the stress lessened, I believe). When a university is said to have 'a <u>student</u> centre', *student* is not marked for number or possession, since the students are not participants in the immediate discourse. Similarly, we have '<u>pedestrian</u> crossing' and '<u>doctor</u> parking', and 'child language acquisition' for 'children's acquisition of language'. Verbs occur in the base form, unmarked for tense and aspect: 'skim milk', 'barb wire', 'carry bag', 'a drink driver'. All part-of-speech forms converge on the uninflected noun form – 'parent rights' for 'parental rights' and 'parents' rights', 'speech language therapy' for 'spoken language therapy', and 'cycle advance stop boxes' for 'boxes [on the roadway] where cyclists can advance and stop [in front of other traffic]'.

It is not obvious that the reduction is a general rule in English, however, for two main reasons. First, many Classifiers are mass nouns or proper nouns or adjectives, without an inflection to lose: 'stainless steel gas cooktop', for example. Second, the apparent exceptions are well motivated, and regular. As Anstey notes (2007: 229), the plural is retained to denote multiple types, not multiple instances (e.g. 'careers guidance' denotes different types of career, where 'career guidance' denotes one person's career).

The reduction in morphology reflects a reduction in semantic structure, as well as in discourse status: the Classifiers just cited have been reduced to the unbounded state (discussed in §3.1.2.2 and §3.2.3). For example, 'a student centre' makes no reference to specific students; the concept STUDENT is conceived without reference to extent in time or space.[5] That reduction and their entities' lack of discourse status help explain why Classifiers are readily confused with the first element of a compound. (Compare §5.8.1.)

The lower status is related to lower 'distinguishability' (Kemmer 2003: 110), 'categoriality' Croft (2003: 213–14) and 'clustering' (Myhill 1988). A more useful concept for our purpose is 'individuation'. Timberlake (1975) defines it as 'the degree to which the participant is characterised as a distinct entity or an individual in the narrated event' (1975: 124). 'John F. Kennedy' will evoke a highly individuated representation of the referent; 'an American president' will evoke a less individuated one, and 'someone' still less so. Different types of noun (proper, count, mass, abstract) establish different degrees of individuation. The semantic reduction of Classifiers to unboundedness, then, will make the referent of the Classifier low in individuation. (Other elements of the phrase also affect individuation, such as indefiniteness and descriptive detail; see Timberlake 1975: 124–7.)

Consider, then, the three references to the World Bank in example (9):

(9)   'If anyone suggested the World Bank did not take global warming seriously, its bosses would bristle: only last October [...] the institution issued a "strategic framework" [...]. This promised more emphasis on noble things like energy efficiency [...] and more bank support for [...].' (*Economist*, 27 June 2009, p. 68)

---

[5] The relatively modern reduction of head nouns to modifying nouns mirrors the much older reduction of nouns to adjectives by affixation (e.g. *manly*, *dirty*, *English*), which achieved the same semantic and discourse reduction.

'The World Bank' individuates the bank fully, where it is the focal participant in the discourse; 'the institution' individuates it rather less, as the focus passes to the strategic framework; 'bank' individuates it much less – its semantic and morphosyntactic reduction give it minimal discourse status. A genitive determiner ('<u>the bank</u>'s support') would individuate the bank a little more fully than the premodifier ('<u>bank</u> support'), and a postmodifier ('the support <u>of the World Bank</u>') would individuate it still more fully.[6]

In conclusion: for the position of an entity, speakers and writers are now regularly choosing among head, premodifier, postmodifier and genitive determiner; they exploit syntactic position along with semantic reduction and morphosyntactic reduction to control participant status, which is part of discourse structure.

9.3.5   Discussion: discourse explanation

9.3.5.1   Language functions
Nearly all of the uses of nominal phrase structure for discourse structure discussed in this section have served the textual metafunction. Structure of Theme and Rheme (§9.3.3) serves the interpersonal function when it orients the hearer. (The experiential function is the dominant function in the basic order; see §3.6.1.)

9.3.5.2   Noun incorporation
Premodifiers in English have many features of noun incorporation, although the 'incorporation' is into a noun, not a verb. The obvious difference, that they are not incorporated morphologically, is not central, since the form of expression reflects the overall morphological character of the language (Mithun 1984: 849), and English is an analytic language. The following discussion is based on Mithun (1984), but similar explanations of incorporation are given by Haiman (1988: 311), Farkas and de Swart (2003: 5) and Dahl (2004: 216–17).

In Mithun's type I, 'lexical compounding', a 'complex lexical item' is derived from 'two or more stems', as in 'He is <u>berry-picking</u>' (1984: 849). 'Noun + noun compounds', such as 'U.S. <u>berry exports</u>', (see chapter 5, §5.8.1) fit that type in the following ways. The incorporated noun has no syntactic status in the clause, cannot be definite, cannot be used for a separate

---

[6] To extend the discussion in chapter 5, §5.8.4: the points made here confirm that Classifiers are now a regular alternative to determiner genitives ('-s genitives') and postposed genitives ('*of*-genitives'), and that they should accordingly be rated as a third form of the genitive: the three forms constitute a paradigm of grammatically related nominals. See Feist (forthcoming). This discussion also suggests that the extensive literature on the genitive variation in English (for example, Rosenbach 2002 and 2006, and work cited there) misunderstands the issues somewhat. Variation according to 'animacy' is better understood as variation according to individuation; and variation according to 'topicality' misses the point that the choice of variant controls the 'topicality', not vice versa.

act of reference, and is tightly bound to the head. The incorporation is used for what is habitual, and for the non-specific. Mithun's type II incorporation is 'manipulation of case', in which an argument – a direct object ('DO') for example – is incorporated into a verb, and an otherwise oblique argument ('OO') takes its place. For example, 'I washed his <u>face</u> [DO]' becomes 'I <u>face</u>-washed him[DO]' (1984: 857). We have seen that manipulation in the use of the Process-head construction (§5.3), where noun premodifiers parallel the subject, object and so on of a clause. For example, 'They've all got <u>child</u> [Goal/DO] restraints for under-fives [OO]' is based on #'They've all got restraints <u>for children</u> [OO] under-five'. In Mithun's type III, 'manipulation of discourse structure', incorporation is used to background known or incidental information – exactly what we saw in §9.3.4.

Since all three types are forms of controlling an entity's discourse status, noun incorporation is part of the discourse-structure explanation given above. It seems to have gone unnoticed.

9.3.5.3   *Typology of English*
The development of discourse structure within nominal phrases is a part of a much larger development in English, noted in §8.5.4: a 'new alignment of grammatical forces' which gives 'relatively less prominence' to the structure of the experience, and more to the structure of the message (Halliday 2000: 228) – a reorientation away from the experiential function and towards the textual function. Du Bois (2003) supports that view. Halliday's instances of this trend are the development of many different patterns of information flow in clauses (entailing Theme and Rheme, and Topic and Comment), the development of phrasal verbs, and the addition of a preposition to a clause element to mark it out for information value. I am asserting that nominal phrases as well as clauses constitute patterns of information flow, and am adding management of participant status to Theme-Rheme and Topic-Comment as patterns. Halliday treats this orientation as a major characteristic of languages. In that view, it constitutes a typology which does not seem to have been considered in the typological literature, and which merits further research.

9.3.6   *Conclusion: discourse explanation*

The conclusions from this section are as follows. Nominal phrases in free and marked order regularly have a discourse structure, and those in unmarked order sometimes do. That structure is one of Topic and Comment, of Theme and Rheme, or of gradation in participant status (which extends beyond premodifiers to postmodifiers and determiners). Since the discourse structures rely on semantic and syntactic principles, without having principles of their own that override the semantic and syntactic ones (except in a few dubious instances), they do not constitute an independent or fundamental explanation of premodifier order. Nevertheless, this discourse explanation supports those semantic and syntactic explanations, and it explains some features of how the order is used. We should note, also, that it is not only clauses that are structured by discourse issues.

In conclusion: structuring information was the motivation for the historical condensation of phrases and clauses discussed in §8.5.4 and §8.7.3; and it remains a motive for free choice among those phrasal alternations, and among the alternations between clauses and Classifier constructions discussed in §5.1.4. In this section, we have seen evidence that Theme-Rheme structure is beginning to control zone position in the premodifier group (§9.3.3), and that participant status is already controlling variation among genitive determiner, premodifier, postmodifier or head (§9.3.4). Just as syntax took over control from morphology in Middle English (§8.3), and semantics to some extent took over from syntax in Early Modern English (§8.4), so discourse structuring is perhaps beginning to take over from semantics. If that is so, then we must add it to our list of current trends (§8.5.4), and rate the trend as a major one.

9.4   Language acquisition

This section supports the main explanations of premodifier order by showing that those explanations also explain the order of children's acquisition of premodifiers: constructionless Classifiers (being experientially basic) are learned first, and other premodifiers are learned in order away from the head. The section uses evidence from general research into children's learning of words and meaning, and into learning processes (§9.4.1), and from research into the development of individual children (§9.4.2).

9.4.1   Evidence from general research

There is general agreement that nouns are learned before adjectives; see Tomasello (2003), Gentner and Boroditsky (2001), Bates and Goodman (1999). Since (to generalise) Classifiers are nouns and Descriptors, Epithets and Reinforcers are adjectives, that suggests strongly that Classifiers like 'baby doll', and 'Thomas engine' are learned first among premodifiers.

The types of meaning are also acquired in sequence. Referential meaning (naming and labelling, as in Classifiers) is learned before descriptive meaning (expressed in Descriptors and Epithets); see Tomasello (2003), Gentner and Boroditsky (2001), Karmiloff and Karmiloff-Smith (2001), Schwanenflugel (1991) and Mervis (1987). Abstract concepts (expressed in Epithets) are acquired after perceptual features (expressed in Descriptors); see Clark (1973), Mervis (1987), Schreuder, Flores d'Arcais and Glazenborg (1985). Grading (which distinguishes Epithets from Descriptors) develops late in children's modifiers: see Nelson (1976).

Bybee (2002: §§9–10) argues that syntax is established gradually, as short phrases memorised without understanding of their construction are reanalysed as progressively more abstract structures. For example, the set phrase 'my mother' becomes understood as '*my* + noun' or 'possessive pronoun + *mother*', and then as 'possessive pronoun + noun'. That fits the precedence of constructionless Classifiers like '<u>Thomas</u> engine', and progression through Epithets to Reinforcers, which rely on the most abstract relation to the head. Much the same process occurs with 'holophrases' – utterances which seem to adults to be single morphemes (e.g. 'Allgone' and even 'No!'), but which in fact express the child's whole response to a situation. Elements of the situation and of meaning are gradually differentiated, and the syntax is expanded (e.g. 'All drink gone', and 'All my drink has gone'). This process of reanalysis and differentiation seems to follow the same order as the complementary process of additive learning of particular words and meanings.

The processes of acquisition are themselves used in an order corresponding to premodifier order. Tomasello (2003), following others' research, shows that children's learning of language begins in the joint attention that the child and caregiver give to things, which would establish referentiality (in Classifiers). Then come pattern-finding, needed for descriptive meaning, in Descriptors and Epithets, and reading others' intentions. Later come using lexical contrast and linguistic context, which characterise Epithets. A still later skill is taking different perspectives, which Epithets need, when they carry attitudinal or social meaning. Tomikawa and Dodd (1980) add that when both perceptual and functional bases for learning are available, children prefer the perceptual one. Gentner and Boroditsky (2001) draw a distinction between cognitive input into language learning, which comes from children's experience of the world, and linguistic input, which comes from the knowledge of language which they have already gained. Gentner and Boroditsky argue that cognitive input dominates the early learning, since children have no knowledge of language when they begin learning words. That first learning is of nouns; cognitive input becomes less dominant as children learn verbs, and linguistic input is dominant as they learn closed-class words, later. That implies that Classifiers (nouns) would be learned before Descriptors (mixed input), before Epithets (dominantly linguistic input), before Reinforcers (closed-class words, with wholly linguistic input – grammatical meaning). Karmiloff-Smith (1992), Hudson and Holmes (2000) and Inchaurralde (2000) give further support for those points.

The order of children's language development, then, mirrors the order of zones. The order of processes of acquisition, and of the learning of parts of speech and types of meaning all correspond to the semantic order we saw in chapter 3 (one of linguistic basicness), to the structure we saw in §9.2.4 on the psycholinguistic explanation (one of cognitive basicness), and to the development of word meaning we saw in chapter 8, on historical explanation.

9.4.2   Evidence from particular children

This section presents conclusions from data of particular children's speech, from the only useful study I have found (Bloom 1970), which reports on observation of three children learning English. The book does not cite all of the children's speech in full; so I rely in part on Bloom's analysis, and in part (where she does cite the utterances) on my own. The section argues that the data, although not conclusive, confirm the conclusion just reached from general studies.

In the time recorded, Kathryn (aged 21 months) used as premodifiers five nouns (Classifiers – for example, '<u>baby</u> book'), and twelve adjectives, almost exclusively perceptual in her use *(big, cold, dirty,* for example). There were no abstract adjectives, or emotive ones, and no grammatical ones, such as *mere.* I conclude that Kathryn was using Classifiers and Descriptors, and not using Epithets (no abstract or emotive premodifiers) or Reinforcers. Gia (at 20 months) used nouns as premodifiers twenty times in the hours of observation ('<u>animal</u> book', for example), and did not use adjectives (in the usual sense of the word) as premodifiers at all. (She seldom used adjectives predicatively, either.) That directly supports the claim that Classifiers come first. Data from the third child, Eric, are inconclusive.

We conclude that Bloom's data support the conclusion reached in the previous section: Classifiers are learned before Descriptors, before Epithets, before Reinforcers.

9.4.3   Conclusion: language acquisition

There is good evidence, though not proof, that children generally acquire the use of the premodification zones in order away from the head. (That should be readily verifiable by further examination of children's early language – a piece of research that seems worth undertaking.) That conclusion confirms the explanations given previously: the same principles underlie the order in which children learn premodifiers, the semantic order of the zones, the way words develop historically, and the way language is processed psycholinguistically. The three-way correlation presented in chapter 1 becomes a four-way correlation: premodifiers' position in the order, their meaning, their historical development, and their development in children.

9.5   Morphological and phonological explanations

This section provides relatively minor support for the earlier chapters, from the levels of language not previously discussed: morphology and phonology.

It seems likely that morphology is useful psycholinguistically in processing nominal phrases, since the inflections that distinguish nouns, adjectives and participles are a useful guide in identifying zone: adjectival suffixes fairly reliably distinguish Epithets and Descriptors from Classifiers; participial suffixes are a useful guide to Descriptor position; and noun form fairly reliably indicates Classifier position. That suggestion is speculative; but it has further support. First, to a significant degree, nonderived adjectives (such as *new, young, slow, thick, green*) are Descriptors, whereas derived adjectives (such as *newfangled, dangerous, horrible, greenish*) are Epithets: again, the morphology is a guide to position (Quirk *et al.* 1985: 1338, note the tendency). Second, there has been a trend from at least the eighteenth century towards replacing adjectival Classifiers with the corresponding nouns, in expressions like '<u>historical</u> lecture' (now '<u>history</u> lecture'), and '<u>geographical</u> book' (now '<u>geography</u> book'); the trend continues, as in the current increase in use of phrases like '<u>science</u> instruments'. That trend makes stricter the part-of-speech distinction between Classifier and Descriptor zones, is part of the systematisation discussed in §8.7.2, and reinforces the trend to reduction discussed in §9.3.4.

Chapter 9 showed that this part-of-speech order was part of the historical explanation. Here, I am not suggesting that it provides an explanation of its own, but that part-of-speech morphology contributes to the psycholinguistic explanation given above, and that it has thus partly motivated the historical survival.

Phonology is probably also useful. It seems clear intuitively that, when spoken, 'splendid old electric trains' (for example) would have more stress on *splendid* than on the other premodifiers; #'splendid **old** electric trains' and #'splendid old **electric** trains' would be marked in stress. Phonological prominence of the first premodifier fits naturally with the semantic importance of Epithets (see §3.6.1), the greater syntactic powers of earlier premodifiers (chapter 4), and their importance in discourse structure (this chapter, §9.3). Moreover, it is widely accepted that semantic and discourse prominence affect phonology. It is said, for example, that stress falls on the most informative word (Oller and Sales 1969: 214); that it marks Topic-Comment structure (Gundel 1988: 230); that it falls on 'the center of interest' (Bolinger 1968: 90); and that new information is made prominent phonologically (Halliday 2004: 61, 89). Phonology expresses or 'realises' the other levels of language. I leave the issues to be resolved by others.[7]

---

[7] Van Donzel (1999) presents research on Dutch, showing that the most prominent words in information structure are most prominent phonologically, in that language.

Phonology has another, less important role in order. 'Sound symbolism' seems to be used more in zones further from the head.[8] Consider, for example, 'a <u>whopping</u> £43m loss' and 'a <u>blithering</u>, hen-pecked twerp', in which sound words precede other premodifiers. This use is commonly disregarded in linguistics. But Marchand (1960/1969: §VII) shows its role in word formation; Rhodes (1994) shows that it has its own syntax and regular meaning; Morton (1994) shows that it has a biological basis and social reality; and the other writers in Hinton, Nichols and Ohala (1994) show how widespread and systematic it is in the languages of the world.

As well as providing some further supporting explanation, this section has helped to show that all levels of language contribute to premodifier order.

9.6 Discussion: supporting explanations

In the literature on premodifier order, a few points have been made on the linguistic areas discussed in this chapter. For example, Martin (1969a, 1969b) suggested that processing affects order; Givón (1990) noted that new information precedes the given; several authors have noted that morphologically longer words tend to precede shorter ones. But the whole of my language-acquisition explanation is new, as far as I am aware, and also the main substance of the other explanations in this chapter.

9.7 Conclusion: supporting explanations

Respected research in psycholinguistics shows that the semantic and syntactic explanations set out in earlier chapters fit the mind's processing abilities and constraints (§9.2). Speakers and writers sometimes exploit the structure determined by semantics and syntax, using it to build a miniature discourse structure, paralleling that of clauses (§9.3). Research indicates that zones furthest from the head are more difficult to learn, and that children learn premodifiers in that order of difficulty (the zone order), learning the furthest from the head last (§9.4). Morphology seems likely to contribute to order psycholinguistically (§9.5). It is likely that phonological prominence matches other forms of prominence – in order to express them (§9.5).

It follows that the principles constituting the basic explanations of premodifier order from semantics and syntax are supported by what we know of the other levels of language (discourse structure, morphology and

---

[8] 'Sound symbolism' is a misleading term, since it includes not only representing real sounds, but also evoking other sensations, and expressing feeling. Semiotically, the meaning is generally indexical rather than symbolic, as shown by the examples given.

phonology), of psycholinguistics and of language acquisition. That supports the main argument of the book, since the correlation of all those levels and approaches implies that the principles are fundamental and all-inclusive. I suggest, further, that that makes the argument comprehensive and fully coherent.

The supporting material given in this chapter has completed the explanation of premodifier order in English nominal phrases. There remain to be considered what explanations others have given, and some wider issues arising from what has been said so far. We turn to that in the next chapter.

10   Discussion

10.1 Introduction

The previous chapters have set out the structure of premodifiers in English, from both synchronic and diachronic points of view. This chapter is broader, discussing the zones themselves, grammaticalisation in the premodifiers, and – more broadly still – other theories of the order. The purpose is to complement the analysis of their structure with discussion of their significance for other areas of linguistics, including particular points of understanding, approaches taken and methodology.

10.2 Premodification zones

10.2.1 Introduction

In chapter 2, zones were presented in little more than assertion – that premodification in English nominal phrases is a structure of zones. This section draws on chapters 3 to 9 to vindicate that assertion, and to show their full significance.

10.2.2 Limits to the importance of zones and of apparent zone structure

The account of zones given so far seems to pose a problem: hearers and readers apparently select a premodifier's sense according to its zone, and rely on its position in premodifier order to identify the zone; but when a word is the only premodifier, they cannot identify its position, and presumably can therefore not identify the zone or the sense. The problem is real, but not as serious as it appears to be.

Many uses of premodifiers are readily interpreted without recourse to zone membership, because they have only one frequent use; and as Hawkins shows (2004), we ignore infrequent possibilities unless they are forced upon us. There is not likely to be any difficulty with *dangerous* and *silly* (since all common uses are Epithets), or with *broken* (Descriptor), or *water* and *leather* (Classifiers). When a word has uses in different zones, the hearer can use the context: in 'a <u>smart</u> person', *smart* must be an Epithet (because of *person*); in 'a <u>smart</u> bomb', it must be a Classifier (because of *bomb*).

There are other guides, noted previously, such as grading submodifiers, which indicate that the word is an Epithet, and inflectional morphology, e.g. *-er* and *-est* which also indicate an Epithet. Derivational morphology is also a guide. For example, in past centuries, *thundery, thunderous, thundering* and *thunderful* were used with varying senses in various zones; but now the usage has been systematised, with *thunder* as the Classifier, *thundery* as the qualitative Descriptor, *thundering* as the verbal Descriptor and colloquial Epithet, and *thunderous* as the regular Epithet *(thunderful* being now archaic). A similar systematisation provides adjectives for descriptive zones (e.g. *childish, birdlike*), and matching nouns as Classifiers (*child, bird*).

If all these interpretive procedures fail, then communication may fail, in part, as a consequence. For example, in 'an ugly, <u>rectilinear</u> old hulk', *rectilinear* must be read as an Epithet (because it is co-ordinated with the Epithet *ugly* and precedes *old* without coordination), so must be interpreted with relevant associations (like those of *ugly*); but if the phrase had been reduced to 'a <u>rectilinear</u> hulk', the reader would take the default reading of *rectilinear*, as a Descriptor, without those associations, and the writer's evocative intention would fail.

10.2.3   Zones as constructions

The discussion of Classifier order (in §5.8.2), showed that the five patterns in the Classifier zone are constructions (in the narrow sense), constituted by more specific constructions such as the qualia. Section 7.5 suggested that each of the other zones constitutes a construction. This section develops those conclusions.

The overall structure of the four zones, as set out in chapters 3 and 4, is a grammatical construction – a quite general and schematic one – with the following features. The order, premodifier + head, signifies the premodification relation, which is the construction's meaning (Goldberg 1995). The unmarked order is rigid (Givón 1979: 108; Haspelmath 2004: 58). The structure consists of categories (namely Reinforcers, Epithets and so on), rather than of particular words (Bybee 2003: 158). The structure has tight subordination (Givón 1979: 98), as shown in chapter 4. The fact that the zones are constructions is shown particularly clearly by the change in meaning that occurs when a word is moved to a different zone, in marked use (see chapter 7): it is the new construction that requires the new interpretation of the word.

There is thus a hierarchy of constructions, of the sort discussed by Croft (2001: ch. 1). The overall premodification (or 'attributive') construction is a schematic one, consisting of the more specific zone constructions (as in

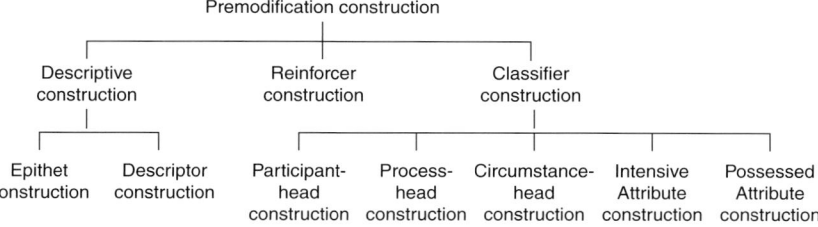

Figure 10.1 Hierarchy of constructions in premodification

§5.8.2). Lowest in the hierarchy come constructions consisting of particular words. Most of the hierarchy is set out in figure 10.1.

Each construction requires its constituents to be of a particular semantic class (see §5.1.3, for the classes), and specifies particular modificational relations. The overall premodification construction requires the premodifiers to be semantic properties. The descriptive construction (with Epithets and Descriptors) therefore takes property adjectives straightforwardly; but participles must be reconstrued as denoting properties instead of events in a narrative. The Classifier construction construes as a property the combination of the object denoted by the word and the constructional meaning; for example, in 'steel knife', the object STEEL + the quale MADE OF are construed as the property which is ascribed to the knife – MADE OF STEEL. The Reinforcer construction construes as property the reinforced contextual content of the word, taken from the descriptive meaning of the head (for example, EXTREME FOLLY, in 'a complete fool'). The Epithet construction (but not the Descriptor construction) allows modification of entities other than the head entity. The overall construction allows modification of the act of ascription (in modal premodifiers).

This account, I suggest, resolves the long-running puzzlement as to why noun premodifiers and some adjectives cannot be used predicatively, although most premodifiers can be; for an example of the discussion, see Quirk *et al.* (1985: §§7.37–39). Predicative use constitutes a different construction from attributive use: it requires words of the property class, and allows only ascription of that property to the head entity (subject of the clause, normally). Epithets and Descriptors fit those requirements, so they can be used predicatively. The following cannot be predicative: (a) Reinforcers, because they do not have property meaning of their own – not *'the fool is <u>utter</u>'; (b) modal premodifiers, because they are ascribed to the act of ascription, not to the head entity' – not *'the murderer is <u>alleged</u>'; (c) Classifiers, because they do not denote properties[1] – not *'the knife is <u>butcher's</u>' (compare §3.2.2 and §5.2.3.)

---

[1] It seems that predicative use is becoming acceptable; compare the discussion of Classifiers in predicative use §5.2.3.

It is crucial to that explanation that the ability to be predicative is deter-mined by the semantic class of each sense of a word; it is not determined by the word as a whole (i.e. by a lexical unit having various senses and syntactic properties). We can say, #'That behaviour is <u>infantile</u>' (Epithet sense), but not *'That paralysis is <u>infantile</u>' (Classifier sense).

10.2.4   Zones as an integrated system

The zones form a linguistic system, integrating the various levels of lan-guage, and integrated with the other parts of the nominal phrase (determin-ers, head, and postmodifiers).

Previous chapters have required a distinction between non-linguistic representations of the world and linguistic ones. (The distinction seems necessary anyway, because linguistic representations are linear in structure and involve features like anaphora, whereas other representations may be like images or networks, for example; see Levinson 2003: 34). The close-ness of the relationship between the linguistic and the non-linguistic rep-resentations varies on the scale of cognitive dominance, discussed in §9.4.1, and based on Gentner and Boroditsky (2001): concrete nouns, for example, are dominated by cognitive input, being relatively directly based on experi-ence of the world; closed-class words are dominated by linguistic input. As we saw (also in §9.4.1), nominal phrases range from cognitive dominance in head nouns, which denote displaced concepts (i.e. concepts independ-ent of the speech situation), to linguistic dominance in determiners (which are bound to the context of the speech situation), with the various types of premodifier as intermediate points in the range. Moreover, words in the different premodifier zones seem to have different mental structures and different processing (see §9.2), and determiners extend those differences, being processed more automatically and less consciously. Fortescue (2009) describes the neurolinguistic units of word processing as scaling from sen-sory, cognitive links at the base of cortical columns to verbal links at the top (the cortex surface). There is thus a coherent psycholinguistic scale right through the nominal phrase (leaving postmodification aside). Children's acquisition of nominal phrase structure follows that scale, starting at the cognitive end (§9.4.1).

That cognitive-linguistic scale is correlated with semantics. The differ-ent zones and subzones have different semantic structures (see chapters 3 and 5): entities, represented from experience, in the Classifier zone; qual-ities, becoming more general and subjective, in the Descriptor and Epithet zones; and wholly abstract and grammatical meaning in the Reinforcer and determiner zones (see chapter 3). They also grade in semantic function served, from naming through describing to pointing (§3.1.2.2), and in syn-tactic scope and function (chapter 4). We saw in chapter 3 that the lexicon is structured through the sense relations of synonymy, hyponymy and so on; we now see that it is structured across the zones in two additional ways. An Epithet, for example, may have Epithet synonyms, of the same semantic type, and Descriptor and Classifier synonyms, of different semantic types; and a single word may have Epithet, Descriptor and Classifier senses. The lexicon is very far from being an unstructured jumble of mere associations, as has often been asserted.

Just as the zones scale in what they represent, so do they scale in their contribution to the representation created by the whole phrase: zones further from the head do more to individuate the entity represented by the phrase. (See chapter 9, §9.3.4, for the concept of individuation.) Classifiers individualise it very little, as in 'those vibrant green <u>gum</u> trees', since they denote entities separate from the head entity, and evoke quite abstract relationships such as type or function. Descriptors are more individuating, being concrete and particular (*green*), and Epithets (*vibrant*) still more so, being subjective and more descriptive (Timberlake 1975: 126). Determiners such as *those* and *the* individuate the entity or entities completely (Timberlake 1975: 126); they will identify the entity on their own ('<u>that</u> tree' or '<u>the</u> tree'). Strikingly, the gradation applies even within the Classifier subzones. The order of subzones was described in chapter 5 as being from the most expected modifier–head relations (close to the head) to the least expected ones. For the qualia relations at least, the Classifiers furthest from the head are also the most individuating, as in #'Westinghouse two-inch brass electronic oil-pressure gauge'. *Oil-pressure* is abstract, and *electronic* is generic, giving little individuation; *brass* is a mass noun giving visual detail; *inch* is a count noun, giving dimensionality in space; *Westinghouse* is a proper noun giving dimensionality in space and time, making the gauge moderately individual.

Individuation is an important element in linguistic structure. It controls the genitive variation in Present-Day English (outlined in §5.8.4, and §9.3.4; see Feist in press for detail), and affects other patterning of the genitive (Timberlake 1975). It is the semantic side of the distinction between accusative, dative and genitive cases (Jacobson 1936/1990): those cases present the participant as progressively less involved in the situation and less individuated. Individuation is an important element in noun types and nominal phrase structure (Rijkhoff 2002), and in clause transitivity (Hopper and Thompson 1980). It affects reciprocal constructions (Lichtenberk 1991: §6). It is perhaps what is often referred to as 'animacy' (§9.3.4). Definiteness is closely related, in some definitions (Timberlake 1975: 125; Lyons 1977: 178). Dahl's 'referential integrity' (2001: 118) is very similar: 'the extent to which an item is associated with a unique individual in the world'. So is 'individuality' (Gentner and Boroditsky 2001), degree of 'referentiality' (Heine, Claudi and Hünnemeyer 1991; Ariel 2000, for example), and degree of elaboration of participants (Kemmer 1993) and of being 'manipulable' in discourse (Hopper and Thompson 1984).

When words at the cognitive end of the scale are dependent on context, that context is our knowledge of the real world; such words serve the experiential function primarily. The context that words at the linguistic end are dependent on is the speech situation – the speaker and hearer and their 'here and now'; they serve the interpersonal function.

This account explains the oddity, noted in §5.8.3, that the Classifier subzones can overlap the other zones in content, just as word senses with the same core content can occur in various zones. Premodification is not structured by content or knowledge of the world, but by our linguistic construal of it.

We conclude that determiners, premodifiers and head form a system with a stepped scale, in which linguistic representations of the world correlate the levels of language, and reflect linguistic development. That linguistic scale parallels the cognitive scale of nonlinguistic representations described by the philosophical distinction between first, second and third order entities, and between extrinsic or accidental properties and inherent, intrinsic or essential properties.

10.2.5   Word classes and gradience in the zones

Throughout the book, it has been explanatorily very useful to refer to the classes of Reinforcers, Epithets, and so on; there has been no occasion at all when the classes of 'adjective', 'noun' and so on have been useful as explanation. Adjectives, nouns and participles occur in most of the zones, changing their semantic and syntactic properties accordingly. Those properties belong to the uses or senses specific to particular zones, not to the words as lexical units; but 'adjective', 'noun', and so on are terms for words as lexical units.

Thus it is natural, and perhaps inevitable, that linguists have been unable to define the parts of speech strictly, treating them instead as 'prototypes' characterised by several features which range from being central to being peripheral. It is not only the variable clustering of features that is problematic; the individual features commonly given for 'adjective' are unsatisfactory, because words have those features in one 'adjectival' use but not in other adjectival uses of the same word. Gradability is given as a feature of adjectives in both standard reference works such as Quirk *et al.* (1985: §7.2), Biber *et al.* (1999: §7.2) and more recent works such as Aarts (2007: §5.1.3). But we have seen (chapter 3) that gradability is a feature of the Epithet senses only; the adjective *positive* <3> (Epithet) is gradable, but not *positive* <1> (Classifier), <2> (Descriptor), or <5b> (Reinforcer). The same oddity applies to a second characteristic, forming comparatives with *-er/-est*, since that depends on gradability. We saw in §10.2.3 above that having both attributive and predicative uses (given as a feature by Quirk *et al.* 1985: §7.2; Biber *et al.* §7.2; and Aarts 2007: §5.1.3) likewise varies with the particular senses. Descriptiveness, the last of Biber *et al.*'s four features, is like predicability in being a feature of words when used in Epithet and Descriptor zones, but not when used in Reinforcer and Classifier zones. The last characteristic in Aarts's list is taking *un-* as prefix; but *complete* and *perfect*, for example, take a negative prefix as Epithets but not as Reinforcers (§3.5.2); and taking a negative prefix is shared by adverbs, verbs, and nouns. It is not only true, then, that the individual features do not apply to all adjectives, as has been recognised: worse, particular adjectives possess their characteristic features on some occasions, but not on others, although they are still 'adjectives'.

Moreover, some adjective uses have none of the claimed characteristics. Reinforcer uses cannot be graded, cannot be inflected, cannot be predicative, and cannot take *un-*; for example, 'utter fool', 'sheer rubbish', 'complete fool'. The same is true of Classifier uses, for example 'infantile paralysis' and 'mental hospital' (although the Epithet uses of *infantile* and *mental* have those characteristics).

These arguments, reinforcing Croft's more general arguments (Croft 2001, 2007) against the traditional concept of form classes, lead to the conclusion that 'adjective' as a prototype concept for a class of whole words has no useful application in the description of Present-Day English. If we want to list words (or senses) in classes, we must recognize that it is no longer the traditional 'parts of speech' that are the linguistically real form classes in English nominal phrases, but Reinforcers, Epithets, Descriptors and Classifiers. The analysis that establishes them needs syntactic classes such as heads and modifiers, semantic classes such as the types and dimensions of meaning, morphological classes such as forms inflected for comparison, and (for some explanations) historical classes such as derived and nonderived. To discuss the constituents of English nominal phrases as 'adjectives' and other 'parts of speech' is to beg the vital question of what categories apply. The term 'adjective' has passed its use-by date.

To draw an analogy: bamboo stalks, lengths of steel rod and sections of water pipe may be used as clubs in the morning and cattle prods in the afternoon, but there is no value in saying that they change class: PROD and CLUB are functions rather than classes, and the same substance can be used for different functions. Similarly, in English nominal phrases, the same semantic 'substance' can be used for different syntactic functions.

The near universality and persistence of such an unsatisfactory concept as 'adjective' needs an explanation. It is simple. Old English had an adjective category strictly definable by its morphology and its position among premodifiers (see §8.2), but the subsequent millennium of change has changed the categories of the language – but not the representations of them in traditional grammar.

The foregoing chapters have shown some sorts of gradience in the zones – of subjectivity, abstractness and range of syntactic scope for example; and it would be easy to describe the zones as prototypes, whose features (subjectivity, abstractness and so on) grade in centrality within each zone and across the zones. But the zones constitute strict categories (if they are 'categories' at all), not areas of gradience, or prototypes: chapter 3 showed that the zones are strictly defined semantically; chapters 2, 6, and 7 showed that they have strict syntactic distinctions; they are not defined by gradient qualities such as subjectivity or abstractness, but by non-gradient qualities such as gradability and meaning type. A pony is no less a horse for being small, and an Epithet is no less an Epithet for being more subjective than others, size being irrelevant to HORSE and subjectivity being irrelevant to EPITHET. There is no 'subsective gradience' (Aarts 2007) within the category in either case. Both Epithets and Descriptors have antonyms, and birds and bees both have wings; but there is no 'intersective gradience' (Aarts 2007) between the categories, antonymy and wings being irrelevant.

There are two ironies here. First, 'prototype' applies reasonably well to the ill-defined and heterogeneous class of words we were all told at school were 'adjectives', just as it applies to the old class of 'fish' which included dolphins and whales. Second, it does have a valid linguistic use, but in its original sense as 'the first type of something', and when applied to the zones' Old English equivalents: genitive nouns as premodifiers, for example, were prototype Classifiers.

Neither prototype nor gradience has been a necessary concept for explaining the grammatical operation of English premodification, though gradience (but not prototype) has been useful in understanding the development and the relationships of the zones. We should conclude that the recent work which treats them as essential concepts in English grammar has mistaken their relevance and exaggerated their importance; and we should wonder whether Wierzbicka (1990: 365) is right in asserting that prototypes have been 'treated as an excuse for intellectual laziness and sloppiness'.

Finally, we should conclude that 'category' is also an unsatisfactory term here. Reinforcers, Epithets, Descriptors, Classifiers and heads are whatever forms can occupy zones. It is senses not words that occupy zones; the senses change a little in different contexts, and are reconstrued for use in different zones. Moreover, the senses may have quite different qualities simultaneously: we saw in §5.3.3, for example, that in 'serotonin reuptake inhibitor', *reuptake* has both 'verb' and 'noun' qualities. 'Category' is a misleading term for such uses – especially since the term variously conflates 'class of object', 'semantic class', 'meaning' and even 'concept' in various uses.

10.2.6   Effect of zone structure on compositionality

The zone structure has implications for the extent to which the meaning of nominal phrases is compositional – that is, the extent to which the meaning is 'a compositional function of the meanings of its grammatical constituents' (Cruse 2004: 65). Several facts from previous chapters lead to the conclusion that nominal phrases are more compositional than has been recognised in cognitive linguistics, even when modal modification, and 'indirect combination' as in 'beautiful dancer', are allowed for, as in Cruse (2004: §4.2).

First, we have seen that the elements of contextual meanings are not created on the occasion of use, but are activations of possible meanings already existing in the network. Second, we have seen that the grammatical meaning of words, interacting with the guidance provided by the zone constructions, instruct hearers on which possible meanings are to be activated; as Harder (1996) notes, the text of an utterance is like a recipe for its meaning, rather than like the cooked product. Third, compositionality depends on the powers of marked usage, as well as those of unmarked usage. The compositional functions of nominal phrases are thus more subtle and more highly specified than has been allowed, even by Cruse (2004). It follows that phrase meanings are more highly compositional. That has been illustrated in the production of neologistic senses in marked order across zones (for example, 'utter' as the meaning of *black*, and 'real' as the meaning of *coffee*, in §7.3.2), and in the complex meaning built up by interaction within and across zones (for example '… all those boisterous, kindly, vulgar people', in §6.5.3). So a further consequence of the productivity is that many common senses need not be stored individually in the lexicon; premodifiers need not be very polysemous, and could perhaps be monosemous.

However, there remain many expressions that are formulaic to some extent (see Wray 2002 and Cruse 2004: §4.3, for example), and constructionless Classifiers cannot be compositional (§5.7). Moreover, psycholinguistic work such as that of Lamb (e.g. 1999) and Barsalou (e.g. 1999) shows that word senses may be formed compositionally on some occasions but retrieved from memory on others. The conclusion is, then, that it is possible for nominal phrase meaning to be highly compositional, not that empirically it always is so. (Dictionary-makers have been strong proponents of polysemy, but even if the argument above is wholly correct, their approach perhaps has a historical justification: before the zone structure evolved, and with it full compositionality, premodifiers must have been polysemous, so it is reasonable to represent later senses polysemously.)

According to Cruse (2004: §4.5), linguists have viewed compositionality as like either building with blocks, or fleshing out a skeleton, or extracting parts of a network. The view here is closest to the network view, but draws on psycholinguistic research to hold that each utterance's network of meaning is not an established part of a static network, but is constructed dynamically for that utterance, in the acts of speaking and responding.

10.2.7   Conclusion: premodification zones

The concept, 'zone', is related to the concept, 'slot': both take 'fillers'. But whereas slots are commonly seen merely as positions in a sequence, without

meaning or powers of their own, this section concludes that the premodification zones of English have significance at most linguistic levels, and in
learning the language, and in processing it.

That importance does not seem to have been recognised previously,
although it was adumbrated by Quirk *et al.* (1985: §94 ff.). Previous writers have failed to see the nature of the relationships among levels, partly
because they have seen syntax as consisting of position and structure, without function for the meaning of the utterance, and have seen semantics as
consisting of concepts and little else.

10.3   Changes in premodifiers, and 'grammaticalisation'

10.3.1   Introduction

We have seen throughout the book that many premodifiers have changed in
types and dimensions of meaning within a sense, have gained new senses,
have changed zone both forward and back, and have changed rank (e.g. from
modifier to head). This section discusses how those changes are related,
beginning from the much-studied process of 'grammaticalisation', with
which these changes have a good deal in common.

The discussion starts (in §10.3.2) with the traditional approach to grammaticalisation[2] – in 'grammaticalisation studies' – arguing that the approach
is unsatisfactory, because by its analysis grammaticalisation appears in so
many places and in so many forms as to be incoherent as a process. The
section then argues (in §10.3.3) for an alternative approach, combining all
linguistic perspectives. It then (in §10.3.4) applies the preceding analysis
to the underlying issue of the fundamental nature of the changes, arguing that what 'grammaticalisation' has been intended to describe is in fact
systematisation.

I will group the changes into two main types. One is change in syntactic
status or 'rank', among head, modifier and submodifier ranks – movement
either 'up' or 'down' – as when the modifier *real* becomes a submodifier ('a
real good idea' or 'a really good idea'); related changes – of meaning, particularly – will be included. The other type is change of zone – movement
along the modifier rank, 'forward' or 'back' – with change in meaning and
so on. The distinction is made because the changes involved are somewhat
different, and because changes of rank include movement to postmodifier,
as well as to premodifier, position.

Two qualifications should be made. There are so many issues in the literature, and so many different approaches to them, that the discussion here

---

[2] I take that tradition to run from Meillet (1912/1958), and to include Lehmann (1982/1995),
Hopper and Traugott (1993, 2003), Bybee, Perkins and Pagliuca (1994), Fischer, Norde and
Perridon (2004) and Norde (2010), for example.

will assume some familiarity with them, and will be general, with only a narrow range of references and very little discussion of secondary issues. The section relies heavily on concepts and assertions established in earlier chapters, especially those on semantics and history.

10.3.2   The changes as viewed in the grammaticalisation-studies approach

10.3.2.1   Introduction

This section demonstrates that the grammaticalisation-studies approach would analyse most movements as grammaticalisation – forward and back, and change of rank – and demonstrates that such an approach is unsatisfactory. It takes Heine and Kuteva (2007) as representative; it uses their definition of grammaticalisation (2007: 32) as 'the development from lexical to grammatical forms, and from grammatical to even more grammatical forms'; and it uses their 'parameters' or criteria (2007: 34) of extension, desemanticisation, decategorialisation, and erosion. Some illustration will be given, but I ask the reader to keep in mind the examples in earlier chapters showing change of meaning and change of zone, especially the word histories given in §3.1.4, and §8.7.1.

10.3.2.2   Analysis of movement forward as grammaticalisation

We begin with how the traditional approach would treat 'movement forward' – which in my account excludes the change from head to Classifier, which is treated as movement down, since its main element is change of status. To represent the examples given previously, I summarise here the movement forward of *perfect* (see §8.7.1). *Perfect* began, in Middle English, with a Classifier-type sense <1a> 'Duly completed' (now obsolete). It developed a concrete and precise Descriptor-type sense <1c> 'Grown-up, adult'; then came a neutral and abstract Epithet sense <2> 'Having all the essential elements'; and then an emotive Epithet sense <4> 'Free from any flaw', which often loses all content and sometimes has informal social meaning. The Reinforcer sense <3e> 'Absolute' in SOED, which has grammatical meaning and no content, developed in the sixteenth century.

Premodifiers moving forward – *perfect*, for example – fit Heine and Kuteva's first criterion, of extension. They extend their syntactic context (by having more zones to modify), and their semantic context (by applying to a wider range of entities, and, as Reinforcers, to virtually any domain); and they gain new grammatical meanings (gradability, the various other grammatical powers described in chapter 4, and finally reinforcement). They also fit the criterion of desemanticisation, as they generalise: Classifiers lose their constructional meaning; Descriptors lose concrete and specific elements, including participles' loss of aspect; Epithets lose any expressive and social meaning and become wholly without content as Reinforcers. The third criterion, decategorialisation, does not apply as widely; it applies only to Epithets losing the adjectival properties of gradability and inflection for comparison as they become Reinforcers. Some criteria given by other writers also apply: chapter 3 showed that premodifiers form increasingly tight paradigms of closed-set words (Lehmann 1982/1995, Croft 2003, Hopper and Traugott 2003), and become more subjective (Traugott 1995, for example).

We conclude that from this approach the movement of premodifiers forward in nominal phrases is grammaticalisation, and, since most English premodifiers move forward (§8.7.1), that this form of grammaticalisation is a normal and regular feature of premodification. It follows also that the standard cline of grammaticalisation should be modified; it is given by Hopper and Traugott (2003: 7) as in (2) (the sign '>' means 'grammaticalises to'):

(2)   Content item > grammatical word > clitic > inflectional affix.

First, the stage 'content item' has two substages: (i) specific content item (the Descriptor zone), and (ii) general content item (the Epithet zone). Second, there is a stage before the content item – that is, naming item (Classifier zone) – which is free of descriptive content, serving a referential and identifying function (§3.2). Thus the cline for grammaticalisation of premodifiers forward is as given in (3), covering the single stage 'content item > grammatical word' in the cline given in (2), above:

(3)   Naming item > specific content item > general content item > grammatical item.

Expressed by zones, that cline is as shown in (4):

(4)   Classifiers > Descriptors > Epithets > Reinforcers.

There is some support for this conclusion in Adamson (2000) and Paradis (2000).

Finally, heads are less grammatical than modifiers (see below), and move 'forward' to Classifier position (§8.7.1); and premodifiers grammaticalise forward into determiners (see Davidse, Brems and De Smedt 2008, for example). It follows that there is a pathway of grammaticalisation from the head all the way forward, as shown in (5):

(5)   Head > Classifiers > Descriptors > Epithets > Reinforcers > determiners.

The pathway presumably continues within determiners, since the post-determiner numeral *one* grammaticalised into the central determiner *a/an*.

10.3.2.3   *Analysis of movement back as grammaticalisation*
This section deals with the way in which the traditional approach treats changes of zone 'back' towards the head. Again, I represent previous examples with *perfect*. Several Classifier senses formed by movement back,

including a physiological sense <10>, 'Developed to the fullest degree', formed from sense <1c> in the seventeenth century, and a bookbinding sense <16>, 'Glued, not sewn', formed in the nineteenth century.

The argument in this section is that, rather surprisingly, the same criteria as used above for movement forward show that movement back is grammaticalisation also. However, there are fewer such changes; and, to my knowledge, there are no changes from Reinforcer to Epithet.

The criteria of Heine and Kuteva (2007) apply. The move from Descriptor or Epithet to Classifier involves extension of the word from the context of descriptive relation with the head to the context of a quale relation with it, or subject or object relation with it, and so on (chapter 5), giving rise to a new grammatical meaning constituted by the quale or other relationship, expressed implicitly by the construction. There is desemanticisation: since Classifiers denote a single bare concept, Epithets must lose almost all their abstract meaning, their evocativeness and expressive and social meaning; and Descriptors must lose their perceptual meaning – the meanings of *perfect* given in §10.3.2.2, for example. The generalisation that brings desemanticisation is seen in the constructional meanings gained as a Classifier, e.g. the qualia. Epithets decategorialise in losing gradability and inflection for comparison as Descriptors, and in the syntactic and morphological reduction to Classifiers (§9.3.4). Erosion occurs as words move to Classifier: the phrase loses stress (compare *swimming animal* Descriptor, and *swimming baths* Classifier); and the parallel loss of a syllable in *swim school* is perhaps a form of erosion, along with the loss of the plural -*s* and genitive -'*s* (§9.3.4).

Other criteria apply, also. Epithets and Reinforcers lose their linguistic paradigmaticity (§3.4.4 and §3.5.6; compare §10.2.4 above) as Descriptors, becoming patterned weakly but more perceptually or experientially, but gain cognitive paradigmaticity as Classifiers (§10.2.4 above; compare Halliday 2004: 320). Words moving back take scope over progressively smaller constructions – 'syntagmatic weight' (Lehmann 1982/1995, and other writers); and they are more closely bound to other words in the construction, both in zone position (chapter 4, particularly §4.7.1), and above all when they become part of a compound or acronym – 'syntagmatic cohesion' (Lehmann 1982/1995, and other writers).

We conclude that movement towards the head is grammaticalisation, also, and that it is fairly frequent (§8.7.1), and regular. In it, the path of grammaticalisation forward is reversed, as in (6):

(6)   Reinforcers > Epithets > Descriptors > Classifiers.

10.3.2.4   Analysis of movement up and down as grammaticalisation
i   Introduction
This section deals with premodifiers changing in their rank status as head, modifier, or submodifier. It argues that by the traditional standards,

movement down is grammaticalisation, and that movement up is regular degrammaticalisation – although the tradition says degrammaticalisation is anomalous and rare. Like the last one, the section invokes the word histories and tables of senses in previous chapters, but begins with a brief general example. The adjective *gentle* rose to a higher rank, with head status as a noun three times: with an affix, it formed *gentleness*, and without an affix it became the noun <1>, '...a person of gentle birth', and the noun <2> 'A maggot' (from the adjectival sense, 'slender'). It also moved to a lower rank, as the first element of a compound (*gentleman*), and as an adverb ('<u>gently</u> rolling hills').

ii   Lowering in rank: movement 'down'
This section argues that from the traditional approach changes downward are a fairly straightforward form of grammaticalisation.

Heads becoming premodifiers undergo extension in gaining a new syntactic context, that of preceding and modifying another word, and in gaining the new grammatical meaning of modification. They desemanticise, in losing the descriptive meaning that head nouns have in descriptive use, e.g. from 'He's just an <u>animal</u>!' to '<u>animal</u> rights', and in losing referentiality (Heine, Claudi and Hünnemeyer 1991: 174), boundedness (see §9.3.4) and degree of individuation (see §10.2.4 above). Modifiers that keep their noun form are decategorialised, in their morphological reduction (§9.3.4); noun heads that become adjectives decategorialise in losing noun properties; but they recategorialise in gaining adjectival properties. They may be said to erode or to not erode, for the same reasons.

Lowering from Classifier includes compounding, e.g. *iron man* to *ironman* and *week's end* to *weekend*, which is regularly considered to be grammaticalisation (reduction to bound morpheme); blending may be included, e.g. from *motor hotel* to *motel*. Epithets lowering becoming submodifiers (e.g. *very*; the adjective 'true' becoming an adverb, and *total*, as in 'a [<u>total</u> maximum [allowable contribution]]'), thereby gaining a new syntactic context and the grammatical meaning of reinforcement. As Epithets become reinforcing words, they desemanticise in losing their descriptive meaning. They decategorialise, since they can no longer inflect for comparison, e.g. 'a <u>real</u> hot day'.

Although the moves between noun, adjective and adverb are changes of category rather than loss of categoriality, they constitute grammaticalisation as usually understood. That is accepted by various writers, including Heine and Kuteva (2007: §2.2.1.1). As grammaticalisation among syntactic ranks, it may perhaps be called 'rank grammaticalisation'.

iii Rise in rank: movement 'up'
The move up from modifier to head contravenes the parameters of traditional grammaticalisation. When the phrases '<u>chinook</u> wind', '<u>chinook</u> jargon' and '<u>chinook</u> salmon' each became the single word *chinook*, the word

gained meaning – the meaning of reference as head of the phrase; when *turkey hen* became *turkey*, it gained descriptive potential, as in 'He's a real turkey, don't you think?', referentiality (Heine, Claudi and Hünnemeyer 1991: 174), and degree of individuation. Such uses were <u>not</u> extensions to a new context, and they <u>lost</u> their grammatical meaning of modification. They <u>gained</u> categorial status, being now able to inflect as nouns for plural and possession, which they could not do as Classifiers. By the traditional standards, then, this change is <u>degrammaticalisation</u>. The change occurred in *gentle* in Old English, and is now common: *my mobile [phone], a red [wine], nuclear [energy]*, and so on.

When prefixes such as *mini-* and *mega-* and elements of a compound such as *sand-dune* and *salt-cellar* become independent modifying words, they degrammaticalise, to the extent that the dependent element gains content of its own, and gains categorial status as an independent word. On the other hand, both forms grammaticalise to the extent that they gain a new grammatical meaning, that of modification.

Other forms of rise in rank are those of *actual* from modifier to discourse particle (§3.5.6), and of *lovely* to use as a 'response particle' (Adamson 2000: 62). Such words degrammaticalise in becoming more independent or 'autonomous', effectively acting at clause level not phrase level; but they grammaticalise in extending their context, generalising and losing their content.

iv   Conclusion to analysis of movement up and down
The conclusions from this discussion of changes in rank are as follows. Grammaticalisation as traditionally understood occurs regularly as words shift from head to modifier and then to submodifier, and perhaps also when they shift to being an element of a compound. Second, degrammaticalisation occurs regularly as submodifiers and compound elements shift to modifier status, and from modifier to head. These changes from rank to rank are different from changes within the modifier rank, and are quite common; so grammaticalisation studies should recognise rank grammaticalisation as an important pathway, distinct from other grammaticalisation.

We have seen that words such as *turkey* and *chinook* moved from head to modifier and back to head (with a new sense). Such cyclic changes are quite common. Other examples include *dwarf*, from noun ('small person') to adjective then noun ('small star'), and *Brie, Camembert* and *Cheddar*, and *Ford, Honda*, etc. The cycle for genitives is more varied: it led from genitive noun modifier in Old English to Classifier noun modifier in Present-Day English, either through postmodifying genitive (e.g. 'business <u>of the school</u>'), or through determiner genitive (e.g. 'the <u>men's</u> shoes', '<u>Ford's</u> cars'), or perhaps through both ('the budget <u>of the university</u>' and 'the <u>university's</u> budget' to 'the <u>university</u> budget'). The role in grammaticalisation of postmodifiers and of genitives (both postmodifying and determining) seems to need further research.

10.3.2.5   Conclusion to viewing the changes traditionally

We see afresh the familiar fact that there are many pathways of grammaticalisation as traditionally understood. We reach the further conclusion, for grammaticalisation within nominal phrases, that other authors have reached for grammaticalisation elsewhere: it is not a unitary phenomenon or process, but occurs in various forms; see, for example, Bybee, Perkins and Pagliuca (1994: §8.10), Tabor and Traugott (1998) and Fischer (2007: §3.2). However, it is more widespread, more frequent and more varied than has been recognised: it occurs right through nominal phrases, from head to determiner, and both towards the determiner and away from it; it occurs also as change in rank downward towards submodifier status; it is a general characteristic of premodifiers, not an incidental process affecting a few words here and there; it has been occurring for many centuries, and is continuing. We see also that degrammaticalisation is a regular process in English.

However, the reader will agree, I trust, that the account given in §10.3.2.2 to §10.3.2.4 is problematic. It is unsatisfactory that so many criteria are available, and that there is no consensus on what they are. Many of the changes have features of grammaticalisation and degrammaticalisation simultaneously, especially loss and gain of meaning. That is perhaps a result of the further problem that many of the subprocesses involved, such as desemanticisation, extension and subjectification, are very varied in nature. We end up with a great deal of analytical data, but not with a great deal of general understanding. We need a different approach.

10.3.3   The changes as viewed in a broader approach

10.3.3.1   Introduction

This section seeks to resolve the problems just summarised. It argues that a better and fuller account of semantics and syntax should be added to the traditional analytical focus on morphemes, and that we should add functional, onomasiological and psycholinguistic perspectives to the analytical perspective. That gives a better general understanding of the changes, and it gives insight into some specific issues such as unidirectionality and gradience.

10.3.3.2   Analytical perspective

The traditional approach, defining grammaticalisation as the development from lexical words or morphemes to grammatical ones, and thus being focused on the morphological level of analysis, gives an inadequate account of the semantic level. The definitions oppose being grammatical and functional to being lexical and having content. Since being lexical and having content generally amounts to having meaning, that implies that grammatical words are meaningless. But chapter 3 showed that Reinforcers, as grammatical words, have meaning, both the grammatical meaning of reinforcement and the 'content' meaning of such abstract concepts as INTENSIFICATION. That chapter showed also that even the most 'lexical' premodifiers are 'grammatical' in having grammatical meaning. It follows that all premodifiers are both 'lexical' and 'grammatical', and that the traditional contrast is misconceived. The types of meaning (chapter 3) and their history (§8.7.1) explain these puzzles about desemanticisation or 'bleaching': when words lose one type of meaning or weaken on one dimension, they may or may not gain in other types or dimensions – for example, they gain emotive meaning in becoming an Epithet, or intensification meaning in becoming a Reinforcer, or constructional meaning in becoming a Classifier.

The traditional view also has an important syntactic implication. Its opposition between being a lexical or content item and being a grammatical or functional one implies that lexical items, such as nouns and verbs, have no grammatical qualities and are not functional. But chapters 3 and 4 have shown that 'lexical' words such as Classifiers and Descriptors have syntactic function (as modifiers). Again, the traditional contrast is misconceived. We would do better to see lexis and morphosyntax ('grammar') as forming a single level of language – 'lexicogrammar', in Halliday's term (2004) – consisting of constructions ranging from schematic to specific (§10.2.3 above), all of which have lexical and morphosyntactic properties. We should see grammaticalisation as consisting of change in constructions, often involving the creation of a new category, such as Reinforcer or article.

Previous chapters have shown that, although the levels of language are (in part) interdependent, they are also (in part) autonomous, not only in having their own units and structures, but also in allowing different 'mappings'. For example, meaning may be mapped onto words (as when PAST is expressed as *past* or *yesterday*), or onto bound morphemes (as when PAST is expressed as *-ed*), or onto constructions (as when IS AGENT OF is mapped onto the subject + predicator construction or the Actor + Goal Classifier construction, not on to words as in 'It is an agent of change'). Different meanings may be mapped onto the same word simultaneously, and one meaning may be mapped onto a grammaticalising morpheme as another one is lost. That helps explain why it is so common for words to be enriched in meaning even while they are being 'bleached'. The semi-independence of the strata also explains why semantics may change without syntactic change, and without morphological change, and so on (Andersen 2006 has an interesting separation of the processes); and it explains why words can grammaticalise in opposite directions.

10.3.3.3   Functional perspective

The paragraph on syntax just above argued that the traditional view gives an inadequate account of function. The functional perspective on language takes that further. For example, Traugott (e.g. 1982) and some others (e.g. the writers in Stein and Wright 1995) have focused on subjectification as part of Halliday's interpersonal metafunction. I believe that the study of grammaticalisation has been weakened by writers' failure to keep in mind that interpersonal function, and the textual function; they have commonly made the assumption that all language is experiential, functioning to communicate information and consisting of conceptual meaning. It has been weakened further by failure to distinguish among the most general functions (the 'metafunctions'), lower-level syntactic functions (such as modifying) and semantic functions (such as naming and describing – §3.1.2.2), and the most basic functions, at content level (such as being an argument of an event).

In particular, the contrast between the different metafunctions explains why both backward and forward grammaticalisation can produce paradigmaticity and the use of closed word classes. The textual and expressive metafunctions form Reinforcers' and Epithets' linguistic paradigms, with grammatical, expressive and social meaning; the experiential function, on the other hand, forms the Classifiers' cognitive paradigms. That contrast also supplies the motivation for the different forms of grammaticalisation. Grammaticalisation forward exploits increased semantic and syntactic range, for its expressive power, serving the interpersonal function; grammaticalisation backward exploits increased precision of words and of the Classifier relations to the head, for their cognitive and logical value, serving the experiential function. Grammaticalisation downward exploits increased structural complexity within the phrase for simplicity of clause structure, serving the textual function; and degrammaticalisation upward simplifies and economises phrase structure – again, serving textual function.

10.3.3.4   Onomasiological perspective

All the approaches discussed so far focus on the expression (word or 'form') alone. Alternatively, we can study the relationship between the expression and what is expressed: whether the meaning or intention is expressed lexically (mapping onto words), grammatically (mapping onto bound morphemes), constructionally, or phonologically (by intonation, for example) – an onomasiological approach, in contrast to the usual semasiological one.

Consider examples of postmodifying phrases being converted to Classifiers, for example when 'a nail 6 inches in length' becomes 'a six inch nail', and when 'sale of arms by Israel' becomes 'Israeli arms sales'. The relational concepts that were previously expressed explicitly by words (as underlined) are expressed implicitly by constructions, instead; they are converted from lexical expression to grammatical expression. In other cases, meanings come to be expressed, where previously no such meaning exists. For example, in grammaticalisation back (e.g. the Descriptor *mobile* becoming the Classifier *mobile*, as in '<u>mobile</u> phone'), the constructional meaning ('of the type called' in that example) is created, not converted; as the Epithets *utter*, *total* and *sheer* grammaticalised forward into Reinforcers, the grammatical meaning 'Reinforce the head word' appeared, along with the abstract concept of REINFORCEMENT entailed in it. Meanings may also vanish (e.g. the Epithet content of *utter*, *total* and *sheer*). Grammaticalisation thus involves not only changes in the word or morpheme, but changes in what is expressed and how – onomasiological changes. Since movement forward entails expressing the grammatical meaning in a single lexical item, and movement back entails expressing it constructionally, the two movements can perhaps be distinguished as 'lexical grammaticalisation' and 'constructional grammaticalisation'.[3]

For lexical expression of grammatical meaning in Reinforcers and of emotive meaning in Epithets and so on to be possible, those types of meaning and their zones had first to be differentiated – just as children learning to speak must differentiate their holophrastic expressions. The formation of the zones in Middle English, and the later formation of the Classifier sub-zones, were thus forms of grammaticalisation; in grammaticalisation, as in language acquisition, differentiation and extension (of constructions and of words) are complementary, and are both needed.[4]

Lack of the onomasiological perspective helps explain why grammaticalisation has generally been understood to consist of weakening of meaning or mere generalisation: linguists have not realised that it entails the lexicalisation or constructionalisation of the grammatical meaning or 'function' – a specific addition to the meaning. It also helps us understand why the development of constructions has been ignored in much of the literature, and why even constructional linguists have missed the emergence of the zones as constructions, along with the whole sets of new categories they entail (§8.7.3).

---

[3] This onomasiological distinction illuminates the different phases of change noted in chapter 8 (§8.5.5). Proto-Indo-European developed the genitive case as a way of relating nominals in a single vague relationship, using constructional expression. Old English or its predecessor developed more precise expression of such relationships, using lexical expression in the suffixes of denominal adjectives, such as *-y* and *-ish*. Later Modern English has reused constructional expression, but this time in a much more complex and precise form, relating nominals in the Classifier constructions.

[4] The importance of differentiation in both history and children's learning of language gives a new perspective on compositionality, as discussed in §10.2.6 above. To the extent that language develops by differentiating holistic situational utterances, rather than by combining words as units of abstract content, we should study differentiability rather than compositionality – the ability of intention and meaning to be differentiated or distinguished. That approach would encounter far fewer difficulties, I believe.

10.3.3.5   Psycholinguistic perspective
The psycholinguistic perspective can contribute two useful points. First, the unconscious processing of grammatical meaning (§9.2) helps explain why linguists have taken grammatical words to be low in meaning, or 'bleached': like other users, they have low awareness of words' grammatical meaning. Second, as words grammaticalise forward, they move along the scale of cognitive dominance (§10.2.4 above) towards its linguistic end, enriching their linguistic value; grammaticalising back takes them closer to the cognitive end, enriching their cognitive value. That understanding supports the explanation of the functional and motivational value given above, and the explanation of enrichment of meaning.

10.3.3.6   Conclusion to the changes as viewed in a broader approach
We conclude, in general, that to understand these changes properly requires us to analyse them on several levels, to allow for the varying relationships among the levels and to see the changes from several complementary perspectives. The changes in a single morpheme, which are the traditional content of grammaticalisation studies, are only part of the historical process. Indeed, many more recent writers define grammaticalisation much more broadly; of the writers on the evolution of language in Christiansen and Kirby (2003), for example, Tomasello (pp. 102–3) describes it as 'loose and redundantly organised discourse structures congealing into tight and less redundantly organised syntactic constructions', and others in that collection agree – Christiansen and Kirby (p. 4), Hurford (p. 51) and Briscoe (p. 305). See also Dahl (2001). Trousdale and Traugott (2010) and some of the other writers in Traugott and Trousdale (2010) go part way to such an understanding, but for most the focus is still on the particular 'grammatical item'; Vincent and Börjars (2010), however, offer a refreshing and satisfying view of 'a multidimensional space within which the properties of an element [i.e. a grammaticalising item] can vary' (2010: 286). Most approaches have been focused too narrowly, I suggest; they have suffered from the difficulty identified by Denison (2010) as 'WYSIWYTCH' – 'What You See Is What Your Theory Can Handle'.

There are many related processes, such as lexicalisation, semanticisation, categorialisation, and development of constructions; most or all of them can be reversed; and they occur with changes in position or independently of them, in various combinations. Nothing seems to be gained by putting them together under the single word, 'grammaticalisation'. The term was useful for labelling certain data when Meillet (1912/1958) and his successors used it, but it seems to have little descriptive or analytical value now; it is another of the 'prototype' concepts found wanting in §10.2.5 above.

The first specific conclusion we may draw is that grammaticalisation as traditionally understood is bi-directional. Many of its elements occur in both movement forward and movement back; and movement up denies even the narrow sense of unidirectionality (that the steps in one grammaticalisation process are not retraced). Degrammaticalisation is completely normal; the different motivations given above also make grammaticalisation and degrammaticalisation equally natural. Even Norde's complete book on the subject (2010) does not recognise those facts. Another conclusion is that grammaticalisation and degrees of synchronic grammaticalness are isomorphic in English nominal phrases, contrary to the expectations of Tabor and Traugott (1998: 263), in both movement across the zones and between the ranks. Further, grammaticalisation occurs abruptly and in the moment of use, in synchronic usage, contrary to the general assumption. In marked order (chapter 7), words are generalised and given new syntactic functions in ad hoc use, as when *X-ray* moved from Classifier forward to Epithet in 'good, penetrating, <u>X-rayish</u> phrases'. Similarly, words are given a new syntactic context and function in marked syntax (§4.8.2.4), as in 'a large **black** sofa'.

A further issue is that of gradience. We see that there is some semantic gradience (or 'gradualness' to some writers, since we are dealing with historical change), as words slowly and gradually acquire new elements of meaning, and I have described the changes as 'clines', because that is customary. But there is no significant gradience syntactically, since the contrasts are between zones, and between ranks, all of which are strict categories; the clines have steps. That reinforces the conclusion on gradience reached in §10.2.5 above.

The final issue to be considered is that of pathways. Grammaticalisation has many pathways, in that it varies significantly between nominal phrases, verbal phrases and so on; but this section and previous chapters have shown that there is only a little variation in the path up and down, i.e. in whether the path involves prefixes or elements of compounds; and that there is a single pathway for movement forward and backward (although various words travel various sections of it).

10.3.4 General conclusion to premodifier changes and grammaticalisation

This section first summarises the changes related to grammaticalisation; then it builds on one element of the summary to conclude that, behind the complexity and apparent contradictions of the four types of change, there is a single unifying change: language becoming more systematic.

The changes may be summarised as in figure 10.2. It represents the zones across the page, and the ranks vertically, with bold arrows for directions of change. Note that the diagram is very schematic, especially in not indicating particular vertical pathways or the distances travelled.

A semantic view of the changes is given in figure 10.3, which is a version of the semantic map given in earlier chapters. It has been revised to show the directions of change, with arrows, and their dominant motivation by the

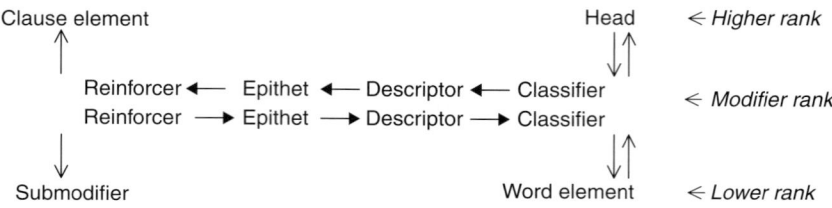

Figure 10.2 Summary of 'grammaticalisation' in nominal phrases

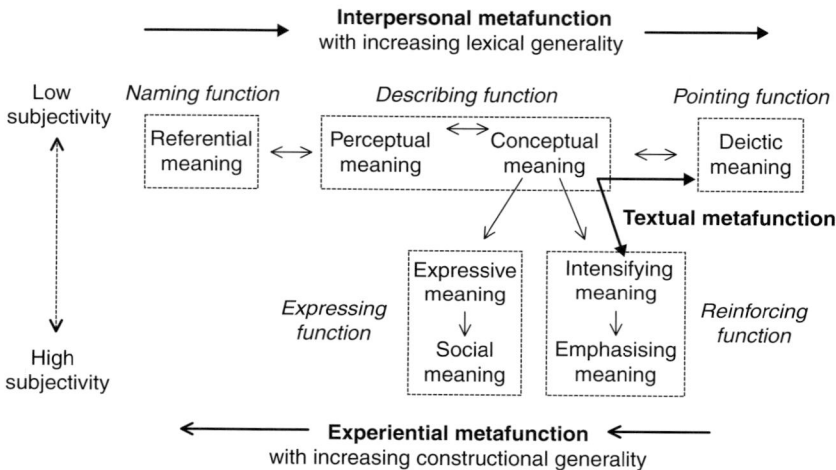

Figure 10.3 Semantic changes in nominal phrases

metafunctions, in bold – equivalent to the bold horizontal arrows in figure 10.2. The diagram shows the semantic nature of English nominal phrases both synchronically and diachronically, and their syntactic nature largely flows from that; so it sums up a good deal of the book – and has been left rather dense accordingly.

Figure 10.2 highlights the role of dependency in the changes, which has been only implicit till now, because the literature has downplayed syntax. It shows fairly clearly that 'vertical' movement is change in the level of dependency, since that goes with syntactic rank. But because of its schematisation, the figure conceals the role of dependency in horizontal movement: the changes of zone entail changes in the level of dependency, since each modifier is dependent on later words in the phrase, the structure being Reinforcer [Epithet [Descriptor [Classifier head]]]; the changes in dependency are small, and within the same syntactic rank. The changes forward, back, down and up therefore have much more unity than has been apparent in the discussion so far, suggesting that the original intuitive concept labelled 'grammaticalisation' had more validity than the developing literature made clear, and that it may be in some way valid to use a single term for most or all of the four movements. Is there, then, a curious state, commonly called 'being more grammatical', which can occur at both ends of the phrase – at opposite ends of the same spectrum – and at top and bottom of the rank scale? The answer to be argued for here is 'yes': what has been described as 'being more grammatical' is better described as being more systematic, where being a system entails, in general, being a set of interdependent parts serving a common purpose or purposes. In language, being more systematic entails having the units and functions operate on more levels of dependency, and with more choices, the choices being linked more closely but more flexibly. Each end of a spectrum can be more or less systematic, since the structuring can be of different kinds, as with the structure of the family and the structure of the nation at the ends of the social spectrum.

At one end of the premodification scale, Reinforcers and Epithets are more systematic than Descriptors and Classifiers, both lexically and grammatically, in several ways. Epithets have many types of meaning available as choices; choices are linked (e.g. choosing to use a Reinforcer requires a further choice among maximiser, minimiser and limiter, and using Epithets' social meaning requires choices among dialect and level of formality). Finally, the choices are closer to being exhaustive and mutually defining, e.g. the sets of synonyms and antonyms in Epithet position. The organisation of these choices as systems depends on the generalised, abstract meaning of the words. At the other end of the scale, Classifiers are more systematic than Descriptors and Epithets, both lexically and grammatically, in having the subzones as choices; in the link between choosing a Classifier of one quale (etc.) and choice of other Classifiers in the phrase; and in their cognitive paradigmaticity (compare §3.2.3.2, and such examples as *fluorescent, phosphorescent, luminescent*). The organisation of these Classifier choices as systems depends on the generalised, rather schematic constructions on which the words depend. On the scale of rank, the bottom of the scale is systematic in the same way that Epithets and Reinforcers are; it offers several degrees or qualities as alternative submodifications of each modifier, and increased grammatical function; its system is organised through abstractions such as intensification.

That account of grammar as systematicity is supported strongly by Systemic Functional Grammar,[5] and less directly by the concepts of relationality (Gentner and Boroditsky 2001), of cohesion as a parameter of grammaticalisation (Lehmann 1982/1995, and others), and of grammar as 'patterns for grouping morphemes into progressively larger configurations' (Langacker 1987: 12).

---

[5] The main difference from Halliday, for example (2004: §1.3), is the use there of 'system' only for what is systematic paradigmatically, and of 'structure' for what is systematic syntagmatically.

What, then, are at the ends of the synchronic spectrum and of the diachronic process, if not 'grammar' and 'lexis'? Synchronically, the answer lies in the linguistic-cognitive scale discussed in §10.2.4. For nominal phrases, at the head end is language that predominantly serves a cognitive or experiential function, directly related to experience, and at the determiner end is language that predominantly serves an expressive or interpersonal function, its units being directly related to other linguistic units and only indirectly to experience. Movement forward and back among premodifier zones has the more cognitively systematic Classifiers at one end and the more linguistically systematic Reinforcers at the other end. (It is the connection between 'linguistic' and 'grammatical' that has led to the changes being called 'grammaticalisation'.) Movement up and down has the more linguistically systematic submodifiers, e.g. intensifiers, at the bottom, and the more cognitively systematic heads at the top. Diachronically, holophrases such as interjections and children's first utterances seem to be at one end of the process and our more fully differentiated and structured present-day language at the other – as in §10.2.4 above, which presented the zones as an integrated system. Seeing 'grammaticalisation' as systematisation also enables us to see why the changes work in both directions: changes in one direction develop cognitive system and serve one function; changes in the other direction develop linguistic system and serve a different function.

Let us sum up. Our understanding would be aided if lexicalisation, desemanticisation, decategorialisation and so on were kept distinct, as related changes that may combine in various ways; and if the various perspectives on language were combined in the study of change. We should see being 'more functional' or 'more grammatical' as being more systematic, cognitively or linguistically.

10.4   Other theories of premodifier order

10.4.1   Introduction

This discussion of other accounts of premodifier order is intended to clarify my own by contrast, to support it by showing that what is of value in others is incorporated in it, and to suggest some wider linguistic significance in the issues raised.

There have been many theories of English premodifier order. They may be classified as follows. Conceptual theories (or 'semantic' or 'ontological' theories) are those that explain premodifier order by the concepts which the modifiers denote. Semantic theories, including my explanation in chapter 3, relate the order to the nature of the relation between words and what they denote or express. Syntactic theories, including my explanation in chapter 4, explain order by structure, as revealed by tree diagrams or constituent analysis, for example. Grammatical theories explain order by part of speech, by transformations underlying the modifiers, or by 'functional projections' in which the modifiers are generated. Functional theories explain order from functions such as 'characterising' and 'classifying'. Psycholinguistic theories explain order by the mental processes that produce it.

This section first discusses those theories as a group, then goes on to particular types of theory, showing how what is valuable in them is incorporated in my own account, showing what is inadequate in them, and suggesting how the theorists went wrong. A fuller exposition and critique of the theories may be found in Feist (2008: chapters 2 and 11).

10.4.2   General discussion of the theories

All the theories I am aware of lack an account of the zones – that is, syntactic positions which take words in specific uses or senses, whose members are co-ordinated with each other and subordinated to those in following zones, and whose members constitute categories. (Quirk *et al.* 1985 describe 'zones', but they take prototypes rather than categories.) That lack has several crippling consequences.

First, without categorial distinctions between positions, the theories must all limit their explanations to being merely 'tendencies', the 'preferred order' and so on. The exceptions are either not explained at all, or are explained by further tendencies and preferences. The theories are consequently not only unsatisfactory as explanations, but create a difficulty they cannot solve in the complexity of processing they imply. For example, in the transformational theory of Vendler (1968), the mind handles twenty-two different transformations and twenty-two different possible premodifier positions, all of which are subject to being overruled by other criteria. According to Quirk *et al.* (1985: 1338–9): within their 'Zone II', nonderived words tend to come before deverbal words, which tend to come before denominal words; and within nonderived words, size and length words tend to come before others. That makes seven positions; but since emotive words tend to precede others in all those positions (two places within each position), there are in effect fourteen positions. Speakers must calculate indefinite probabilities for fourteen positions, within the single zone. It seems extremely unlikely that the mind can operate such systems.

Other consequences of having no provision for strict zones are that the theories cannot explain the regular variation in meaning among uses of the same word in different positions, especially when the uses have a single core meaning in common, as illustrated in table 10.1. (The table shows that the variation can extend even to determiners.) Nor can they explain the coerced change of meaning in marked order, or the effects possible in free order; and they have no principled way of explaining the co-ordinated historical changes in position and meaning.

Table 10.1 *Word uses with a single core meaning, in different positions*

Word	Determiner	Epithet	Descriptor	Classifier	Head
main	*a*	*self-supporting*	*woody*	*main*	*stem*
	the	*popular*	*main*	*dining*	*room*
	the	*main*	*independent*	*AIDS homecare*	*provider*
red		*small*	*dried*	*red*	*chiles*
	a	*big*	*red*	*question*	*mark*
	a	*bright red[,] gorgeous*	*[old]*	*fire*	*engine*
single	*a*		*booming*	*8-watt single*	*speaker*
	the	*new*	*single*	*European*	*currency*
		fine[,] single	*white*		*border*
	the single	*biggest*	*stationary*	*air*	*polluter*

A second general weakness in other theories is that they are not based on a wide enough range of data – although Quirk *et al.* (1985) is perhaps an exception. Because the theorists did not examine phrases with several Classifiers, for example, they could not account for Classifier constructions, and because they did not examine multiple uses of particular premodifiers, they did not realise that they must account for the use of one word in several zones, as illustrated in table 10.1. They over-generalise useful observations.

Most theories give a statement of the order, but do not say why one class of concept, one part of speech, one function, or the product of one transformation should precede another. Their 'explanation' itself requires explanation.

A final general weakness is that most theories have been based on an unsatisfactory understanding of how the forms of explanation are related. The most obvious instance of that is their reliance on the understanding of the levels of language embodied in the traditional 'parts of speech' (see §10.2.5 above). As a consequence, many writers have considered only adjectives, implicitly equating them with premodifiers; thus, they have treated adjectival postdeterminers such as *same* and *other* as modifiers, treated noun premodifiers as if they were not modifiers at all, and ignored adverbial and participial premodifiers. Some writers have considered syntax to be fully autonomous, leading them to misunderstand the relationship of position and meaning. Quirk and his colleagues (1985), in spite of their wealth of data and rich insight, made the converse error of failing to understand that semantics and syntax, acting together as described in chapters 3 and 4, have enough autonomy in unmarked order to constitute strict rules and withstand the pressures of phonology and stylistic considerations; that contributed to their complex web of tendencies described above. Some theories, including those from parts of speech and from transformations, seem to have misunderstood the relation between synchronic and diachronic explanations, and

Table 10.2 *Dixon's theory of premodifier order*

		Adjectival modifiers					Post-adjectival modifiers	
Value	Dimension	Physical property	Speed	Human propensity	Age	Colour	Origin/ composition	Purpose/ beneficiary
good	*wide*	*hard*	*fast*	*wicked*	*new*	*white*	*oatmeal*	*dog*
bad	*big*	*heavy*	*slow*	*clever*	*old*	*brown*		
delicious	*long*	*hot*	*quick*	*jealous*	*young*	*black*		

none that I know of have seen that history itself is a partial explanation. Others again have given primacy to either a psycholinguistic explanation or a strictly linguistic one, instead of ensuring that the explanation conforms to linguistic and psycholinguistic criteria equally.

10.4.3   Particular types of theory

10.4.3.1   Conceptual theories
Some conceptual theories explain order by the concepts themselves. Dixon (1982), for example, asserts that value words precede dimension words, which precede physical property words, and so on, as set out in table 10.2. (The last two columns represent phrases like 'oatmeal dog food'.) Huddleston and Pullum (2002) give a similar account. Other works include those conceptual classes as a subordinate part of their theory, (e.g. Hetzron 1978, Quirk *et al.* 1985, and Bache 2000).

Some theories explain the order as a gradation in a certain property of the concepts: for example, certain premodifiers come close to the head because their concepts are more iconic (e.g. Haiman 1985), more particular (e.g. Givón 1990), more inherent (e.g. Givón 1990 and Whorf 1945/1956), or more intrinsic (e.g. Byrne 1979).

All these conceptual theories err in following the philosophical tradition which sees language as symbolising knowledge directly (and knowledge as representing the world directly), ignoring the practical, expressive and social functions of language, and unaware of the important differences between knowledge and meaning. In particular, the theorists seem to have been unaware of the subtle and complex cognitive-linguistic scale discussed in §10.2.4 above. That, I suggest, is why they do not account for premodifiers that have only grammatical meaning (Reinforcers), premodifiers that have purely attitudinal or emotive meaning, or premodifiers which do not denote properties (denoting actions or events, as in 'a dying soldier', or direction, place or time, as in 'upward movement', 'the above statement', and 'early riser'). However, there is important validity in the degrees of generality, and some validity in degrees of being extrinsic or non-inherent if those qualities approximate being subjective; see chapter 3.

10.4.3.2   Semantic theories
Semantic theories, including Hetzron (1978), Quirk *et al.* (1985), Adamson (2000) and Vandelanotte (2002), attribute the order to the gradation in subjectivity noted in chapter 3. They are correct as far as they go, then, but have over-generalised one element of the explanation.

10.4.3.3   Syntactic theories
Halliday (2004: 322) seems to include a syntactic principle along with his semantic principle of subcategorisation. For example, *splendid* is the first premodifier in 'those [splendid [old [electric trains]]]' because it has 'the greatest specifying potential'. Ziff (1960: 201) gives the same principle, in addition to his conceptual principle of definiteness. This account is my syntactic explanation, in chapter 4. It is very striking that, although many authors are aware of the syntactic structure of nominal phrases – for example, in referring to 'right-branching' structure – no others I have surveyed give syntactic structure as a fundamental explanation of premodifier order.

10.4.3.4   Grammatical theories
According to Biber *et al.* (1999: 598), the order is by part of speech, as given in (7) (the sign '>' means 'comes before'):

(7)   Adverb > adjective > colour adjective > participle > noun (> head).

The theory does accurately describe some phrases; but we have seen repeatedly that it simply does not hold regularly. Moreover, the parts of speech are not defined, so we cannot apply the theory reliably (to 'an interesting remark', for example); and the theory cannot even account for most successions of adjectives. I suggest that these theorists have been misled by the prototype concept discussed in §10.2.5. They have over-extended the concept originally applied to natural categories, which are characterised by perceptual features, to abstractions which are functions or paradigms rather than categories, and certainly not perceptible natural categories.

According to Vendler (1968), attributive adjectives are placed in their positions by transformations which move them from the predicative position in which they are first placed (in the base structure); the first to be moved is placed nearest the head, and so on; there are twenty-two possible positions. Martin (e.g. 1970) and Levi (1978) give transformations as part of the explanation. As argued by Martin (1969a: 698), there is no explanation or support for the postulated order of transformations, other than the order of the adjectives, so Vendler's argument appears to be circular.

Nor can the theory account for words that can be used only in attributive position: Reinforcers, certain other adjectives (as listed by Huddleston and Pullum 2002: 553) and nouns. Some noteworthy proponents of transformational grammar have apparently felt unable to explain premodifier order at all: Haegeman (1994), a comprehensive textbook of government and binding theory, does not discuss the issue; and Chomsky wrote, as late as 1995 (1995: 382), 'We still have no good phrase structure theory for such simple matters as attributive adjectives.' (Some recent transformational theorists have offered non-transformational explanations instead, e.g. Scott 2002). It seems possible that Vendler was influenced by historical 'transformations', such as the movement of genitive nouns from post-position to pre-position in the Old English period and the later conversion of postmodifier phrases to premodifiers (chapter 8). His theory would be more convincing if stated historically.

Crisma (1995) and Scott (2002), building on the work of Cinque (e.g. 1994), suggest that the order is that of the 'functional projections' in which the adjectives are generated; the adjectives are not moved by transformations. Each functional projection is associated with a conceptual class (much like those of Dixon 1982), adding something to the interpretation of the adjective. For example, in 'the old man', the projection adds AGE; but in 'my old boss' ('former'), *old* is generated in a different projection, which adds TEMPORAL, and *old* will be placed in a different position. The theory accounts for changes in meaning with change in position; and it allows for what I call 'constructional' meaning, in what the projection adds.

10.4.3.5 Functional theories
In functional theories, as set out by Teyssier (1968), 'identifying' words, such as numbers and quantifiers, come first; next come 'characterising' premodifiers, that is (in my terms), descriptive ones; last come 'classifying' premodifiers, that is, restrictive ones. The theory is correct for many phrases, and is accounted for as discourse explanation, in chapter 9. It is supported by Coates (1971), McGregor (1997), Bache (2000), Adamson (2000) and Ghesquière (2009).

For other theorists, a single functional principle determines the order. Their theory explains the syntactic principle that each premodifier modifies the rest of the phrase by the further principle that 'the most discriminative adjective tends to be placed first'; what is 'discriminative' is 'determined by the pragmatic demands of the communicative situation' (Danks and Glucksberg 1971: 66). So (to use the example given by Danks and Glucksberg), if there are two red tables, only one of which is Swiss, we say 'the Swiss red table' (not 'the red Swiss table'). This principle is used by some other authors to explain exceptions to the order prescribed by their main principle: Vendler (1968: 130), Martin (1970: 379), Crystal (1971), Huddleston and Pullum (2002: 452, 454), for example. The authors

Table 10.3 *Approximate number of occurrences of established and reversed order*

Author(s)	Established order			Reversed order		
	Wording	BNC	COCA	Wording	BNC	COCA
Martin (1970)	*large red*	40	260	*red large*	0	0
Huddleston and Pullum (2002)	*large black*	80	360	*black large*	0	0
Crystal (1971)	*long black*	110	640	*black long*	0	1

Note: The Corpus of Contemporary American English has other phrases with 'black long', but with the words in other senses (e.g. *black* 'African-American'); the relevant use of 'black long' is colloquial.

give no evidence that the principle is followed in real usage. Martin (1970) gives laboratory evidence; the other authors appear to be giving invented examples. The evidence of usage supplied by large corpora contradicts them, since the supposedly variable phrases they give occur there in only a single order. Table 10.3 illustrates the point from expressions given by these authors, by showing the fairly frequent occurrence of the established order in the British National Corpus (BNC) and the Corpus of Contemporary American English (COCA), and the non-occurrence of the allegedly acceptable reversed order. On this evidence, the reversed order is not acceptable to users of English.

10.4.3.6   Psycholinguistic theories
Some scholars explain premodifier order partly or wholly through psycholinguistic processing. To Martin (1969a, 1969b, 1970), the order of adjectives is determined partly by their relative accessibility. To Sproat and Shih (1988), the order of conceptual classes is determined by the number of computations each needs in processing. Both theories leave important questions unanswered and do not seem to have been sustained by later work. Hawkins (2004) has a thorough psycholinguistic study of order in general, based on recent research, but gives no discussion of premodifiers. (It is used in chapter 9, §9.2.)

10.4.3.7   Theories of Classifier order
Chapter 5, §5.8.1, noted that there has been a long and inconclusive discussion of Classifiers, under terms such as 'nominal compounds' (Lees 1970, Anstey 2007), 'compound nouns' (Downing 1977), 'complex nominals' (Levi 1978), 'classifying adjectives' (Warren 1984), 'noun-noun compounds' (Ryder 1994). See also Bundgaard, Ostergaard and Stjernfelt (2008). The approach used has varied widely. Some works note the Process-head structure (with Agent and Patient; §5.3), in phrases such as 'opposition corruption allegations' (e.g. Radford 1993: 75), usually attributing it to an underlying

'sentence'. However, they are alike, except for Anstey (2007), in concluding that there is no syntactic structure among Classifiers as a whole – only an indefinitely large set of semantic relations: Ryder (1994), in her book title, describes the situation as 'chaos'. Anstey (2007) identifies three Classifier constructions, which denote property, relation, and type; but they are independent, and such phrases have only one Classifier each.

Perhaps the main mistake of most of the authors was methodological: they considered Classifiers individually, therefore missing the patterns that appear when long Classifier groups are compared (as in my tables in chapter 5). They were also handicapped, I suggest, by their assumption that (because they are nouns) noun premodifiers are fundamentally like noun heads, and not like adjectival premodifiers, even though Quirk *et al.* (1972: §13.65) had shown that to be wrong before most of those works were written.

10.4.3.8 Multi-factorial theories
Multi-factorial theories correlate explanations of many kinds. Wulff (2003), for example, considers phonological, syntactic, semantic and pragmatic factors given by previous theorists; it calculates their relative influence in determining order, with the result that the order observed in the corpus analysed can be predicted with 73.5 percent accuracy. It does not explain why or how any of the factors influence order, or any connections among them; so for our purpose, the 'explanation' itself needs to be explained.

10.4.4 Conclusion to other theories

This review of what has gone wrong in other theories of premodifier order reinforces some underlying themes that emerge from previous chapters: methodologically, we need to work empirically with a very wide range of data, and to not presuppose that certain categories, such as parts of speech, will explain the data; analysis should occur at all levels of language; interpretation of the analysis must keep a fine balance between the levels' degree of dependence on each other and their degree of independence; to be illuminating, theories must specify the connections among the various levels and various approaches.

10.5   Conclusion to discussion

Previous chapters of the book have given my own account of premodifiers. This chapter has amplified it by discussing the nature of the zones, and grammaticalisation across the zones, and it has reviewed what other writers have said. We are ready to conclude the book.

11   Conclusion

11.1   Summary

This section summarises the book in one paragraph and in order of importance to the argument developed, and then offers a summary chapter by chapter.

There is a normal, grammatically required unmarked order in English nominal premodifiers which consists of the order of the zones in which the words occur. There are four zones, each of which may have one word, many words (co-ordinated with each other), or none. The order of zones is at once semantic (that is, of words' constituent types and dimensions of meaning – their 'semantic structure'), and syntactic (that is, earlier words modify all the later words as a group and are subordinated to them). The normal order can be varied, in marked order: moving a word into a zone for which it has no conventionalised use gives the word emphasis, and requires the reader to interpret it with a new meaning of the type appropriate to its zone. When there are two or more words in a zone, speakers may grammatically put them in any order, but sometimes speakers choose to follow a stylistic principle for the order. Premodifier order has evolved historically, with the syntactic order developing in Middle English and the semantic order developing as an extra dimension by early in the Modern English period. The principles given just above are confirmed by information structure in the phrase, by the processes of grammaticalisation, and by what we know of psycholinguistic processing and of children's acquisition of nominal phrase structure.

The 'zones' chapter (chapter 2) outlined the four zones, as in '*Your actual* [Reinforcer] *tinny* [Epithet] *round* [Descriptor] *percussion* [Classifier] *instrument*'. The order of premodifiers is determined primarily by their zone membership, and it is the specific use of the word that determines its zone – many words belong in different zones in different uses, e.g. *pure* in table 11.1. The zone order constitutes a grammatically required, unmarked order; but usage has established an optional marked order, in which a word is placed in an abnormal position. Words in the same zone may be used in any order, there being no grammatically required order.

Table 11.1 Pure *in different zones.*

Det.	Reinforcer	Epithet	Descriptor	Classifier	Head
				Shetland <u>pure</u>	wool
a			new and <u>pure</u>	German	identity
her		<u>pure</u>	unforced	natural	soprano
a	pure	disgusted [=disgusting] shameless	young		woman

Chapter 3 argued that the unmarked order is in part semantic. Each zone has its own type of semantic structure – that is, combination of types and dimensions of meaning. Reinforcers' meaning is purely grammatical, e.g. *actual*, in 'Your actual tinny round percussion instrument'. Epithets have scalar descriptive meaning, and only they can have expressive or social meaning, e.g. *tinny* (on a scale from slightly tinny to very tinny, and with unfavourable and colloquial meaning). Descriptors have nonscalar descriptive meaning, e.g. *round*. Classifiers have referential meaning, and relate to the head by a constructional meaning, e.g. *percussion* (naming something not describing it, and related to *instrument* by the constructional meaning, OF THE [percussion] TYPE). Premodifiers grade in steps forward from the head: Classifiers are the most cognitively basic, the simplest and the least linguistic; Epithets and Reinforcers are the most complex, the most subjective and sophisticated, and the most linguistic. The most directly referential words (Classifiers) are next to the head, which is the focus for any act of reference made through the whole phase.

Chapter 4 argued that the unmarked order is in part syntactic. Each premodifier precedes the group of words it modifies, as in 'Your [actual [tinny [round [percussion instrument]]]]' and 'her [pure [unforced [natural soprano]]]'. The zones further forward have wider syntactic powers: they can semantically modify more entities than the later zones can – even modifying entities represented outside the nominal phrase. Normally, the requirements for order of semantic structure and modification structure coincide. If they conflict in a particular situation of use, users must in general follow the semantic rule; for example, the syntactic structure for contrasting a new German identity with a new French one would be *'a German new identity', but the semantic rule disallows that. Modal premodifiers such as *fake* and *supposed* form an exception to that generalisation.

Chapter 5 showed that the Classifier zone, distinctive in denoting entities not properties, has a distinctive unmarked order within the zone. There are five alternative constructions, which express semantic relations between the head entity and the premodifier entity, parallel to those of clauses. The two commonest constructions can be illustrated as follows. 'An <u>electric soldering</u> iron' parallels 'The iron <u>is for soldering</u> and is <u>of the electric type</u>', having modifiers and head in qualia relations. 'U.S. law enforcement' has the modifiers and head related as event and its arguments – *The U.S.* [Actor] *enforces* [event] *the law* [Goal]. Many Classifiers, however, are used singly, in no such construction.

Chapter 6 discussed the grammatically free order of several premodifiers in one zone. It showed that speakers and writers often give the modifiers a stylistic order, such as achieving climax, with the most forceful word last (e.g. 'a small, very modern, even spare house'), or developing the integrity and cohesiveness of the text, with the key word first (e.g. 'her stagnant but peaceful Yugoslav homeland', where *stagnant* gives the feeling and theme of the whole passage).

Chapter 7 discussed marked order. Moving a word into a new zone makes it salient, and gives it a temporary new meaning appropriate to its new zone and its context. For example, in 'the ruby, sweet-tasting Parma ham' (contrasted with the unmarked order, 'sweet-tasting ruby Parma ham'), *ruby* is no longer simply a colour word (Descriptor), but an evocative Epithet.

Chapter 8 showed that the present unmarked order of premodifiers has evolved through the history of English, in three main stages. In Old English, the order was adjective + participle + genitive noun, with all premodifiers modifying the head directly, as in #'[poor] and [old] [of-London] men'. In Middle English, the Old English order was reanalysed as a syntactic structure; for example, 'old [poor [London men]]' restricted the reference of 'poor London men', and 'poor [old [London men]]' (with changed order), restricted the reference of 'old London men'; *poor*, *old* and *London* were similar semantically (being factually descriptive). By Early Modern English, the order had been reanalysed again, as having a semantic structure as well as the syntactic one, and as being fixed by the semantic structure of the words; 'poor [old [London men]]' was required as the order; and *poor* was an Epithet, *old* was a Descriptor, and *London* was a Classifier, having different semantic structures; that change created the zones. In the nineteenth and twentieth centuries, several constructions evolved in the Classifier zone, each forming its own structure of subzones. The history provides a general explanation of the order, parallel with the synchronic ones; but it also explains specific features such as the frequency of adjective-participle-noun sequences, and the existence of borderline examples.

Chapter 9 gave support from other areas of linguistic study. Modern understanding of language processing makes the explanations in earlier chapters psycholinguistically credible. Discourse study shows that the semantic and syntactic structures are used to create a discourse structure in some nominal phrases, paralleling that of clauses. What we know of the order in which children acquire premodifiers mirrors the semantic and syntactic order: Classifiers (closest to the head, and most basic) are learned first, and the others in succession. It seems probable that phonological structure mirrors semantic and syntactic structure, and that morphological structure fits the order as well, as a processing aid.

Chapter 10 dealt mainly with the significance of premodifier structure for other areas of linguistic study. It discussed the zones as a structure that integrates the linguistic levels. It discussed historical changes such as grammaticalisation, as words move towards head position or towards determiner position. It discussed other theories of premodifier structure, seeking to show how the theory given here goes beyond them, while including their insights.

11.2   Conclusion

So far in the book, explanation has been by linguistic level (semantics, syntax, and so on), and from synchronic and diachronic approaches; the explanations have consequently been numerous and so varied as to perhaps seem heterogeneous. This section sets out to integrate them – and to do so in a fresh way – using several principles that have so far been incidental; then those principles are further integrated through a single principle, that of language function.

Language is fundamentally constrained by the mind's ability to process the structure and content of language. (The subtitle of Givón 1979 encapsulates the point: 'grammar as a processing strategy'.) The processing of premodifiers in unmarked order is automatic and unconscious, since the order is constituted simply by four zones and is fixed by grammatical rule. Premodifiers in free order (in the same zone) are often arranged unconsciously, but sometimes speakers work more deliberately, following a stylistic principle. Marked order is a relatively deliberate structure, not produced by routine automatic processing; it mostly occurs in writing.

The processing is assisted very greatly by Givón's 'discretization': 'Syntax tends to *discretize* the scalar cognitive dimensions that underlie it... Such *discretization* is an absolute necessity for information processing under real-world time constraints.' (1988: 278; the italics are in the original.) Subject, predicator and object discretise the flow of a clause. Similarly, the zones discretise semantic gradients of several kinds: specific to general, content-oriented to 'grammatical' and monosemous to polysemous, for example. The syntax is also structured by discrete units: word units within the zone unit. So is the discourse structure: Topic and Comment discretise the gradient from Given to New. (§3.4.2.3 noted that Descriptors discretise qualities that Epithets represent as scalar – 'continuous'.) Premodifiers in English thus have a formal explanation, in the sense that they work as units in a hierarchy, are controlled by rules, and can be represented diagrammatically.

The gradients (such as from specific senses to general ones) are formed historically by repeated fresh construal; we construe experience into meanings, and reconstrue the meanings; we add or remove types and dimensions of meaning, giving a word a new semantic structure. We have seen that it is semantic structure, not content (i.e. knowledge, or the world that is known), that distinguishes the zones semantically, and that in principle almost any word can occur in different positions – an important characteristic of the zones and one that has generally been missed in the literature. (This reconstrual is analogous to giving words new relations and functions by derivation of adjectives from nouns, and so on; premodifiers are reconstrued similarly, without derivation.) Likewise, words' syntactic relations are reconstrued: first, within the four main zones, from modifying simply the head entity (Descriptors) to modifying some other participant or the whole situation (Epithets), for example; and second, within the Classifier subzones, among the five constructions. The history of individual premodifiers, and of the premodification structure itself, is characterised by reconstrual.

Another element of the gradience in premodification is that, as a default principle, more important words come further from the head. Semantically, the most forceful or informative word comes first; syntactically, the word making the crucial discrimination comes first; in discourse structure, the word with most information value comes first. Those are the principle's application in unmarked order: in free order, it may be the most important for the textual theme that comes first; in marked order, it is first position that most often gives the word prominence and forces the semantic change. The default order can be overruled by deliberate processing: for example, free order may put the important last, as climax, and marked order may move a word to last position, to gain preciseness.

The gradients (including that of 'important first') constitute a synchronic developmental order, from Classifiers forward. Cognitively, Classifiers are conceptually most basic and Descriptors experientially most basic; Reinforcers are most sophisticated, and thus advanced. Semantically, the zones develop forward in generality and subjectivity, and thereby in grammaticalness. They are part of the larger sequence from referential, naming, and heavily cognitive heads, through partly abstract and descriptive premodifiers, to determining, fully abstract and wholly linguistic determiners.

Historically, development has mirrored the cognitive and semantic sequence, with the most sophisticated and grammatical developing last, on the whole; that applies to both the zones (broadly) and to individual words – as grammaticalisation. The developmental order appears also in child development, with children evidently learning Classifiers first and Reinforcers last.

The historical development has had many 'triggers' or 'causes' for the innovations that contributed to it; but the adoption and spread of the innovations has (I have argued) been motivated by a deeper and more personal need: finding nominal phrase structures that satisfyingly realise deeper structures and intentions. For example, the zones realise different semantic structures. That is highlighted by the changes in the role of what were once fairly fixed parts of speech; for example, a participle in Classifier position realises an object, in Epithet position it realises a property, and only in Descriptor position does it realise an event. The syntactic modification structure realises the semantic modification (perceptual Descriptors modifying referential Classifier + head, conceptual Epithets modifying both of them, and so on.) Phonological stress appears to realise the important-first structure, just as contrastive stress realises conceptual contrast.

To some extent, however, a complementary process has been at work: a structure that developed to realise a deeper intention or structure is then exploited in the development of a further structure. For example, the syntactic structure has been exploited in modern times by both semantic structure and discourse structure.

There is a still more general principle beyond those principles of processing constraint, gradience, construal, exploitation, importance of what is first, developmental sequence, and realisation. To that we now turn.

Premodifier semantics and syntax are constrained – 'from below', as it were – by the nature and limitations of the mind's processing system, which require a well-structured system (and a formal explanation), as noted above. But premodifier structure is managed – from 'above' – by the purposes I have identified as language functions. The experiential and textual functions are realised through the semantic and syntactic units into which the gradients have been discretised; and, where necessary, those units are provided by the functions' reconstrual of more fundamental units. The expressive function exploits the gradients themselves (which also constitute the synchronic and diachronic developmental sequence), putting first what is important for personal and interpersonal expression. These functions also require a well-structured system, to be carried out consistently and reliably. Premodifiers in English need not only a formal explanation, but also a functional one.

Of English premodifiers, and particularly of their order, Cruse wrote (2004: 302): 'Various partial explanations have been put forward, but none is comprehensively convincing.' The principles outlined in this section summarise what is intended to be a comprehensive and convincing explanation.

References

Aarts, Bas 2007 *Syntactic Gradience: The Nature of Grammatical Indeterminacy.* Oxford: Oxford University Press.

Adamson, Sylvia 1998 'Literary language.' In Romaine (ed.), pp. 598–692.

  1999 'Literary language.' In Lass (ed.), pp. 187–331.

  2000 'A lovely little example: word order options and category shift in the pre-modifying string.' In Olga Fischer, Anette Rosenbach and Dieter Stein (eds.), *Pathways of Change: Grammaticalization in English.* Amsterdam / Philadelphia: Benjamins, pp. 39–66.

Aijmer, Karin 2002 *English Discourse Particles: Evidence from a Corpus.* Amsterdam / Philadelphia: Benjamins.

Aitchison, Jean 2001 *Language Change: Progress or Decay?* 3rd edn. [1st edn Fontana, 1981]. Cambridge: Cambridge University Press.

Al-Karabsheh, Aladdin 2005 'Interpretation of terminological constructions: the case of technico-scientific nominal compounds.' *Journal of Language and Linguistics* 4 (2): 161–82.

Altenberg, Bengt 1980 'Binominal NP's in a thematic perspective: genitive vs. *of*-construction in 17th century English.' In Jacobson (ed.), pp. 149–72.

Andersen, Henning 2006 'Grammation, regrammation, and degrammation: tense loss in Russian.' *Diachronica* 23 (2): 231–58.

Anderson, John M. 1997 *A Notional Theory of Syntactic Categories.* Cambridge: Cambridge University Press.

  2003 'On the structure of names.' *Folia Linguistica* 37 (3–4): 347–98.

Anstey, Matthew 2007 '*Tree tigers* and *tree elephants*: a constructional account of English nominal compounds.' In Mike Hannay and Gerard J. Steen (eds.), *Structural-Functional Studies in English Grammar: In Honour of Lachlan Mackenzie.* Amsterdam / Philadelphia: Benjamins, pp. 227–46.

Ariel, Mira 2000 'The development of person agreement markers: from pronouns to higher accessibility markers.' In Michael Barlow and Suzanne Kemmer (eds.), *Usage-based Models of Language.* Stanford: CSLI Publications, pp. 197–260.

Baars, Bernard J. 1988 *A Cognitive Theory of Consciousness.* Cambridge: Cambridge University Press.

Bache, Carl 1978 *The Order of Premodifying Adjectives in Present-Day English.* Odense: Odense University Press.

  2000 *Essentials of Mastering English: A Concise Grammar.* Berlin: Mouton de Gruyter.

Baker, Mona, Gill Francis and Elena Tognini-Bonelli (eds.) 1993 *Text and Technology*. Philadelphia / Amsterdam: Benjamins.

Barsalou, Lawrence W. 1987 'The instability of graded structure: implications for the nature of concepts.' In Neisser (ed.), pp. 101–40.

1992 *Cognitive Psychology: an Overview for Cognitive Scientists*. Hillsdale, NJ: Erlbaum.

1999 'Perceptual symbol systems.' *Behavioural and Brain Sciences* 22: 577–660.

Bates, E. and J. Goodman 1999 'On the emergence of grammar from the lexicon.' In B. MacWhinney (ed.), *Emergence of Language*. Mahwah, NJ: Erlbaum, pp. 29–80.

Bauer, Laurie 1978 *The Grammar of Nominal Compounding: With Special Reference to Danish, English and French*. Odense: Odense University Press.

1983 *English Word-Formation*. Cambridge: Cambridge University Press.

1998 'When is a sequence of two nouns a compound in English?' *English Language and Linguistics* 2: 65–86.

2004 'Adjectives, compounds and words.' *Nordic Journal of English Studies* 3 (1) (special issue, *World of Words: A Tribute to Arne Zettersten*): 7–22.

Bergs, Alexander and Gabriele Diewald 2008 'Introduction: constructions and language change.' In Alexander Bergs and Gabriele Diewald (eds.), *Constructions and Language Change*. Berlin / New York: Mouton de Gruyter, pp. 1–21.

Biber, Douglas, Stig Johansson, Geoffrey Leech, Susan Conrad, and Edward Finegan 1999 *Longman Grammar of Spoken and Written English*. Harlow: Longman.

Bloom, Lois 1970 *Language Development: Form and Function in Emerging Grammars*. Cambridge, MA: MIT Press.

Boas, Hans C. 2003 *A Constructional Approach to Resultatives*. Stanford: CSLI Publications.

Bolinger, Dwight 1967 'Adjectives in English: attribution and predication.' *Lingua* 18: 1–34.

1986 *Intonation and its Parts: Melody*. Stanford: Stanford University Press.

Bouchard, Denis 2002 *Adjectives, Number and Interfaces*. Amsterdam: Elsevier.

Bouillon, Pierrette and Federica Busa (eds.) 2001 *The Language of Word Meaning*. Cambridge: Cambridge University Press.

Bowerman, Melissa and Stephen C. Levinson (eds.) 2001 *Language Acquisition and Conceptual Development*. Cambridge: Cambridge University Press.

Brinton, Laurel J. and Elizabeth Closs Traugott 2005 *Lexicalization and Language Change*. Cambridge: Cambridge University Press.

British National Corpus 100 million words, UK, 1980s–1993. Available online at www.americancorpus.org.

Bryant, Arthur 1938 *Samuel Pepys: The Saviour of the Navy*. London: Reprint Society edition (1953).

Bundgaard, Peer F., Svend Ostergaard and Frederik Stjernfelt 2008 'Multi safe compound constructions: a reply to Anders Søgaard.' *Semiotica* 172: 363–93.

Burnley, David 1992 'Lexis and semantics.' In Norman Blake (ed.), *Cambridge History of the English Language, Volume II, 1066–1476*. Cambridge: Cambridge University Press, pp. 409–99.

Bybee, Joan 2002 'Sequentiality as the basis of constituent structure.' In Givón and Malle (eds.), pp. 109–34.

2003 'Cognitive processes in grammaticalization.' In Michael Tomasello (ed.), *The New Psychology of Language: Cognitive and Functional Approaches to Language Structure*, Mahwah, NJ: Erlbaum, pp. 145–67.

Bybee, Joan, and Paul Hopper 2001 *Frequency and the Emergence of Linguistic Structure*. Amsterdam / Philadelphia: Benjamins.

Bybee, Joan, Revere Perkins and William Pagliuca 1994 *The Evolution of Grammar: Tense, Aspect, and Modality in the Languages of the World*. Chicago and London: University of Chicago Press.

Byrne, Brian 1979 'Rules of prenominal adjective order and the interpretation of 'incompatible' adjective pairs.' *Journal of Verbal Learning and Verbal Behaviour* 18: 73–8.

Carlton, Charles 1963 'Word order of noun modifiers in Old English prose.' *Journal of English and Germanic Philology* LXII: 778–83.

Chatman, Seymour 1960 'Pre-adjectivals in the English nominal phrase.' *American Speech* 35: 83–100.

Chomsky, Noam 1965 *Aspects of Syntactic Theory*. Cambridge, MA: MIT Press.

1995 *The Minimalist Program*. Cambridge, MA: MIT Press.

Christiansen, Morten H. and Simon Kirby 2003 *Language Evolution*. Oxford: Oxford University Press.

Cinque, Guglielmo 1994 'On the evidence for partial N-movement in the Romance DP.' In Guglielmo Cinque, Jan Koster, Jean-Yves Pollock, Luigi Rizzi and Raffaella Zanuttini (eds.), *Paths Towards Universal Grammar: Studies in Honor of Richard S. Kayne*. Washington, DC: Georgetown University Press, pp. 85–110.

Clark, Eve 1973 ' "What's in a name?" On the child's acquisition of semantics in his first language.' In Timothy E. Moore (ed.), *Cognitive Development and the Acquisition of Language*. New York: Academic Press, pp. 65–110.

Coates, Jennifer 1971 'Denominal adjectives: a study in syntactic relationships between modifier and head.' *Lingua* 27: 160–9.

Coates, Richard 2000 'Singular definite expressions with a unique denotatum and the limits of properhood.' *Linguistics: An Interdisciplinary Journal of the Language Sciences* 38: 1161–71.

Conrad, Joseph 1902 *Typhoon*. Pickering. In 1993, *The Complete Short Fiction of Joseph Conrad, Volume 3*, ed. Samuel Hyner. London: Pickering ad chatto.

1925a *Youth*. London: Gresham.

1925b 'Nigger of the Narcissus.' In *The Collected Works of Joseph Conrad 1925–28*, Medallion edition (1995). London: Routledge/Thommes.

Corpus of Contemporary American English 2008- Mark Davies (ed.) 400+ million words, 1990-present. Available online at www.americancorpus.org.

Crisma, Paola 1995 'On the configurational nature of adjectival modification.' In Karen Zagona (ed.), *Grammatical Theory and Romance Languages: Selected Papers from the 25th Linguistic Symposium on Romance Languages (LSRL XXV), Seattle, 2–4 March 1995*. Amsterdam / Philadelphia: Benjamins, pp. 59–72.

Croft, William 1991 *Syntactic Categories and Grammatical Relations*. Chicago / London: University of Chicago Press.

1998 'Event structure in argument linking.' In Miriam Butt and Wilhelm Geuder (eds.), *The Projection of Arguments: Lexical and Compositional Factors*. Stanford: CSLI Publications, pp. 12–63.

1999 'Some contributions of typology to cognitive linguistics and vice versa.' In Theo Janssen and Gisela Redeker (eds.), *Cognitive Linguistics: Foundations, Scope, and Methodology*. Berlin / New York: Mouton de Gruyter, pp. 61–94.

2000 *Explaining Language Change*. Harlow: Longman.

2001 *Radical Construction Grammar: Syntactic Theory in Typological Perspective*. Oxford: Oxford University Press.

2003 *Typology and Universals*. 2nd edn [1st edn 1990]. Cambridge: Cambridge University Press.

2007 'Beyond Aristotle and gradience: a reply to Aarts.' *Studies in Language* 31 (2): 409–30.

Croft, William, and D. Alan Cruse 2004 *Cognitive Linguistics*. Cambridge: Cambridge University Press.

Cruse, Alan 2004 *Meaning in Language: An Introduction to Semantics and Pragmatics*. 2nd edn [1st edn 2004]. Oxford: Oxford University Press.

Crystal, David 1971 *Linguistics*. London: Penguin.

Curme, George O. 1931 *Syntax*. Boston: Heath.

Cuyckens, Hubert and Britta Zawada (eds.) 2001 *Polysemy in Cognitive Linguistics: Selected Papers from the Fifth International Cognitive Linguistics Conference*. Amsterdam / Philadelphia: Benjamins.

Dahl, Östen 2001 'Grammaticalization and the life cycles of constructions.' *RASK – Internationalt Tidsschrift for Sprog og Kommunikation* 14: 19–134.

2004 *The Growth and Maintenance of Linguistic Complexity*. Amsterdam / Philadelphia: Benjamins.

Dalrymple, Mary 2001 *Syntax and Semantics, Volume 34, Lexical Functional Grammar*. San Diego: Academic Press.

Danks, Joseph H. and Sam Glucksberg 1971 'Psychological scaling of adjective orders.' *Journal of Verbal Learning and Verbal Behaviour* 10: 63–7.

Davidse, Kristin, Lieselotte Brems and Liesbeth De Smedt 2008 'Type noun uses in the English NP: a case of right to left layering.' *International Journal of Corpus Linguistics* 13 (2): 139–64.

Davies, Eirian 2007 'Problems in NP structure: an example from British tabloid journalism.' In Christopher Butler, Raquel Hidalgo Downing and Julia Lavid (eds.), *Functional Perspectives on Grammar and Discourse in honour of Angela Downing*. Amsterdam / Philadelphia: Benjamins, pp. 205–16.

Denison, David 2010 'Category change in English with and without structural change.' In Traugott and Trousdale (eds.), pp. 105–28.

Dixon, R. M. W. 1982 *Where Have all the Adjectives Gone?* Berlin: Mouton de Gruyter.

Downing, Pamela 1977 'On the creation and use of English compound nouns.' *Language* 53: 810–42.

Du Bois, John W. 2003 'Discourse and grammar.' In Michael Tomasello (ed.), *The New Psychology of Language: Cognitive and Functional Approaches to Language Structure*, Mahwah, NJ: Erlbaum, pp. 17–88.

Eble, Connie 2000 'Slang and lexicography.' In Lockwood, Fries and Copeland (eds.), pp. 499–512.

Eckardt, Regine 2006 *Meaning Change in Grammaticalization: An Enquiry into Semantic Reanalysis*. Oxford: Oxford University Press.

Eichenwald, Kurt 2005 *Conspiracy of Fools*. New York: Broadway Books.

Farkas, Donka and Henriette de Swart 2003 *The Semantics of Incorporation: From Argument Structure to Discourse Transparency.* Stanford: CSLI Publications.

Feist, Jim 2008 *The Order of Premodifiers in English Nominal Phrases.* University of Auckland: doctoral dissertation. researchspace.auckland.ac.nz/handle/ 2292/3301

   Forthcoming 'What controls the "genitive variation" in English?' *Studies in Language.*

Ferris, Connor 1993 *The Meaning of Syntax: A Study of the Adjectives in English.* London / New York: Longman.

Fillenbaum, Samuel and Amnon Rapoport 1971 *Structures in the Subjective Lexicon.* New York / London: Academic Press.

Finegan, Edward 1998 'English grammar and usage.' In Romaine (ed.), pp. 536–88.

Fischer, Olga, Muriel Norde, and Harry Perridon (eds.) 2004 *Up and Down the Cline – the Nature of Grammaticalization.* Amsterdam / Philadelphia: Benjamins.

Fischer, Olga, Ans van Kemenade, Willem Koopman and Wim van der Wurff 2007 *Morphosyntactic Change: Functional and Formal Perspectives.* Oxford: Oxford University Press.

Fortescue, Michael 2009 *A Neural Network Model of Lexical Organisation.* London: Continuum.

Fraser, George McDonald 1969 *Flashman.* London: Penguin.

Fries, Peter H. 1986 'Toward a discussion of the ordering of adjectives in the English noun phrase.' In Benjamin F. Elson (ed.), *Language in Global Perspective: Papers in Honor of the 50th Anniversary of the Summer Institute of Linguistics.* Dallas, TX: Summer Institute of Linguistics, pp. 123–33.

   2000 'Some peculiar adjectives in the English nominal group.' In Lockwood, Fries and Copeland (eds.), pp. 289–322.

Furnivall, Frederick J. (ed.) 1868 *Early English Meals and Manners.* London: Trubner.

Geeraerts, Dirk 1993 'Vagueness's puzzles, polysemy's vagaries.' *Cognitive Linguistics* 4 (3): 223–73.

Geeraerts, Dirk (ed.) 2006 *Cognitive Linguistics: Basic Readings.* Berlin / New York: Mouton de Gruyter.

Gentner, Dedre and Lera Boroditsky 2001 *Individuation, Relativity, and Early Word Learning.* In Bowerman and Levinson (eds.), pp. 215–50.

Gentner, Dedre, and Susan Goldin-Meadow (eds.) 2003 *Language in Mind: Advances in the Study of Language and Thought.* Cambridge, MA: MIT.

Ghesquière, Lobke 2009 'From determining to emphasising meanings: the adjectives of specificity.' *Folia Linguistica* 43 (2): 311–43.

Ghomeshi, Jila, Ray Jackendoff, Nicole Rosen and Kevin Rusell 2004/2010 'Contrastive focus reduplication in English (the salad-salad paper) (2004).' In Ray Jackendoff, *Meaning and the Lexicon: The Parallel Architecture 1975–2010.* Oxford: Oxford University Press, chapter 11.

Gibbs, Raymond W. and Herbert L. Colston 2006 'Image schemas: the cognitive psychological reality of image schemas and their transformations.' In Geeraerts (ed.), pp. 239–68. First published 1995, in *Cognitive Linguistics* 6 (4): 347–78.

Giegerich, Heinz J. 2005 'Associative adjectives in English and the lexicon–syntax interface.' *Journal of Linguistics* 41: 571–91.

Givón, Talmy 1979 'From discourse to syntax: grammar as a processing strategy.' In Talmy Givón (ed.), *Syntax and Semantics, Volume 12, Discourse and Syntax*, New York: Academic Press, pp. 81–110.

1984 *Syntax: A Functional-Typological Introduction, Volume 1*. Amsterdam / Philadelphia: Benjamins.

1988 'Pragmatics of word order: predictability, importance and attention.' In Hammond, Moravcsik and Wirth (eds.), pp. 243–84.

1990 *Syntax: A Functional-Typological Introduction, Volume 2*. Amsterdam / Philadelphia: Benjamins.

Givón, Talmy and Bertram F. Malle (eds.) 2002 *Evolution of Language out of Pre-language*. Amsterdam / Philadelphia: Benjamins.

Goldberg, Adele E. 1995 *Constructions: A Construction Grammar Approach to Argument Structure*. Chicago and London: Chicago University Press.

Görlach, Manfred 1978 *Introduction to Early Modern English*. Cambridge: Cambridge University Press.

1999 'Regional and social variation.' In Lass (ed.), pp. 459–538.

Grimshaw, Jane 2005 *Words and Structure*. Stanford: CSLI Publications.

Gundel, Jeannette K. 1988 'Universals of topic-comment structure.' In Hammond, Moravcsik and Wirth (eds.), pp. 209–42.

Haegeman, Liliane 1994 *Introduction to Government and Binding Theory*. 2nd edn [1st edn 1991]. Oxford: Blackwell.

Haiman, John 1985 *Natural Syntax: Iconicity and Erosion*. Cambridge: Cambridge University Press.

1988 'Incorporation, parallelism and focus.' In Hammond, Moravcsik and Wirth (eds.), pp. 303–20.

Halliday, M. A. K. 1977 'Text as semantic choice in social contexts.' In Teun A. van Dijk and Janos S. Petöfi (eds.), *Grammars and Descriptions (Studies in Text Theory and Text Analysis)*. Berlin/New York: Walter de Gruyter, pp. 176–225.

1978 *Language as Social Semiotic: The Social Interpretation of Language and Meaning*. London: Arnold.

2000 'Grammar and daily life.' In Lockwood, Fries and Copeland (eds.), pp. 221–38.

2004 *An Introduction to Functional Grammar*. 3rd edn [1st edn 1985]. London: Hodder Arnold.

Halliday, M. A. K. and Ruqaiya Hasan 1976 *Cohesion in English*. London / New York: Longman.

Hammond, Michael, Edith Moravcsik and Jessica Wirth (eds.) 1988 *Studies in Syntactic Typology*. Amsterdam / Philadelphia: Benjamins.

Harder, Peter 1996 *Functional Semantics: A Theory of Meaning, Structure and Tense in English*. Berlin /New York: Mouton de Gruyter.

Harker, Peter 2005 *Random Shots*. Auckland: Halcyon Press.

Haspelmath, Martin 1999 'Why is grammaticalization irreversible?' *Linguistics* 37 (6): 1043–68.

2004 'On directionality in language change with particular reference to grammaticalization.' In Fischer, Norde and Perridon (eds.), pp. 17–44.

Hawkins, John A. 2004 *Efficiency and Complexity in Grammars*. Oxford: Oxford University Press.

Heine, Bernd and Tania Kuteva 2007 *The Genesis of Grammar: A Reconstruction.* Oxford: Oxford University Press.

Heine, Bernd, Ulrike Claudi and Friederike Hünnemeyer 1991 'From cognition to grammar: evidence from African languages.' In Elizabeth Closs Traugott and Bernd Heine (eds.), *Approaches to Grammaticalization, Volume I, Focus on Theoretical and Methodical Issues.* Amsterdam / Philadelphia: Benjamins, pp. 149–88.

Hengeveld, Kees 2008 'Prototypical and non-prototypical noun phrases in Functional Discourse Grammar.' In Daniel García Velasco and Jan Rijkhoff (eds.), *The Noun Phrase in Functional Discourse Grammar.* Berlin / New York: Mouton de Gruyter, pp. 51–62.

Hetzron, Robert 1978 'On the relative order of adjectives.' In Hansjakob Seiler (ed.), *Language Universals: Papers from the Conference held at Gummersbach / Cologne, Germany, October 3–8, 1976.* Tübingen: Gunter Narr Verlag, pp. 165–4.

Hinton, Leanne, Johanna Nichols and John J. Ohala (eds.) 1994 *Sound Symbolism.* Cambridge: Cambridge University Press.

Hogg, Richard M. (ed.) 1992–1999 *The Cambridge History of the English Language.* 4 volumes. Cambridge: Cambridge University Press.

Hopper, Paul J. and Sandra A. Thompson 1980 'Transitivity in grammar and discourse.' *Language* **56** (2): 251–99.

1984 'The discourse basis for lexical categories in universal grammar.' *Language* **60** (4): 703–52.

Hopper, Paul J. and Elizabeth Closs Traugott 1993 *Grammaticalization.* Cambridge: Cambridge University Press.

2003 *Grammaticalization.* 2nd edn [1st edn 1993]. Cambridge: Cambridge University Press.

Huddleston, Rodney 1984 *Introduction to the Grammar of English.* Cambridge: Cambridge University Press.

Huddleston, Rodney and Geoffrey K. Pullum 2002 *The Cambridge Grammar of the English Language.* Cambridge: Cambridge University Press.

Hudson, Richard and Jasper Holmes 2000 'Re-cycling in the encyclopedia.' In Peeters (ed.), pp. 259–90.

Huxley, Aldous 1932 *Brave New World.* London: Penguin.

Inchaurralde, Carlos 2000 *Lexicopedia.* In Peeters (ed.), pp. 97–114.

Jackendoff, Ray 1997 *The Architecture of the Language Faculty.* Cambridge, MA: MIT Press.

Jacobson, Roman 1936/1990. 'Contribution to the general theory of case.' In Linda R. Waugh and Monique Monville-Burston (eds.), *On Language*, Cambridge, MA: Harvard University Press, pp. 332–85 (combining the 1936 paper with parts of the 1958 revised paper; translated from German).

Jacobson, Sven (ed.) 1980 *Papers from the Scandinavian Symposium on Syntactic Variation.* Stockholm: Almqvist and Wiksell International.

Johnston, Michael, and Federica Busa 1999 'Qualia structure and the compositional interpretation of compounds.' In Evelyne Viegas (ed.), *Breadth and Depth of Semantic Lexicons.* Dordrecht: Kluwer, pp. 167–87.

Kamp, Hans and Barbara Partee 1995 'Prototype theory and compositionality.' *Cognition* **57**: 129–91.

Karmiloff, Kyra and Annette Karmiloff-Smith 2001 *Pathways to Language: From Fetus to Adolescent.* Cambridge, MA and London: Harvard University Press.

Karmiloff-Smith, Annette 1992 *Beyond Modularity: A Developmental Perspective on Cognitive Science.* Cambridge, MA: MIT Press.

Katz, Jerrold J. 1972 *Semantic Theory.* New York: Harper and Row.

Keenan, Edward L. and Bernard Comrie 1977 'Noun phrase accessibility and universal grammar.' *Linguistic Inquiry* 8: 63–99.

Keller, Rudi 1994 *On Language Change: The Invisible Hand in Language.* Translated by Brigitte Nerlich. London / New York: Routledge.

Kemmer, Suzanne 1993 *The Middle Voice.* Amsterdam / Philadelphia: Benjamins.

　　2003 'Human cognition and the elaboration of events: some universal conceptual categories.' In Michael Tomasello (ed.), *The New Psychology of Language: Cognitive and Functional Approaches to Language Structure*, Mahwah, NJ: Erlbaum, pp. 89–118.

Kemmerer, David 2000 'Selective impairment of knowledge underlying pronominal adjective order: evidence for the autonomy of grammatical semantics.' *Journal of Neurolinguistics* 13 (1): 57–82.

Kurath, Hans (ed.) 1963 *Middle English Dictionary.* Ann Arbor: University of Michigan Press.

Lamb, Sydney M. 1999 *Pathways of the Brain: The Neurocognitive Basis of the Brain.* Amsterdam / Philadelphia: Benjamins.

　　2004 *Language and Reality.* London / New York: Continuum.

Langacker, Ronald W. 1987 *Foundations of Cognitive Grammar, Volume 1, Theoretical Prerequisites.* Stanford: Stanford University Press.

　　2003 'Conceptualization, symbolization, and grammar.' In Michael Tomasello (ed.), *The New Psychology of Language: Cognitive and Functional Approaches to Language Structure*, Mahwah, NJ: Erlbaum, pp. 1–40.

　　2004 'Remarks on nominal grounding.' *Functions of Language* 11 (1): 77–113.

　　2006 'On the continuous debate about discreteness.' *Cognitive Linguistics* 17 (1): 107–51.

Lass, Roger (ed.) 1999 *Cambridge History of the English Language, Volume III, 1476–1776.* Cambridge: Cambridge University Press.

Leech, Geoffrey 1974 *Semantics.* London: Pelican.

Leech, Geoffrey, Marianne Hundt, Christian Mair and Nicholas Smith 2009 *Change in Contemporary English: A Grammatical Study.* Cambridge: Cambridge University Press.

Lees, Robert B. 1970 'Problems in the grammatical analysis of English nominal compounds.' In Manfried Bierwisch and Karl Erich Heidolph (eds.), *Progress in Linguistics: A Collection of Papers.* The Hague / Paris: Mouton, pp. 174–86.

Lehmann, Christian 1982/1995 *Thoughts on Grammaticalization.* (First available in 1982; revised and expanded version 1995.) Munich / Newcastle: Lincom Europa.

Lehmann, Winfred 1974 *Proto-Indo-European Syntax.* Austin/London: University of Texas Press.

Lehrer, Adrienne 1974 *Semantic Fields and Lexicalisation.* Amsterdam / London: North Holland.

Lessing, Doris 1973 *The Summer Before the Dark.* London: Jonathan Cape.

Levi, Judith 1978 *The Syntax and Semantics of Complex Nominals*. New York: Academic Press.

Levinson, Stephen C. 2003 'Language and mind: let's get the issues straight!' In Gentner and Goldin-Meadow (eds.), pp. 25–46.

Lichtenberk, Frantisek 1991 'Semantic change and heterosemy in grammaticalization.' *Language* **67** (3): 475–509.

Löbner, Sebastian 2002 *Understanding Semantics*. London: Arnold.

Lockwood, David G., Peter H. Fries and James E. Copeland (eds.) 2000 *Functional Approaches to Language, Culture and Cognition: Papers in Honour of Sydney M. Lamb*. Amsterdam / Philadelphia: Benjamins.

Longobardi, Giuseppe 2001 'Structure of DPs: some principles, parameters, and problems.' In Mark Baltin and Chris Collins (eds.), *Handbook of Contemporary Syntactic Theory*. Oxford: Blackwell, pp. 562–604.

Lyons, John 1975 *Formal Semantics of Natural Language: Papers from a Colloquium Sponsored by the King's College Research Centre, Cambridge*. Cambridge: Cambridge University Press.

    1977 *Semantics*. Cambridge: Cambridge University Press.

McClelland, James L. and David E. Rumelhart 1986 *Parallel Distributed Processing: Explorations in the Microstructure of Cognition, Volume 2, Psychological Models*. (Written with the PDP Research Group.) Cambridge, MA: MIT Press.

McClelland, James L., David E. Rumelhart and G. E. Hinton 1986 'The appeal of parallel distributed processing.' In Rumelhart and McClelland, pp. 3–44.

McGregor, William B. 1997 *Semiotic Grammar*. Oxford: Clarendon Press.

MacMahon, Michael K. C. 1998 'Phonology.' In Romaine (ed.), pp. 373–535.

Malt, Barbara C., Steven A. Sloman, Silvia P. Gennari, Meiyi Shi and Yuan Wang 1999 'Knowing versus naming: similarity and the linguistic categorization of artifacts.' *Journal of Memory and Language* **40**: 230–62.

Malt, Barbara C., Steven A. Sloman and Silvia P. Gennari 2003 'Speaking versus thinking about objects and actions.' In Gentner and Goldin-Meadow (eds.), pp. 81–112.

Marchand, Hans 1960/1969 *The Categories and Types of Present-Day English Word-Formation: A Synchronic-Diachronic Approach*. 2nd edn revised, 1969 [1st edn 1960]. Munich: Beck'sche Verlagsbuchhandlung.

Martin, J. E. 1969a 'Some competence-process relationships in noun phrases with prenominal and postnominal adjectives.' *Journal of Verbal Learning and Verbal Behaviour* **8**: 471–80.

    1969b 'Semantic determinants of preferred adjective order.' *Journal of Verbal Learning and Verbal Behaviour* **8**: 697–704.

    1970 'Adjective order and juncture.' *Journal of Verbal Learning and Verbal Behaviour* **9**: 379–83.

Matthews, P. H. 1981 *Syntax*. Cambridge: Cambridge University Press.

Meillet, Antoine 1912/1958 'L'évolution des formes grammaticales.' First printed in 1912; reprinted in *Linguistique Historique et Linguistique Générale*. Paris: Champion, pp. 130–48.

Mel'cuk, Igor A. 1988 *Dependency Syntax: Theory and Practice*. Albany, NY: State University of New York Press.

Mervis, Carolyn B. 1987 'Child-basic object categories and early lexical development.' In Neisser (ed.), pp. 201–33.

Miller, Jim Forthcoming 'English in the 21st century.' In Laurel Brinton and Alex Bergs (eds.), *History of English, Volume* 2. Berlin / New York: Mouton de Gruyter.

Mitchell, Bruce 1985 *Old English Syntax*. Oxford: Clarendon Press.

Mithun, Marianne 1984 'The evolution of noun incorporation.' *Language* **60**: 847–92.

Morris, Richard. (ed.) 1871 *Legends of the Holy Rood: Symbols of the Passion and Cross-Poems*. London: Early English Text Society.

Morton, Eugene S. 1994 'Sound symbolism and its role in non-human vertebrate communication.' In Hinton, Nichols and Ohara (eds.), pp. 348–65.

Mossé, Fernand 1952 *A Handbook of Middle English*. Baltimore: Johns Hopkins Press.

Mustanoja, Tauno F. 1960 *A Middle English Syntax*. Helsinki: Société Néophilologique.

Myhill, John 1988 'Categoriality and clustering.' *Studies in Language* **12**: 261–97.

Neisser, Ulric (ed.) 1987 *Concepts and Conceptual Development: Ecological and Intellectual Factors in Categorization*. Cambridge: Cambridge University Press.

Nelson, Katherine 1976 'Some attributes of adjectives used by young children.' *Cognition* **4**: 13–30.

Nevalainen, Terttu 1999 'Lexis and semantics.' In Lass (ed.), pp. 332–459.

Norde, Muriel 2010 *Degrammaticalization*. Oxford: Oxford Books Online. (Print edn, 2009.).

OED – *Oxford English Dictionary*. Online edition.

Oller, John W. and B. Dennis Sales 1969 'Conceptual restrictions on English: a psycholinguistic study.' *Lingua* **23**: 209–32.

Paradis, Carita 2000 'Reinforcing adjectives: a cognitive semantic perspective on grammaticalisaton.' In Ricardo Bermúdez-Otero, David Denison, Richard M. Hogg and C. B. McCully (eds.), *Generative Theory and Corpus Studies*. Berlin / New York: Mouton de Gruyter, pp. 233–58.

 2001 'Adjectives and boundedness.' *Cognitive Linguistics* **12** (1): 47–65.

Partington, Alan 1993 'Corpus evidence of language change.' In Baker, Francis and Tognini-Bonelli (eds.), pp. 177–2.

Partridge, Eric 1970 *A Dictionary of Slang and Unconventional English*. 7th edn [1st edn 1937]. New York: Macmillan.

Peeters, Bert (ed.) 2000 *The Lexicon-Encyclopedia Interface*. Oxford: Elsevier.

Plank, Frans 2006 'DP-internal information structure: topic, focus and other illocutionary forces.' Paper delivered at the Workshop on DP-Internal Information Structure, Utrecht, 17–18 November, 2006.

Pustejovsky, James 1995 *The Generative Lexicon*. Cambridge, MA: MIT Press.

 2001 'Type construction and the logic of concepts.' In Bouillon and Busa (eds.), pp. 91–123.

Quirk, Randolph, Sidney Greenbaum, Geoffrey Leech and Jan Svartvik 1972 *A Grammar of Contemporary English*. London: Longman.

 1985 *A Comprehensive Grammar of Contemporary English*. London: Longman.

Radford, Andrew 1993 'Head-hunting: on the trail of the nominal Janus.' In Greville G. Corbett, Norman R. Fraser and Scott McGlashan (eds.), *Heads in Grammatical Theory*. Cambridge: Cambridge University Press, pp. 73–113.

Ramsey, Violeta 1987 'The functional distribution of preposed and postposed "if" and "when" clauses in written discourse.' In Russell S. Tomlin (ed.), *Coherence and Grounding in Discourse: Outcome of a Symposium, Eugene, Oregon, June 1984*. Amsterdam/Philadelphia: Benjamins, pp. 383–408.

Raumolin-Brunberg, Helena 1991 *The Noun Phrase in Early Sixteenth-Century English: A Study Based on Sir Thomas More's Writings*. Helsinki: Société Néophilologique.

Reboul, Anne 2000 'Words, concepts, mental representations and other biological categories.' In Peeters (ed.), pp. 55–95.

Rhodes, Richard 1994 'Aural images.' In Hinton, Nichols and Ohara (eds.), pp. 276–92.

Richardson, Henry Handel 1930 *The Fortunes of Richard Mahoney*. London: Penguin.

Rijkhoff, J. 2002 *The Noun Phrase*. Oxford: Oxford University Press.

Romaine, Suzanne (ed.) 1998 *Cambridge History of the English Language, Volume IV, 1776–1997*. Cambridge: Cambridge University Press.

Rosenbach, Anette 2002 *Genitive Variation in English: Conceptual Factors in Synchronic and Diachronic Studies*. Berlin / New York: Mouton de Gruyter.

2006 'Descriptive genitives in English: a case study on constructional gradience.' *English Language and Linguistics* **10**: 77–118.

Ross, Woodburn O. 1940 *Middle English Sermons*. London: Oxford University Press. (For Early English Texts Society.)

Ruhl, Charles 1989 *On Monosemy: A Study in Linguistic Semantics*. Albany, NY: State University of New York Press.

Rumelhart, David E. and James L. McClelland 1986 *Parallel Distributed Processing: Explorations in the Microstructure of Cognition, Volume 1, Foundations*. (Written with the PDP Research Group.) Cambridge, MA: MIT Press.

Ryder, Mary Ellen 1994 *Ordered Chaos: the Interpretation of English Noun-Noun Compounds*. Berkeley: University of California Press.

Salmon, Vivian 1999 'Orthography and punctuation.' In Lass (ed.), pp. 13–55.

Schiffrin, Deborah 1987 *Discourse Markers*. Cambridge: Cambridge University Press.

Schreuder, Robert and Giovanni B. Flores d'Arcais 1989 'Psycholinguistic issues in the lexical representation of meaning.' In William Marslen-Wilson (ed.), *Lexical Representation and Process*. Cambridge, MA: MIT Press, pp. 409–36.

Schreuder, Robert, Giovanni B. Flores d'Arcais and Ge Glazenborg 1985 'Semantic decomposition and word recognition.' In G. A. J. Hoppenbrouwers, P. A. M. Seuren and A. J. M. M. Weijters (eds.), *Meaning and the Lexicon*. Dordrecht: Foris, pp. 108–14.

Schwanenflugel, Paula J. 1991 'Why are abstract concepts hard to understand?' In Paula J. Schwanenflugel (ed.), *The Psychology of Word Meanings*. Hillsdale, NJ: Lawrence Erlbaum and Associates, pp. 223–50.

Scott, Gary John 2002 'Stacked adjectival modification and the structure of nominal phrases.' In Guglielmo Cinque (ed.), *Functional Structure in DP and IP: The Cartography of Syntactic Structures, Volume 1*. Oxford: Oxford University Press, pp. 91–120.

Sears, Donald A. 1971 'The noun adjuncts of modern English'. *Linguistics: An International Review* **72**: 31–60.

Seuren, Pieter A. M. 1998 *Western Linguistics: An Historical Introduction*. Oxford: Blackwell.

Seuren, Pieter S. 1975 'Referential constraints on lexical items.' In Edward L. Keenan (ed.), *Formal Semantics of Natural Languages*. Cambridge: Cambridge University Press, pp. 84–98.

SOED – 2002 *Shorter Oxford English Dictionary on Historical Principles*. 5th edn. Oxford: Oxford University Press.

Sørensen, Knud 1980 'From postmodification to premodification.' In Jacobson (ed.), pp. 77–84.

Sproat, Richard and Chilin Shih 1988 'Prenominal adjectival ordering in English and Mandarin.' *Proceedings of the 18th Annual General Meeting of the North East Linguistic Society*, pp. 465–89.

Stefanowitsch, Anatol 2003 'Constructional semantics as a limit to grammatical alternation: the two genitives of English.' In Gunter Rohdenburg and Britta Mondorf (eds.), *Determinants of Grammatical Variation in English*. Berlin/ New York: Mouton de Gruyter, pp. 413–44.

Stein, Dieter 1995 'Subjective meanings and the history of inversions in English.' In Stein and Wright (eds.), pp. 129–50.

Stein, Dieter and Susan Wright (eds.) 1995 *Subjectivity and Subjectivisation*. Cambridge: Cambridge University Press.

Strang, Barbara M. H. 1962 *Modern English Structure*. London: Arnold.
1970 *A History of English*. London: Methuen.

Stubbs, Michael 1996 *Text and Corpus Analysis: Computer-Assisted Studies of Language and Culture*. Oxford: Blackwell.

Sussex, Roland 1974 'The deep structure of adjectives in noun phrases.' *Journal of Linguistics* **10**: 112–31.

Svoboda, Aleš 1968 'The hierarchy of communicative units and fields as illustrated by English attributive constructions.' *Brno Studies on English, Volume 7*. Brno: Universita J. E. Purkyne, pp. 49–101.

Sweetser, Eve 1999 'Compositionality and blending: semantic composition in a cognitively realistic setting.' In Theo Janssen and Gisela Redeker (eds.), *Cognitive Linguistics: Foundations, Scope, and Methodology*. Berlin / New York: Mouton de Gruyter, pp. 129–62.

Szendrói, Kriszta 2006 'A flexible approach to discourse-related word order variations in the DP.' Paper delivered at the Workshop on DP-Internal Information Structure, Utrecht, 17–18 November, 2006.

Tabor, Whitney and Elizabeth Closs Traugott 1998 'Structural scope expansion and grammaticalization.' In Anna Giacalone Ramat and Paul J. Hopper (eds.), *The Limits of Grammaticalization*. Philadelphia / Amsterdam: Benjamins, pp. 229–66.

Talmy, Leonard 2001 *Toward a Cognitive Semantics, Volume 1, Concept Structuring Systems*. Cambridge, MA: MIT.

Taylor, John R. 1992 'Old problems: adjectives in Cognitive Grammar.' *Cognitive Linguistics* **3** (1): 1–35.
2002 *Cognitive Grammar*. Oxford: Oxford University Press.

Teyssier, J. 1968 'Notes on the syntax of the adjective in modern English.' *Lingua* **20**: 225–49.

Timberlake, Alan 1975 'Hierarchies in the genitive of negation.' *Slavic and East European Journal* **19** (2): 123–38.

Tognini-Bonelli, Elena 1993 'Interpretative nodes in discourse: the case of the intensifier.' In Baker, Francis and Tognini-Bonelli (eds.), pp. 177–92.

Tomasello, Michael 2003 *Constructing a Language: A Usage-Based Theory of Language Acquisition.* Cambridge, MA, and London: Harvard University Press.

Tomikawa, Sandra A. and David H. Dodd 1980 'Early word meanings: perceptually or functionally based?' *Child Development* **51**: 1103–09.

Trapp, J. B., J. Hollander, F. Kermode and M. Price 1973 *The Oxford Anthology of English Literature, Volume I.* New York: Oxford University Press.

Traugott, Elizabeth Closs 1982 'From propositional to textual and expressive meanings: some semantic-pragmatic aspects of grammaticalization.' In Winfred P. Lehmann and Yakov Malkiel (eds.), *Perspectives on Historical Linguistics.* Amsterdam / Philadelphia: Benjamins, pp. 245–71.

  1995 'Subjectification in grammaticalisation.' In Stein and Wright (eds.), pp. 31–54.

  1999 'The rhetoric of counter-expectation in semantic change: a study in subjectification.' In Andreas Blank and Peter Koch (eds.), *Historical Semantics and Cognition.* Berlin/New York: Mouton de Gruyter, pp. 177–93.

  2003 'From subjectification to intersubjectification.' In R. Hickey (ed.), *Motives for Language Change.* Cambridge: Cambridge University Press, pp. 124–39.

  2006 'Grammaticalization, emergent constructions, and the notion of "newness".' Paper delivered at High Desert Linguistics Society Conference 7, November 2006.

Traugott, Elizabeth Closs and Richard B. Dasher 2002 *Regularity in Semantic Change.* Cambridge: Cambridge University Press.

Traugott, Elizabeth Closs and Graeme Trousdale 2010 *Gradience, Gradualness and Grammaticalization.* Amsterdam / Philadelphia: Benjamins.

Trousdale, Graeme and Elizabeth Closs Traugott 2010 'Preface'. In Traugott and Trousdale (eds.), pp. 1–18.

Tucker, Don M. 2002 'Embodied meaning: an evolutionary-developmental analysis of adaptive semantics.' In Givón and Malle (eds.), pp. 51–82.

Van de Velde, Freek 2007 'Interpersonal modification in the English noun phrase.' *Functions of Language* **14** (2): 203–30.

van Donzel, Monique Elisabeth 1999 *Prosodic Aspects of Information Structure in Discourse.* PhD thesis, Universiteit van Amsterdam. The Hague: Academic Graphics.

Vandelanotte, Lieven 2002 'Prenominal adjectives in English: structures and ordering.' *Folia Linguistica* **36**: 219–59.

Varantola, Krista 1984 *On Noun Phrase Structures in Engineering English.* Turku: Turun Yliopisto.

Vendler, Zeno 1968 *Adjectives and Nominalizations.* The Hague / Paris: Mouton.

Vincent, Nigel and Kersti Börjars 2010 'Grammaticalisation and models of language.' In Traugott and Trousdale (eds.), pp. 280–99.

Warren, Beatrice 1978 *Semantic Patterns of Noun-Noun Compounds.* Göteborg: Acta Universitatis Gothoburgensis.

  1984 *Classifying Adjectives.* Göteborg: Acta Universitatis Gothoburgensis.

Whorf, Benjamin Lee 1945/1956 'Grammatical categories.' In John B. Carroll (ed.), *Language, Thought and Reality: Selected Writings of Benjamin Lee Whorf.* Cambridge, MA: MIT, New York: Wiley, London: Chapman and Hall, pp. 87–101. Reprinted from *Language* 21 (1945): 1–11.

Wierzbicka, Anna 1990 '"Prototypes save": on the uses and abuses of the notion of "prototype" in linguistics and related fields.' In S. L. Tsohatzidis (ed.), *Meanings and Prototypes: Studies in Linguistic Categorisation*, London / New York: Routledge, pp. 347–67.

Wray, Alison 2002 *Formulaic Language and the Lexicon.* Cambridge: Cambridge University Press.

Wroe, Ann 1991 *Lives, Lies and The Iran-Contra Affair.* London: I.B. Tauris.

Wulff, Stefanie 2003 'A multifactorial corpus analysis of adjective order in English.' *International Journal of Corpus Linguistics* 8 (2): 245–82.

Ziff, P. 1960 *Semantic Analysis.* Cambridge: Cambridge University Press.

Index